D1610784

THE CISTERCIANS IN THE MIDDLE AGES

Monastic Orders

ISSN 1749–4974

General Editor: Janet Burton

Monastic houses – houses of monks, regular canons, nuns, and friars – were a familiar part of the medieval landscape in both urban and rural areas, and members of the religious orders played an important role in many aspects of medieval life. The volumes in this series provide authoritative and accessible guides to the origins of each of these orders, to their expansion, and to their main characteristics.

ALREADY PUBLISHED

The Franciscans in the Middle Ages
Michael Robson

The Other Friars
The Carmelite, Augustinian, Sack and Pied Friars in the Middle Ages
Frances Andrews

The Benedictines in the Middle Ages
James G. Clark

FORTHCOMING VOLUMES

The Canons Regular
Janet Burton and Karen Stöber

The Carthusians
Julian Luxford

The Cistercians
in the Middle Ages

Janet Burton and Julie Kerr

THE BOYDELL PRESS

First published 2011
The Boydell Press, Woodbridge

ISBN 978–1–84383–667–4

The Boydell Press is an imprint of Boydell & Brewer Ltd
PO Box 9, Woodbridge, Suffolk IP12 3DF, UK
and of Boydell & Brewer Inc.
Mt Hope Avenue, Rochester, NY 14620, USA
website: www.boydellandbrewer.com

A CIP catalogue record for this title is available
from the British Library

The publisher has no responsibility for the continued existence or accuracy of URLs
for external or third-party internet websites referred to in this book, and does not
guarantee that any content on such websites is, or will remain, accurate or appropriate.

Papers used by Boydell & Brewer Ltd are natural, recyclable products
made from wood grown in sustainable forests

Printed in Great Britain by
CPI Antony Rowe, Chippenham and Eastbourne

Contents

Illustrations

Acknowledgements

This book is the result of close collaboration between the two authors and each of us has been reliant on the other; however, Janet Burton is responsible for the introduction and chapter 1 and 2, and Julie Kerr for chapters 3 to 8. A number of people have supported and assisted us with the writing of this book and we are indebted to them. We are particularly grateful to Stuart Harrison who so willingly and generously offered his advice on Cistercian architecture, alerted us to important new developments in this field and, not least, provided us with a number of images from his collection of photographs which have been reproduced as plates. Dr Karen Stöber kindly read and commented on several draft chapters and has offered tremendous encouragement during the entire undertaking. The West Yorkshire Archive, Leeds, generously waived copyright and reproduction charges and we are immensely grateful for their kindness. We are indebted to Martin Crampin for drawing the map of Cistercian houses in Europe, and thank the Walters Art Museum, Baltimore, for allowing us to use the image from the Beaupré Antiphonary on the cover. Janet Burton would like to thank colleagues in the School of Archaeology, History and Anthropology at University of Wales Trinity Saint David for stimulating discussion of matters monastic, and in particular Professor David Austin, Dr Andrew Abram and Dr Jemma Bezant. Her thanks also go to the students who over the years have taken her 'Cistercians' special subject, and who have kept her on her toes with searching questions. Julie Kerr benefited greatly from her work on the Cistercians in Yorkshire project (http://cistercians.shef.ac.uk) at the University of Sheffield, under the direction of Professor Sarah Foot, and would like to thank Sarah, the project team, and indeed all those who offered their advice and support during these three years. We thank Caroline Palmer of Boydell & Brewer for her guidance throughout the writing process and her patience when this took rather longer than anticipated. Our greatest debt is to our husbands, both fellow medievalists, for their support and interest. Whether casting a critical eye over the text, offering advice on their own areas of expertise or couriering much-needed texts across the country, their help and encouragement have been invaluable.

Janet Burton
Julie Kerr
January 2011

Abbreviations

BL	London, British Library
Dugdale, *Monasticon*	W. Dugdale, *Monasticon Anglicanum*, ed. J. Caley, H. Ellis and B. Bandinel, 6 vols in 8 (London, 1817–30)
Ecclesiastica Officia	*Les Ecclesiastica Officia Cisterciens du xiième siècle,* ed. D. Choisselet and P. Vernet (Reiningue, 1989)
NLT	*Narrative and Legislative Texts from Early Cîteaux,* ed. Chrysogonus Waddell, Cîteaux: Commentarii Cistercienses, Studia et documenta, 9 (Cîteaux, 1999)
NMT	Nelson's Medieval Texts
ODNB	*Oxford Dictionary of National Biography in Association with the British Academy, from the Earliest Times to the Year 2000,* ed. H. D. G. Matthew and B. Harrison (Oxford, 2004)
OMT	Oxford Medieval Texts
PL	Patrologia Latina
RB	Regula Benedicti/Rule of St Benedict
RS	Rolls Series
Twelfth-Century Statutes	*Twelfth-Century Statutes from the Cistercian General Chapter,* ed. Chrysogonus Waddell, Cîteaux: Commentarii Cistercienses, Studia et documenta, 12 (Brecht, 2002)

Introduction

Reform and Renewal

In 1098 a small band of monks established themselves in a spot which became known as Cîteaux, just a few kilometres from the ducal centre of Dijon in Burgundy. Over the half century that followed the way of life that developed there spread to all parts of Christendom, and the Cistercian Order became a powerful congregation. This book seeks to explore the dynamics of the phenomenon that was the Cistercian Order. But Cîteaux was not unique; indeed, it did not appear from nowhere. Cîteaux was but one experiment – a highly successful one – in a series of attempts to find the most perfect form of monastic life and observance. The context out of which Cîteaux and similar movements emerged was one of intellectual ferment, in which the very nature of the monastic life was investigated and debated. It was also one of increasing wealth and prosperity, which provoked among many a desire for the simpler life of their forbears. An understanding of this context is a necessary prelude to a discussion of the Cistercians and the Cistercian Order.

All accounts of forms of monastic life in the medieval West, however, must begin with that great written monument, the Rule of St Benedict, the 'little rule for beginners' compiled by the Italian abbot in the first half of the sixth century for his monastery at Monte Cassino.[1] Although Benedict envisaged a wider circulation for the Rule than just this one abbey, it was not for over two centuries that political ambition, harnessed to the Rule's own intrinsic merits, propelled it to the position of the pre-eminent monastic code in Europe. It was Louis the Pious (814–40), heir to the vast empire of his father, Charlemagne, along with his ecclesiastical adviser, Benedict of Aniane, who made the Rule of St Benedict the dominant code in Western Europe. Their promotion of the Rule at the councils of Aachen (816–17) reminds us that the importance of monasteries to medieval society stretched far beyond the communities that were housed within their walls. Benedict's daily cycle of prayer, inspired by the verses from Psalm 118 (Vulgate) 'seven times a day have I given praise to thee ... at midnight I rose to give praise to thee', was a corporate act of

---

[1] For a comprehensive discussion of the emergence and development of the Benedictines see the volume by James Clark in this series: *The Benedictines in the Middle Ages* (Woodbridge, 2011).

worship and, for individual monks and for the community, it was the spiritual pathway to God.[2] However, by the ninth century if not before monastic prayer had acquired an intercessory, indeed a social, function. To the medieval mind, monks and nuns existed not just to fulfil their own spiritual journeys but to pray for the well-being of humankind, and more especially for earthly rulers, that is, for kings and emperors. Louis the Pious and Benedict of Aniane envisaged a monastic order, united by the common observance of the Rule of St Benedict, to mirror the political unity of the empire, interceding for Louis and for the success of his government and the safety of his lands.

Medieval monasteries, far from being cut off from society, were embedded within it; as the *oratores*, whose function was to pray, monks served its spiritual needs and promoted the success of its ruling elites, the *bellatores*, supported by the third section of that society, the *laboratores*.[3] Monks prayed for peace, and they both suffered and prospered in time of war. After the partition of the empire following the death of Louis, and its subsequent breakdown under the twin pressures of internal implosion and external raids, monastic houses were robbed, burnt – even abandoned – but they also reaped the rewards of benefactions from those who were involved in warfare. It was the most politically unstable of the imperial lands, the Middle Kingdom, or Lotharingia, that saw the greatest flowering of monastic life, in particular that associated with the renowned abbey of Cluny. Founded in 910 by William of Aquitaine – one of a growing number of great lay lords who, like emperors and kings, came to sponsor monastic foundations – Cluny developed in a number of ways that met the needs of contemporary society of the tenth century. In a time of violence and disorder it provided a haven of beauty – the famous phrase 'the beauty of holiness' has above all come to be associated with Cluny, with its lavish architecture and elaborate decoration. Moreover, in an attempt to free itself from the stranglehold of lay patrons, who had come to supplement their own resources by using their role as advocates and protectors of monasteries to annex monastic estates, Cluny sought a close relationship with the papacy. Protected by the See of Peter from the clutches of an often predatory aristocracy and also exempt from the control of the local episcopate, an autonomous Cluny gradually, over the next two centuries, flourished and in reciprocal fashion provided a firm ally for the papacy in the development of its own power and authority. Standing at the head of a congregation that came to embrace both established houses which adopted Cluniac customs and houses founded *de novo*

---

2 RB, chapter 16.
3 The traditional view of medieval society was that of a tripartite division: those who fought (*bellatores*), those who prayed (*oratores*) and those who worked (*laboratores*).

by admirers of the new monastic order, Cluny elaborated and extended the liturgical life of the monastery so that there was little time for any other activity. Thus Cluny effectively put an end to the carefully balanced timetable of the Rule of St Benedict, which wove periods of manual work and sacred reading (*lectio divina*) around the seven canonical hours and the night office. At Cluny and its associated houses, as in many of the other abbeys of Western Europe, the monastic life became wholly liturgical, the basic hours embellished and supplemented by masses for the dead, which were increasingly demanded by patrons and benefactors. Manual labour was either eliminated or reduced to a token. Moreover, by the eleventh century monasteries were often founded in towns – or towns grew up around their walls to serve their needs – increasing the interaction between monastic houses and the world outside. Although there was a great diversity in the location, size and resources of the monastic houses of medieval Europe, many were wealthy, supported by estates granted by the faithful and by the repentant who sought to redeem their sins, and by the peasantry that worked these lands.

In many ways medieval monasticism reflected the broader political, social, economic and cultural environments in which it existed. By the late eleventh century there emerged different outlooks on, and concepts of, the monastic life. There can be no doubt that in part these developments marked a reaction to liturgical and other practices in the great abbeys like Cluny. The reformer Peter Damian was a critic of the way in which contemporary churches were decked with costly ornaments, and after a visit to Cluny in 1063 in a reference to the excessive liturgy he remarked on the 'unnecessary sounding of bells … protracted chanting of hymns … conspicuous use of ornament';[4] there was too much splendour and too little penance and mortification. Others drew attention to the distortion of the Rule of St Benedict through the loss of manual labour. The considerable wealth of abbeys brought criticism for its incompatibility with monastic vows of poverty, for the way in which monks enjoyed sources of income, such as tithes, which were intended for others, and for the way in which great wealth involved them in secular affairs. However, there was more to the explosion of forms of the monastic life in the eleventh and twelfth centuries than dissatisfaction with contemporary practice. The eleventh and twelfth centuries were ones of great social and economic change as well as that intellectual ferment which long ago acquired the title of the 'twelfth-century renaissance'. There was a growing debate about what was the purest form of the monastic life, as

---

4 Quoted in L. J. Lekai, *The Cistercians: Ideals and Reality* (Kent State, Ohio, 1977), p. 4.

writers sought to find and define the origins of their beliefs and practices and to establish historical precedent for their way of life.

Historians have tended to use the word 'new' to describe the reformed orders and congregations of the eleventh and twelfth centuries. The word 'novelty', however, was not one which would have carried connotations of approval or praise at the time. When Abbot Geoffrey of St Mary's Abbey, York, used the word to describe the practices of the Cistercians he did so with horror.[5] The spirit of intellectual enquiry led to debates about 'renewal' or 'revival', and to a search for the primitive form of monastic life.[6] This search became manifest in a number of ways. The first was an emphasis on, even a rediscovery of, the 'desert', gleaned through close attention to the lives of the pioneer monks of Egypt and Palestine where the story of monasticism began. Writers sought to root the reformed monasticism of the eleventh century within a tradition that went back even beyond Benedict to the very origins of the monastic life, and the desert became a powerful theme in their rhetoric. The second tool in the intellectual armoury of the reformers was a desire for apostolic poverty, as the gospel texts called for renewed attention to what they said about the earliest form of communal living and about voluntary poverty. Although by the late eleventh century the word 'apostolic' was ceasing to be applied solely to the monastic way of life, renewed emphasis on Acts 4.32 ('and the multitude of them that believed were of one heart and of one soul: neither said any of them that ought of the things which he possessed was his own; but they had all things in common') gave impetus to monastic reform.[7] The third aspect of renewal lay in inspiration from that landmark in the history of the monastic order, the Rule of St Benedict, and demanded a return to stricter observance of its tenets. Indeed, the Rule brought together the eremitic and cenobitic, or communal, origins of monastic life in its very first chapter, in which Benedict underlined the importance of the cenobium and communal life as a preparation for the higher calling of the desert. The Rule describes the first type of monks as those who lived in a monastery, and the second as the hermits or anchorites, 'who not in the first fervour of their conversion, but after long probation in a monastery, having learnt in association with many brethren how to fight against the devil, go out well-armed from the ranks of the community to the solitary combat of the desert'.[8] All these ideas, underpinned by the desire to discover exemplars for their way of life,

---

5 *Narratio de Fundatione of Fountains Abbey*, in *Memorials of the Abbey of St Mary of Fountains*, I, ed. J. R. Walbran, Surtees Society, 42 (1863), p. 2.
6 On these themes see Giles Constable, 'Renewal and Reform in Religious Life', in *Renaissance and Renewal in the Twelfth Century*, ed. Robert L. Benson and Giles Constable (Oxford, 1982), pp. 37–67.
7 Quotation from the King James Version of the Bible.
8 RB, chapter 1.

informed the monastic renewal that emerged in Europe from the latter decades of the eleventh century. The desert, or the eremitic origins of the monastic life in the East, and the cenobitic, or communal, traditions of the Rule of St Benedict, could be fused; they need not be at opposite extremes of the monastic experience.

Thus into a monastic world dominated by Benedictine houses sprang new monasteries and congregations such as Fonte Avellana, Camaldoli and Vallombrosa in Italy, and La Grande Chartreuse, Tiron, Savigny, Fontevraud and Grandmont in France. In different ways they exemplified the spirit of renewal and desire to return to past practices and ideologies. At Camaldoli, for instance, the founder, Romuald of Ravenna, constructed two buildings, one a communal monastery and the other, in the hills above, a secluded hermitage; together they were almost an embodiment of chapter 1 of the Rule of St Benedict. At Vallombrosa John Gualbert introduced a class of lay brothers in order to free the monks from outside concerns so that they could concentrate on a life of contemplation; it would be the Cistercians who would use these *conversi* to their full potential. Other founders were inspired, to greater or lesser degrees, by the desire to return to the Rule in all its simplicity, to live a more secluded life, or to live in poverty.

Many of these movements seem to have owed their origins to inspired individuals, men who withdrew from the world to live a stricter life than they thought possible within the organised, communal monasticism of their day – men whose devoutness, humility, extraordinariness and example others sought to emulate. In the hills of Tuscany and the forests of France the hermit settlements grew, first to communities, then to groups and orders. One such pioneer was Bernard of Tiron, who turned his back on high office as abbot of a Benedictine monastery and sought the solitude of the forests of Craon, where he lived by the labour of his hands, eschewing even the touch of money, and preaching salvation to those who came to him. Inspired by his call to repentance, people joined him, and Bernard found himself once again an abbot, and, in time, head of a substantial group of abbeys that spread from northern France into Wales and Scotland, and not many years later into England. The written lives of these pioneers stress, in varying degrees, their commitment to poverty, to solitude or the desert, and to the Rule of St Benedict.[9] However much we may be inclined to read these lives as constructs of monastic sanctity rather than reflections of reality, the persistence of these motifs in the

---

9 For instance, the life of Bernard of Tiron by Geoffrey 'Grossus', PL, 172, cols 1362–1446, trans. Bernard Beck, *Saint Bernard de Tiron, l'ermite, le moine et le monde* (Cormeilles-le-Royal, 1998). For these themes in the reformed monasticism see Lester K. Little, *Religious Poverty and the Profit Economy in Medieval Europe* (London, 1978); Giles Constable, *The Reformation of the Twelfth Century* (Cambridge, 1996).

literature is testimony to the chords that Bernard, along with Vitalis of Savigny, Romuald of Ravenna, John Gualbert of Vallombrosa and their like, struck in the mentality of the eleventh and twelfth centuries.[10]

For all the criticism – implied or real – of the contemporary order, these new monasteries and congregations did not displace the traditional monastic establishment, represented by the autonomous Benedictine houses and the abbeys and priories of the congregation of Cluny and their like. However, the apparent divergence of the emergent monastic movements from contemporary practices – their emphasis on poverty, strict adherence to the Rule, manual labour, and isolated locations as opposed to urban sites – has led some historians to identify a 'crisis of monasticism', or more strictly a 'crisis of cenobitism'. The new monasticism posed a direct challenge to the old and indeed grew out of its weaknesses. Van Engen has argued convincingly that any 'crisis' lay less in the failure of traditional houses and more in the challenge of the new, or more accurately in renewal and revival.[11] Benedictine and Cluniac houses continued to thrive, to secure both recruits and benefactors, and to embrace into confraternity those lay people who sought association with them. But there can be no doubt that the new orders of the eleventh and twelfth centuries brought a richness and vibrancy to the monastic world. It was a process that proved at times to be a painful one. It was a process that by 1215 the ecclesiastical hierarchy, represented by the Fourth Lateran Council, sought to curb and indeed to bring to an end, with its injunction that 'lest too great a diversity of religious orders lead to grave confusion in the Church of God, we strictly forbid anyone in the future to found a new order, but whoever should wish to enter an order, let him choose one already approved. Similarly, he who would wish to found a new monastery, must accept a rule already proved.'[12]

Among all the new congregations to emerge at this time the name of Cîteaux and the Cistercian Order dominates. The Cistercians, as we shall see, shared many of the.characteristic features of the other new monastic movements, but there were two crucial differences. The first is that unlike so many of these congregations the origins of Cîteaux did

10   A recent reassessment of Bernard, for instance, sees him as a 'career churchman' working within existing structures of power and patronage. See Kathleen Thompson, 'The Other Saint Bernard: the "Troubled and Varied Career" of Bernard of Abbeville, Abbot of Tiron', *Journal of Ecclesiastical History* 60 (2009), 657–72.

11   J. Van Engen, 'The "Crisis of Cenobitism" Reconsidered: Benedictine Monasticism in the Years 1050–1150', *Speculum* 61 (1986), 269–304. See also Norman F. Cantor, 'The Crisis of Western Monasticism, 1050–1130', *American Historical Review* 66 (1960), 47–67; J. Leclercq, 'The Monastic Crisis of the Eleventh and Twelfth Centuries', in *Cluniac Monasticism in the Central Middle Ages*, ed. N. Hunt (Hamden, CN / London, 1971), pp. 217–37.

12   Canon 13, Fourth Lateran Council. The decrees of the council are conveniently translated in *English Historical Documents, 1189–1327*, ed. H. Rothwell (London, 1975), pp. 643–75.

not lie in the aspirations and actions of one holy man supposedly seeking poverty and seclusion: Cîteaux came about as the result of the secession of a substantial group of monks from an established monastery, Molesme. Those who left went on to found a monastery which was not a solitary hermitage, however much their literature might talk of the *heremum*, that is, the 'desert' or 'solitude'. The second is that the Cistercian Order, which developed and began to coalesce from the second decade of the twelfth century, created and sustained a cohesive congregation – an 'order' in the fullest sense – which made it far and away the most prolific and enduring experiment to emerge from the tumultuous intellectual and monastic fervour of the eleventh and twelfth centuries. The chapters that follow seek to discuss what it was that made the Cistercians distinctive. Chapter 1 explores the historical debates around the events that led to the foundation of the New Monastery in 1098; as many of these arguments hinge on the nature and dating of key narratives, close attention is given to these documents. Chapter 2 considers the phenomenon of the expansion of the Cistercian Order throughout Christendom. Subsequent chapters explore the physical setting of Cistercian monasteries, their sites and their buildings; the administration of the Order; life within the cloister; Cistercian spirituality; and the economic basis of Cistercian abbeys. The final chapter seeks to explore aspects of the interaction between the White Monks and the world outside their cloisters.

CHAPTER ONE

The 'desert-place called Cîteaux'

After these things, supported by so distinguished and so important an authority, the aforesaid abbot and his own returned to Molesme, and from that fraternity of monks selected from their own company devotees of the Rule, so that between those who had spoken to the legate in Lyon and the others called from the monastery, there were twenty-one monks; and thus escorted by so goodly a company they headed eagerly for the desert-place called Cîteaux.[1]

The monastery which became known as Cîteaux lay within the duchy of Burgundy, in the heart of the fragmented Middle Kingdom, or Lotharingia. Ruled by the semi-autonomous dukes, the region had seen the emergence of movements, such as the Peace of God and the Truce of God, designed to curb private warfare. It had also seen the foundation of monasteries, notably Cluny, and the alienation of property to them, which allowed them to prosper. Located on the fringes of the kingdom of the Capetian kings of France to the west, and the German lands to the east, Burgundy was on one of the main routes south into Italy. Remote it was not. Yet it was here that Cîteaux was founded and flourished, claiming to be a community that strenuously upheld the Rule of St Benedict, and, moreover, to be a desert place, a wilderness, 'removed from populated areas'.[2]

The foundation of Cîteaux: the historical debate

For students of Cistercian history there is one plain, but all too familiar, fact of life: to turn one's back on the subject, even for a moment, is to lose the plot.[3]

David Robinson's comment on the enduring appeal of the Cistercians to scholars of all disciplines – and the difficulties it can cause – was in 2006, and is still, an appropriate one. In recent years, however, it has been

[1] *Exordium Parvum, NLT*, p. 421.
[2] *Ibid.*, p. 435.
[3] David Robinson, *The Cistercians in Wales: Architecture and Archaeology 1130–1540*, Reports of the Research Committee of the Society of Antiquaries of London, 73 (London, 2006), p. x.

the very nature of the Cistercian movement in its first half century and beyond, and the emergence of the Cistercian 'Order', that have caused most controversy. To a large extent the problems are embedded in the documentary sources themselves, and an appreciation of those sources must be our starting point.

The narrative sources
At one time it seemed as if the story of the origins and growth of Cistercian monasticism represented one of the 'certainties' of medieval scholarship. Although it was recognised from an early date that the two narratives that tell the story of the foundation from the Cistercian perspective, the *Exordium Parvum* and the shorter *Exordium Cistercii*, posed problems relating to their authorship, date, and relationship to each other, nevertheless it seemed to historians that the basic outline of 'what happened' was clear enough.[4] This is the story they tell.

In 1098 a group of monks from the prosperous monastery of Molesme, in the diocese of Langres, led by their abbot, Robert, appeared before the archbishop of Lyon, then papal legate. They voiced their deep discontent with monastic practices at Molesme, particularly the poor observance of the Rule of St Benedict. Accordingly the monks sought, and received, permission to leave Molesme, and they founded a new monastery in a remote spot in the diocese of Chalon, near Dijon. Indeed in its first years it was known as the *Novum Monasterium*, the 'New Monastery', and only later as Cîteaux. In this desolate and secluded spot – 'the desert-place called Cîteaux' – undistracted by the world outside, the monks would worship God in simplicity and poverty. The place suited their purposes well in that it was remote, 'rarely approached by men back in those days because of the thickness of grove and thornbush' and 'inhabited only by wild beasts'. After clearing away the dense thickets, they began the construction of a wooden monastery with the support of the local lord, Odo I, duke of Burgundy. The bishop of Chalon-sur-Saône, who approved the foundation, released the monks from their vow of stability at Molesme and, in the correct and canonical way, blessed Robert as abbot of the New Monastery.

An early threat to the new community came from Molesme, whose monks demanded of Pope Urban II the return of Robert on the grounds that his departure had caused scandal in the neighbourhood, and at a council held at Port d'Anselle, convened to discuss weighty matters, it was decided that they should have their wish. Robert resumed office at

---

4   The latest editions and translations of these two narratives are to be found in *NLT*, pp. 177–91, 232–59 (Latin text), and pp. 399–413, 417–40 (Latin text and translation). All quotations are from this edition and translation. The following brief summary is from the *Exordium Parvum*.

Molesme. In his stead Alberic, former prior of Molesme, was elected abbot (1099–1109). Chapter XV of the *Exordium Parvum*, entitled 'The institutes of the monks of Cîteaux who came from Molesme', lays down in some detail what are seen as many of the defining features of Cistercian monasticism: the close adherence to the Rule of St Benedict, the rejection of certain types of revenues, economic organisation through granges and *conversi* (lay brothers) and the siting of abbeys 'in places removed from populated areas'.[5] The text continues with the death of Alberic (1109) and the election of the third abbot of Cîteaux, the Englishman Stephen Harding.[6] Stephen, who had been one of the original party to leave Molesme, was responsible for two significant measures. The first was the exclusion of secular lords such as the duke of Burgundy from holding court in the monastery at important feasts; the second was the introduction of greater physical austerity into the church through the banning of gold and silver. Chapter XVI of the *Exordium Parvum* speaks of a period of uncertainty, even despair: although the monks attracted donations and landed endowments they failed to secure new recruits, a failure that the author put down to the harsh physical demands of the way of life at Cîteaux. But the final two chapters end on a triumphant and optimistic note, with an upturn in the monastery's fortunes, as thirty recruits – 'so many clerics, learned and noble, so many laymen, powerful in the world and likewise noble' – entered its gates. This led to the beginnings of the expansion through the foundation of daughter houses. The *Exordium Parvum* accordingly crafts a careful history, giving authenticity to the narrative by the inclusion of documents. Of eighteen chapters, nine are narrative and nine take the form of letters, privileges or statutes.

The *Exordium Cistercii* also tells the tale of the departure of Robert and his companions, but in a much shorter text – a bare two chapters – which have none of the fierce criticism of Molesme found in the *Exordium Parvum*. The problem with the monastery, which caused Robert and his colleagues to leave, was not, as in the *Exordium Parvum*, failure to observe the Rule of St Benedict. On the contrary, Molesme was 'of the most celebrated renown, and remarkable for monastic observance'. However, it was also rich, 'ample in possessions', but 'association of possessions with virtues is not usually longlasting', and this led Robert and others

---

[5] The traditional meaning of the word *conversus* in monastic contexts was an adult convert to the monastic life. Within the emerging monastic congregations it took on a new meaning, that of a member of a second group within an abbey, who took vows after a period of noviciate, but as a worker rather than a monk. On these see below, pp. 151–60.

[6] *Exordium Parvum*, chapter XVII, *NLT*, p. 438. The rubric of this chapter calls Alberic and Stephen first and second abbot respectively, thus ignoring Robert of Molesme, even though he was blessed as abbot of Cîteaux. The text states that Alberic ruled nine and a half years, and his death, which took place on 26 January, is sometimes given as 1108 and sometimes as 1109.

to ponder 'poverty, fruitful mother of a virile stock'.[7] True, observation of the Rule according to their profession was a concern, but the main reason for departure was to seek poverty, and it was thus that, armed by the authority of church officials and with the backing of the duke of Burgundy, they sought 'a desert place', 'a place of horror and of vast solitude'.[8] Internal evidence in both *exordia* – the apparent reference to the number of abbots at the time of writing[9] – might suggest a date for the composition of the texts in the early 1120s, some quarter century after the secession, but this has not been universally accepted. It was early in the last century that scholars began to address these issues, and the controversy continues. The debate, which has centred on the dating of the early Cistercian documents, is, more broadly, about how soon the monks of the New Monastery set a radical agenda for reform, how soon a monastic order – the Cistercian Order – emerged with an identity based on a set of uniform ideas and principles, and indeed whether 'uniformity', so often considered the hallmark of Cistercian monasticism, was ever really seen as an achievable aim.

A recent reassessment of the authorship, date and intention of the early Cistercian documents has been that of Chrysogonus Waddell in his edition of the early Cistercian documents.[10] Waddell's hypothesis is that the *Exordium Cistercii* is the earlier of the two texts and that its composition can be linked to the revision of the Cistercian liturgical customary, known as the *Ecclesiastica Officia*, that is, the detailed instructions for the performance of the canonical hours. In an important manuscript, Trento MS 1711, the *Exordium Cistercii* appears in sequence with the *Summa Carte Caritatis*, *Capitula* (rulings by the General Chapter), along with the second recension or revision of the *Ecclesiastica Officia*, thus bringing

---

[7] *NLT*, pp. 399–400.
[8] *Ibid.*, pp. 399–401. For further comment on the phrase 'in loco horroris et vaste solitudinis' see below, pp. 15–16, 57–8.
[9] *NLT*, p. 402 (*Exordium Cistercii*) and p. 439 (*Exordium Parvum*).
[10] Space does not permit a detailed discussion of these arguments. They are summarised in Waddell, *NLT*, pp. 137–55 (*Exordium Cistercii*) and 199–205 (*Exordium Parvum*); for his own arguments see pp. 156–61, 205–31. See also the review article of Waddell's edition by Christopher Holdsworth, *Cîteaux: Commentarii Cistercienses* 51 (2000), 157–66. Holdsworth is not convinced by Waddell's arguments as to authorship and suggests (p. 165) that the *Exordium Parvum* could be in its entirety the work of Stephen Harding, probably completed in two stages by 1119. J. -B. Auberger, in a review in the same issue (pp. 193–7), is also unconvinced by Waddell's arguments about authorship. See also J. -B. Auberger, *L'Unanimité Cistercienne primitive: mythe ou réalité?*, Cîteaux: Commentarii Cistercienses, Studia et Documenta, 3 (Achel, 1986). To these discussions of the narratives should be added Constance Berman's controversial dating of the documents in *The Cistercian Evolution: the Invention of a Religious Order in Twelfth-Century Europe* (Philadelphia, 2000) and the reviews by Brian Patrick McGuire, 'Charity and Unanimity: the Invention of the Cistercian Order: a Review Article', and Chrysogonus Waddell, 'The Myth of Cistercian Origins: C. H. Berman and the Manuscript Sources', *Cîteaux: Commentarii Cistercienses* 51 (2000), 285–97 and 299–386.

together a range of historical, constitutional and liturgical texts.[11] Waddell
has argued that the *Exordium Cistercii* was the work of Raynard du Bar,
a monk of Clairvaux who was elected abbot of Cîteaux, probably in 1134,
and who died in 1150. It took the form it did because it was designed as a
brief historical narrative leading into the legal and liturgical texts, which
were revised early in Raynard's abbacy. As a historical text, therefore, the
Exordium Cistercii represents a view of the origins of Cîteaux from nearly
forty years after the event.

The *Exordium Parvum* in the form in which we have it, on the other
hand, Waddell considers to be an even later creation, but one based on
earlier tradition. He is not the first to have considered it a hybrid document but his hypothesis differs slightly from earlier ones, in that he sees
the core of the *Exordium Parvum* – a hypothetical primitive *exordium*
– as the prologue and chapters I–II and IV–XIV, possibly written by
Abbot Stephen Harding as a 'postulants' guide' around 1113 when the
first daughter houses were being set up.[12] The remainder – that is, chapter
III, which contains the most damning criticism of Molesme, chapter XV,
the statutes which set the Cistercian agenda, and chapters XVI–XVIII,
the account of the lack of success of the New Monastery in attracting
recruits, and the turnaround under Stephen Harding himself – were also,
for Waddell, the work of Raynard du Bar, composed not long before 1147.
If he is correct we may see the production of the *Exordium Parvum* as
coming at a time of great change; that is, that as a result of the incorporation of a number of smaller monastic groups – Obazine, Coyrouz and
Savigny – the Cistercians produced yet another recension of the liturgical customs, that now known as RIII. The controversies about monastic
practices, initiated by Bernard of Clairvaux's letter to his nephew (traditionally dated to c. 1119) and his *Apologia* (c. 1125), were still alive, and the
White Monks found themselves fully immersed in ecclesiastical politics
with the first Cistercian pope elevated to the See of St Peter in 1145. Such
circumstances may well have produced a fuller and more self-conscious
account of the foundation of Cîteaux and its early years.

Whatever the fine tuning of the dating of these texts, the significance
is that they are later representations, or reworkings of the Cistercian story.
The Cistercians revised their foundation narrative – or their 'origin myth',

---

[11] MS Trento 1711 is described by Waddell, *NLT*, pp. 92–3. Its provenance is the abbey of Villers-
Betnach (dioc. Metz), and it dates from c. 1138/40. Berman considers the texts of *EC, SCC* and
Instituta (i.e. *Capitula*) to be additions to the manuscript of 'later than 1161' and dates the *Exordium
Cistercii* and *Summa Carte Caritatis* to between 1163 and 1165: see *Cistercian Evolution*, pp. 56–67; but
see also the discussion of the manuscript by Waddell himself in 'The Myth of Cistercian Origins',
pp. 304–6. The second revision or recension of the liturgical texts is generally known as RII.
[12] Auberger, *L'Unanimité*, pp. 42–52, considered *Exordium Parvum* as a hybrid, but with the earlier
version represented by the prologue and diplomatic texts, linked by the narrative of chapters I, and
III–V. Additions were therefore chapters IX–XIII, XV–XVIII. See *NLT*, p. 204.

perhaps – in different historical circumstances. Reading the prologue of the *Exordium Parvum* with this in mind makes it clear that the Cistercians were in some ways seeking to justify their foundation; that is, this was written at a time of controversy. It takes a defensive tone:

> We Cistercians, the first founders of this church, by this present document, are notifying our successors how canonically, and with what authority, and also by whom and by what stages their monastery and tenor of life took their beginning, so that, with the sincere truth of this matter made public, they may the more tenaciously love both the place and the observance of the Holy Rule there initiated …[13]

This prologue sets the scene for a narrative that will argue that Cîteaux was a canonical and legitimate foundation. Waddell is correct to point out that it is not until late in the twelfth century, with the *Exordium Magnum* of Conrad of Eberbach, that there is evidence of overt charges – from the German Benedictines – that as an order the Cistercians were illegal.[14] Nevertheless, there were earlier circumstances in which the White Monks might have felt defensive and crafted their history accordingly. So, what can we learn from these accounts, read in their broader context, about the early Cistercians?

The foundation of Cîteaux in context

A key feature of the narratives, particularly the *Exordium Parvum*, is the failure of the monks of Molesme to adhere strictly to the Rule of St Benedict. In chapter III, a section that Waddell would credit to Raynard du Bar c. 1147, the monks accuse themselves of perjury in failing to observe the Rule as they should, and the need to observe the Rule is a consistent feature of the text. Close adherence to Benedict's *horarium* (the monastic timetable for the day) was also an aspiration of other new monastic movements of the period. It meant reducing the liturgical accretions that had crept in over the centuries since Benedict wrote, as patrons and special friends came to expect lengthy masses for the dead; these reductions allowed for the restoration into the *horarium* of the periods of manual labour expected by Benedict. We do not have to rely solely on these Cistercian accounts, however, to understand the importance, for the early Cistercians, of adherence to the Rule. An English Benedictine monk, William of Malmesbury, writing before 1124 and possibly deriving his knowledge of the White Monks from the French Cistercian monastery of

---

[13] *NLT*, p. 417.

[14] *Exordium Magnum Cisterciense sive Narratio de Initio Cisterciensis Ordinis*, ed. Bruno Griesser, Corpus Christianorum Continuatio Medievalis, 138 (Turnhout, 1994).

L'Aumône, described how Stephen Harding, while a monk at Molesme and a leading protagonist in the debate that led to the secession, had proposed that the abbey should 'abandon superfluities and explore the very marrow of the Rule and nothing else', and noted that the Cistercians held to the Rule 'so closely … that they think it wrong to diverge by one letter, one iota'.[15] Another Benedictine monk, Orderic Vitalis, writing at a Norman monastery, St Evroul, and somewhat later (c. 1135) made the contemporary Benedictine abandonment of manual labour a keystone of the imagined debate at Molesme on the eve of the departure for Cîteaux.[16] Chapter XV of the *Exordium Parvum* contains perhaps the most explicit statement of the need to conform strictly to the tenets of the Rule in terms of food and drink, bedding and clothing, and all other details of the monastic life, and, even if Waddell is correct in his dating and this was an editorial addition to the text of c. 1147, the evidence of William and Orderic is clear: by the 1120s and 1130s the Cistercians were seen as the upholders of the Rule in its primitive form. That the witnesses are Benedictine monks makes their evidence the more compelling. This is how they understood Cistercian practices.

The insistence on the strict observance of the Rule linked the early Cistercians with the most powerful written monument in the monastic tradition. But they were aware – as indeed was Benedict himself – that what lay behind the cenobitic or communal way of life for which the Rule was written was the call of the desert, the cradle of the hermit monks of the third and fourth centuries who were seen as the real founders of the monastic way of life.[17] The eremitic monastic tradition was transmitted to the West through John Cassian, through the anonymous author of the *Regula Magistri*, and through Benedict himself. Part of the enduring Cistercian myth was the taming of the desert, whether in terms of monastic sites on the edges of society, or the opening up of new lands to cultivation. The *Exordium Cistercii* uses a phrase to describe the site of the New Monastery, which was to become a topos in Cistercian writing. Cîteaux, writes the author, was founded 'in loco horroris et vaste solitudinis', 'in a place of horror and vast solitude' (Deuteronomy

---

[15] William of Malmesbury, *Gesta Regum Anglorum: the History of the English Kings*, ed. and trans. R. A. B. Mynors, R. M. Thomson and M. Winterbottom, 2 vols, OMT (Oxford, 1998–9), I, 576–85 (p. 581) and note at II, 291. For further discussion of the Cistercians and the Rule see Janet Burton, 'Past Models and Contemporary Concerns: the Foundation and Growth of the Cistercian Order', in *Revival and Resurgence in Christian History*, ed. Kate Cooper and Jeremy Gregory, Studies in Church History, 44 (Woodbridge, 2008), pp. 27–45.

[16] *The Ecclesiastical History of Orderic Vitalis*, ed. and trans. M. Chibnall, 6 vols, OMT (Oxford, 1969–80), IV, 312–27.

[17] RB, chapter 1.

32.10).[18] In the *Exordium Parvum* the author makes use of the word *heremum*, 'desert', to encapsulate the theme of isolation and marginality. The early Cistercians accordingly transmitted to their successors the idea that they were the inheritors of the desert tradition. In an eloquent passage in his *Vita Prima* of St Bernard, William of St Thierry extolled the site of Clairvaux, the third daughter house of Cîteaux, in a way that linked both the eastern and the Benedictine traditions:

> I was amazed to see as it were a new heaven and a new earth, and the well worn path trodden by the monks of old, our fathers in Egypt, bearing the footprints of men of our own time…. There was a sense in which the solitude of that valley, strangled and overshadowed by its thickly wooded hills, in which God's servants lived their hidden lives, stood for the cave in which our father St Benedict was once discovered by shepherds – the sense in which those who were patterning their lives on his could be said to be living in a kind of solitude. They were indeed a crowd of solitaries. Under the rule of love ordered by reason, the valley became a desert for each of the many men who dwelt there.[19]

The *exordia*, therefore, portrayed Cîteaux as an institution that followed the Rule strictly, called to mind the tradition of the desert, which was symbolically portrayed by the very site of the house, and embraced that poverty which – characteristic of the emergent monastic movements of the period – at one and the same time evoked the notion of apostolic poverty (making the 'new monks' the successors of the apostles as well as the early monks) and criticised the great wealth and ostentation of contemporary houses of Black Monks. But was this construction of the monastic life the intention of the founder fathers of the *Novum Monasterium* or a later justification? Just how different was Cîteaux?

The *Exordium Parvum* has a number of heroes, the earliest of which is the founder abbot, Robert of Molesme. The author – no doubt with an eye to the criticism that in abandoning their abbey the monks had breached their vow of stability – makes a point of recording the canonical election and benediction of Robert as abbot of the New Monastery.[20] But Robert was ordered to return to Molesme, and the phrasing of the report of the council of Port d'Anselle, which refers to Robert's 'usual

---

[18] This is part of the 'Song of Moses' in which God is praised as a bulwark and defence of his people. The phrase appears in other Cistercian narratives, such as the *Vita Prima*, where it is applied to Clairvaux (PL, 185, col. 241) and in the early thirteenth-century foundation history of the Yorkshire monastery of Fountains, the *Narratio de Fundatione: Memorials of Fountains*, I, 2. On Cistercian sites see below, pp. 56–66.

[19] *Vita Prima Sancti Bernardi*, PL, 185, cols 247–8. The translation here is that in *The Cistercian World: Monastic Writings of the Twelfth Century*, ed. P. Matarasso (Harmondsworth, 1993), pp. 30–1.

[20] *NLT*, pp. 239–40, 422.

inconstancy', suggests that his career was unorthodox.[21] Indeed, putting the foundation of Cîteaux in its broader context makes it clear that it was the last of a number of experiments through which Robert had attempted to devise a combination of the eremitic and the cenobitic traditions.

Robert had entered the monastic life at Montier-la-Celle and risen to hold the office of prior, during which time he had helped to organise a group of hermits in the forest of Colan.[22] In 1068 he was elected abbot of Saint-Michel-de-Tonnerre, which he attempted to reform, despite the requests of the hermits of Colan that he become their leader. He was also sought, as prior, by Saint-Avoul-en-Provins, but was ordered by Pope Gregory VII to accede to the request of the hermits, and in 1075 he relocated them to Molesme, probably with the intention of transforming the community into a Benedictine abbey. Molesme attracted patronage – an important benefactor being Duke Odo I of Burgundy – and grew wealthy. Robert was fully conversant with other contemporary reform movements. He provided assistance, for example, to Bruno of Cologne in his search for a new form of religious life which was to result in the foundation of La Grande Chartreuse. Increasingly restless at Molesme, Robert attempted to introduce reform there but left once again to live with a group of hermits at Aux. In an action that was to prefigure events of late 1098 the monks petitioned Pope Urban II to order Robert to return to them, which he did, probably in 1094. Robert once more attempted to reform Molesme, this time assisted by the man who in 1094 or 1095 was named claustral prior, Alberic. Robert now embarked on a journey which took him through Flanders, visiting abbeys such as Saint-Vaast-la-Haut and Tournai, which were also undergoing reform. In 1097, just a year before the secession, Molesme's cell of Aulps was raised to the status of abbey, three witnesses of which were the 'three founders of Cîteaux': Robert, Alberic and Stephen. In one sense, therefore, Cîteaux marked not a beginning but an ending: it was to be the last of Robert's many experiments in making monastic foundations.

Robert's career speaks of his commitment to reform of monastic houses, and also his interest in the eremitic tradition in the monastic life. He was a man driven by the same need to question, to challenge and to reassess the meaning of the monastic life as other reformers who flourished in this time of intellectual ferment. However, for all the Cistercians' professed desire – so evident in the *Exordium Cistercii* – to withdraw from

---

[21] *Ibid.*, pp. 242, 425. William of Malmesbury implies that Robert was not unwilling to return to Molesme (*Gesta Regum*, I, 583; see also Orderic Vitalis, *Ecclesiastical History*, IV, 323–4). Robert was not counted as first abbot of Cîteaux until his canonisation in 1220.

[22] This account of Robert's earlier career is drawn from Jean-Baptiste Van Damme, *The Three Founders of Cîteaux*, trans. Nicholas Groves and Christian Carr, Cistercian Studies Series, 176 (Kalamazoo, 1998), pp. 19–52.

the world, the establishment of Cîteaux was rooted in that co-operation between the secular and ecclesiastical authorities that generally marked successful monastic foundations. The *Exordium Parvum* opens with the appearance of the monks before the archbishop of Lyon, a papal legate, and throughout the text the monks are shown to have secured ecclesiastical sanction for their foundation. Now, read one way this could be seen as a later Cistercian attempt to give the whole order canonical authority and legitimacy. Read in another way, however, it indicates that the early Cistercians were fully aware of the implications of what they were doing, and that they were locating their actions firmly within the agenda of the reforming papacy. Pope Urban II (1088–99) – the pope who launched the First Crusade – knew of Robert and his past career, and was supportive of the new foundation. He it was who ordered investigation into the petition of the monks of Molesme for the restoration of Robert, and that Robert should be returned there. However, he also supported the continuation of the community of those 'who love the desert'.[23] Although a Cluniac before his elevation to the See of St Peter and therefore a member of the congregation that would later become seen as the antithesis – and opponent – of the White Monks, Urban was a reformer and may have seen in the new groups that were springing up a force for good and an agent of change. The early years of Cîteaux coincided with a second wave of the struggles between the Empire and the Papacy, but Pope Paschal II, despite his difficulties, was able to lend his authority to the *Novum Monasterium* by granting the papal privilege.[24]

The *Exordium Parvum* makes two brief mentions of the lay founders of Cîteaux. In chapter III the author tells of the help given by the duke of Burgundy in raising the first wooden monastery and in supplying the monks with land and animals. In chapter XVII Abbot Stephen Harding forbade 'the duke of that region or any other lord to hold court in the church at any time, as had formerly been their practice on solemnities'. This last phrase is a telling one, because it suggests that in its early years – to 1109 at the earliest and maybe for some time later – Cîteaux was used to entertaining its lay patrons in traditional Benedictine fashion. Indeed, what the *Exordium Parvum* does not tell us is that the lay founder (in the sense of the provider of the site) was Reynard, viscount de Beaune, and his wife Hodierna. With the assent of their sons and daughter they granted to Abbot Robert 'and the brothers, who with him are desirous of observing the Rule of St Benedict more strictly and faithfully than they

---

23 *Exordium Parvum*, chapter VI, *NLT*, p. 423.
24 *Exordium Parvum*, chapter XIV, *NLT*, pp. 432–4. Chapter X (p. 428) refers to Alberic seeking the privilege 'before Pope Paschal, imprisoned by the Emperor, had committed his sin'. His 'sin' was to complete the coronation of Emperor Henry V after a period of imprisonment. For comment on this see *ibid.*, p. 429.

have hitherto done' their estate at Cîteaux, together with buildings and all things necessary for the monastery.[25] The estate was an allod; that is, it did not carry with it any service or obligations. Reynard also renounced any claim to the chapel on the site, since the monks did not feel it right to accept such a grant from a layman.[26] That he and his lord, the duke of Burgundy, were both committed to help the new foundation is shown by Reynard's further endowment of it, at the request of the duke of Burgundy. The evidence of Reynard's charter is consistent with that of the *Exordium Parvum* in that it stresses the desire of the monks to live more fully in accordance with the Rule of St Benedict. However, at the same time it suggests that the *Exordium*'s 'thickness of grove and thornbush … inhabited only by wild beasts' was a rhetorical device, intended to suggest a metaphorical desert; the reality of the site of the New Monastery was that it was far from remote but was integrated into the territorial holdings of Burgundy, not many kilometres from the ducal and ecclesiastical centre of Dijon, and settled enough to have a rural population. By 1106 work on the site was advanced enough for the church to be consecrated.[27]

The New Monastery was born, then, with the full cooperation of the ecclesiastical and temporal authorities, harnessed to the restless spiritual adventures of Robert of Molesme who in 1098 – and in contrast to his earlier endeavours – was able to convince a sizeable portion of his convent to join him in his latest monastic adventure. The foundation of Cîteaux therefore stands in sharp relief to that of the other reformed orders of the period, which grew up around individuals. The departure from Molesme was a true schism; Cîteaux grew out of division and dissent.

Chapter XV of the *Exordium Parvum* is headed 'The Institutes of the monks of Cîteaux who came from Molesme', but, as we have seen, both the content and the heading may be later additions inserted around 1147. The monks who left under Robert would have had no such clearly articulated programme as we find in chapter XV; rather, they were motivated by more general concerns linked to monastic practices and ecclesiastical reform. The presence of Robert at the New Monastery was short and his direct input into the development of Cistercian thought after 1098 must have been minimal. His successor, Alberic, had been prior at Molesme, and the *Exordium Parvum* notes his devotion to the Rule of St Benedict,

---

[25]   Translated in *The New Monastery; Texts and Studies on the Early Cistercians*, ed. E. Rozanne Elder, Cistercian Fathers Series, 60 (Kalamazoo, 1998), pp. 11–12, from *Chartes et documents concernant L'Abbaye de Cîteaux 1098–1182*, ed. J. Marilier, Bibliotheca Cisterciensis, 1 (Rome, 1961), no. 23 (pp. 49–51).

[26]   Auberger, *L'Unanimité*, pp. 91–2, discusses the site of the New Monastery, pointing out that as it was an allod it was not difficult to acquire. He takes the reference to the church, or chapel, to be the first church built by the monks and not one in existence at the time of Reynard's grant.

[27]   Marilier, *Chartes et documents*, no. 27 (p. 53).

suggesting that he may have been a formative influence in this part of the Cistercian agenda. It is clear from charter evidence that Alberic was successful in building the material base of the new abbey.[28] A glimpse of the evolution of Cistercian thought can be seen in the *Exordium Parvum*'s account of the abbacy of Stephen Harding. Like Robert, Stephen had a background marked by lack of stability. Born in England he entered the monastic life at the Benedictine abbey of Sherborne, only to leave and spend several years wandering: to Scotland, to France and to Rome. It was on his return from Rome that he became a monk of Molesme. Out of pride for 'the worthy man who was the author and agent of that monastic observance', or, as the *Exordium Parvum* describes him, 'a certain brother, Stephen by name, English by birth', William of Malmesbury assigns to Abbot Stephen a leading role in the secession from Molesme and the formation of Cistercian thought. The impression given in the *Exordium Parvum* is one of a decisive leader. Stephen is not only recorded as taking a stand about the presence of lay patrons in the monastery, but he defined that austerity with which the Cistercians were to become associated, and which was noted by William of Malmesbury as early as 1124 as being characteristic of Cîteaux:

> It is an index of his self-denial that in those houses you nowhere see, as you do in other monasteries, the glitter of gold or flashing gems or gleaming silver; for as the pagan poet says, 'To what purpose gold in holy places?' The rest of us think our sacred vessels fall far short unless a solid sheet of precious metal is outshone by glorious gems ... But the Cistercians put in second place what other mortals wrongly think most important; their efforts are all spent on the adornment of the character and they prefer pure minds to gold-embroidered vestments, knowing that the best return for a life well spent is the enjoyment of a clear conscience.[29]

Here then we begin to perceive a sense of 'us and them': by the third decade of the twelfth century, before even a single Cistercian foundation had been made on English soil, the Cistercians were perceived, by an English observer, to be different, to be distinctive and worthy of comment. Given that Stephen presided over the beginnings of the expansion of the congregation and the formation of the earliest constitution, there are good grounds for seeing his abbacy as a seminal point in the beginnings of the creation of a Cistercian identity.

---

[28] Van Damme, *Three Founders*, pp. 62–4; Marilier, *Chartes et Documents*, nos 22–3, 33–5 (pp. 49–51, 57).
[29] William of Malmesbury, *Gesta Regum*, I, 584–5.

CHAPTER TWO

'In mountain valleys and plains':
the Spread of the Cistercian Order

Here begins the narrative of the beginning of the Cistercian Order, how our fathers left the monastery of Molesme in order to recover the purity of the Order according to the Rule of St Benedict and founded the fertile house of Cîteaux which is the mother of all our houses, since from her, as if from the purest fountain, the rivers of all the churches of our Order flow.[1]

In his opening sentence of the third and most ambitious of the Cistercian *exordia*, the *Exordium Magnum*, Conrad of Eberbach makes two points.[2] The first is that within the Cistercian tradition the impetus for the secession from Molesme was now firmly seen as the desire to bring monastic life back to the Rule of St Benedict. The second is that Cîteaux itself was the mother house of all Cistercian abbeys – in other words the head of an order. The close and tightly knit relationship among Cistercian houses has always been seen as one of the hallmarks of the Order. So, too, has the rapid spread of the reputation of the White Monks and, as a result of this, the equally rapid foundation of Cistercian houses throughout Europe. The received narrative of modern scholarship on the Middle Ages tells us that the novelty and the attraction of their way of life meant that the monks of the New Monastery were not left alone to enjoy the solitude: between 1113 and 1115 four daughter houses were founded; in 1119 the then abbot, Stephen Harding, drew up the *Carta Caritatis*, the 'constitution' of the Order; and over the next thirty years the Cistercians were so overwhelmed both by recruits seeking the 'high road of supreme progress toward Heaven'[3] and by men and women wanting to found Cistercian houses that the congregation's numbers exploded, and in 1152 a halt had to be called.[4] The Order – theoretically but not in practice – had reached its fullest extent. Held together by common usages in all areas of

---

[1] *Exordium Magnum*, p. 5 (our translation). The quotation in the title for this chapter is from Orderic Vitalis, *Ecclesiastical History*, IV, 311, where Orderic begins his description of the foundation of Cîteaux and the spread of the Cistercians. Here he comments on their ubiquity.

[2] Conrad began the *Exordium Magnum* at Clairvaux between 1177 and 1193 and completed it at Eberbach between 1206 and 1221.

[3] A phrase used by William of Malmesbury in his essay on the Cistercians. See *Gesta Regum*, I, 577.

[4] See below, pp. 45–7.

monastic observance, the Cistercians continued to develop and became a powerful voice in ecclesiastical reform.

Although in traditional scholarship there have been some areas of debate, the chronology and nature of Cistercian growth were not seriously challenged: the beginnings of expansion by 'apostolic gestation', that is, from 1113 the deliberate colonisation or sending out of daughter houses containing twelve monks and an abbot; the development of a cohesive Order sharing common values and practices; from 1119 the governmental and jurisdictional mechanisms of General Chapter and visitation; and a fully fledged Order by the end of the first phase of expansion (1152), which was closely followed by the death of the most influential of the second generation of Cistercians, St Bernard (1153). However, recent historiography has questioned more closely both the 'neat' pattern of expansion from one generation to the next, and the myth of the ubiquity of Cistercian uniformity. This chapter examines the nature of the dispersal of the Order and indeed explores the very notion of 'order'.

The First Daughter Houses, 1113–21

As we have seen, the *Exordium Parvum* ends on an optimistic note: the entry of thirty noblemen and clerics into the 'cell of novices' which was said to have saved the New Monastery from extinction. In this narrative one name is conspicuous by its absence: that of Bernard of Fontaines, who was to become the most vociferous and well-known Cistercian of the twelfth century. According to the *Vita Prima* Bernard entered Cîteaux, along with thirty of his relatives and friends – the number coinciding with that given in the *Exordium Parvum*. The date is given in the *Vita Prima* as 1112, but it may have been 1113, the year in which the first daughter house was sent to La Ferté (Saône-et-Loire), some miles south of Cîteaux and roughly equidistant from Cîteaux and Lyon.[5] The foundation charter links the establishment of La Ferté to growing numbers at the New Monastery:

> There was so great a number of brothers at Cîteaux that the supplies were not sufficient for all of them, nor could the place where they lived adequately support them. It pleased the abbot of the place, Stephen by name, and the other brothers to seek another place at which some of them might serve God devoutly and according to the Rule, separated

[5] *Vita Prima*, PL, 185, cols 237–41. The *Vita Prima* was the work of three authors, William of St Thierry, Arnold of Bonneval and Geoffrey of Auxerre. Modern scholars prefer the date 1113 for Bernard's conversion, suggesting that the *Vita Prima* used 1112 as a way of indicating that the arrival of Bernard and his colleagues stimulated the foundation of the first daughter house the following year. See Matarasso, *Cistercian World*, p. 305.

from the others in body though not in spirit. While the abbot was diligently searching for such a place, the undertaking came to the ears of Lord Walter, bishop of Châlons, and of the canons of that same city, and to the ears of two counts, Savery and William, and of other highborn men. Rejoicing greatly and surveying the lands in the area, by God's will, they discovered the perfect spot for the monks to serve God and live according to the Rule ...[6]

This 'perfect spot' was in the forest of Bragny, on the banks of the Grosne, and there the colony settled under Abbot Philibert. Bishop Walter, mentioned in this passage, was by no means unknown to the Cistercians, for he it was who had welcomed the first monks from Molesme into his diocese in 1098. La Ferté, it would seem, was founded on the initiative of Stephen Harding as a result of the growth in numbers at Cîteaux, but with the close co-operation of both ecclesiastical and secular authorities. La Ferté was followed in May 1114 by Pontigny in the diocese of Auxerre. A priest, Ansius, who, like Stephen, is said to have recognised the implications of the growth of Cîteaux, offered his chapel to the New Monastery, with the approval of Bishop Humbald of Auxerre, for the foundation of a second colony.[7] Pontigny was by no means a 'place of horror and vast solitude'; on the contrary it was situated close to a network of roads and on one of the major routes to Italy.[8] A year later, so William of St Thierry records, 'God put it into the heart of Abbot Stephen to build a new house of Clairvaux'. The site is described by William: 'It had once been a hide-out of robbers and was known as the Vale of Wormwood either because the plant grew there in abundance or because of the bitter ordeal of those who fell into the robbers' clutches.'[9] The Cistercians brought redemption to the place in more ways than one. It was on his return from overseeing the foundation of Pontigny that Stephen had encountered and discussed the possibility of this third daughter house with Bishop Josseran of Langres and Josbert, lord of La Ferté and a kinsman of Bernard. Josbert, together with Bernard's own father, Tecelin, made possible this new foundation (June 1115). According to the *Vita Prima* of Bernard it was to the amazement of the brothers of Cîteaux who were experienced in the monastic life that Stephen appointed as founding abbot of Cîteaux's

---

[6] Translated in Elder, *The New Monastery*, p. 188, from Marilier, *Chartes et documents*, no. 42 (pp. 65–6), a partial transcript from the original charter. Note here the emphasis on the Rule and the phrase 'separated from others in body though not in spirit', which is reminiscent of *Carta Caritatis Prior*, on which see below, pp. 29–32.

[7] Translated in Elder, *The New Monastery*, pp. 188–9, from Marilier, *Chartes et documents*, no. 43 (p. 66), a twelfth-century copy of the foundation charter.

[8] William Chester Jordan, 'The English Holy Men of Pontigny', *Cistercian Studies Quarterly* 44 (2009), 63–75.

[9] *Vita Prima*, PL, 185, cols 241–2, translated in Matarasso, *Cistercian World*, p. 26.

third daughter house the youthful, and as yet untried, Bernard.[10] Given his connections with the lay founders of the house, however, his rapid elevation looks less surprising, and indeed the founding convent included four brothers of the new abbot, an uncle, two cousins and four friends.[11] Although Clairvaux was in the diocese of Langres it was a neighbouring churchman, William of Champeaux, formerly a regular canon of the reformed house of St Victor in Paris and now bishop of Châlons-sur-Marne, who blessed Bernard as abbot. William was to become a key figure in Cistercian expansion.

Cistercian tradition has assigned the very same foundation date both to Clairvaux and to the fourth daughter house, Morimond, the latter the result of negotiations between a hermit, a layman named John, a local lord from whom land was obtained, and Bishop Josseran.[12] However, Michel Parisse has argued for the likelihood of a rather later date for Morimond. The earliest surviving version of the *Carta Caritatis*, discussed below, gives prominence to the first three daughter houses of the New Monastery, but not Morimond, making it unlikely that it was in existence when Stephen Harding first conceived the *Carta*. However, a date for the foundation much later than 1115 is unlikely, since Morimond seems to have been substantial enough to send out its first colony in 1120 (Bellevaux); Parisse suggests a foundation date of c. 1117, with an 'official' Cistercian date to coincide with that of Clairvaux being introduced later to raise Morimond's standing in the Order.[13] The case of Morimond teaches us to treat with caution official Cistercian dates of foundation, affiliation and status, which may have developed over a number of decades. As we shall see, Morimond played a vital and substantial role in the Cistercian dispersal, and it may have been because of this – and probably as late as the 1150s – that it acquired the status of La Ferté, Pontigny and Clairvaux, and then as a result of its role as the head of a family rather than its early foundation.[14] What we can say, however, is that within about five years, if not three as usually supposed, the New Monastery had acquired it first four daughters, located in three dioceses.

The detailed evidence for these foundations is significant in that it demonstrates from the very start the proactive nature of the Cistercian expansion: the New Monastery grew, and the monks actively sought sites

10   *Vita Prima*, PL, 185, cols 245–6.
11   Marcel Pacaut, *Les moines blancs: histoire de l'ordre de Cîteaux* (Saint-Armond-Cher, 1993), p. 60.
12   Marilier, *Chartes et documents*, no. 45 (p. 67).
13   For a detailed discussion see Michel Parisse, 'La formation de la branche de Morimond', in *Unanimité et diversité Cisterciennes: filiations – reseaux – relectures du XIIe au XVIIe siècle*, Actes de Quatrième Colloque International du C.E.R.C.O.R., Dijon, 23–25 Septembre 1998, ed. N. Bouter (St Étienne, 2000), pp. 87–101.
14   *Ibid.*

– and those who would grant them – for further foundations. Moreover, they make abundantly clear the co-operation of secular patrons and the ecclesiastical authorities in the dispersal of the colonies of the New Monastery. As Martha Newman has pointed out, in contrast to the Cluniacs of previous centuries, who had purposefully sought to distance themselves from diocesan bishops, the early Cistercians consciously courted them and relied on their support. She has astutely drawn attention to the significance of the geographical location of Cîteaux and its four eldest daughters in relation to the dioceses of the area. Cîteaux itself lay at the northern extremity of Chalon-sur-Saône, near the dioceses of Langres and Autun, and La Ferté at its southern edge. Pontigny was located in the north-east of the diocese of Auxerre, near to the borders of Sens and Langres. Clairvaux lay in the diocese of Langres, near Châlons-sur-Marne and Troyes; and Morimond was in the eastern part of Langres. The Cistercians accordingly occupied liminal sites in terms of their dioceses; they may have been distant from the main centres of episcopal power, but their situation on the borders and fringes brought them into contact with more than just their own diocesan. 'Thus, rather than avoiding relations with the episcopacy, the first five Cistercian monasteries developed ties with ten bishops.'[15]

The expansion from Cîteaux continued in 1118 and four further houses were established before 1121. Preuilly, in the diocese of Sens, was founded in 1118 by Adela, daughter of William I of England, and her son, Theobald, count of Blois. Adela had known Robert of Molesme and was an early benefactor of Pontigny; for the foundation of Preuilly she acquired lands from a network of families. As LoPrete has argued, the new abbey not only consolidated the connectivity between these families, but occupied a strategic position on the frontiers of the lands of Blois with those of the Capetian kings.[16] A second family foundation followed: in 1121, probably on the initiative of Count Theobald, Cîteaux's daughter house of l'Aumône (Loir-et-Cher) was founded in the western comital domains and within the diocese of Chartres. Bishop Geoffrey of Chartres, who lent his approval to the establishment of the house, was an associate of Bishop William of Champeaux of Châlons-sur-Marne, who after the

[15] Martha G. Newman, *The Boundaries of Charity: Cistercian Culture and Ecclesiastical Reform 1098–1180* (Stanford, 1996), p. 143.

[16] Marilier, *Chartes et documents*, no. 63 (p. 78). See the important discussion of Adela's monastic patronage in Kimberley A. LoPrete, *Adela of Blois: Countess and Lord (c. 1067–1137)* (Dublin, 2007), and on Preuilly especially pp. 366–8, 403, 433, 502–3. See also Jean A. Truax, '*Miles Christi*: Count Theobald IV of Blois and Saint Bernard of Clairvaux', *Cistercian Studies Quarterly* 44 (2009), 299–320. Truax traces the relationship between the count and the abbot, who probably met before 1120, though Bernard is not mentioned in the foundation charter of Preuilly. For Preuilly and the foundations discussed below see Pacaut, *Les moines blancs*, pp. 62–3.

foundation of Clairvaux had developed a close friendship with Bernard. Loroux (Anjou), the ninth daughter house of Cîteaux, appears to have been founded in 1121 by Fulk, count of Anjou,[17] one of a growing number of the French aristocracy to see the potential in patronising the Cistercian monks, both as a way of obtaining their spiritual services and at the same time using them to cement political power. However, the close dependence of the early Cistercians on the French episcopate continued. In 1119 the bishop of Orleans requested from Stephen Harding a group of monks to establish Le Cour-Dieu, and the same year saw the formal foundation of Bonnevaux. Preparations for Bonnevaux had been in progress since 1117 when Archbishop Guy of Vienne, returning from a council at Dijon, had visited the New Monastery and requested of Abbot Stephen a colony of monks.[18] In 1119 Guy would become pope as Calixtus II. Given the prominence of bishops in the early spread of the Cistercian movement it is small wonder that the *Carta Caritatis*, to which we will turn shortly, insisted that the permission of the local bishop be obtained before a foundation was made in his diocese.[19]

Significantly, 1118 saw the beginning of houses of the next generation. In that year William of Champeaux encouraged Bernard to make a foundation in his diocese of Châlons-sur-Marne and so was born Trois Fontaines, the first 'granddaughter' of Cîteaux, established on land obtained from the son of the count of Champagne. Trois Fontaines was followed by Fontenay, a second daughter of Clairvaux (1119); and in 1121, with the assistance of the bishop of Laon, Clairvaux founded Foigny in the archdiocese of Reims. In 1120 foundations began from Morimond (Bellevaux, in the diocese of Besançon) and from Pontigny (Bourras, in the diocese of Auxerre). The momentum continued, with the foundation in 1121 from Morimond of La Creste (La Crête), in the diocese of Langres. But as with Morimond, a further note of warning as to the reliability of official dates of foundation is sounded by Cadouin in south-west France. Later lines of affiliation accorded to Cadouin the status of the eleventh house in line from Cîteaux, via Pontigny, and a foundation date of 1119. However, it was not until a date much later than 1119 that Cadouin became formally affiliated to the Cistercians. In origin it was one of a number of hermitages associated with Gerald de Salles. This group seems to have broken up after Gerald's death c. 1120 and re-formed around two houses, Cadouin and Dalon. Cadouin had been elevated to the status of abbey in 1119 with a monk of Pontigny named Henry as its abbot, but subsequent papal bulls make it clear that full incorporation into the

[17]   Marilier, *Chartes et documents*, no. 72 (p. 83).
[18]   Marilier, *Chartes et documents*, nos 62, 64–5 (pp. 78–9, 204).
[19]   *NLT*, pp. 274, 442.

Order was a long time coming, as indeed it was with Dalon. To accord Cadouin a foundation date of 1119 as a daughter house of Pontigny is therefore misleading.[20] As we shall see, it represents a later Cistercian attempt to 'tidy up' the lines of affiliation.

One of the greatest advances of recent historiography has been to dispose of the myth that the Cistercians were hostile to women and that women had no place in the history of the Cistercian expansion. Constance Berman's researches have done much to write women back into the history of the Cistercian Order, remedying a deficiency that she puts down to the male-dominated Cistercian narratives: 'That this [omission] is so should not be surprising given how much the discourse concerning medieval religious women was controlled by the men who wrote the earliest histories of the Cistercian Order and other orders.' The invisibility of women in the male-authored 'self-glorifying texts called *exordia*, which Cistercian men wrote and from which they excluded women' has been balanced as a result of Berman's delving into the cartularies and other administrative records of local houses to argue for female participation in the Cistercian movement from an early date.[21]

It is, indeed, in the *Vita Prima* of Bernard of Clairvaux that we find early evidence of the presence of women in houses associated with the Cistercians. In describing the entry of Bernard and his companions into Cîteaux, William of St Thierry notes that some of the postulants were married, and that their wives took vows at the same time. He continues to tell how Bernard built a nunnery at Jully for these women.[22] Although Bernard is credited with the foundation, and his sister-in-law, Elizabeth, was first prioress, and his sister, Humbeline, second head of the house, the land had originally been granted to Molesme. Moreover, at a date that cannot be determined more precisely than between 1118 and 1132, the abbot of Molesme, with the counsel of those of Pontigny, Clairvaux, Morimond and Fontenay, is said to have drawn up customs to be followed at the nunnery which closely resembled those of the Cistercian Order. This suggests that Jully continued under the oversight of Molesme, though with close contacts with Bernard and with Clairvaux

---

20 For a discussion see Berman, *Cistercian Evolution*, pp. 123–6, 138–40; see also B. Barrière, 'Les abbayes issues de l'érémitisme', in *Les Cisterciens de Languedoc (XIIIᵉ–XIVᵉ siècle)*, Cahiers de Fanjeaux, 21 (Toulouse, 1986), pp. 71–105, on Cadouin especially pp. 80–81 and on Dalon pp. 79–80. See the latter also (pp. 82, 94–8) on the evidence of the letters of Bernard and papal bulls suggesting the slow adoption of full Cistercian association.

21 Constance Hoffman Berman, 'Were there Twelfth-Century Cistercian Nuns?', in *Medieval Religion: New Approaches*, ed. Constance Hoffman Berman (New York/London, 2005), pp. 217–48. See also her *Cistercian Evolution*.

22 *Vita Prima*, PL, 185, col. 237; Berman, 'Were there Cistercian Nuns?', pp. 228–9.

as well as other Cistercian houses; perhaps significantly these did not include Cîteaux itself.[23]

More importantly, in 1120 Josseran, bishop of Langres, who had been associated with the foundation of Clairvaux, oversaw the foundation of a nunnery at Tart by a nun of Jully, Elizabeth, daughter of a great benefactress of Cîteaux, Elizabeth de Vergy. The project, as Elizabeth Connor has demonstrated, involved a far wider network of people, lay, monastic and ecclesiastical, than just these two. Moreover, a charter of a later abbot of Cîteaux, Guy, makes it clear that a close relationship had been forged between the nunnery and Cîteaux: Tart was described as a daughter house of Cîteaux, living according to the institutes of Cîteaux, and fully under the oversight of the father abbot.[24] It is clear that women were associated with the emerging Order from the second decade of the twelfth century if not earlier.

By 1121, of the first daughter houses of Cîteaux only La Ferté had failed to make a foundation, and there were sixteen abbeys for men (if we do not count Cadouin), including the New Monastery itself.[25] Cîteaux had nine daughter houses, and six granddaughters, three of the line of Clairvaux, two of Morimond and one of Pontigny. The association of an existing hermitage at Cadouin with the Cistercians is significant, even if it was not fully effective for some time. As we will see, not all Cistercian houses were foundations *de novo*: the Order also grew by incorporation. Moreover, the knowledge and influence of the Cistercians were beginning to disperse more widely in geographical terms: Cadouin lies in the Bordeaux region of south-eastern France, a world away – politically, socially and ecclesiastically – from the Burgundian cradle of the nascent Order.

This is an appropriate point to break into this account of the geographical dispersal of the daughter houses of the 'Order' to ask: was there an 'Order' in 1121, and what do the sources tell us of how the monks of the mother house viewed its satellite houses?

---

[23] Berman ('Were there Cistercian Nuns?', pp. 218–19) suggests that Molesme had oversight of Jully until 1145 when it passed to Clairvaux, but it is not made clear why this should have happened.

[24] See Elizabeth Connor, 'The Abbey of Tart', in Elder, *The New Monastery*, pp. 211–18; Berman, 'Were there Cistercian Nuns?', p. 219, points out that Tart had at least eighteen daughter houses by the late twelfth century. See also Laurent Veyssiere, 'Les différences de vue et de réalisation chez Étienne Harding et Saint Bernard à propos des premières moniales cisterciennes', in Bouter, *Unanimité et diversité*, pp. 133–47. See below (pp. 51–4) for further discussion of nunneries.

[25] Significantly sixteen houses, with seven more already begun, is the number given by William of Malmesbury, writing before 1124: *Gesta Regum*, I, 582–3.

The Beginnings of a Monastic Order? The Carta Caritatis and Cistercian 'Identity'

In the opening sentence of that version of the *Carta Caritatis* known as *Carta Caritatis Prior* (*CC1*) the text tells how the charter was drawn up by Stephen Harding 'before the Cistercian abbeys began to flourish'. It continues:

> In this decree, then, the aforesaid brethren, taking precaution against future shipwreck of their mutual peace, elucidated and decreed for their posterity by what covenant, or in what manner, indeed with what charity their monks throughout abbeys in various parts of the world, though separated in body, could be indissolubly knit together in mind. They considered that this decree should be called the *Charter of Charity*, because, averting the burdensome levying of all exactions, its statute pursues only charity and the advantage of souls in things human and divine.[26]

The *Carta* is not mentioned in the *Exordium Parvum* but the author of the *Exordium Cistercii* is secure in his own mind about both its authorship and its early date, and indeed its purpose:

> from the very beginning, when the new planting had begun bourgeoning with new branches, the venerable father Stephen, with a keenly watchful sagacity, had provided in advance a document of admirable discernment, as a sort of pruning hook, namely, to cut off the budding shoots of schism which, springing up, could at some time choke the burgeoning fruit of mutual peace. So it was that he wished this document to be given the appropriate name, *Charter of Charity* – because its every article is redolent of only what pertains to charity.[27]

This is quite explicit: the author of the *Carta Caritatis* was Stephen Harding; the date of composition coincided with and indeed may have preceded the first foundations from the New Monastery; and the dynamic behind the text was the preservation of peace and love. The text that follows indicates Stephen's conviction that such was achieved through uniformity of observance. The two short chapters of the *Exordium Cistercii* thus move seamlessly from a narrative of the origins of Cîteaux to the first step, taken by Stephen Harding, to create a monastic order, one in which administrative arrangements would be underpinned by *caritas*, charity, or love. Chapter III of the sequence of texts begins

[26] *NLT*, p. 442. The phrase 'before the Cistercian abbeys began to flourish' confirms that the prologue or preface was added at a later date.
[27] *NLT*, p. 402.

29

with a summary or abridgement of the charter, known as *Summa Carte Caritatis.*

As with the narratives discussed in chapter 1 above, there is considerable debate about the evolution of the texts of the *Carta Caritatis* that are extant, namely *Carta Caritatis Prior* (*CC1*), *Summa Carte Caritatis* and *Carta Caritatis Posterior* (*CC2*).[28] It is generally accepted that any version of the *carta* composed by Stephen c. 1113 is not recoverable. However, Waddell argues that *Carta Caritatis Prior* represents the developed text that was presented to Pope Calixtus II at Saulieu in 1119 for confirmation, which produced the papal bull *Ad hoc in apostolicae*.[29] *Carta Caritatis Prior* was replaced by a later version in 1152, which was confirmed by Pope Eugenius III. *Carta Caritatis Posterior* (*CC2*), while not this precise text, is a version that was confirmed in 1165 by Pope Alexander III.[30]

The question of the dating of the documents is not just a pedantic one. It has profound implications for the question of a Cistercian 'Order'. If Waddell is correct in thinking that *CC1* is – shorn of its preface or prologue – to all intents and purposes the same as Stephen Harding's *Carta Caritatis*, then the notion of 'Order' in terms of a cohesive body, following the same regulations and held together constitutionally, came very early on in the expansion of houses following the way of life of the New Monastery. In her radical reappraisal of the Cistercians in the half century or so following the foundation in 1098, Constance Berman has argued that all the documents on which we construct our arguments are either forgeries or of a later date.[31] The Cistercian Order, she would argue, did not exist until after mid century, and the phrase *ordo Cisterciensis* or *ordo noster* meant not an order in the constitutional sense, but something more akin to 'the Cistercian way of life'. For Berman, what she designates proto-Cistercian houses (those founded or incorporated before about 1150) were not part of an order, but were simply houses following – fairly loosely – the same customs. There are two issues here. The first is uniformity of observance – *ordo Cisterciensis* as Berman would interpret it. The second is the mechanism, or series of mechanisms, by which uniformity would be enforced.

Let us examine the text of *Carta Caritatis Prior* more closely. The underlying dynamic of its eleven chapters is uniformity, and this is surely

---

[28] These texts are printed and translated in *NLT*, pp. 183–5, 404–7 (*Summa Carte Caritatis*), 274–82, 442–50 (*Carta Caritatis Prior*), 381–8, 500–5 (*Carta Caritatis Posterior*).
[29] Marilier, *Chartes et documents*, no. 69 (pp. 81–2); *NLT*, pp. 261–82 and 442–50. See also Auberger, *L'Unanimité*, pp. 26–8. Even *Ad hoc in apostolicae* is not free from controversy. Waddell and others accept the authenticity of the pope's confirmation, but Berman does not. The preface of *Carta Caritatis Prior*, quoted above, was not part of the original, but was added much later.
[30] *NLT*, pp. 371–94 and 498–505.
[31] Berman, *Cistercian Evolution*, pp. 97–110.

one hallmark of what we would understand as a monastic order, even if it is aspirational rather than achievable in practice. *Carta Caritatis Prior* lays down that all should use the same books and follow the same interpretation of the Rule:

> we will and we command them, that they observe the Rule of St Benedict in everything just as it is observed in the New Monastery. Let them not introduce a different meaning in the interpretation of the Holy Rule; but as our predecessors, the holy fathers – that is to say the monks of the New Monastery – understood and kept it, as we today understand and keep it.[32]

Such desire for uniformity of observance, based on long tradition, can be seen in two other documents. The first relates to Stephen's reform of the hymnal, sometime between 1109 and 1112, in which Stephen, describing himself as 'second minister of the New Monastery', ordered that the community and its successors were to use only the hymns known to have been composed by Archbishop Ambrose of Milan because they were the ones known to have been prescribed by Benedict.[33] The second, dated internally to 1109 and therefore early in his abbacy, is Stephen's *monitum* relating to the Bible. It explains his careful examination of copies of the Bible in pursuit of an authentic text, which he then had copied for use by all. His *monitum* drew attention to the corrections and justified them.[34] These documents are reflected in *Carta Caritatis Prior*, chapter III, which requires the deployment of the 'usages and chant and all the books necessary for the day and night Hours and for Mass according to the form of the usages and books of the New Monastery, so that there may be no discord in our conduct, but that we may live by one charity, one Rule, and like usages'.[35]

Carta Caritatis Prior also introduces the mechanisms by which such uniformity would be enforced: the annual visitation of each daughter house by the Father Immediate, and the required attendance by all abbots at the annual General Chapter, which came to be held at Cîteaux in September.[36] The Chapter was to serve a number of functions. It was to

---

[32] *NLT*, p. 444.

[33] Marilier, *Chartes et documents*, no. 31 (p. 55); see also M. Chrysogonus Waddell, 'Abbot Stephan [sic] Reforms the Hymnal', and 'The Molesme – Cistercian Hymnal', in Elder, *The New Monastery*, pp. 78–86, reprinted from the introduction to Waddell's edition and translation, *The Twelfth-Century Cistercian Hymnal*, I, Cistercian Liturgy Series, 1 (Gethsemani, 1984), pp. 7–22.

[34] Marilier, *Chartes et documents*, nos 31–2 (pp. 55–6). See Van Damme, *Three Founders*, pp. 80–1.

[35] *NLT*, p. 444.

[36] *NLT*, pp. 445–7. For the date of 14 September, the Feast of the Exaltation of the Holy Cross, see the statute for 1186/8: *Twelfth-Century Statutes*, pp. 37, 134. On the operation of visitation and the General Chapter, see below, pp. 88–95.

be the forum for the disciplining of wayward abbots. It was to maintain the bonds of love and charity that underpinned the Order. It was its legislative body, and it was to take responsibility for the relief of poverty of any one of its houses. The notion of 'order' is further cemented by the development of the procedure laid down in the Rule of St Benedict for the election of the head of the community, the abbot. The Rule established the principle of the choice of the superior by the community.[37] However much, in practice, such election was subject to external pressures,[38] this principle remained. The *Carta Caritatis*, however, extended the notion of community by making it the responsibility of the Father Immediate to oversee the election of the abbot of a daughter house, and by widening the circle of potential candidates to make it possible for any Cistercian monk to be elected to the headship of a Cistercian abbey. Such scrutiny of elections – as indeed in the conduct of visitation – was a 'top-down' process, with Cîteaux at the apex. But the mother house of the Order was not exempt from oversight. She was visited by the abbots of her three eldest daughters,[39] and participation in the election of a new abbot of the mother house of the Order was extended to any abbot who could get to Cîteaux within three weeks of the announcement of the death of its abbot.

But how far were these ideas about an Order as such in place at that date at which we have paused in our narrative to ask these questions about Cistercian identity, that is, around 1121? This is a matter of great debate. Berman has argued that these measures came late, much later than Stephen Harding's *Carta*, and probably around the middle of the twelfth century.[40] If she is correct, then the annual General Chapter and visitation came into being just as the Order was (as we shall see) trying to halt further expansion. A counter argument is that it would have been precisely at this time that such a system would have been seen as unworkable. The whole notion of abbots travelling twice a year, once on a series of visitations and again for the Chapter, suggests that these ideas date from when the congregation was largely confined to its Burgundian heartlands. It needs to be acknowledged, however, that records of the operation of the Chapter and of visitation are rare before the middle of the twelfth century, but this does not mean that they cannot be found.[41]

[37] RB, chapter 64.
[38] For pressures on elections in an English context see David Knowles, *The Monastic Order in England: a History of its Development from the Times of St Dunstan to the Fourth Lateran Council, 940–1216*, 2nd edn (Cambridge, 1963), pp. 395–410.
[39] *Carta Caritatis Posterior* added Morimond to the first three daughter houses.
[40] Berman, *Cistercian Evolution*, pp. 46–92.
[41] On visitation see below, pp. 91–5.

A suggestive example comes from the letters of St Bernard and it relates to the second of Clairvaux's English daughter houses.

In 1131 Bernard had been instrumental in sending the Cistercian message to the north of England with the foundation of Rievaulx near Helmsley. As a direct result of the mission a group of monks from the Benedictine abbey of St Mary's, York, had left their community, in an action that resulted in the foundation of Fountains Abbey, a second Yorkshire daughter house of Clairvaux. The thirteenth-century *Narratio de Fundatione* of Fountains records how Bernard, having agreed that the community should be a daughter house of Clairvaux, sent Geoffrey of Ainai, a monk, to instruct the brethren: 'ut instituat eos prima ordinis elimenta, modum vivendi, et mores conservandi, secundum ordinis disciplinam' ('so that he might teach them the elements of the Order, the way to live and keep the customs, according to the discipline of the Order'). They received his teaching 'as warm wax does the impress of the seal'.[42] This passage may be taken to lend support to Berman's interpretation of *ordo Cisterciensis*. But there is also evidence in the early sources of the second and more concrete meaning of *ordo*. At a point before the death of the second abbot of Fountains, Richard, in 1143, Bernard wrote jointly to him and Abbot William of Rievaulx. He stated his obligation to visit them:

> I am obliged to go out of my house on visitations by the Rule of our Order ... [but] ... the way is hard and difficult, and my body is weak. Because of this, beloved, I am sending for your visitation my brother and dear friend Henry, Abbot of Vauclair. Hear him, I beg you, as if he were myself. He is an upright and reasonable man who has taken on his shoulders some of my own cares and burdens and shares my powers for the correction of faults and the maintenance of the Order.[43]

Further, on Richard's death Bernard wrote to Prior Alexander of Fountains and his monks, and his letter is significant in a number of ways. One is that Bernard clearly understood that, as Father Immediate, he had responsibility to oversee the election of Richard's successor, but instead he sent a proxy, Henry Murdac, abbot of Vauclair: 'I would have sent someone to you long ago, but I have been waiting until I could do so conveniently and helpfully', he wrote, adding that he had given Henry 'full authority to act in the matter of this election and in anything that may need regularizing or correcting in your monastery or the others'. Moreover, the election of Henry Murdac, which can be seen as Bernard's imposition of his own preferred candidate on the Fountains commu-

---

[42] *Memorials of Fountains*, I, 46–7 (our translation).
[43] Bernard of Clairvaux, *The Letters of St Bernard of Clairvaux*, trans. B. S. James (London, 1953; repr. with intro. B. Kienzle, Stroud, 1998), no. 201 (pp. 269–70).

nity at a critical point in the York election dispute, can also be seen to reflect the *Carta*'s provision for the election of any Cistercian monk to the abbacy of any house.[44] Although the evidence is not conclusive that what was being practised in 1143 was in place in 1121 or 1119, nevertheless Bernard's instructions concerning both visitation and election bear the hallmarks of a system of some maturity.

The *Carta* accordingly points to a desire, or aspiration, on the part of Stephen and his successors to ensure that all Cistercians followed the same customs. Two further writings, emanating from Clairvaux rather than Cîteaux, tell us of an evolving sense of 'what made a Cistercian', although they could not be more different from the juridical nature of the *Carta Caritatis*. These are Bernard's *Apologia* (c. 1125) and his earlier letter written to his nephew, Robert, who had left the Cistercians to join – or, as the counter claim would have it, rejoin – the Cluniacs. In the letter Bernard draws some sharp contrasts between the Cistercians and the Cluniacs. The Cluniacs claimed that Robert had been promised to them as a child oblate and that although as an adult he had joined the Cistercians, nevertheless he should be bound by the earlier vow. Bernard's attitude is that even if this were true – and of this he was unsure – the adult vocation should take precedence over the vow made by parents on behalf of a child. He signals here the Cistercian breach of the tradition of oblation and insistence on adult vocation. Further, he contrasts Cluniac indulgence with Cistercian austerity in matters of food and clothing, claiming for his own brothers a line of descent from the earliest monks:

> Does salvation rest rather in soft raiment and high living than in frugal fare and moderate clothing? If warm and comfortable furs, if fine and precious cloth, if long sleeves and ample hoods, if dainty coverlets and soft woollen shirts make a saint, why do I delay and not follow you at once? But these things are comforts for the weak, not the arms of fighting men … Wine and white bread, honey-wine and pittances, benefit the body not the soul. The soul is not fattened out of frying pans! Many monks in Egypt served God for a long time without fish. Pepper, ginger, cumin, sage, and all the thousand other spices may please the palate but they inflame lust. And would you make my safety dependent on such things?[45]

These themes were developed in the *Apologia*, written at the request of William, Benedictine abbot of St Thierry, who was to become one of Bernard's biographers. William was concerned that Bernard should refute

---

44 *Ibid.*, nos 173–4 (pp. 242–4). For the York election, see below, pp. 39–40.
45 *Letters of St Bernard of Clairvaux*, no. 1 (pp. 1–10, especially p. 8). For the copying of this letter by Bernard's secretary, William, later abbot of Rievaulx, see *Vita Prima*, PL, 185, cols 255–6.

a charge that he had been slandering the Cluniacs.[46] In his response to William, the *Apologia*, Bernard made it clear that he was not condemning the Cluniacs as a whole, merely abuse within their order. In so doing he further polarised the White Monks and the Black, and we may say that Bernard was instrumental in the 1120s in creating and shaping a Cistercian identity, and those features that were recognised as quintessentially Cistercian. While it was not his purpose to give his audience a detailed description of the structure of the Cistercian Order, the way in which he refers in the *Apologia* to monks of 'our Order' suggests something beyond the notion of *ordo* as simply a way of life.

Cistercian identity was created in different ways. It was about how the Cistercians perceived themselves and how they portrayed themselves to others. This was a gradual process; the General Chapter, in its role as legislator, created a body of rules and regulations, the *capitula* and *statuta* which came to define all manner of Cistercian activity, and which will be explored in the chapters that follow.[47]

'Sixteen monasteries he has built': further dispersal under Stephen Harding

William of Malmesbury wrote this of Stephen Harding some time before 1124 – just two years before the first Cistercian prelate was elected[48] – and the Cistercian expansion was sustained until and beyond Stephen's resignation in 1133. Even allowing for the difficulties in establishing the precise nature of the earliest *Carta Caritatis*, and therefore exercising a reasonable amount of caution, we may suggest that by this time the White Monks had begun to develop a sense of distinctiveness and a sense of self-identity, as well as mechanisms to transmit them. These notions were further defined – albeit in a negative sense of 'what Cistercians are not' – by Bernard. For the mother house of Cîteaux itself the 1120s

---

[46] The *Apologia* is translated in *Cistercians and Cluniacs: St Bernard's Apologia to Abbot William*, trans. Michael Casey, with an intro. by Jean Leclercq, Cistercian Fathers Series, 1 (Kalamazoo, 1970).

[47] The earliest *capitula* are to be found in the Trento MS in the sequence of texts with *Exordium Cistercii* and *Summa Carte Caritatis*. These are described by Waddell as a 'summary and thematic arrangements of the General Chapter statutes'. They are an abridged version of the first group of institutes (27 in number) which appear with two other series (12 unnumbered and 48 numbered chapters) in the sequence of texts with *Exordium Parvum* and *Carta Caritatis Prior*. This suggests that all these institutes had been decided by the General Chapter before c. 1136 when they were codified by Raynard du Bar for the introduction to the revision of the customary known as RII (on which see above, pp. 12–13). All 87 appear in the 1147 redaction known as RIII. All the *capitula* were subsequently modified or in some cases eliminated. The dating is complex and it is not possible to recover the earliest ones. Waddell separated the twelfth-century series into: A: earliest, possibly ?1136; B: 1157–61; C: 1180–89; D: 1190–1201.

[48] William of Malmesbury, *Gesta Regum*, I, 582–3, where he also noted that a further seven had been begun. The first Cistercian to hold episcopal office was Abbot Peter of La Ferté (1121–26), archbishop of Tarentaise (1126–40).

was a decade of consolidation rather than expansion and between 1121 and 1130 it made no further foundations.[49] By contrast Cîteaux's daughters flourished, although Morimond experienced temporary disruption and scandal caused by its abandonment by Abbot Arnold, a situation remedied by the installation as abbot, by Stephen Harding on Bernard's suggestion, of Walter, prior of Clairvaux.[50] The geographical areas that experienced Cistercian influence now widened. Cistercian houses might be founded *de novo* or – as we have seen in the case of Cadouin – by incorporation; the latter might involve the taking over of an informal eremitic group, or the adoption of Cistercian customs by an existing Benedictine or Augustinian house. The establishment of a new abbey might be the result of complex relationships between the White Monks themselves and churchmen, kings, princes and members of the lay aristocracy; often it was a network of associations that brought a foundation to fruition. And all of these people had their own motives and agenda; all had their own ideas of what they could do for the Cistercians, and what the Cistercians could do for them. This fusion of interests took the Cistercians to the borders of Christendom and beyond.

After France the first push into 'foreign' territory was into Italy, into what was very much a divided region. The north was part of the Empire, which, following the death of Emperor Henry V in 1125 saw fierce factional fighting between Guelf and Ghibelline. Further south, in central Italy, the Papal States were emerging under a more purposeful papal monarchy, while the cities of the north were flexing their muscles. The first expansion in Italy came from La Ferté, which made two early foundations, Tiglieto in Liguria (1120) and Locedio (1124) in the diocese of Vercelli and Piedmont.[51] Of the four daughters of Cîteaux that enjoyed pre-eminence, however, La Ferté was the least successful in numerical terms, counting only eight foundations by 1153.

The White Monks also began to expand into the German-speaking lands. Just before the crisis at Morimond its German abbot had sent monks to Camp (Altenkamp) to the west of Cologne in 1123. Camp itself made foundations at Walkenried (1130) and Volkenrode (1131), both between the rivers Elbe and Weser, Amelunxborn (1135), to the west of the Weser, and to Hardehausen (forming a triangle with Amelunxborn

49 In 1131 Cîteaux established three new monasteries: La Bussière (dioc. Autun), to the west of Cîteaux, Le Miroir (dioc. Lyons), and St Andrew de Sestri, not far from Genoa. The latter was a significant foundation in that it was the conversion of a Benedictine house.

50 The problems at Morimond were caused by Arnold's desire, opposed by the Cistercian hierarchy, to make a foundation in the Holy Land. Of note at this date (1124) was the dominant role of Bernard in the affair. See Pacaut, *Les moines blancs*, p. 81. See also *Letters of St Bernard of Clairvaux*, no. 6 (pp. 24–5).

51 Tiglieto became the mother house of Staffarda (1135) and Casanova (1151).

and Walkenried) and Michelstein, to the east of Walkenried, both in 1140. The affiliation of Morimond, largely through Camp, dominated in the north of the German-speaking lands, but it also colonised southern Germany with the foundation of Ebrach in Bavaria in 1127, Ebrach itself growing enough to found Rein in Austria two years later.[52] The expansion of Morimond's family was not confined to Germany; its daughter house of Bellevaux gave rise to Lützell (Lucelle) in Alsace (now France), and Lutzell to Neuburg (France, 1131), Kaisheim (Germany, 1134) and others.[53]

In 1128 L'Aumône became the springhead of Cistercian expansion in England, dispatching monks to Waverley at the behest of the aged bishop of Winchester, William Giffard,[54] and it also sent monks to staff the first Welsh house, Tintern, near the border with England, at the invitation of the Clare lord of Chepstow in 1131. Whereas Tintern could number only two daughter houses, Kingswood in Gloucestershire and Tintern Parva in Ireland, the senior English house, Waverley, gave rise to a substantial family of daughter and granddaughter houses. L'Aumône was also the mother or grandmother of over half of the fourteen abbeys in Brittany.[55]

It was, however, Bernard's Clairvaux which from the 1120s became the most successful springboard of Cistercian expansion. Bernard, a charismatic preacher, inveterate letter writer and, with the publication of his *Apologia* in 1125, a powerful figurehead in monastic circles, was never going to be ignored. His European status was further enhanced by his involvement in the controversy over the disputed election to the papacy following the death of Honorius II in 1130. Bernard backed a winner – Innocent II over Anacletus II – and that Innocent prevailed over his rival was due in no small part to Bernard, who brought to his side the kings of France and England. Nor was he – despite the Benedictine and hence Cistercian emphasis on stability – a stay-at-home abbot. And there can be

---

[52] On the German houses see Klaus Wollenberg, 'Die Deutschen Zisterzienserklöster zwischen Rhein und Elbe', in Bouter, *Unanimité et diversité*, pp. 321–44. For the filiation of Morimond see Parisse, 'La formation de la branche de Morimond'. For the dates of foundation and for discussion see Pacaut, *Les moines blancs*, pp. 81–4, 367–82.

[53] Ernst Kemp, 'La presence cistercienne dans la Suisse médiévale', in Bouter, *Unanimité et diversité*, pp. 400–18.

[54] Although Waverley was the earliest English Cistercian foundation, the Savigniac foundation of Furness, established in 1124 at Tulketh, was not slow to claim to be the senior house in England after the merger of the two orders.

[55] For an account of the Cistercians in England and Wales see Janet Burton, 'The Foundation of the British Cistercian Houses', in *Cistercian Art and Architecture in the British Isles*, ed. C. Norton and D. Park (Cambridge, 1986), pp. 24–39; and '*Homines sanctitatis eximiae religionis consummatae*: the Cistercians in England and Wales', *Archaeologia Cambrensis* 154 (2007 for 2005), 27–49; Glyn Coppack, *The White Monks: the Cistercians in Britain 1128–1540* (Stroud, 1998); and *Fountains Abbey: the Cistercians in Northern England* (Stroud, 2003); Robinson, *Cistercians in Wales*. On L'Aumône and Brittany see André Dufief, 'Filiations des abbayes cisterciennes bretonnes', in Bouter, *Unanimité et diversité*, pp. 121–8.

no doubt as to the impact wrought both by his political involvement and his journeys beyond the confines of the cloister. Bernard accompanied Innocent on his travels in 1130–31. It was probably a meeting between Bernard and Henry I of England in 1131, at which Henry was persuaded to lend his support to Innocent, that led to the famous letter written by Bernard to the king announcing his intention to make a Cistercian settlement in his realm.[56] When the foundation was made – at Rievaulx in north Yorkshire the following year by one of Henry's leading northern barons, Walter Espec – it received the backing not only of the king, but of Pope Innocent and of Henry's archbishop of York, Thurstan.[57] Thurstan, appointed to his see in 1114 by the king, had spent the first seven years of his archiepiscopate in exile. From 1119 to 1121 he was in the household of Pope Calixtus II, and had been with the pope in 1119 when he had confirmed the *Carta Cartitatis* – Thurstan effectively witnessed the official birth of the Cistercian Order. The archbishop undoubtedly eased the path of the Cistercians into England and into his diocese.[58] Such were the networks of power and influence on which the Cistercians relied. Archbishop Thurstan was also a key influence behind, indeed could be regarded as the founder of, Fountains Abbey, whose unorthodox origin in a schism from St Mary's, York, was apparently provoked by the sight of the Clairvaux monks *en route* for Rievaulx. Fountains came to be seen as the English Cîteaux, and St Mary's the English Molesme.[59] In the years to come Rievaulx and Fountains were to be mothers and grandmothers to two further generations of daughter houses and retained a pre-eminence among the English abbeys. Fountains and one of its daughter houses, Kirkstead, also produced offshoots in Norway, respectively Lyse (1146) and Hovedøya (1147). Rievaulx's influence spread north of the border into Scotland, with the foundation of Melrose and Dundrennan by the Scottish king, David I. His son, Prince Henry of Scotland, founded Holm Cultram from Melrose as a marker of political supremacy on the very border of England, and Holm Cultram in turn sent monks to establish Grey Abbey in Ireland (1193).

1132 saw Bernard in the Midi, and 1133 in Genoa and Pisa. He accompanied Innocent II to Rome, and was there again in 1137 and 1138 at the

---

56 *Letters of St Bernard of Clairvaux*, no. 95 (pp. 141–2).
57 *Cartularium Abbathiae de Rievalle*, ed. J. C. Atkinson, Surtees Society, 83 (1889), no. 1.
58 For his career see D. Nichol, *Thurstan, Archbishop of York 1114–1140* (York, 1964), and on his relations with the Cistercians, pp. 151–91.
59 On Rievaulx and Fountains see in particular Janet Burton, *The Monastic Order in Yorkshire 1069–1215*, Cambridge Studies in Medieval Life and Thought, fourth series, 40 (Cambridge, 1999), pp. 98–124; and 'Rievaulx Abbey: the Early Years', in *Perspectives for an Architecture of Solitude: Essays on Cistercians, Art, and Architecture in Honour of Peter Fergusson*, ed. T. N. Kinder (Turnhout, 2004), pp. 47–53; Coppack, *Fountains Abbey*; Emilia Jamroziak, *Rievaulx Abbey in its Social Context 1132–1300: Memory, Locality, and Networks* (Turnhout, 2005).

end of the schism. In Italy, as elsewhere, Bernard's high profile produced results and a number of foundations followed his visits, their very names resonant of their affilation: Chiaravalle near Milan (1135), and Chiaravalle della Columba (1137) in the diocese of Piacenza. These were foundations *de novo* but there was also reform of existing houses. St Vincent and St Columba in Rome was offered to Bernard by Innocent II in 1140 – a favour repaid, one might think, for Bernard's support – and in its Cistercian life was known as Tre Fontane. Its first abbot was Bernardo Paganelli of Pisa, later to be the first Cistercian pope, Eugenius III. Also reformed was Casamari (1140), a former Benedictine abbey. Like Morimond, Clairvaux was active in the German-speaking lands and made foundations in the southern Rhineland at Himmerod (1134) and Eberbach (1135).

From Stephen Harding to the death of Bernard: 1133–53

In 1133 old age and blindness led Abbot Stephen Harding to resign, and his death the following year must have removed one of the last, if not the last, of the founder fathers of the New Monastery. But his death and the election of the unfortunate and short-lived Abbot Guy did not see any abatement in the spread of the Order. Indeed in England the greatest expansion was between 1133 and the death of Bernard in 1153. In English political terms this coincided with the reign of Stephen (1135–54), a period usually characterised either as one of civil war or of anarchy.[60] As Stephen and his cousin, the Empress Matilda, battled for the throne, the Cistercians flourished, finding their patrons among those loyal to the king but more especially those who supported the Angevin cause. From the early 1140s the Yorkshire Cistercians of Fountains and Rievaulx, some of them local men who had entered the monastic life in Burgundy and spearheaded the Cistercian settlement of the north of England, entered into an ecclesiastical dispute which had political connotations. Following the death of Archbishop Thurstan in 1140 the Chapter of York Minster had, under royal pressure, elected as his successor William fitz Herbert, treasurer of York. Not for the first time the Cistercians intervened to prevent the succession of one they saw as an unworthy minister of the Church.[61] The difference this time was that the elect was the king's candidate, and opposition at a time of political conflict was potentially damaging to royal authority. The appeal of the abbots of Rievaulx and Fountains against the election rocked the ecclesiastical world, and trained

---

[60] The bibliography on the reign of Stephen is abundant. For recent treatments see, for instance, David Crouch, *The Reign of Stephen 1135–1154* (London, 2000); Edmund King, *King Stephen* (London, 2010).

[61] On the Cistercians as church reformers see Newman, *Boundaries of Charity*, especially pp. 191–218.

the attention of Bernard on the realm. It is small wonder that in the years that followed the Cistercians in England received heightened attention. This did not diminish when the Cistercian pope – Eugenius III, a former monk of Clairvaux – deposed William and ordered a fresh election, and when the new elect was Henry Murdac, a former monk of Clairvaux who had been sent in 1143 or 1144 by Bernard to be elected as abbot of Fountains.[62] It was in these inflammatory years that David I of Scotland, whose predilection for patronising new and fashionable movements was matched only by his political ambitions to redraw the Scottish border further south, began to found Cistercian houses in Scotland. He drew his colonies from the northern powerhouse of Rievaulx, where from 1134 his former steward, Aelred, had been a monk and, from 1147 to 1167, abbot.[63] From David's two foundations, Melrose and Dundrennan, derived all the Scottish Cistercian houses.

Few English and Welsh Cistercian houses were founded direct from continental abbeys. Apart from Waverley and Tintern from L'Aumône, and Rievaulx from Clairvaux, the only other direct foundations from overseas were those of Boxley in Kent (1143 or 1146) and the Welsh houses of Whitland (?1140) and Margam (1147) from Clairvaux.[64] All the rest – until the late foundation of Beaulieu from Cîteaux in 1202 – were the result of internal colonisation.[65] A few English houses, like Kirkstall and Radmore, appear to have absorbed earlier communities of hermits but most were founded as Cistercian houses, their foundation charters often specifying that land had been given 'for the foundation of an abbey of the Cistercian Order'. A significant boost to the number of Cistercian houses in France, England and Wales, however, came with the incorporation of the order of Savigny, traditionally dated to 1147, the same date as the incorporation of the congregation of Obazine.[66] Savigny was

---

[62] The fullest discussion of the York election is now Christopher Norton, *St William of York* (York, 2006), pp. 76–148. See also Janet Burton, 'English Monasteries and the Continent', in *King Stephen's Reign (1135–1154)*, ed. Paul Dalton and Graeme J. White (Woodbridge, 2008), pp. 98–114 (pp. 109–13).

[63] Burton, *Monastic Order in Yorkshire*, pp. 99–109 and 'Rievaulx Abbey: the Early Years'. For the broader political context see Paul Dalton, *Conquest, Anarchy and Lordship: Yorkshire 1066–1154*, Cambridge Studies in Medieval Life and Thought, fourth series, 27 (1994). On David see Christopher Brooke, 'Princes and Kings as Patrons of Monasteries', in *Il Monachesimo e la Riforma Ecclesiastica 1049–1122*, Miscellanea del centro di studi medievali, 6 (Milan, 1971), pp. 125–52.

[64] For a recent reappraisal of the circumstances surrounding the foundation of Whitland see Huw Pryce, 'Patrons and Patronage among the Cistercians in Wales', *Archaeologia Cambrensis* 154 (2007 for 2005), 81–95, especially 83–4.

[65] Beaulieu, founded at Faringdon in 1202 and transferred to Beaulieu in the New Forest, is notable not only as the only English daughter of Cîteaux, but as a royal foundation made by King John, who before that date and indeed after had shown himself to be no friend of the White Monks. See S. F. Hockey, *Beaulieu: King John's Abbey* (Beaulieu, 1976).

[66] The date of 1147 is discounted by Berman (*Cistercian Evolution*, pp. 142–8) but she does not take account of the late twelfth-century *Historia Fundationis* of the English Savigniac abbeys of Byland and Jervaulx, which is explicit about the date. The *Historia* is a good source for the history of the

another of those reform movements of the eleventh and twelfth centuries, described above, that was rooted in the eremitic aspirations of an individual reformer, in this case Vitalis.[67] The success of his experiment led to the foundation first of an abbey at Savigny, on the borders of Brittany, Normandy and Maine, then a series of daughter houses. By the fifth decade of the twelfth century the Savigniac houses numbered over thirty, with thirteen in England and Wales. The history of the English Savigniacs highlights the lack of Savigniac control over its houses, and this weakness, along with his admiration of the White Monks, is said to have prompted Abbot Serlo to seek a merger with the Cistercians. There was some opposition, notably in England from Furness Abbey, the oldest of the English houses of the Order, which was indeed founded four years before the arrival of the Cistercians at Waverley.[68] The unease of the Furness monks may have resulted from the prospect of a loss of independence under the more cohesive government of the White Monks, but in the wake of the York election dispute, with the Cistercians increasingly identified with the Angevin opponents of the king, they would presumably have been mindful of the attitude of their patron – King Stephen himself – to the merger. The incorporation of Savigny was a significant event, since it brought into the Cistercian organisation a substantial number of houses whose customs and culture would have been familiar to, but not identical with, its own.[69]

This raises the broader question of incorporation, and its significance for the development of the character of the Cistercian Order. Berman argues on the basis of the evidence from France that only forty of the houses in existence in 1152 were foundations *de novo*, and that the Order grew largely as a result of the adoption of Cistercian customs by existing houses rather than by colonisation. As McGuire rightly points out, Berman's assessment is distorted by her concentration on France,[70] and certainly the evidence from Scandinavia, or indeed that from England and Wales, discussed above, does not support her argument that incorporation was a general phenomenon. However, there were areas where incorporation of existing houses was important, either individually or

---

English Savigniacs in the period leading up to the merger. See *The Foundation History of the Abbeys of Byland and Jervaulx*, ed. and trans. Janet Burton, Borthwick Texts and Studies, 35 (York, 2006), pp. xxv–xxvii, 23, 45.

[67] See above, pp. 5–6.

[68] Burton, *Foundation History of Byland and Jervaulx*, pp. xviii–xxvii.

[69] In his life of Aelred of Rievaulx the monk Walter Daniel notes that Aelred sent Walter's father, Daniel, and other monks of Rievaulx to Swineshead, a Savigniac house in Lincolnshire 'to illuminate it with the Cistercian way of life'. The chronology suggests a time shortly after Aelred's election as abbot of Rievaulx in 1147: see *The Life of Aelred of Rievaulx by Walter Daniel*, ed. and trans. F. M. Powicke, NMT/OMT (London, 1950; repr. Oxford, 1978), p. 35.

[70] McGuire, 'Charity and Unanimity', p. 292.

en masse. An example is the house of Sylvanès in southern France, an account of the foundation of which was written by a monk of the house in the 1170s.[71] The origins of Sylvanès lie in a hermitage founded in the 1130s by the converted brigand Pons of Léras. Subsequently and with the patronage of a local castellan it developed into a cenobitic foundation. The narrative tells how the monks debated which *ordo* – the Carthusian or Cistercian – they should adopt. On the advice of the Carthusians they decided to take up the Cistercian way of life, and approached the abbey of Mazan, the nearest Cistercian house (1136). This is the story as it was recorded in the 1170s. But Berman argues that in the 1130s Mazan itself was not yet Cistercian: it was still a hermitage, and its adoption of Sylvanès therefore marked the expansion of its hermit congregation – which also included two of the three sisters of Provence, Le Thoronet (1136) and Sénanque (1148) – not of the Cistercian Order.[72] Mazan and its associated houses together sought incorporation at a later date. Seeking to interpret the history of Sylvanès further underlines the difficulties of unravelling later foundation narratives that sought to root the Cistercian origins of their monastery in an earlier period.

Two further incorporated abbeys, both in south-west France, became springboards for Cistercian expansion into Spain. The abbey of Fontfroide near Narbonne, which had been founded in 1093, was reformed and refounded as a daughter house of Grandselve in 1144 just before Bernard's visit in 1145.[73] L'Escale Dieu was in origin a hermitage and became a daughter house of Morimond, bringing with it satellite houses on either side of the Pyrenees.[74] Because of their geographical location, both Fontfroide and L'Escale Dieu were well placed to spread the Cistercian message into the lands beyond the Pyrenees.

By the death of Bernard in 1153 the Cistercian Order had swelled to somewhere in the region of three hundred and fifty abbeys. It is small wonder that Marcel Pacaut subtitled his chapter on 'le temps de saint Bernard' 'les années triumphales'.[75] Like others he defined forty years of Cistercian history by reference to one man. Yet it is important to realise

71 Berman, *Cistercian Evolution*, pp. 110–17. Beverly May Kienzle, 'The Tract on the Conversion of Pons of Léras and the True Account of the Beginning of the Monastery at Sylvanès', *Cistercian Studies Quarterly* 30 (1995), 219–43. On these houses see B. Wildhaber, 'Catalogue des établissements cisterciens en Languedoc aux XIIIᵉ et XIVᵉ siécles', in *Les Cisterciens de Languedoc (XIIIᵉ–XIVᵉ siècle)*, pp. 21–44 (p. 35), and Barrière, 'Les abbayes issues de l'érémitisme', *ibid.*, pp. 83–7.
72 The third 'sister', Sylvacane, was an eleventh-century foundation which is attested as a Cistercian house from the 1190s and not before.
73 Wildhaber, 'Catalogue des établissements cisterciens en Languedoc', pp. 31–2 (Fontfroide), p. 33 (Grandselve).
74 Beverly May Kienzle, *Cistercians, Heresy and Crusade in Occitania 1145–1229: Preaching in the Lord's Vineyard* (York, 2001); *Les Cisterciens de Languedoc XIIIᵉ-XIVᵉ siècle*, p. 29; its family numbered two houses in the Languedoc and eleven in Spain.
75 *Les moines blancs*, pp. 103–40.

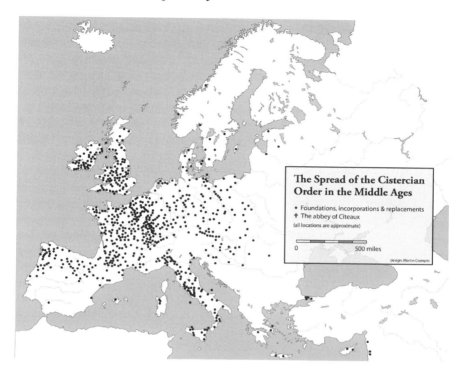

that the apparent cohesion of the Order may not have seemed as real at the time as it does in retrospect. The first half of the twelfth century was a period of growth and of experiment. As we have seen, many houses came to Cîteaux through incorporation, and that process – witness Cadouin – might be a lengthy one. The neat lines of affiliation belong to a later period, as the Order, perhaps under the pressure of incorporated houses – which themselves needed a 'mother' – came to place a growing premium on the importance of filiation. For one thing, the whole system of visitation depended on the well-established relationship between mother and daughter houses; for another, precedence of abbots within the General Chapter was important and depended on the seniority of foundation. As Christopher Brooke wrote, 'we know that there were complex disputes in later times as to who was truly the parent of whom', and the neat lines of descent and precise dates of foundation were a product of attempts to confront such issues.[76]

---

[76] C. Brooke, *The Age of the Cloister: the Story of Monastic Life in the Middle Ages* (Stroud, 2003), p. 11, where he refers his readers to the dispute between Tintern and Kingswood Abbeys over paternity,

1152 and Beyond: Reform, Christianisation and Conquest

A retrospective account attributes to the year 1152 a potentially important pronouncement by the General Chapter:

> In the year of our Lord 1152 it was decreed in the General Chapter of abbots that in the future no new abbey of our Order would be constructed anywhere, nor would any place of different observance be joined to our Order by means of annexation.[77]

The statute did allow the removal of an existing abbey to another location with the consent of the Father Immediate but was careful to specify that it had to be ten Burgundian leagues (about forty kilometres) from other abbeys. It also permitted abbeys already begun to be completed. However, its intention seems to have been to draw a line under further Cistercian expansion. This statement is, as Waddell has demonstrated, a retrospective commentary, and the earliest manuscript in which it survives dates to around 1180. Nevertheless its assertion is corroborated by two passages in the chronicle of Robert of Torigni,[78] and there seems to be little doubt that in 1152 a bold – though as it turned out ineffective – decision was made to halt further dispersal.

That it was ineffective was due to the continued desire on the part of founders and patrons to establish Cistercian houses. This desire was fuelled not only by considerations of salvation and commemoration, but by compelling political reasons on the part of the laity, and by reasons of ecclesiastical reform, evidenced by the continued patronage of the episcopate. It is impossible to separate out all the motives behind monastic foundation and patronage; these are complex issues. However, the remainder of this chapter seeks to explore some of the reasons why founders and patrons continued to be drawn to the White Monks. The important point to note is that if the Cistercians themselves seriously intended to halt further foundations, then the spiritual agenda must have passed to others, non-Cistercians, who determined the future shape of the Order. This can be demonstrated with respect to a number of distinct regions.

Aggression, defence and state-formation: Wales and Ireland

As we have seen, the Cistercian landfall in Wales came only three years after England, in 1131 with the foundation of Tintern on the very borders of south Wales and England, within striking distance of the castle of the

---

recorded in *The Letters and Charters of Gilbert Foliot*, ed. Z. N. Brooke, A. Morey and C. N. L. Brooke (Cambridge, 1967), pp. 510–13.
[77] *NLT*, pp. 364, 492–3.
[78] *Ibid.*, pp. 310–11.

founder at Chepstow.[79] Walter fitz Richard de Clare was of the second generation of Norman settlers in Wales, and Tintern followed the pattern, established by an earlier generation of Benedictine priories, of the foundation of religious houses by a ruling elite eager to assert its authority. The dominance of Anglo-Welsh or Anglo-Norman founders persisted, with two daughter houses of Clairvaux, Whitland and Margam, the latter founded just before his death by Earl Robert of Gloucester, the half-brother of the Empress Matilda, in 1147. In 1147 as well – a true *annus mirabilis* for the Order – was founded Abbey Dore on the borders of England and Wales, the only English daughter house of Morimond; and two houses of the order of Savigny, Basingwerk in the north and Neath in the south, swelled the number of Welsh houses.

In 1164, a dozen years after the General Chapter's attempt to ban further foundations, the Norman castellan of Cardigan, Robert fitz Stephen, established monks from Whitland at Strata Florida in Ceredigion, under the shadow of the Cambrian Mountains. This was to be a momentous foundation but not for reasons that would have been apparent to its founder. The following year, in a resurgence of native Welsh power, Lord Rhys of Deheubarth overran parts of south and mid Wales. He seized control of the new foundation of Strata Florida, and, in the words of his charter of 1184, he 'loved and cherished' it. Certainly he endowed it with extensive moorland and mountain pasture.[80] There must have been more to Rhys's enthusiastic embracing of the Cistercians than what is often termed 'conventional piety', that is, his concern for salvation. For an aspiring Welsh ruler Cistercian monasteries offered more than spiritual support. As members of a European-wide religious order which, unlike the Benedictine foundations of an earlier phase of monastic expansion in Wales, had no links with English or Norman houses, no connotations of alien settlement, they brought international contacts, prestige and status for a monastic patron to rival that of other rulers, and more material benefits. As native rulers such as Rhys sought to extend and consolidate their political power, the Cistercians could bring administrative support as well as financial recompense in return for grants of land.

Following the adoption of Strata Florida by the Lord Rhys the second phase of Cistercian expansion in Wales, which lasted until 1201, was dominated by the native Welsh rulers, and inextricably bound with their territorial ambitions and state building. Second and third daughters of Whitland were Strata Marcella, founded by Owain Cyfeilog, ruler of

---

[79] Robinson, *Cistercians in Wales*, pp. 267–74.
[80] See *The Acts of the Welsh Rulers 1120–1283*, ed. Huw Pryce with the assistance of Charles Insley (Cardiff, 2005), no. 28 (pp. 171–5). Pryce notes ('Patrons and Patronage among the Welsh Cistercians', 84) that Whitland also passed into Rhys's patronage, though probably some little time later.

southern Powys, and Abbey Cwmhir, founded by the lord of Ceri and Maelienydd.[81] Strata Florida itself sent colonies to Llantarnam in the south and Aberconwy in the north, both founded by native lords in periods of resurgence of Welsh power. Cistercian expansionism, joined to the aspiring ambitions of Madog ap Gruffudd Maelor, ruler of Powys, accounts for the final Welsh foundation at Valle Crucis, established by Madog but at the request of the abbots of Whitland, Strata Florida, Strata Marcella and Abbey Cwmhir.[82] The process of foundation followed precise negotiations both locally and at the centre of the powerful Cistercian organisation. In 1198 the General Chapter had referred to the abbot of Clairvaux the request of one 'Grifin' to found a Cistercian abbey; the following year it delegated to the abbot of Margam, along with those of Buildwas (Shropshire) and Whitland, the task of inspecting the site that had been offered by 'Grifin', who on this occasion was described as 'prince of North Wales'.[83] In reviewing the ubiquity of the Cistercians in Wales we should not forget that still more foundations were intended. In the same way as the first attempt to settle Cwmhir, so too did an early foundation at Pendar fail to thrive; and in 1203 a request by the 'king of Wales' to make a Cistercian foundation was referred to the abbots of Margam and Buildwas, who were to enquire *sollicite* (carefully) as to the resources the 'king' was prepared to commit, but the project was never realised.[84]

The Cistercian houses of Welsh Wales amply repaid the generosity of their lordly benefactors. They did so by recording their deeds and writing their history; by preserving Welsh culture through the copying of manuscripts; by providing them with hospitality; and by safeguarding their muniments. The monks offered spiritual support for their regimes and practical expertise and assistance in the formation of their political power. At the end they offered them the solace of entry *ad succurrendum* and burial within their walls.[85] At Strata Florida the graves of the princes of Deheubarth may still be seen. Not so at Aberconwy. When the principality of Gwynedd fell to the armies to Edward I after the death of the last prince of Wales, Llywelyn ap Gruffudd (the Last), the English king in a master stroke of psychological warfare had Aberconwy dismantled to

---

81 An earlier attempt had been made to colonise Cwmhir in 1143, but it failed.
82 Pryce, *Acts of the Welsh Rulers*, no. 499 (pp. 698–700).
83 *Twelfth-Century Statutes*, pp. 415–16 (1198: 38), 428–9 (1199: 20); *Statuta Capitulorum Generalium Ordinis Cisterciensis ab Anno 1116 ad Annum 1786*, ed. J. M. Canivez, 8 vols (Louvain, 1933–41), I, 230 (1198: 41), 236 (1199: 21). 'Grifin' can be identified as Madog ap Gruffudd.
84 Canivez, *Statuta*, I, 294 (1203: 48).
85 As Huw Pryce notes ('Patrons and Patronage among the Welsh Cistercians', 85) the 'choice of Cistercian abbeys as their final resting places represented a substantial vote of confidence by native rulers in the spiritual efficacy of the communities they patronized'.

make way for his new castle of Conwy, and its stones – and the mausolea of the princes of Gwynedd who rested there – moved to a new site of Maenan.[86]

As in Wales, so too in Ireland the Cistercians, who arrived there in 1140, came to a land with a complex political geography, a 'patchwork of kingdoms'. There the native church was seen by outsiders as backward and in need of reform.[87] As in so many other regions, it was a member of the ecclesiastical hierarchy who took the first steps towards Cistercian plantation. In 1140 Bishop Malachy of Down, already a keen patron of the Augustinian canons, visited Clairvaux, and so great was the affection that he developed for it that he was buried there in 1148. It was from Clairvaux that Malachy brought Cistercian monks – both Frenchmen and Irish novices trained by Bernard – to Mellifont, to make a Cistercian foundation and take the first steps towards bringing control and order to the Irish Church through association with the broader international Church. It is worth remembering, however, that Malachy did not act alone, for the land on which Mellifont was founded was given by its chief benefactor, Donough O'Carroll, king of Oriel.[88] Between 1140 and 1180 a further fifteen Cistercian houses were established, largely from Mellifont, by the native Irish kings. In the 1170s Ireland was invaded and settled by Anglo-Norman adventurers, and after 1180, though the native Irish continued to found Cistercian houses, so too did the newcomers.[89] As elsewhere the foundation of Cistercian houses might have been part of a strategy of aggressive state building, or a defensive mechanism. Donal Mor O'Brien, king of Munster, founded four abbeys between 1170 and 1195 when his lands were under attack by the Anglo-Normans, three of them – Fermoy, Holycross and Kilcooly – in particularly threatened areas. The Anglo-Normans made their own foundations, filled them with English monks, and laid claim to their newly found lands. Native or newcomer, each founder hoped to create, consolidate and protect his political influence, and what developed in Ireland were two separate Cistercian orders, a situation not unlike that in Wales.

---

[86] The parish church of St Mary, Conwy, is the former abbey church. See Robinson, *Cistercians in Wales*, pp. 223–5. On the transfer to Maenan see Rhŷs W. Hays, *The History of the Abbey of Aberconway 1186–1537* (Cardiff, 1963), pp. 61–77. The negotiations were complex and designed to win the support of the monks for the English king.

[87] For a useful overview of the Cistercian settlement of Ireland see Roger Stalley, *The Cistercian Monasteries of Ireland: an Account of the History, Art and Architecture of the White Monks in Ireland from 1142 to 1540* (London/New Haven, 1987).

[88] *Ibid.*, p. 10. On the selection of the site see below, p. 60.

[89] In all there were to be 36 houses in Ireland, two of the affiliation of Savigny. Of the 34 Cistercian houses, 24 had Irish founders and 10 Anglo-Norman: *ibid.*, pp. 12–13.

Reform and ambition: the case of Scandinavia

In Scandinavia there came to be twenty houses for men and ten for women.[90] The germ that gave rise to the spread of the Order to Sweden (1143), Denmark (1144) and Norway (1146) can be traced to the synod held at Lund in 1139, a meeting of Scandinavian bishops called by Archbishop Eskil of Lund in an attempt to integrate these lands – in parts of which Christianity was still superficial – into the mainstream of the Western Church. Eskil was concerned more particularly to consolidate the recently won independence of his church of Lund from the archbishopric of Hamburg. The council was also attended by Danish and Norwegian bishops as well as a papal legate, Theodignus, the latter very probably the conduit for the idea of bringing the Cistercians to Scandinavia as a missionary force to strengthen and reform the local church. Present at the council were the three founder bishops of the first Cistercian houses: Eskil himself, Gisle of Linköping and Sigurd of Bergen.

The first foundation was Alvastra in Sweden, settled direct by Bishop Gisle from Clairvaux in 1143, and it became the mother of three daughter houses. Gisle's enthusiasm for the White Monks is demonstrated by a second establishment at Nydala in the same year, also from Clairvaux. The circumstances of the foundation of Alvastra in particular, however, indicate that what lay behind it was more than the desire of a bishop to introduce reforming monks to his diocese. Alvastra depended on royal support. King Sverker and his queen granted the land on which the house was founded and supported it with resources. Indeed Alvastra became renowned as the burial place of the Swedish royal family. As in so many other cases it was a fusion of interests that promoted the spread of the Order. Eskil of Lund was a close friend of Bernard, and was to die at Clairvaux in 1181. Despite this it was to Cîteaux that Eskil turned for the first monks of Herrevad (Denmark, now southern Sweden, 1144), but his second foundation, that of Esrum (1153) on the island of Zealand, was made by monks of Clairvaux, brought, so Eskil's charter tells, 'despite the great difficulties and expense … the seed from which a

---

[90] On the Cistercians in Scandinavia see B. P. McGuire, 'Why Scandinavia? Bernard, Eskil and Cistercian Expansion in the North', in *Goad and Nail: Studies in Medieval Cistercian History*, 10, ed. E. Rozanne Elder, Cistercian Studies Series, 84 (Kalamazoo, 1985), pp. 251–81, and *The Cistercians in Denmark: Their Attitudes, Roles and Functions in Medieval Society*, Cistercian Studies Series, 35 (Kalamazoo, 1982); James France, *The Cistercians in Scandinavia*, Cistercian Studies Series, 131 (Kalamazoo, 1992), 'St Bernard, Eskil and the Danish Cistercians', *Cîteaux: Commentarii Cistercienses* 39 (1988), 232–48, 'The Coming of the Cistercians to Scandinavia – *ad exteras et barbaras regiones*', *Cîteaux: Commentarii Cistercienses* 48 (1997), 5–15, and 'The Cistercians in Scandinavia', in *Norm und Realität: Kontinuität und Wandel der Zisterzienser im Mittelalter*, Vita regularis Ordnungen und Deutungen religiosen Lebens im Mittelalter, 42, ed. Franz J. Felten and Werner Rosener (Berlin, 2009), pp. 475–87.

harvest of souls of the faithful may be prepared'.[91] There they replaced a community of Benedictine monks. The third episcopal founder, Sigurd of Bergen, brought a colony from the Yorkshire abbey of Fountains which he visited, to create the first Norwegian abbey at Lyse (1146); another bishop, William of Oslo, turned to a daughter house of Fountains, Kirk-stead, to establish Hovedøya (1147).[92]

Cistercian expansion into Scandinavia thus owed much to its bishops, who saw in the White Monks agents of consolidation – the *Exordium Magnum* speaks of their mission as the strengthening of Christianity – and reform of the Church.[93] Like Esrum, its granddaughter house of Sorø also replaced a community of Benedictine monks, though the representation of the Benedictines as corrupt and in decline has been shown to be a Cistercian myth, perpetuated in order to justify their arrival.[94] But the success of the Cistercian settlements also depended on the backing of royalty and aristocracy. Esrum received privileges from King Valdemar at the end of his victorious conclusion to a civil war in exchange for promoting the cult of his murdered father. Alvastra could, as we have seen, claim to be a royal as well as an episcopal foundation, and its daughter house, which after a series of moves settled on its final site of Varnhem, became the greatest of the Swedish monasteries.[95] Vitskøl, a foundation made by the Danish king, was engineered by Eskil. King and bishop worked hand in hand.[96] Tvis Abbey was founded from Herrevad in 1163 by Duke Buris Henriksen, a claimant to the throne, probably as a marker of his political ambitions. But, as McGuire has argued, the Danish Cistercians were not merely the pawns of the political ambitions of kings and nobles. They were seen as bringers of peace, men who could lend spiritual authority to political power. The coming of the Cistercians to Scandinavia coincided with consolidation of royal power, economic growth, and the presence of archbishops and bishops with an agenda of implanting reform.

[91] Quoted in France, 'Cistercians in Scandinavia', p. 476; for a discussion of the historiography of Eskil's role and the significance of his friendship with Bernard see McGuire, *Cistercians in Denmark*, pp. 38–40.

[92] The maintenance of the links between Fountains and Lyse proved difficult and in the early thirteenth century Lyse was transferred by the General Chapter to Alvastra: Canivez, *Statuta*, I, 406. See below, p. 94.

[93] McGuire, *Cistercians in Denmark* (p. 37), makes the point that although Denmark had been converted for over a century Christianisation may have been confined to the nobility.

[94] *Ibid.*, pp. 74–9. For historical narratives written by the Cistercians in Scandinavia see James France, 'Cistercian Foundation Narratives in Scandinavia in their Wider Context', *Cîteaux: Commentarii Cistercienses* 43 (1992), 119–60, and Brian Patrick McGuire, *Conflict and Continuity at Øm Abbey: a Cistercian Experience in Medieval Denmark* (Copenhagen, 1976).

[95] France, 'Cistercians in Scandinavia', p. 481; McGuire, *Cistercians in Denmark*, p. 41.

[96] *Ibid.*, pp. 57–9 (p. 57).

Conquest, conversion and Christianisation: the Baltic, east of the Elbe, and Iberia

A Cistercian monastery could be a marker of power and authority, and in some areas it was part of a push to colonise new lands, especially ones that had been recently converted. In eastern Europe the advance into the Slavic lands east of the Elbe, and their conversion to Christianity, was accompanied by the foundation of Cistercian as well as Premonstratensian houses. Cistercian expansion east of the Oder helped to cement German influence. The Cistercians were similarly used as markers of political power along the Baltic. During his expeditions in the 1170s King Valdemar I of Denmark brought Danish monks from Esrum to found Dargun (1172). Two years later Kołbacz was established by Warcisław Świętobrzyc, a close relative of the duke of Stettin, also from Esrum. In between these two foundations, in 1173, Valdemar had captured Stettin. Clearly more than one noble saw political value in the implantation of the Cistercians, Valdemar in the extension of Danish influence, and Warcisław in asserting his independence from Stettin. A major benefactor of Dargun was Duke Kazamir I of Pomerania, who in two great charters granted forests, lakes, meadows and a mill, with an invitation to colonise the lands by settling Germans, Slavs and Danes.[97] Although Cistercian foundations were being made in the twelfth century, the great period of expansion in central and eastern Europe was to be in the 'long' thirteenth century. Kołbacz was to give birth to Oliwa (1186), but continued to expand with Marienwalde, founded c. 1280 by Margraves Otto IV and Conrad, and Himmelstädt, founded in 1300 by Margrave Albrecht III, indicating sustained Cistercian infiltration into Poland from the twelfth to the fourteenth centuries. Cistercian success depended on both episcopal and royal or aristocratic backing, and their founders and patrons benefited from the houses' economic activities.[98] By 1300 there were around fifteen abbeys in Germany east of the Elbe, twenty-three abbeys in Poland (including Silesia), and fourteen in Bohemia.

In the Iberian Peninsula the Cistercian settlement became part of the Reconquista of Moorish lands by the kings of the north.[99] In c. 1153 Alfonso I of Portugal founded Alcobaça as a thanksgiving for victory over the Moors at Santarem and as a stronghold of royal power in his emerging

---

97 McGuire, *Cistercians in Denmark*, pp. 80–1. On Dargun see also *Das Zisterzienserkloster Dargun in Stammesgebeit der Zirzipanen*, ed. H. Brachmann, E. Foster, C. Kratzke and H. Reimann (Stuttgart, 2003).

98 Jerzy Kloczowski, 'Les Cisterciens en Europe du Centre-Est au moyen âge', in Bouter, *Unanimité et diversité*, pp. 421–39; see p. 452 for a table of the principal founders of 53 monasteries in Bohemia, Hungary and Poland. See also, in the same collection (pp. 441–51), Zbigniew Pilat, 'Le réseau des cisterciens en Europe du Centre-Est du XIIᵉ au XVᵉ siècle'.

99 See Adeline Rucquoi, 'Les Cisterciens dans la peninsula ibérique', in Bouter, *Unanimité et diversité*, pp. 487–523.

kingdom. All thirteen houses in Portugal were either royal foundations or had royal backing. In Spain Kings Alfonso VII (1126–57) and VIII (1158–1214) of Castile founded nearly twenty houses. Although there are some problems of chronology of foundation of certain houses, the earliest was probably Fitero, founded in 1140 by Alfonso VII of Castile from the Gascon house of L'Escale Dieu, which made five other foundations in Spain. Clairvaux's influence came through the French houses of Grand-selve and Fontfroide with their daughter houses in Catalonia, newly recovered from the Muslims. The most significant of these was Poblet (1150), located on the no-man's land of the political frontier, to which monks were brought from Fontfroide by Count Raymond Berengar of Barcelona after victories against the Moors. The lands newly conquered from the Moors proved ideal Cistercian territory, and this helped to establish them as Christian lands. The Cistercians became part of a strategy of securing new lands for their founders and patrons. They also participated in missions against heretics, notably against the Cathars in the Albigensian Crusade, thus helping to consolidate both papal authority and local political power.[100] In all these areas Cistercian settlement formed part of the creation of states and of identities.

One final, remarkable, example of conversion is the settlement by the Cistercians in the Holy Land in the wake of the Crusades, the second of which (1147) was preached by St Bernard on behalf of the Cistercian pope, Eugenius III. As early as 1157 Morimond settled Deir Balamand (Belmont) south-east of Tripoli. Later the Syrian orthodox monastery of St George of Jubin was incorporated as a daughter house of La Ferté by a former monk of the mother house, Peter, when he became patriarch of Antioch in 1209; and two Cistercian nunneries were established in Acre and Tripoli, dedicated to St Mary Magdalene.[101]

Moniales albe

The year 1213 has often been seen as marking a significant shift in Cistercian attitudes towards women. In that year the General Chapter laid down that houses of nuns which were already incorporated into the Order should not, nevertheless, have free admittance unless licensed by the abbot under whose care they lived; that any nunneries incorporated in the future were to be fully enclosed; that no new nunneries were to be founded without the consent of the Chapter; and that these provisions were to be enforced by abbots who had female houses under their supervision.[102] This is clear acknowledgement by the Chapter that there

---

[100] On Cistercian influence on and participation in the Crusades see below, pp. 194–200.
[101] D. H. Williams, *The Cistercians in the Early Middle Ages* (Leominster, 1998), p. 19.
[102] Canivez, *Statuta*, I, 405 (1213: 3).

were already Cistercian nunneries,[103] whether those, like Tart, founded in association with Cîteaux or Clairvaux in the early years of the Order, or those, like Coyroux, which joined the Order with their congregation.[104] Elsewhere in Europe throughout the twelfth century houses of Cistercian nuns came into being. In England in the last three decades of the twelfth century a number of female houses received papal bulls which refer to them following the Rule of St Benedict and the institutes of the Cistercian brethren;[105] the Welsh nunnery of Llanllŷr, founded by the Lord Rhys of Deheubarth, was under the supervision of Rhys's foundation of Strata Florida, and Gerald of Wales had no doubt that it was Cistercian.[106] There was a powerful nunnery at Las Huelgas in Spain, founded in 1187 by King Alfonso VIII of Castile and claimed by him to be a special daughter of Cîteaux, and in 1191 the Spanish abbesses were holding their own chapter. It is generally argued that pressure from these aristocratic nuns and patrons forced a reluctant General Chapter formally to recognise the status of nunneries as members of the Cistercian Order. Cistercian men, or their corporate representative, the General Chapter, were seen at best to be reluctant to admit women into their ranks, at worst misogynist.[107]

More recently it has been argued that modern historians have been misled into thinking that twelfth-century Cistercian abbots and monks were antagonistic towards religious women. On the contrary, many of them encouraged women's vocation; and the refusal to accept that these women were fully Cistercian lies rather with the authors of the Cistercian foundation narratives, such as the *Exordium Magnum*, which were male constructs of Cistercian history, and which effectively wrote women out of the picture. This has had the effect that female participation in the Order has been significantly underestimated. Moreover, as Berman suggests, it is possible that modern historians have also been misled by statements such as that of Herman of Laon (c. 1130), who spoke of women

---

103 A point made by Elizabeth Freeman, 'Houses of a Peculiar Order: Cistercian Nunneries in Medieval England, with Special Attention to the Fifteenth and Sixteenth Centuries', *Cîteaux: Commentarii Cistercienses* 55 (2004), 245–87 (p. 247).

104 Coyroux was a member the congregation of Obazine, incorporated in 1147, and the merger of Savigny in the same year brought two female houses, l'Abbaye-Blanche and Villers-Canivet.

105 For instance see Burton, *Monastic Order in Yorkshire*, pp. 147–52.

106 Janet Burton, '*Moniales* and *Ordo Cisterciensis* in Medieval England and Wales', in *Female 'vita religiosa' between Late Antiquity and the High Middle Ages. Structures, Developments and Spacial Contexts*, ed. G. Melville and A. Müller, Vita regularis Ordnungen und Deutungen religiosen Lebens im Mittelalter, 46 (Berlin, 2011), pp. 375–89. Only two English female houses, Tarrant and Marham, were accorded the status of abbey and were fully incorporated. There were just two houses in Wales, Llanllŷr and Llanllugan, which were, respectively, under the supervision or the abbots of the male Cistercian houses of Strata Florida and Strata Marcella.

107 See, for example, Sally Thompson, *Women Religious: the Founding of English Nunneries after the Norman Conquest* (Oxford, 1991), p. 94: 'The early Cistercians were remarkable for their hostility to women.'

of the reformed monastery of Montreuil-les-Dames living 'according to the *ordo* of Cîteaux, which is difficult even for men' and showing themselves 'imitating in all things the monks of Clairvaux'.[108] For Berman, the significant word here is 'imitating', which seems to downplay female participation: women were not 'proper' Cistercians; they merely emulated Cistercian men. In reality, she argues, the word 'imitating' is often used in charters of both male and female communities: it is gender neutral. Cistercian nunneries, it can be argued, were as fully members of the Cistercian Order from an early date as were houses of White Monks, and the decree of 1213 merely regularised the position of women within the Order in the same way as the drawing up of lines of affiliation did for male houses at a slightly earlier date.

1213 may seem to mark the beginning of formal Cistercian recognition of the existence of Cistercian nuns, but it is more appropriate to see the legislation of that year as marking the first time there is record of the General Chapter dealing specifically with issues relating to its female members. These were matters that it would return to again and again, and just as 1152 saw an (unsuccessful) attempt to ban further Cistercian foundations, so 1228 saw an equally unsuccessful moratorium on the acceptance of further female houses and interaction between Cistercian men and women: mother abbesses were not to be present at visitations made by abbots and, if they themselves made subsequent visitations they were not to change anything that had been ordained by the male visitor; nuns not willing to submit to the judgement of the Order were to be expelled, and abbesses were not to hear confessions; no new monasteries of nuns were to be made, nor existing houses joined to the Order, but houses not yet incorporated or even built might emulate the institutes of the Cistercians, although the Order would not undertake the cure of their souls or the office of visitation.[109]

Much historiographical debate has centred on whether there was any real difference between houses founded before 1213 and the supposed 'official' admittance of female houses by the General Chapter. It is a distinction implied by the 1228 decree, which seems to have drawn a line between houses over which it had jurisdiction and those which 'emulated' its customs. In many ways, given that the lives of medieval nuns and nunneries are often poorly documented, this is a difficult question to answer. It was impossible, to be sure, for women to be part of the General Chapter held at Cîteaux, and the whole question of visitation was, as the

---

[108] Berman, 'Were there Cistercian Nuns?', p. 229. See also C. H. Berman, ed., *Women and Monasticism in Medieval Europe: Sisters and Patrons of the Cistercian Reform* (Kalamazoo, 2002).

[109] Canivez, *Statuta*, II, 67–8 (1228: 13, 15–16).

decrees of the Chapter show, problematic. To be 'emulating' or 'imitating' the institutes of the Cistercians may imply that in some ways nunneries were not adopting the full range of activities of the White Monks, but this is not to see them in a negative light. The English evidence suggests that some nunneries may indeed have followed Cistercian customs, but that they were inventive enough to graft on to them administrative structures that suited their situation.[110] It was the period from about 1190 to 1250 that saw the greatest expansion of houses for Cistercian women, and their numbers came to equal those of abbeys of Cistercian monks.[111]

At the death of St Bernard, a turning point in Cistercian history which came only a year after the attempt to halt new foundations, there were in the region of three hundred and fifty monasteries that could be counted as Cistercian. But the Order continued to expand after the watershed of 1152, perhaps not at the same rate or intensity, but in a sustained way, so that by the end of the Middle Ages the number had doubled. Most pronounced in the later periods of expansion was the drive east and north, into the Baltic, Poland and east of the Elbe and the Oder. Encouraged by archbishops and bishops as agents of reform and Christianisation, patronised by kings, princes and nobles as adjuncts of their efforts at statebuilding and consolidation of political power, and indeed as a part of the process of conquest, the White Monks did indeed spread throughout the world; as the *Exordium Magnum* put it:

> Monastic life [was] transplanted across many seas [...] in order to foster the practice of true religious devotion [...] and bring the mould of religion and discipline to uncultivated and wild men.[112]

But was life the same in all these monasteries? We have seen how the *Carta Caritatis* seems to lay great store by uniformity, and provides the means by which it could be enforced. The following chapters will explore the defining features of Cistercian monastic practice. They will also question the notion of Cistercian ubiquity of observance. Was their

---

110 Janet Burton, 'The Chariot of Aminadab and the Yorkshire Nunnery of Swine', in R. Horrox and S. R. Jones, ed., *Pragmatic Utopias: Ideals and Communities, 1200–1630* (Cambridge, 2001), pp. 26–42 (p. 28).

111 See Franz J. Felten, 'Waren die Zisterzienser frauenfeindlich? Die Zisterzienser und die religiöse Frauenbewegung im 12. und frühen 13. Jahrhundert. Versuch einer Bestandsaufnahme der Forschung seit 1980', in *Norm und Realität: Kontinuität und Wandel der Zisterzienser im Mittelalter*, Vita Regularis, 42, ed. Franz J. Felten and Werner Rosener (Berlin, 2009), pp. 179–223, and Alixis Grélois, 'L'expansion cistercienne en France: la part des affiliations et des moniales', in *ibid.*, pp. 287–324 (pp. 312–23).

112 *Exordium Magnum*, pp. 258–9, quoted in France, 'Cistercians in Scandinavia', p. 479.

uniformity real? Was it aspirational, in that it provided a goal to which the Cistercians could strive? Or was uniformity more of a veneer for diversity of practice, dictated by local conditions? It is to these questions that we must now turn.

CHAPTER THREE

'Lonely wooded places':
The Cistercians, their Sites and their Buildings

You will find much more labouring amongst the woods than you ever will amongst books. Woods and stones will teach you what you can never hear from any master. Do you imagine you cannot suck honey from the rocks and oil from the hardest stone; that the mountains do not drop sweetness and the hills flow with milk and honey; that the valleys are not filled with corn?[1]

The Cistercians had a strong affinity with their surroundings. The physical environment was 'a window onto the Divine' and the taming of the landscape was symbolic of the soul's return to God.[2] The name of the monastery often evoked its setting. Cîteaux likely stems from the Latin *cisterna* which can mean a marsh or bog,[3] while Clairvaux translates as 'Valley of Light' and Roche alludes to its rocky environs. There is evidence for monks identifying their abbey with its surroundings. An example is Ralph of Fountains who was sent from Yorkshire to Norway in 1146 to preside as founding abbot of Lyse, south of Bergen. Each time Ralph saw the sun setting on the fjords, he would be reminded of the Skelldale valley at Fountains and feel nostalgia for his home community. Ralph, like others who were sent to distant houses, returned to die at his own abbey and to be buried in familiar surroundings.[4]

The White Monks favoured rural sites and were particularly associated with valleys. Early Cistercian legislation stipulated that houses should be built 'in places removed from human habitation' and not in cities, walled towns or villages; as previously noted no abbey was to be closer than ten Burgundian leagues (c. forty kilometres) from another monastery.[5] But

---

[1] Bernard of Clairvaux to Henry Murdac (1128 (?)): *Letters of St Bernard of Clairvaux*, no. 107 (pp. 155–6). The phrase 'lonely, wooded places' in the title of this chapter comes from Orderic Vitalis, *Ecclesiastical History*, IV, 327.

[2] Elizabeth Freeman, *Narratives of a New Order: Cistercian Historical Writing in England, 1150–1220* (Turnhout, 2002), pp. 141–2.

[3] See T. N. Kinder, *Cistercian Europe: Architecture of Contemplation* (Grand Rapids/Cambridge/Kalamazoo, 2002), p. 32, who also suggests other possible origins of the name.

[4] France, *Cistercians in Scandinavia*, p. 112. This is discussed further in chapter 5.

[5] 'Institutes of the General Chapter', no. 1, *NLT*, pp. 325, 458, and *Exordium Parvum*, chapter XV, *ibid.*, p. 435, where this is stated to be in accordance with St Benedict; 'Institutes of the General Chapter', no. 33, *ibid.*, pp. 338, 469. See also above, p. 44.

the Cistercians were contemplatives rather than solitaries and their sites were more secluded than remote. Accordingly, the monks were sheltered but not cut off from the world and most houses were relatively near to transport links and communication routes. The Hungarian abbey of Pilis, for instance, looked out onto a secluded landscape yet was within twenty kilometres of three urban centres.[6] Melrose Abbey stood on the Roman road linking England to Tweeddale and the Lothians, whilst Tautra, in the Trondheim Fjord, was on the north-east side of a small island but close to a shipping lane.[7] The monks of Øm (Denmark) actually relocated as their site at Kalvø on Lake Skanderborg was too isolated. In bad weather the community might be cut off for a week or longer.[8]

This chapter looks more closely at the Cistercians and the buildings they constructed. The first part explores how their sites were chosen and developed to meet the needs of a growing community in a changing world. The second considers the design and décor of Cistercian buildings and how the White Monks were both conveyors of new ideas and techniques, and assimilators of local practice.

'A vast solitude'

> ... they eagerly headed for the desert-place called Cîteaux. This place, situated in the episcopate of Chalon, and rarely approached by men back in those days because of the thickness of grove and thornbush, was inhabited only by wild beasts.[9]

Chapter one considered how the monks of Molesme, who settled in woods south of Dijon and established the community from which Cîteaux would spring, are portrayed in Cistercian literature as pioneers. This image which became synonymous with the Cistercians and integral to the Order's identity is evoked in a number of foundation histories and related documents. They include the bishop of Kilkenny's letter to the General Chapter, c. 1204, about the Irish site of Duiske (Graignamanagh) which he described as 'a place of horror and of vast solitude, a cave of robbers, and the lair of those who lie in wait for blood'.[10] The *Vita Prima* (c. 1145) depicts Clairvaux as a den of robbers ('the Valley of Wormwood') which the monks made into 'God's temple and a house of

6 These were Esztergon, Buda and Visegrád; see P. Szabó, *Woodland and Forests in Medieval Hungary*, British Archaeological Reports, International Series, 1348 (Oxford, 2005), p. 114.
7 R. Oram, 'The History of the Abbey', in R. Fawcett and R. Oram, *Melrose Abbey* (Stroud, 2004), pp. 11–67 (pp. 50, 54, 58); France, *Cistercians in Scandinavia*, p. 89.
8 This was in 1172. See McGuire, *Conflict and Continuity*, p. 39.
9 *Exordium Parvum*, chapter III, *NLT*, p. 421.
10 Stalley, *Cistercian Monasteries of Ireland*, p. 38.

prayer', whilst the *Narratio de fundatione* of Fountains Abbey compares the spot at Skelldale, Yorkshire, where the monks settled, to 'a place of horror and vast solitude'.[11] This imagery linked the Order as a whole to the early desert monks and, importantly, connected the later Cistercians to their founding fathers.[12] But the image embodied the very essence of Cistercian life which was based on simplicity and poverty and was conducive to contemplation. It symbolised the monks' mental withdrawal from the world, for as Aelred of Rievaulx (d. 1167) reflected, to enter solitude meant 'to consider this whole world a desert' and to desire the Fatherland.[13]

The desert imagery was therefore intended as a metaphor rather than a visual description of the site and was charged with symbolic overtones. This explains the seeming paradox in the Book of Henryków (Heinrichau) which in book two (c. 1310) portrays the founding community of monks as pioneers who tamed the 'savage' landscape, whereas the original compiler, Abbot Peter (c. 1268), makes it clear that the site had been cultivated and settled for at least a century before their arrival.[14]

As the Cistercians expanded throughout Europe and Western Christendom they encountered differing landscapes and had to adapt accordingly. In Scandinavia, for instance, a number of Cistercian abbeys were located on islands since there were few rivers but plenty of lakes and coast; this made the setting of the Scandinavian houses quite distinctive.[15] The incorporation of houses and orders meant that the Cistercians might inherit sites they would otherwise have eschewed, notably those in or near to urban centres. Examples include the former Savigniac monasteries of Stratford Langthorne, London,[16] as well as St Mary's, Dublin;[17] and the nunnery of St Antoine-des-Champs-lèz-Paris, which was previously

---

[11] Matthew 21.13; Mark 11.17; Luke 19.46; see *Vita Prima*, Book I (William of St Thierry), chapter 5, PL, 185, cols 241–2, trans. Matarasso, *Cistercian World*, p. 26; *Memorials of Fountains*, I, 33–4.

[12] For instance, the origins of Fountains Abbey in a breakaway group from St Mary's, York, could be directly compared to the departure of the monks of Molesme for Cîteaux and, as Freeman argues, enabled Archbishop Thurstan to present the Yorkshire house as 'the Cîteaux of the North': Freeman, *Narratives of a New Order*, p. 155. See above, p. 38.

[13] *Aelred of Rievaulx, The Liturgical Sermons: the First Clairvaux Collection*, trans. T. Berkeley and M. B. Pennington, Cistercian Fathers Series, 58 (Kalamazoo, 2001), sermon 6, pp. 129–41 (p. 140).

[14] *Henryków Book*, trans. P. Górecki, *A Local Society in Transition: the Henryków Book and Related Documents* (Toronto, 2002), pp. 85, 101–5, 147.

[15] France, *Cistercians in Scandinavia*, p. 24. But there was variation within Scandinavia on account of each country's unique circumstances. In Norway, the only suitable areas for habitation were by the coast and all three houses there were situated in coastal places. In Sweden, the Cistercians settled on the lower, more fertile southern lands rather than on the northern mountainous lands, while in Denmark, fear of Wendish pirates meant that the monks settled inland, with sites at Øm and Esrum: *ibid.*, p. 63.

[16] For an overview of this site see *The Cistercian Abbeys of Britain: Far from the Concourse of Men*, ed. David Robinson (London, 1998), pp. 180–1.

[17] The abbey was founded in 1139 on the north bank of the River Liffey, directly opposite the Hiberno-Norse trading port: Stalley, *Cistercian Monasteries of Ireland*, p. 38.

a hospital for prostitutes and repentant usurers, but may have originated as a hermitage.[18] It was not uncommon for nunneries to be closer to civilisation since a number had previously been hospitals or had belonged to another order.[19] But their urban setting might lead to an influx of guests and prompt them to relocate. It was for this reason that the nuns of Byarum (Sweden) moved to Sko and the nuns of Gudhem (Sweden) to Jönköping.[20]

Although the Cistercians might inherit urban locations few of their abbeys were founded in such places. One rare example, and the only one in England, is St Mary Graces, London, which was founded in 1350 by Edward III. This abbey in east Smithfield was on the site of a plague cemetery; a chapel there was later incorporated within the monastic precinct.[21] Recent research suggests that this location may have been chosen specifically to facilitate regular contact with the royal court at the Tower of London, and that the abbey's success is a testimony to the White Monks' ability to adapt to their circumstances.[22]

The choice of site

> Adam found at Meaux the very place he sought; it was well planted with woods and orchards, surrounded by waters and rivers, and blessed with a fertile soil. Rising in its midst was St Mary's hill, where the church was later founded. Climbing the hill, Adam struck his staff on the ground with great force saying, 'Let this place be called a palace of the heavenly king and a celestial vineyard and a gate of life. Here, let there be established followers of Christ.'[23]

[18] The nunnery of St Antoine-des-Champs-lèz-Paris was outside the east walls of the city and was a hospital from c. 1198 until the Cistercians took it over as a nunnery in 1208: Berman, *Women and Monasticism*, p. 38; C. H. Berman, 'Cistercian Nuns and the Development of the Order: the Abbey of St Antoine-des-Champs outside Paris', in *The Joy of Learning and the Love of God*, ed. E. R. Elder, Cistercian Studies Series, 160 (Kalamazoo, 1995), pp. 121–56.

[19] For example see, Berman, *Women and Monasticism*, p. 10, and Paulo Pereira, *Abbey of Santa Maria: Alcobaça* (London, 2007), pp. 16–17.

[20] France, *Cistercians in Scandinavia*, p. 179.

[21] For an overview of the site, see Robinson, *Cistercian Abbeys of Britain*, pp. 136–7. The site may be compared to the Carthusian charterhouse in London, on which see B. Barber and C. Thomas, *The London Charterhouse*, Museum of London Archaeological Service Monograph, 10 (London, 2002); D. Knowles and W. F. Grimes, *Charterhouse: the Medieval Foundation in the Light of Recent Discoveries* (London/Toronto/New York, 1954); J. Kerr, 'The Symbolic Significance of Hospitality', in *Self-Representation of Medieval Religious Communities: the British Isles in Context*, ed. A. Müller and K. Stöber, Vita regularis Ordnungen und Deutungen religiosen Lebens im Mittelalter, 40 (Berlin, 2009), pp. 125–42 (pp. 136–9).

[22] Emilia Jamroziak, 'St Mary Graces: a Cistercian House in Later Medieval London', in *The Use and Abuse of Sacred Places in Late Medieval Towns*, ed. P. Trio and M. de Smet (Leuven, 2006), pp. 153–64 (p. 154).

[23] *Chronica Monasterii de Melsa*, ed. E. A. Bond, 3 vols, RS (London, 1866–68), I, xiv–xv, 76–7. The chronicle was compiled by Thomas Burton (d. 1437), a former abbot of the house.

When preparations were under way for the Cistercians' expansion into Ireland, Bernard of Clairvaux wrote to Malachy, at that time the bishop of Down, with advice on how to select an appropriate location for the new foundation. He suggested that Malachy look for a site based on what he had seen at Clairvaux and 'far removed from the turmoil of the world'.[24] Malachy duly chose a spot on the banks of the River Mattock, some five miles north-west of Drogheda. This land belonged to Donough O'Carroll, king of Oriel, and the bishop probably entered into negotiations with O'Carroll to secure the site for his monks.[25] Malachy was evidently successful for in 1142 the Cistercians arrived in Ireland and settled at Mellifont, which was founded as a daughter house of Clairvaux. Mellifont was the first of over thirty Cistercian abbeys established in Ireland. Whilst Malachy sought out a suitable location for his new community – and there is evidence for others acting similarly[26] – in many cases the Cistercians did not actively look for a site but received an offer of land from a prospective founder who invited the monks to settle on his domain, perhaps for political rather than spiritual reasons.[27] Representatives from the Order then visited the site to assess whether or not it was appropriate and if the endowment could adequately support a community. The foundation was subsequently sanctioned or aborted.[28] Plans by Buildwas Abbey (Shropshire) to found a daughter house at Dunbrody, c. 1175, were abandoned when the lay brother of the house sent to survey the Irish site returned with an unfavourable report of what he considered a desolate, sterile and barbarous place. Although Buildwas decided against sending a colony to Dunbrody, it released the land to St Mary's, Dublin, in 1182, which founded a daughter house there.[29]

The decision as to where precisely on the founder's land the monastery should be built was often made by the monks. This was the case at two twelfth-century Yorkshire houses, Meaux and Roche. In the passage quoted above, the fourteenth-century chronicle of Meaux describes how its founding abbot, Adam of Fountains, surveyed William le Gros's lands in Holderness to find the ideal spot for his abbey. He chose the site of Meaux, an area surrounded by woods, orchards and rivers and where St

24 *Letters of St Bernard of Clairvaux*, no. 383 (p. 452).
25 Stalley, *Cistercian Monasteries of Ireland*, p. 37; see above, p. 47.
26 Note, for example, the relocation of the monks of Kalvø to Øm in 1172 (see McGuire, *Conflict and Continuity*, pp. 39–40, and France, *Cistercians in Scandinavia*, pp. 18–19) and the relocation of the Yorkshire community from Barnoldswick to Kirkstall (*The Foundation of Kirkstall Abbey*, ed. and trans. E. Clark, *Miscellanea*, Publications of the Thoresby Society, 4 (Leeds, 1895)).
27 See below, pp. 63–4.
28 See, for instance, Bernard of Clairvaux's letter to Henry I about the party from Clairvaux who in 1131 visited the Yorkshire site where Rievaulx was founded: *Letters of St Bernard of Clairvaux*, no. 95 (pp. 141–2) and discussed above, p. 38.
29 Stalley, *Cistercian Monasteries of Ireland*, pp. 35–7.

Mary's hill rose from the ground. Adam believed that divine providence had guided him to this lofty spot. This was rather unfortunate for Count William who had earmarked the land for hunting and he endeavoured to persuade Adam to reconsider his choice. But the abbot stood firm and the site was duly released to the brethren who settled at Meaux in 1150.[30] The monks of Roche were allowed to choose which side of the River Beck they wished to inhabit, either that of Richard de Busli (lord of Maltby) or that of Richard fitz Turgis (lord of Hooten). Whatever their decision they would receive the support of both men who would be regarded as equal founders. The monks decided on de Busli's land which lay on the north, a site that bordered on Bruneswald (Sherwood Forest) and was enclosed by steep limestone cliffs. The colony arrived at Roche in 1147.[31] Conversely, when the monks of Byland moved from their first site at Hood to Old Byland (Byland on the Moor) in 1142,[32] it was Roger de Mowbray (d. 1188) who decided on the location. According to the abbey's foundation history, Roger wished that, 'if it could be done appropriately', the monks should build their abbey on the southern side of the River Rye, so that they might utilise the water as the monks of Rievaulx did on the north. Old Byland did not provide a permanent home for the monks who relocated to Stocking several years later.[33]

Several Cistercian houses are known to have been founded on sites of established spiritual significance and were likely chosen by the White Monks for this very reason. Some had been occupied by another religious settlement, such as Kirkstall near Leeds, which was home to a group of hermits who made way for the Cistercians from Barnoldswick. The island of Hovedøya on the Oslo Fjord had a church dedicated to St Edmund which the Cistercians took over when they settled there in 1147.[34] Elsewhere the existence of holy wells may have been an attraction, and perhaps suggested to the monks of Strata Florida that they establish their monastery on the present site.[35] Moreover, at both Strata Florida

---

[30] *Chron. Melsa*, I, 76–7, 81. According to the chronicle, on reaching the summit Adam cited Micah 4.1 ('In the last days it shall come to pass that the mountain of the Lord's house shall be established on the top of the mountains'). As Adam had recited that verse the very same day he took this as a sign from God that this was where the new monastery should be established.

[31] J. W. Aveling, *The History of Roche Abbey from its Foundation to its Dissolution* (Worksop, 1870), pp. 4–6; P. Fergusson, *Roche Abbey*, English Heritage Guide (London, 1990; rep. 1999), p. 27.

[32] Burton explains that the date should be 1142 and not 1143 as stated in the text: *Foundation History of Byland and Jervaulx*, p. 10, note, 11.

[33] Burton, *Foundation History of Byland and Jervaulx*, pp. 13, 16. The account, compiled by Philip of Byland in 1197, describes how Roger himself realised that the site was inappropriate and duly extended the monks' endowment to enable them to move: *ibid.*, pp. 16–19. In 1177 the monks moved yet again to their final site of New Byland. See below, pp. 63–4, for further discussion.

[34] France, *Cistercians in Scandinavia*, p. 87.

[35] See the discussion of the site at: www.trinitysaintdavid.ac.uk/en/schoolofarchaeologyhistoryandanthropology/stratafloridaproject (accessed December 2010).

and Neath, and especially at Margam, the presence of early Christian memorial stones in the vicinity may be indicative of Cistercian settlement at sites of existing spiritual significance.[36] In such cases the Cistercians were important agents of transition and transformation.

The choice of site might be divinely inspired – or at least presented as such.[37] Tintern Parva (Ireland) allegedly owed its location to a vow made by William Marshall (d. 1219) when caught up in a storm at sea. William, who was earl of Pembrokeshire and lord of Leinster, swore that he would found a monastery wherever he could land safely. The earl was brought to shore at Bannow Bay where Tintern Parva – also known as Tintern de Voto (Tintern of the Vow) – was founded as a daughter house of Tintern Abbey in Monmouthshire.[38] Heavenly association with sites is not uncommon in Cistercian literature and is particularly striking in the foundation history of Jervaulx Abbey.[39] This describes a vision that occurred in the cloister at Byland Abbey in 1150, when a group of monks was departing to colonise its daughter house at Fors, later known as Jervaulx (Yorkshire). The recipient of this vision was John who was to become the founding abbot of the new house. Just as the party was leaving Byland, John saw the Virgin and Christ Child in the cloister and watched the boy pluck a branch from the small tree that stood in the centre. Later, en route to Fors, the monks became lost in a wood but according to the narrative they were helped by the reappearance of these heavenly figures. Mary consoled the group and explained that she was often to be found in desert places, adding that she had recently been at both Byland and Rievaulx but was now to go to a new abbey, to cheer the community there. The Christ Child then held up the branch which he had taken earlier from Byland and directed the monks to their new site.[40] The account of this vision therefore reinforces the idea that the abbey site had divine endorsement and was under the care of Heaven and particularly Mary. But the vision is also rich in imagery of planting and fruition, so strongly associated with the Cistercians and which, as is discussed later, was evoked to describe their familial bonds.[41]

[36]   Robinson, *Cistercians in Wales*, p. 49.
[37]   See above, note 30, for Adam of Meaux's selection of a site.
[38]   William founded both Tintern and Duiske (Graignamanagh) on land that had been conquered by the English; the abbeys subsequently became part of the new Anglo-Norman lordship of Ireland: Stalley, *Cistercian Monasteries of Ireland*, p. 16.
[39]   See Janet Burton's discussion of the source: *Foundation History of Byland and Jervaulx*, especially p. ix.
[40]   Burton, *Foundation History of Byland and Jervaulx*, pp. 58–60; see also Burton's discussion, pp. xxxiv–xxxv.
[41]   For further discussion, see below pp. 96–7.

Relocation

Whilst considerable effort might be taken to choose an appropriate location it was not uncommon for communities to move. The site might prove too small, as at Clairvaux c. 1135;[42] it might be exposed to adverse weather conditions, vulnerable to local turmoil or caught up in lordly politics and state-building strategies. Relocation was time-consuming and costly, and indeed occasionally it brought cultural and linguistic change. The nuns of La Ramée originally settled at Kerkom (Belgium) which was Dutch-speaking, but as the land was arid they relocated to La Ramée and were helped by Abbot Walter (c. 1214–31) of Villers. The new house was in a French-speaking area and as most of the nuns spoke Dutch they required a bilingual chaplain and also relied on their French-speaking sister, Ida, to help with interpretation.[43] In some cases the community relocated several times before finding a permanent place to settle. The monks of Boyle (Ireland) moved four times within sixteen years,[44] while the Byland monks occupied a total of five sites.[45] This Yorkshire community had its origins as a Savigniac house at Calder (Cumbria) in 1135, but was forced to leave when the area was devastated by the Scots. The monks resided temporarily at Hood before relocating to Old Byland in 1142 and five years later moved to Stocking; in the same year they became part of the Cistercian family. The abbey's foundation history suggests that the unsuitability of the site at Old Byland and its proximity to the Cistercians at Rievaulx necessitated the move to Stocking. But Burton argues that there may have been political strategies at play for it was surely no coincidence that Roger de Mowbray's gift of the Stocking site, which was disputed territory, coincided with the Stuteville family's resurgence of power in the area. Stocking had until 1106 belonged to the Stutevilles when they forfeited it as a consequence of their loyalty to Robert Curthose who was defeated at the Battle of Tinchebrai. The land duly passed to the Mowbrays. By 1147 the Stutevilles were reasserting their authority and seeking to reclaim this territory; Roger's grant of the site to the monks of Byland should perhaps be seen as his attempt to block

---

42   *Vita Prima*, Book II (Arnold of Bonneval), PL, 185, cols 283–5; *Bernard of Clairvaux: Early Biographies*, trans. M. Cawley, Guadalupe Translations (Lafayette, 2000), chapters 30–1 (pp. 79–80).

43   Goswin of Bossut, 'Life of Ida the Compassionate of Nivelles', chapter 2, in *Send Me God: the Lives of Ida the Compassionate of Nivelles, Nun of La Ramée, Arnulf, Lay Brother of Villers, and Abundus, Monk of Villers, by Goswin of Bossut*, trans. and intro. M. Cawley, preface B. Newman (Turnhout, 2003; repr. as paperback, University Park, Pennsylvania, 2006), pp. 29–99 (pp. 34–6, 60). Cawley, *ibid.*, p. 10, argues that Ida was likely sent to Kerkom for the very reason that she spoke French and could learn Dutch and thereby act as a translator for the women when they relocated and joined a community of French-speaking religious women from Nivelles.

44   J-F. Leroux-Dhuys, *Cistercian Abbeys: History and Architecture* (Paris, 1998), p. 156.

45   Their various travels and moves are described in the foundation history of the house: see Burton, *Foundation History of Byland and Jervaulx*, pp. 1–35.

a rival's territorial claims.[46] Thirty years after the move to Stocking the monks transferred to their final site at Byland where they built one of the finest and most ambitious churches of the time in medieval Europe.[47]

Some sites were only intended as temporary locations and provided the monks with a base while the permanent site was developed. This might take many years. The monks of Vale Royal (Cheshire) spent fifty years at a rather dilapidated makeshift monastery before moving to their new facilities in 1330, which even then were incomplete.[48]

The development of the site

> A new abbot is not to be sent to a new place without at least twelve monks … nor without having first constructed these places: oratory, refectory, dormitory, guest quarters, gatehouse – so that they may straightaway serve God there and live in keeping with the Rule.[49]

Early Cistercian legislation ruled that before any community arrived at its new site there should be certain buildings in situ, so that monastic observance might commence immediately. They were an oratory where the monks could pray, a dormitory and refectory for their living accommodation, a guest house so that visitors would not intrude on claustral life and a gatehouse to control access to the precinct. In most cases these first buildings would have been rather primitive structures which served the community until more substantial provision could be made in stone. The monks of Meaux resided at first in mud and wattle huts,[50] whilst the colony from Beaulieu that settled at Hailes (Gloucestershire) in June 1246 initially slept in tents at Hailes Mill.[51] It is unclear whether the patron or the founding house was responsible for the construction of these buildings. There is evidence both for advance parties of lay brothers being sent to prepare the site and for patrons agreeing to make sure that the

---

[46] Burton, *Foundation History of Byland and Jervaulx*, pp. 20–3.
[47] S. Harrison, *Byland Abbey*, English Heritage Guide (London, 1995), p. 3; P. Fergusson, *Architecture of Solitude: Cistercian Abbeys in Twelfth-Century England* (Princeton, 1984), pp. 83–8.
[48] T. Bostock and S. Hogg, *Vale Royal Abbey and the Cistercians 1277–1538* (Northwich, 1998), pp. 1–3; Robinson, *Cistercian Abbeys of Britain*, pp. 192–3.
[49] *Capitula*, no. 9, *NLT*, p. 408.
[50] *Chron. Melsa*, I, 82. The chronicle describes how the lay brothers initially lived in a wattle and mud house beside a two-storey chapel; the monks used the ground floor as a dormitory while the first floor accommodated their refectory and oratory. For discussion see G. Coppack, "According to the Form of the Order"? The Earliest Cistercian Buildings in England and their Context', in Kinder, *Perspectives for an Architecture of Solitude*, pp. 35–45.
[51] D. Winkless, *Hailes Abbey Gloucestershire: the Story of a Medieval Abbey* (Stocksfield, 1990, repr. London, 2001), p. 9, citing the Hailes Chronicle. Winkless thinks it likely that the monks used the parish church as their oratory. Indeed the founder's infant son was buried there in 1246 but reburied in the abbey church once it had been built (p. 17).

place was suitably equipped for the monks' arrival and even providing the group with an escort and provisions on its journey.[52] It may well be that there was no official stance and that practices varied. However, as Fergusson argues, it is likely that many founders accepted some responsibility for ensuring that the site was ready for the monks, even if this meant no more than using lay brothers from the founding house to erect rudimentary accommodation.[53]

The foundation history of Fountains Abbey describes how the dissident monks from St Mary's, York, who arrived in the Skelldale Valley in October 1132, at first sought shelter under an elm tree and then a rock. Thereafter they occupied a simple hut. The community was not at this time part of the Cistercian Order but the following summer St Bernard adopted the Yorkshire monastery as a daughter house of Clairvaux. He subsequently sent one of his monks to offer guidance on the layout of the site, to ensure that the buildings were set out 'according to the form of the Order'.[54] This was Geoffrey of Ainai, who was responsible for the temporary wooden buildings at Fountains. During his time at the Yorkshire abbey, Geoffrey instructed two monks of the house, Adam who was subsequently the founding abbot of Meaux, and Robert, the first abbot of Newminster. They in turn passed on an understanding of Cistercian requirements and between them oversaw the construction of Kirkstead (1147–49), Woburn (1145), Vaudey (1147), Meaux (1150), Newminster (1138) and Sawley (1147). It was in this way that knowledge of the Cistercian remit and presumably the benefits of experience were transmitted throughout Europe.[55]

The recovery of some of these early timber structures, notably at Fountains and Sawley (Lancashire), has greatly increased our understanding of the planning of Cistercian sites and the phases of construction. The buildings at Fountains date from Geoffrey of Ainai's supervision of the site in 1133 and are the earliest Cistercian timber buildings known in Europe. They seemingly comprised a simple rectangular chapel with domestic buildings to the south.[56] The temporary buildings at Sawley are the most extensive remains of this kind and date from between 1150 and

---

[52] Robinson, *Cistercians in Wales*, p. 51. According to the Hailes Chronicle, Richard of Cornwall provided the Beaulieu monks with an escort and provisions for their journey to Hailes: Winkless, *Hailes Abbey*, p. 8.

[53] Fergusson, *Architecture of Solitude*, p. 24; Robinson, *Cistercians in Wales*, p. 51.

[54] *Memorials of Fountains*, I, 10–48.

[55] In addition to Geoffrey, Bernard sent two more of his monks to Europe to offer instruction. They were Achard, who oversaw the building of Himmerod (see *Exordium Magnum*, III, 22 (p. 208)), and Robert, who went to Ireland to help with the construction of Mellifont (see *Letters of St Bernard of Clairvaux*, no. 385 (pp. 454–5)).

[56] For further discussion, see Coppack, '"According to the Form of the Order"?', pp. 38–40.

1180. Five buildings were excavated and showed that these were quality structures with clay walls and a lead-pipe water supply.[57]

The process of construction

Workmen were speedily hired. The brethren too engaged themselves on the job in every way. Some hewed timber, some shaped stone; some laid walls. Others busied themselves channelling the river into a network of flumes, sustaining its level high enough for the overshot wheels. The fullers too, and the bakers and tanners, the carpenters and other craftsmen all fashioned machinery adapted to their tasks, harnessing the gurgling waters to stream through their buildings, banked up and welling forth from the underground channels wherever it was needed … As for the walls, which spaciously encircle all the surroundings of the monastery, they were completed with quite unforeseeable speed.[58]

Arnold of Bonneval's description of the building of Clairvaux II, c. 1133,[59] offers a vivid insight into the process of construction as well as the speed with which this was effected and the diversity of workers engaged. Monks, lay brothers, hired labourers and artisans worked together to develop the new site.[60] The fourteenth-century chronicle of Meaux records how the first monks, cowled, helped with the building work and carried out their liturgical duties.[61] The monks of Louis IX's foundation, La Royaumont, were similarly active in the construction of their house. Louis's canonisation records present a striking image of the king helping the community during his visit to the house in December 1244. On seeing the brethren wheeling barrows full of stones, Louis was allegedly compelled to join them and urged his entourage to do likewise – but warned them to maintain an appropriate silence.[62] The impressive church at Hailes Abbey, Gloucestershire, was overseen by Brother John, a monk of the house, who is described as *cementarius* and was almost seventy when the church was dedicated in 1251.[63]

---

[57] *Ibid.*, pp. 40–2.

[58] The building of Clairvaux II, c. 1133, followed the relocation of the monastery down the valley: see *Vita Prima*, Book II (Arnold of Bonneval), PL, 185, col. 285, and Cawley, *Bernard of Clairvaux: Early Biographies*, chapter 31 (p. 80).

[59] There is considerable discussion and debate regarding the date of construction; this is the date suggested by Stuart Harrison and Christopher Holdsworth. We are indebted to Stuart Harrison for his generous advice on this.

[60] *Vita Prima*, Book 2 (Arnold of Bonneval), PL, 185, col. 285; Cawley, *Bernard of Clairvaux: Early Biographies*, chapter 31 (p. 80).

[61] *Chron. Melsa*, I, 83.

[62] W. Jordan, 'The Representation of Monastic-Lay Relations in the Canonization Records for Louis IX', in *Religious and Laity in Western Europe 1000–1400: Interaction, Negotiation and Power*, ed. E. Jamroziak and J. Burton (Turnhout, 2006), pp. 225–40 (pp. 232–3).

[63] Winkless, *Hailes Abbey*, p. 11.

These are fairly isolated examples and the extent to which monks (and indeed lay brothers) were involved in the actual building work is rather uncertain and is likely to have varied considerably. In many cases the monks may have had little to do with the construction work but relied on hired laymen to help the *conversi* while they focused on the daily liturgical round. Coppack suggests that at both Sawley and Fountains local artisans were brought in to carry out the work.[64] They probably helped the lay brothers who would have been busy developing the abbey's agriculture and industry.[65] There is both documentary and architectural evidence for parties of masons and artisans moving from one religious site to another, bringing with them experience and also fresh ideas. Stalley suggests that differences in style in the church at Boyle Abbey (Roscommon) indicate the arrival of new craftsmen who were familiar with work in the west of England, while sculpture in the abbey shows similarities with the Augustinian house at Ballintubber (Galway).[66] It can probably be assumed that Walter, the master builder, as well as the masons, Geoffrey and Miles, and Vitalis, the carpenter, who all witnessed a charter pertaining to Fontenay (Burgundy) in the 1140s, were involved in construction work at the abbey, perhaps the church.[67] The fourteenth-century ledger book of Vale Royal Abbey, founded in 1274 by Edward I, suggests that a number of the masons who worked on the abbey came from afar and were thus itinerant as well as experienced; they had likely worked on other monastic sites. A royal clerk was custodian of works at Vale Royal and the building work was supervised by a master mason of Hereford, who had previously designed castles in Wales.[68] The fourteenth-century accounts for the rebuilding of the church of the Cistercian *studium* in Paris (Collège Saint-Bernard) reveal much about the acquisition of materials and the nexus of people involved in this enterprise. The accounts were drawn up by Pons, a lay brother of Boulbonne who replaced the disgraced cleric Bertrand Auseti as head of works (*operarius operis*).[69] The *studium*'s location in Paris meant that it could draw on a wide range of suppliers as well as a team of experienced and clearly effi-

[64] Coppack, '"According to the Form of the Order"?', p. 41.
[65] See chapter 7 for further discussion of the *conversi* or lay brothers.
[66] He notes that 'an impressive team of professional masons' carried out the reconstruction of Mellifont in the thirteenth century: Stalley, *Cistercian Monasteries of Ireland*, pp. 40–1.
[67] See S. Harrison, 'The Abbey Church of Fontenay: a Reassessment of the Evidence', forthcoming *Cîteaux: Commentarii Cistercienses*. We are grateful to Stuart Harrison for making available a copy of his article prior to publication and for advising us on current thinking on architectural developments.
[68] Bostock and Hogg, *Vale Royal Abbey*, p. 2.
[69] Bertrand had been accused of fraud by the college's patron, Benedict XII, and was duly sacked: Michael T. Davis, 'The Church of the Collège Saint-Bernard', in Kinder, *Perspectives for an Architecture of Solitude*, pp. 223–34 (p. 228).

cient builders; indeed, to save time they sent templates to the quarries to cut stone to the right size.[70]

The speed of construction

Building work was effectively ongoing in the monastery. It might take many years to complete the initial structures and thereafter there were repairs, renovations and rebuilding. It has been estimated that the average church took some twenty years to construct and the claustral complex about forty.[71] But the timescale varied greatly, depending on the generosity and interest of the patron, the availability of materials and workers, and not least, the scale of the plan. Thanks to the munificence of its founder, Richard of Cornwall, building work at Hailes progressed swiftly and by 1251, only five years after its foundation, the church was dedicated.[72] After the ceremony Matthew Paris, a Benedictine monk of St Albans, asked the earl just how much money he had expended on the building and was told that this amounted to some 10,000 marks (c. £6,600).[73] The claustral complex at Kirkstall, near Leeds, was finished within thirty years as a result of the liberal support it received from its founder, Henry de Lacy.[74] Where the patron lacked interest or finances, the building suffered. This was the case at Vale Royal which was founded by Edward I in 1274 as 'a celebration of royal prestige'.[75] Edward had ambitious plans for his abbey and initially poured a considerable amount of money into its construction. The church was as long as Westminster Abbey internally and was the largest in Britain; it was richly decorated with Purbeck marble which the king ordered specially and Edward bestowed various relics on the house including a piece of the True Cross. In 1283 the church was sufficiently ready for its dedication – that is, the east end was complete – but by 1290 Edward had lost interest in the building project. He withdrew his financial support for further construction and left it to the community to fund additional work. Little was done until 1353 when the Black Prince supported the construction of a thirteen-chapel chevet in the east end

---

70 This work was financed by Benedict XII, a former monk of the Cistercian abbey of Fontfroide and a brilliant theologian of the university. The foundation stone was laid by Queen Jeanne de Bourgogne in 1335: Davis, 'The Church of the Collège Saint-Bernard'.

71 Stalley, *Cistercian Monasteries of Ireland*, pp. 44, 264 note 55.

72 Once the east end had been constructed a church could effectively be consecrated; it is unlikely that the entire church building at Hailes was complete in 1251.

73 Cited Winkless, *Hailes Abbey*, p. 12. Richard was at this time at the height of his power and had therefore the means to inject funding.

74 G. G. Astill and S. M. Wright, 'Perceiving Patronage in the Archaeological Record: Bordesley Abbey', in *In Search of Cult, University of York Archaeological Papers*, ed. M. Carver (Woodbridge, 1993), pp. 125–37 (p. 128).

75 See J. Denton, 'From the Foundation of Vale Royal Abbey to the Statute of Carlisle: Edward I and Ecclesiastical Patronage', in *Thirteenth Century England IV: Proceedings of the Newcastle Upon Tyne Conference 1991*, ed. P. R. Coss and S. D. Lloyd (Woodbridge, 1992), pp. 123–37.

of the church. Progress, however, was short-lived for in 1364 a gale blew down most of the nave and prompted a reconsideration of the elaborate plans. Building was pursued along more modest lines.[76]

Water management within the precinct

Whether the community took over an inhabited or an uncultivated site, its first concern was water management. This involved bringing fresh water to the precinct, providing a strong current to remove waste and to power industry, and, not least, controlling flooding. The thirteenth-century Chronicle of Øm[77] reveals the careful consideration that preceded the relocation of the Danish abbey from Kalvø to Øm in 1172. An ideal spot was found between two lakes, and Martin, a monk of the house, looked into ways of securing a water supply. By using a plumb Martin discovered that the water level in Lake Mossø was higher than that in Lake Gudensø; running water could thus be created by digging a canal between the two. In the event, two canals were dug, forming an island.[78] At Maulbronn Abbey in Baden-Württemberg some twenty natural and artificial lakes and ponds were linked by a complex system of canals and trenches.[79] The creation of a hydraulic system preceded the laying out of the buildings within the precinct and largely determined how they were set out. Thus, whilst the cloister was generally south-facing to make best use of the sun, in some cases the nature of the landscape and the design of the water system meant it had instead to face north. Examples include Melrose (Scotland), Alcobaça (Portugal) and also Pontigny (Burgundy) where the cloister was trapezial to accommodate the mill stream which bisected the east range.[80]

A fresh piped water supply was essential for washing, drinking, cooking and liturgical functions. This was generally secured by channelling water from uphill springs and either piping it to the monastery, as at Fountains and Pontigny, or bringing it via an open channel. The water was then

[76] Denton, 'From the Foundation of Vale Royal Abbey', pp. 124–6, 128; Bostock and Hogg, *Vale Royal Abbey*, p. 3; Robinson, *Cistercian Abbeys of Britain*, pp. 192–3.

[77] For discussion of this source and dating of the various parts, see McGuire, *Conflict and Continuity*, pp. 20–6.

[78] *Exordium Monasterii Carae Insulae*, chapter 19, in *Scriptores Minores Historiae Danicae*, 2, ed. M. Cl. Gertz (Copenhagen, 1970), pp. 153–264 (pp. 175–6); see also France, *Cistercians in Scandinavia*, pp. 14, 18–19; McGuire, *Conflict and Continuity*, pp. 39–40. A similar system was created at Søro (Denmark), where a canal was dug to link the abbey with Lake Tuel: see France, *Cistercians in Scandinavia*, p. 16 and McGuire, *Conflict and Continuity*, p. 39.

[79] Maulbronn Monastery: www.kloster-maulbronn.de/en/maulbronn-monastary/Cistercian-water-management/372499.html (accessed December 2010).

[80] T. N. Kinder, 'Living in a Vale of Tears: Cistercians and Site Management in France: Pontigny and Fontfroide', in *Monastic Archaeology*, ed. G. Keevil, M. Aston and T. Hall (Oxford, 2001), pp. 37–53 (pp. 42–5). For further discussion see T. Kinder, 'Aménagement d'une vallée de larmes: les Cisterciens et l'eau à Pontigny', in *L'hydraulique monastique* (*Actes* of the colloquium L'hydraulique monastique, Royaumont, 1992), ed. A. Bonis and M. Wabont (Grâne, 1996), pp. 383–95.

filtered in settling tanks and plumbed, often feeding two parts of the precinct – the lay brothers in the west and the monks in the east. The basins of both fountains survive at Pontigny, although they have been moved from their original location.[81] An essential part of the hydraulic system was the removal of sewage from the precinct. At Fountains Abbey the River Skell was canalised to flush water through the various toilet blocks as it ran west to east through the cloister. A branch of the river ran through each latrine block and the privies were arranged so that waste passed through a chute into the water below, where it was conducted away from the precinct.[82] Water power was harnessed to drive the abbey's forges and mills, such as the corn mill at Fountains, which was located in the outer court.[83] The Cistercians were quick to exploit this new technology and as such contributed to the advancement of water power for industrial purposes.[84]

The management of water could be extremely complex, demanding skill and expertise. The construction of the thirteenth-century infirmary drain at Fountains presented particular problems for Abbot John of Kent (1220–47) and required him to divert the river by canalising it through four parallel stone-vaulted tunnels. They in turn supported a level platform upon which an infirmary for the lay brothers was built.[85] Excavations at the Portuguese Abbey of Alcobaça uncovered a system of channels which fed water to the kitchen and supplied a large water tank in the floor.[86] In some places the Cistercians acquired a reputation for their knowledge of hydraulic engineering and were called upon to advise neighbouring religious. The Victorine canon St William of Eskilsø (d. 1203) secured the help of the Esrum Cistercians in Zealand to lay water pipes at his house of St Thomas in Æbelholt.[87] Once the water system had been laid out the rest of the precinct could be planned accordingly.

[81] Kinder, 'Living in a Vale of Tears', pp. 43–4.

[82] C. J. Bond, 'Water Management in the Rural Monastery', in *The Archaeology of Rural Monasteries*, ed. R. Gilchrist and H. Mytum, British Archaeological Reports, British Series, 203 (Oxford, 1989), pp. 83–111 (pp. 91–6).

[83] Bond, 'Water Management in the Rural Monastery', and C. J. Bond, 'Monastic Water Management in Great Britain: a Review', in Keevil *et al.*, *Monastic Archaeology*, pp. 88–136; G. Coppack, *Fountains Abbey Yorkshire*, English Heritage Guide (London, 1993), p. 120; G. Coppack, 'The Water-driven Corn Mill at Fountains Abbey: a Major Cistercian Mill of the Twelfth and Thirteenth Centuries', in *Studies in Cistercian Art and Architecture*, 5, ed. M. Parsons Lillich, Cistercian Studies Series, 167 (Kalamazoo, 1998), pp. 270–96.

[84] Bond, 'Monastic Water Management in Great Britain', p. 114. For discussion of water power at Bordesley Abbey see *A Medieval Industrial Complex and its Landscape: the Metalworking, Watermills and Workshops of Bordesley Abbey*, ed. G. G. Astill (York, 1993).

[85] Bond, 'Water Management in the Rural Monastery', pp. 95–6.

[86] Pereira, *Abbey of Santa Maria: Alcobaça*, pp. 73–5.

[87] France, *Cistercians in Scandinavia*, p. 18; McGuire, *Conflict and Continuity*, p. 40.

The precinct

Recent research suggests that at early Cistercian sites the domestic buildings were rather loosely arranged around a timber church. It was not until
the mid 1130s that the White Monks adopted the typical Benedictine plan
and started to build in stone.[88] From this time the church stood at the
core of the precinct and adjoined the cloister with its various ranges. The
claustral area was the nerve centre of monastic observance and was sheltered from distraction. Access was restricted and initially prohibited to
all females, but regulations were revised to accommodate changing needs
and new expectations. The layout of the church and claustral ranges was
fairly standard in Cistercian houses. The church was divided in two with
the monks occupying the presbytery in the east and the lay brothers the
nave in the west. These two distinct areas were separated by a rood screen.
Later, when the number of lay brothers declined, their part of the church
might be used for lay burials and processions, or to provide additional
private altars for the growing number of monk priests.[89] The cloister itself
was the hub of daily monastic life and the monks had little need to
leave this area other than to carry out their chores or if sickness required
them to go to the infirmary. The cloister garth was usually rectangular or
square and was put to practical use. The brethren were shaved here and
could hang out their washing; manuscripts might be set out to dry and
small tasks may have been carried out such as the mending of clothes.
Indeed, a thimble and copper buttons were uncovered during excavation
of the cloister at Rievaulx Abbey.[90] But the cloister was also a place of
ritual – there were processions as well as the weekly Maundy[91] – and it
was charged with symbolic significance.[92] As a place of contemplation the
cloister was identified with Paradise (or as 'a paradise'[93]) and was, accordingly, to be well maintained. In 1394, Abbot Herman of Stratford reprimanded the monks of Hailes (Gloucestershire) for their unkempt cloister
which was full of weeds. Herman reminded them that the cloister should
be a thing of beauty rather than of shame.[94] Paradoxically, the cloister was

---

[88]   We are grateful to Stuart Harrison for his advice on this matter.
[89]   As, for example, at the Yorkshire abbey of Rievaulx. At neighbouring Fountains, the nave was modi-
       fied to create side chantries.
[90]   Kinder, *Cistercian Europe*, p. 132; J. Kerr, *Life in the Medieval Cloister* (London/New York, 2009),
       p. 21.
[91]   The ritual washing of the monks' feet by the abbot, after the example of Christ (John 13.14–15).
[92]   See Megan Cassidy-Welch, *Monastic Spaces and their Meanings: Thirteenth-Century English Cistercian
       Monasteries* (Turnhout, 2001), pp. 58–65.
[93]   See E. Gilson, *The Mystical Theology of St Bernard*, trans. A. H. C. Downes, Cistercian Studies Series,
       120 (Kalamazoo, 1990), p. 91.
[94]   C. Harper-Bill, 'Cistercian Visitation in the Late Middle Ages: the Case of Hailes Abbey', *Bulletin of
       the Institute of Historical Research* 53 (1980), 103–14 (p. 109). For the cloister as symbolic of Paradise,
       see Cassidy-Welch, *Monastic Spaces*, pp. 65–71.

also equated with Purgatory; it was a place where sins could be cleansed and the brethren purged in preparation for their heavenly journey. This is vividly depicted in a vision experienced by an English Cistercian in the late twelfth or early thirteenth century who was led into a cloister by St Benedict. There he saw one row of monks and lay brothers 'rained upon by melted metal' and another charred in a fire. Mary circled the cloister, saving some of the brethren and sending a cool wind to others, to alleviate their sweating. The monk learned that this cloister was the Order's purgatory where brethren who had sinned while they lived were tortured, to fit them for salvation.[95]

The north claustral walk abutted the church.[96] The monks might read and write here and this was where the whole community gathered for the daily Collations reading.[97] The ground floor of the east range housed the sacristy, as well as a book cupboard or library, and the chapterhouse.[98] The community assembled in the chapterhouse each morning for a meeting which opened with the reading of a chapter from the Rule of St Benedict. This was followed by discussion of monastery business and thereafter disciplinary matters were addressed. Misdemeanours were confessed (or reported) and miscreants punished. A small slype (passage) adjoined the chapterhouse and was known as the parlour. It was the one place in the cloister where a little necessary conversation was permitted. Each day the monks gathered in the parlour to receive their work tools from the prior, before embarking on their stint of manual labour. A multifunctional room, generally referred to as the day-room or solar, was incorporated within the eastern range. This often vast room might be used for any number of activities or even by the novices, as was the case at Alcobaça in the fifteenth century.[99] The monks' dormitory and latrine block (reredorter) occupied the upper floor of the range. The dormitory was connected to the presbytery via nightstairs, which provided covered access to the church for the night Office of Vigils. The southern claustral range housed the calefactory (warming house), as well as the refectory and the kitchen. From a date around the 1170s the Cistercians often built their refectories perpendicular to the cloister rather than parallel to it.[100]

95 This is cited in Brian P. McGuire, 'Purgatory, the Communion of Saints and Medieval Change', *Viator* 20 (1989), 61–84 (pp. 76–7), and discussed by A. Müller, 'Presenting Identity in the Cloister', in Müller and Stöber, *Self-Representation of Medieval Religious Communities*, pp. 167–88 (pp. 167–8). The collection was seemingly written c. 1200: *ibid.*, p. 168.
96 Where the cloister was north-facing this was the south claustral walk.
97 The office of Collations consisted of a reading from John Cassian's *Conferences* and other edifying works and was heard in the north claustral walk before Compline.
98 For a useful summary see Kinder, *Cistercian Europe*, pp. 135–6.
99 Pereira, *Abbey of Santa Maria: Alcobaça*, p. 69.
100 Harrison, 'The Abbey Church of Fontenay', forthcoming. For recent discussion of this see S. Harrison, 'L'abbaye de Longuay: une évaluation architecturale', *Cîteaux: Commentarii Cistercienses* 58 (2007), 279–97, especially pp. 287–90, 295, 297. See also P. Fergusson, 'The Twelfth-Century

This meant that the kitchen could now be accommodated within the southern range and accessed directly from the cloister. It also gave scope for creating larger and lighter refectories since the size of the building was no longer restricted by the length of the range. It could extend as far southwards as the community wished and, as at Rievaulx Abbey, windows might be inserted along the length of the building, flooding it with light.[101] The western range linked the cloister to the outside world and was occupied by the lay brothers who had their own refectory and dormitory here. There was also cellarage for storing provisions and a parlour where visitors or merchants might meet and where business was transacted. In some houses a lane or courtyard separated the western range from the rest of the cloister, reinforcing the division between the two communities. Examples include Clairvaux, Mellifont and Alcobaça.

The composition and arrangement of the rest of the precinct varied considerably, for the use of space not only differed from house to house but changed over time depending on the community's needs and resources. Still, some general points can be made. The infirmary complex was usually to the east of the cloister, near to the cemetery, and might be connected to the cloister by a covered passage. The inmates were thus physically removed from the monastery yet linked to the community, symbolic of their status of being 'outside the convent' whilst infirm. [102] The infirmary provided more comfortable accommodation with better heating and bedding and a more relaxed regime. The complex was often substantial, having its own chapel, kitchen, latrine block and hall – the aisled hall of the monks' infirmary at Fountains was one of the largest in medieval Britain.[103] There might be a garden for the monks to recuperate. Later, when it was common for abbots to have private lodgings, these were often in the eastern part of the precinct, near, adjacent to or incorporated within the infirmary. This was the case at Villers (Brabant) from the late thirteenth century until 1487, when an abbatial suite was fash-

Refectories at Rievaulx and Byland Abbeys', in Norton and Park, *Cistercian Art and Architecture*, pp. 160–80; Robinson, *Cistercians in Wales*, p. 156. Harrison questions Fergusson's suggestion that this new design was initiated by Clairvaux c. 1150 and argues that although the perpendicular refectory at Clairvaux likely influenced its adoption in other Cistercian houses it may not have been the first of this kind: Harrison, 'L'abbaye de Longuay', 297.

[101] For discussion of Rievaulx's refectory, see Fergusson, 'The Twelfth-Century Refectories at Rievaulx and Byland Abbeys'; P. Fergusson and S. Harrison, *Rievaulx Abbey: Community, Architecture and Memory* (New Haven, 1999), pp. 42–3.
[102] For an incisive discussion of the location and significance of the infirmary, see D. Bell, 'The Siting and Size of Cistercian Infirmaries in England and Wales', in Lillich, *Studies in Cistercian Art and Architecture*, 5, pp. 211–38. A separate infirmary for the lay brothers was usually in the western part of the precinct as, for example, at Villers, Fountains, Roche and Clairvaux: see Robinson, *Cistercians in Wales*, p. 161.
[103] Coppack, *Fountains Abbey*, pp. 78–80.

ioned from the former lay brothers' infirmary.[104] The regulation of meat-eating in 1439 meant that monasteries now required a special room where members of the community took turns to enjoy a fleshy repast since no meat was to be eaten within the refectory. This was the misericord and it was generally placed near to the infirmary where meat had long since been cooked for the sick.[105] The western part of the precinct was usually occupied by an inner and outer court which housed guest accommodation, barns, stables and workshops, as well as mills and forges. There might be a tannery and dovecots, fish stews or vineyards. But facilities varied. The Burgundian abbey of Fontenay, for instance, had a forge;[106] there were beehives at Beaulieu (Hampshire) and Buckfast (Devon),[107] whilst both Clairvaux and Longpont had icehouses.[108]

Access to the precinct was by a gatehouse which was under the management of the monastic porter, who also served as the community's almoner.[109] There was often a chapel at the gate or within the gatehouse that could be used by women or the poor who were restricted from entering the monastic precinct.[110] But it might also serve for lay burial, as at Hailes, or for pilgrimage. At some houses the laity gathered in the gatehouse chapel to hear a sermon. In December 1344 the bishop of Lincoln granted forty days' indulgence to everyone who devoutly visited the chapel of St Mary outside the gate at Furness Abbey (Lancashire) to hear the monks preach there.[111] The entire precinct was sometimes surrounded by a boundary wall, both to control access and to demarcate the extent of the monks' territory. At the Yorkshire abbey of Fountains remains of the great precinct wall survive to the south and west of the monastery. It was built in the first half of the thirteenth century and extended over three metres high.[112] Some abbeys were later fortified, although this required special permission. Clairvaux was crenellated in

[104] See Kinder, *Cistercian Europe*, p. 385. Previously the abbot had occupied a small room adjacent to the dormitory. The infirmary complex at Longuay was similarly converted to make an abbatial suite: see Harrison, 'L'abbaye de Longuay', 283. J. Hall, 'East of the Cloister: Infirmaries, Abbots' Lodgings and Other Chambers', in Kinder, *Perspectives for an Architecture of Solitude*, pp. 199–211, reiterates the 'mutable nature' of these chambers to the east of the cloister and the frequent link between the infirmary and the abbot's lodgings.

[105] Lekai, *Cistercians: Ideals and Reality*, p. 370.

[106] Kinder, *Cistercian Europe*, p. 372.

[107] *The Account Book of Beaulieu Abbey*, ed. S. F. Hockey, Camden fourth series, 16 (London, 1975), pp. 73, 93, 124, 135, 175, 177, 184, 193, 194; E. Crane, *The Archaeology of Beekeeping* (London, 1983), pp. 133, 264. Bee boles – recesses built into the wall for basket hives ('skeps') – thought to date from the twelfth century survive at Abbey Farm, Buckfast.

[108] See Kinder, *Cistercian Europe*, p. 372, for the egg-shaped ice-houses at Clairvaux and Longpont.

[109] The distribution of charity is considered in chapter 8, pp. 191–4.

[110] For gatehouse chapels see Kinder, *Cistercian Europe*, p. 369 and J. Hall, 'English Cistercian Gatehouse Chapels', *Cîteaux: Commentarii Cistercienses* 52 (2001), 61–91.

[111] *The Coucher Book of Furness Abbey*, ed. J. C. Atkinson and J. Brownbill, Chetham Society, 3 vols (1886–88), II (iii), 803–4.

[112] Coppack, *Fountains Abbey*, pp. 79–81.

the fourteenth century during the Hundred Years War, while there was a drawbridge at Maulbronn Abbey which was enclosed by a stone wall connected to five towers.[113]

The design and use of buildings continually evolved and, as Kinder underlines, the monastery never stood still; it was a living monument. Legislative changes, economic developments and the social composition of the community might all have an impact on the use of space. Thus, with the demise of the *conversi* from the thirteenth century, their quarters were often refashioned. At Marienfeld (Germany) the lay brothers' refectory was converted into a monastic library in the early fifteenth century, while at Bebenhausen (Baden-Württemberg) it was turned into a winter refectory for the monks since it could be heated.[114] Falling numbers within the monastic community might lead to a similar restructuring of space. Robinson demonstrates how the southern end of the eastern range at Neath Abbey (West Glamorgan) was remodelled c. 1500 to accommodate an abbatial suite and its reworking is indicative of the growing importance of the abbot and his household at this time. Part of the monks' dormitory, dayroom and toilet block was converted to house the new facilities.[115]

The remainder of this chapter moves from the use of space within the precinct to the nature of the Cistercians' buildings and considers the various factors which influenced their design and décor.

The buildings: design and décor[116]

> They resolved to retain no crosses of gold or silver, but only painted wooden ones; no candelabra except a single one of iron; no thuribles except of copper or iron; no chasuble except of plain cloth or linen, and without silk, gold, and silver; no albs or amices except of linen; and likewise without silk, gold, and silver. As for all mantles and copes and dalmatics and tunics, these they rejected entirely. They did, however, retain chalices, not of gold, but of silver, and, if possible, gilded … As for altar cloths, they explicitly decreed that they be of linen, without pictorial ornamentation, and that the wine cruets be without gold or silver.[117]

---

[113] Kinder, *Cistercian Europe*, pp. 367, 371; P. R. Anstett, *Maulbronn Monastery*, 2nd edn (Munich, 1995), pp. 9, 70–2.

[114] Leroux-Dhuys, *Cistercian Abbeys*, p. 150. The lay brothers' dormitory at Altzelle (Germany) became a library in 1514: Kinder, *Cistercian Europe*, p. 329.

[115] Robinson, *Cistercians in Wales*, p. 219.

[116] For useful discussions of Cistercian architecture and the phases of constructions, see Kinder, *Cistercian Europe*; Robinson, *Cistercians in Wales*; N. Coldstream, 'The Mark of Eternity: the Cistercians as Builders', in Robinson, *Cistercian Abbeys of Britain*, pp. 35–51; Stalley, *Cistercian Monasteries of Ireland*; and Fergusson, *Architecture of Solitude*.

[117] *Exordium Parvum*, chapter XVII, *NLT*, p. 438.

When Innocent II visited Clairvaux in 1131 he was struck by the starkness of the high altar. There were no jewels, lavish fabrics or hangings, just a bare wooden cross. This simplicity and lack of adornment characterised the design and décor of Cistercian buildings, which were rather minimalist. The Order eschewed highly ornate buildings and rich furnishings. These were regarded as unnecessary and ostentatious but, crucially, were likely to distract the eye and excite the senses. Conversely, Cistercian buildings were to subdue the senses and focus the mind, thereby aiding contemplation.[118] Moreover, as Bernard of Clairvaux warned in his *Apologia*, c. 1125, such lavishness was vanity and even a form of idolatry. It might impress visitors and prompt them to open their purses but did little to augment devotion or arouse compunction.[119]

Early legislation prohibited the use of colour and fabrics, ruling against stained glass, carpets, wall-hangings and paintings.[120] Internally, buildings were bare. They were generally lime-washed white and might have mock masonry lines picked out. A greenish clear glass known as grisaille was used and natural lighting was preferred to artificial both for reasons of economy and its spiritual significance. As Kinder explains, the soft subtle light animated these buildings as it slowly moved through them and provided a fitting setting for contemplation.[121] But also, and importantly, it evoked Christ who was the Light of the World. As time progressed changes were made. The use of coloured glass, for example, became common and was eventually allowed, while prescriptions relating to vessels, ornaments, paintings and sculptures were relaxed.[122] Stone bell towers were initially forbidden and a small timber structure was to suffice. This was not always adhered to and in some places proved impractical, notably in France where wooden towers could not withstand the mistral; the General Chapter had to revise its stance to permit modest stone towers there.[123] The evolution of practices did not necessarily mean that ideals were forsaken. Carter has recently argued that although the art

---

[118] For a helpful discussion see Kinder, *Cistercian Europe*, especially pp. 141–61.

[119] *St Bernard's Apologia to Abbot William*, pp. 63–6. Bernard wrote this tract at the instigation of William of St Thierry, largely to undermine rumours that the Cistercians were slandering the Cluniacs; Bernard was critical of the vices of both orders in this work. See above, pp. 34–5.

[120] See *Exordium Parvum*, chapter VII, *NLT*, p. 438.

[121] Kinder, *Cistercian Europe*, pp. 219, 385–6.

[122] See C. Norton, 'Table of Cistercian Legislation on Art and Architecture', in Norton and Park, *Cistercian Art and Architecture*, pp. 315–93; Kinder, *Cistercian Europe*, pp. 219–20.

[123] Kinder, *Cistercian Europe*, p. 195. For important discussion on the tower, see P. Fergusson, 'Early Cistercian Churches in Yorkshire and the Problem of the Cistercian Crossing Tower', *Journal of the Society of Architectural Historians* 29 (1970), 211–21, and S. Harrison, '"I lift up mine eyes": a Re-evaluation of the Tower in Cistercian Architecture in Britain', in Kinder, *Perspectives for an Architecture of Solitude*, pp. 125–35. Stalley, *Cistercian Monasteries of Ireland*, p. 141, explains that whilst the ruling was generally adhered to on the continent, this was not the case in England where it became 'a standard feature'.

and décor in the northern English houses of the later Middle Ages were often more elaborate than earlier in the period, this development was not incompatible with Cistercian ideology. Rather, these embellishments were in keeping with the Order's identity, for where saints were depicted they were from the Cistercian calendar; liturgical inscriptions that were inscribed on towers as well as on vestments were from its breviary.[124]

This simplicity defined Cistercian architecture. But, as Kinder warns, the term needs to be used cautiously for their buildings could be complex and costly, drawing on high-quality materials and expertise and utilising new technologies and styles. The Cistercians may have been noted for their unity and cohesion but there was no set of prescriptions defining the Order's architecture, which was characterised by its fluidity and receptivity to change. It is thus less appropriate to talk of Cistercian architecture than a Cistercian spirit or, as Stalley suggests, 'a Cistercian attitude towards architecture'.[125] Accordingly, there was a tremendous variety in the design and décor of the White Monks' buildings. No two abbeys were the same: they might share similar ground-plans and a 'linear simplicity', but the elevations, mouldings, materials and style gave each monastery its own particular character.[126]

An evolving style: the Cistercians as conveyors and assimilators

Cistercian architecture was progressive. It moved with the times and in accordance with advances in technology and design. The Order acted as a conduit, advancing new ideas, but it also assimilated regional practice, making use of local materials and workers, and employing traditional methods. The church at Maulbronn Abbey combined Burgundian elements with Swabian traditions 'of the Hirsau style', seen, for example, in the uniformity of the pillars and the rectangular frame of the nave arcades.[127] The twelfth-century nave of the church was not vaulted but followed local practice and had a flat wood-beam ceiling. Similar examples include Tre Fontane in Rome and Melleray in Brittany.[128] The evolution of Cistercian building is here considered first through an analysis of the church and then through the impact of local influence and individuals on the design and décor of the buildings.

---

[124] Michael Carter, 'The Cistercians' Use of Devotional Images in Late Medieval England: Some Northern Evidence', paper given at the International Medieval Congress, Leeds, July 2010. See also his published papers, 'Late Medieval Relief Sculptures of the Annunciation to the Virgin from the Cistercian Abbeys of Rievaulx and Fountains', *Cîteaux: Commentarii Cistercienses* 60 (2009), 1–22, and 'Remembrance, Liturgy and Status in a Late Medieval English Cistercian Abbey: the Mourning Vestment of Abbot Robert Thorton of Jervaulx (1510–33)', *Textile History* 41 (2010), 3–18.

[125] Stalley, *Cistercian Monasteries of Ireland*, p. 2.

[126] Kinder, *Cistercian Europe*, pp. 108, 143.

[127] Anstett, *Maulbronn Monastery*, pp. 5–6.

[128] Kinder, *Cistercian Europe*, pp. 199, 217.

There is little solid evidence for the design and construction of early Cistercian churches, that is, buildings belonging to the first twenty years or so of the Order's history. But, as we noted earlier, recent excavations suggest that these were small timber buildings which were later replaced with stone, and that the domestic buildings were 'loosely arranged' around the church. From c. 1130 the Cistercians built modest churches with adjoining claustral ranges and adopted the Benedictine plan. They were simple, even austere, structures and were either aisleless, as at Tintern in Monmouthshire, or had aisles which were effectively corridors, as well as square presbyteries and narrow transepts; but there was no crossing tower. Examples include Fountains (Yorkshire), Vauclair (Aisne) and l'Escale Dieu (Haute Pyrénées). Until recently the Burgundian abbey of Fontenay has been regarded as the oldest surviving Cistercian church in France and was thought to reflect the archetypal early Cistercian church. Stuart Harrison's reassessment of the dating of the abbey church builds on Thomas Coomans's work and challenges this paradigm.[129] Harrison suggests a later period of construction than previously held. He argues that building was probably begun c. 1140 rather than 1139 and finished in the 1160s instead of 1147. This would mean that Fontenay belongs to a second, 'more mature phase' of Cistercian church building that took place in the 1140s and 1150s. Indeed, the church at Fontenay, 'solidly Romanesque', is larger and more elaborate than the early buildings at Vauclair and l'Escale Dieu, having wider nave aisles, developed pier bases and both transverse and high barrel vaults. This reassessment of the church at Fontenay has significant implications since the abbey's architecture has been used as a benchmark to date other monastic churches. Some of these may in fact be later than hitherto thought.[130]

Towards the latter part of the twelfth century Cistercian architecture was influenced by a new style – the Early Gothic. This is thought to have originated in north-east France, with Abbot Suger's rebuilding of St Denis, Paris, c. 1135.[131] With its rib vaults, lancet windows, moulded piers and three-storey elevations, the Early Gothic created buildings which were loftier and lighter than those in the Romanesque Burgundian style. Further, it required less stone, making this a more efficient way of building. The Cistercians embraced change and were quick to adopt the new form of architecture. In doing so they helped to propagate the Early Gothic style throughout Europe. There are numerous examples.

---

[129] Coomans questioned just how much of the abbey church had been completed at its dedication in 1147: see T. Coomans, 'Fontenay au-delà de Saint Bernard: à propos de deux publications récentes sur l'abbaye et son architecture', *Cîteaux: Commentarii Cistercienses* 54 (2003), 171–86.

[130] See Harrison, 'The Abbey Church of Fontenay', for extensive discussion of the dating.

[131] Robinson, *Cistercians in Wales*, p. 78; C. Wilson, *The Gothic Cathedral: the Architecture of the Great Church 1130–1530* (London, 1990, rev. 2000), pp. 13–90.

The nave at Pontigny, for instance, is the earliest example of rib vaulting in Burgundy,[132] while the church at Alcobaça was the first and largest Early Gothic building in Portugal.[133] The White Monks brought Gothic to Ireland with the building of Grey (Down), Inch (Down) and Duiske (Kilkenny), and the narthex of Maulbronn Abbey was the first example of this style of architecture in Germany; it was built by the so-called 'Master of the Paradise' who was trained in Paris.[134] For this reason the Cistercians were dubbed by some as 'missionaries of Gothic'. But the use of this term has generated considerable discussion and is now regarded as inappropriate and inaccurate.[135] Robinson concludes that the White Monks on occasion introduced or promoted 'a rather evolved strain of early French Gothic' that was quite different to the architectural style of the Burgundian mother houses.[136] They fused the new style with traditional Romanesque and also regional design. Thus the church at Maulbronn combines Romanesque, Early Gothic and Late Gothic features; at Alcobaça, the semi-circular Romanesque arches in the door of the chapterhouse are set beside colonnettes and capitals 'of decidedly Gothic proportions'.[137]

Whilst the Cistercians disseminated knowledge of new styles or methods of construction, often they incorporated native traditions and were influenced by contemporary developments in the region.[138] At Jerpoint Abbey (Kilkenny) the distinctively Irish dumbbell design survives in the cloister. This comprises two shafts cut from a single block and connected by 'thin plate or web'. It was taken on by the Cistercians in Ireland and distinguished them from their counterparts in Britain and Europe.[139] The dumbbell design at Jerpoint linked the house to other Cistercian abbeys in the country, but the series of late-medieval carvings in its cloister – 'a chaotic mixture of the sacred and the profane', depicting knights, abbots, saints, ladies, dragons and nut-eating squirrels – is unique both in an Irish and a Cistercian context. Stalley describes the carvings as 'a rare

---

[132] Kinder, *Cistercian Europe*, pp. 199, 222.
[133] Pereira, *Abbey of Santa Maria: Alcobaça*, p. 34; the abbey had the first Gothic flying buttresses in Portugal which were to support the chevet in the church.
[134] Stalley, *Cistercian Monasteries of Ireland*, pp. 2, 77–8; Anstett, *Maulbronn Monastery*, p. 20.
[135] Christopher Wilson, 'Gothic Architecture Transplanted: the Nave of the Temple Church', in *The Temple Church in London: History, Architecture, Art*, ed. R. Griffith-Jones and D. Park (Woodbridge, 2010), pp. 19–44, now considers the Temple Church in London rather than the northern English Cistercian abbeys as the key transmitter of the style; Stuart Harrison argues that in the north of England the archbishops of York and not the Cistercians were fundamental in promoting the style and that the choir at York Minster, initiated under Roger Pont l'Evêque (1154–81), preceded any other Cistercian Gothic building. We are indebted to Stuart Harrison for this information.
[136] Robinson, *Cistercians in Wales*, pp. 92–103.
[137] Anstett, *Maulbronn Monastery*, especially pp. 2, 4–16; Pereira, *Abbey of Santa Maria: Alcobaça*, pp. 59, 66.
[138] For a particularly useful discussion in the context of Britain, see Coldstream, 'The Mark of Eternity', especially pp. 42ff.
[139] See Stalley, *Cistercian Monasteries of Ireland*, pp. 154–6, 160.

spectacular rejection of Cistercian austerity' and compares them to the English Court Style of the reign of Richard II (1377–99), particularly the tomb of Edward III (d. 1377) in Westminster Abbey. Although the Jerpoint carvings are less skilful than those in Westminster, they draw on the same motifs and Stalley suggests that the men who worked at Jerpoint were likely experienced in tomb sculpture.[140]

The nature of the workmen's experience could clearly have a significant impact on the monastery's architecture. The influence of an abbot or patron might be equally decisive and contribute to the individuality of the building. The two-storey chapterhouse at Rievaulx, built in the time of Abbot Aelred (d. 1167), was exceptional in a Cistercian context, having an apsidal east end, tiered seating and an ambulatory that was probably intended to accommodate the lay brothers. It is thought to have been influenced by the basilicas outside the walls of Rome.[141] A 'unique feature' at St Mary Graces, London, is the Lady Chapel, built before 1492 by one of Richard III's councillors, Sir Thomas Montgomery, who wished to establish his family mausoleum at the abbey.[142] The star-shaped abaci in the east claustral range of Le Trésor – 'in the Royannant design' – are the earliest examples of this kind of decoration in Normandy. Lindy Grant attributes their appearance to the nunnery's royal patrons, Blanche of Castile and her son, Louis IX, and their concern to make the building seem more French than Norman.[143]

Patrons, benefactors and abbots might leave their imprint on the abbey by incorporating heraldic devices within the architecture, either on walls or on floor tiles. As Stöber argues, monasteries could function as monuments to the living and the dead.[144] A striking example is Marmaduke Huby's Tower at Fountains Abbey, which was erected by one of the leading abbots in the country. Abbot Huby (1495–1526) personalised this great tower with an inscription of his shield bearing his initials, 'MH', between a mitre and crozier, and his motto, 'Honour and glory to God alone' (*Soli Deo Honor et Gloria*). A carving of a head on the second storey may be a representation of St Bernard or perhaps of the

---

[140] *Ibid.*, pp. 189–93.

[141] P. Fergusson and S. Harrison, 'The Rievaulx Abbey Chapter-House', *Antiquaries Journal* 74 (1994), 216–53, and Fergusson and Harrison, *Rievaulx Abbey: Community, Architecture and Memory*, pp. 57–68, 94–9, suggest that the Romanesque chapterhouse at Rievaulx may be a miniature version of these basilicas. However, the design of the chapterhouse has aroused considerable debate and others hold that Aelred may have been influenced by the architecture in Burgundy, Durham or Normandy.

[142] Jamroziak, 'St Mary Graces', pp. 159–60.

[143] Lindy Grant, *Architecture and Society in Normandy 1120–1270* (New Haven/London, 2005), pp. 144, 207–8; L. Hicks, *Religious Life in Normandy, 1050–1300: Space, Gender and Social Pressure* (Woodbridge, 2007), p. 10.

[144] K. Stöber, 'The Role of Late Medieval English Monasteries as Expressions of Patronal Authority: Some Case Studies', in Trio and de Smet, *The Use and Abuse of Sacred Places in Late Medieval Towns*, pp. 189–207 (p. 206).

abbot himself.[145] More common are the coats of arms of benefactors and
abbots, such as those painted on the nave walls at Maulbronn and on
the refectory floor at Cleeve (Somerset). The latter includes the royal
arms of Henry III, the arms of Poitou and the arms of Clare to celebrate
the marriage of Henry III's nephew, Edmund of Cornwall, to Margaret
de Clare in 1272.[146] Some of the most impressive heraldic devices are
at Hailes Abbey, Gloucestershire, founded in 1246 by Richard, earl of
Cornwall and king of Germany. Tiles in the church depict an eagle to
represent the German kingdom and are thought to lie near the burial
spot of Richard and his wife, Sanchia. The walls of the parish church at
the abbey gate bear Richard's arms, as well as the arms of his wives and
various relatives and notables; heraldic bosses in the west claustral area
include those of Henry Percy, earl of Northumberland (d. 1527), and
Sir John Huddleston who was constable of the castles of Sudeley and
Gloucester and was buried at the abbey c. 1511. John left instructions that
his grave should be covered with a marble slab bearing his image and his
name, as a reminder to everyone who passed his remains.[147] Tombs and
shrines could similarly affect the design and décor of monastic buildings
and, as Coldstream argues, in this way benefactors 'invaded Cistercian
churches'.[148]

The physical setting of their monasteries and the design of their buildings were highly significant to the Cistercians, having symbolic as well as
practical importance. The rural settings that they preferred provided the
monks with the solitude that they craved and provided space to develop
substantial precincts. This environment also marked them out from the
Benedictines whose houses were often in urban centres. As the Order
expanded across Europe and the Cistercians incorporated houses of
other orders they were confronted with a variety of landscapes but as we
have seen, they adapted accordingly and were equally responsive to new
ideas in architecture and design. The Cistercians took on and promoted
developments in style yet retained a simplicity and purity that defined
the Order. They accommodated change whilst preserving the Cistercian
spirit.

Having considered the organisation of space within the monastery it is
appropriate to turn now to the organisation of the Order, to examine its
administrative structure and the daily running of the monastery.

[145] W. St John Hope, 'Fountains Abbey', *Yorkshire Archaeological Journal* 15 (1898–99), 269–402 (p. 314).
[146] Anstett, *Maulbronn Monastery*, p. 14; S. Harrison, *Cleeve Abbey, Somerset*, English Heritage Guide (London, 2000), p. 13.
[147] Winkless, *Hailes Abbey*, pp. 17, 49–53.
[148] Coldstream, 'The Mark of Eternity', p. 37.

CHAPTER FOUR

Unity and Concord:
The Administration of the Order

United in one church, one order and finally one body in Christ.[1]

One of the distinguishing features of the Cistercian Order has always been held to be its tight organisation. The structure was set down in the constitution of the Order, the *Carta Caritatis*, which was discussed above in chapter two.[2] Individual Cistercian houses were joined together in familial bonds and arranged in a hierarchy. The abbot of Cîteaux stood at the head of the Order; below him were the abbots of the four eldest daughter houses of La Ferté, Pontigny, Clairvaux and Morimond. Thereafter all abbeys were organised according to their affiliation. Bouchard has recently argued that this structure was inspired by Gregory VII's 'vision' of the papacy, whereby the pope stood at the apex of the pyramid, the archbishops were beneath, followed by the bishops and so on. By taking on the papal model the Cistercians not only adopted this hierarchical structure for themselves but acted as a conduit by transmitting it further both to monastic and to secular circles. Thus, under Peter the Venerable (1122–56) Cluny was organised according to a hierarchy, while Emperor Frederick Barbarossa (1152–90), the first German king to convert the great German counties and duchies into royal fiefs, was advised by the White Monks.[3]

The organisational structure of the Cistercian Order was an effective way to promote unity and conformity of practice. This was implemented chiefly through the General Chapter and the annual visitation of each daughter house by its Father Immediate, who was not only to make sure that standards were upheld but to offer the brethren advice. The success of this system was widely acknowledged and was adopted by other orders. The Gilbertines and Premonstratensians took on both of these elements, while the Carthusians and Cluniacs introduced the practice of holding

---

[1] *Exordium Magnum*, I, 29 (p. 57).
[2] See above, pp. 31–5.
[3] C. Bouchard, '"Feudalism", Cluny and the Investiture Controversy', in *Medieval Monks and their World: Ideas and Realities. Studies in Honor of Richard E. Sullivan*, ed. D. Blanks, M. Frassetto and A. Livingstone, Brill's Series in Church History, 25 (Leiden, 2006), pp. 81–92.

a general chapter. In 1215 Cistercian administration received the papal seal of approval at the Fourth Lateran Council, where Innocent III held this up as a model to the Benedictines and regular canons. He ruled that henceforth all orders should hold a general assembly every three years and that the Cistercians should guide them on how to implement this.[4]

Before looking further at these two aspects of Cistercian organisation it is appropriate to consider, briefly, the internal management of the monastery, namely, how discipline was maintained within each house and how the abbey was run. This largely fell on the abbot as father (*abba*) of the community and the chief authority within the monastery. But power was devolved and he was assisted by senior monks who held administrative posts or 'obediences'; they were known as obedientiaries.

The Cistercians were at heart Benedictines. They sought to return to a purer interpretation of the Rule of St Benedict and took these tenets as their basis for regulating monastic life. The Rule was only ever intended to be a starting point and the Cistercians elaborated on it in their legislative texts to provide more extensive and explicit instruction that was needed to administer the growing Order.

Internal administration

The power of the abbot

Reprove, entreat, rebuke. (2 Timothy 4.2)[5]

Obedience was the bedrock of monastic observance and one of the three vows that the monk made at his profession.[6] He was to show obedience to God, to the Rule of St Benedict and to his abbot who stood in place of Christ within the cloister and was to be adhered to in all matters. As the supreme authority within the monastery, the abbot was responsible for maintaining discipline and ensuring that all the brethren atoned for their wrongs, since only those who were unfettered by sin could receive the heavenly reward of salvation. It was the abbot's duty to make sure that each member of the community attained this goal. He was to be the shepherd who led his flock to pasture and protected it from the devil's wiles. As Bernard of Clairvaux warned, the abbot should be vigilant and do everything to prevent the devil from finding a way into the monastery to 'snatch a lamb' from his very hands.[7] Given that the abbot was to guard the monks from temptation and correct abuses, he was ultimately

---

[4] *Decrees of the Ecumenical Councils*, I, ed. N. P. Tanner (Georgetown, 1990), pp. 240–1 (cl. 12).
[5] RB, chapter 2.
[6] These were stability, conversion of his life and obedience: RB, chapter 58.
[7] *Letters of St Bernard of Clairvaux*, no. 103 (p. 150).

liable for their wrongs and, as the Rule of St Benedict warned, on the
Day of Judgement the abbot would be held accountable for the brethren's
sins as well as his own:

> Let him know that to the fact of the shepherd should be imputed any
> lack of profit which the father of the household may find in his sheep.
> Only then shall he be acquitted, if he shall have bestowed all pastoral
> diligence on his unquiet and disobedient flock and employed all his
> care to amend their corrupt way of life.[8]

The abbot's accountability for the brethren's conduct is clearly illustrated
in an anecdote concerning an abbot of Clairvaux and a knight who
entered the house as a novice. The newcomer made a promising start
but soon fell by the wayside and became disruptive. The abbot blamed
himself for the novice's demise which he regarded as his personal failure.
He offered to take on full responsibility for the novice's sins since he
considered himself a poor shepherd who had allowed the wolf to carry
off his sheep. His actions brought about a change in the novice who duly
mended his ways and persisted in the monastic life. Later, the novice had
a vision which revealed to him the abbot's reward for his sacrifice; he saw
two couches awaiting his abbot in heaven since he, like Christ, had laid
down his life for his sheep.[9]

The abbot therefore had a difficult task, for he was to show compassion
and inspire love yet also command authority and preserve order if he was
to help the monks secure salvation. How then did he maintain discipline
and effect remorse amongst the brethren?

Discipline in the cloister
> We who are in this vale of tears have to weep. And because we sin every
> day, we need daily penance.[10]

Each monk was obliged to exercise self-discipline. He was to be his own
judge and to be guided by his conscience which would compel him to
resist sin and, importantly, to confess wrongdoings. William of St Thierry
(d. 1148) advised brethren to examine their consciences every day and
stand before God to see the reasons for joy and sorrow in their actions,
and to feel true remorse for their sins.[11] Whilst discipline was to come

8   RB, chapter 2.
9   Matarasso, *Cistercian World*, pp. 301–4; Kerr, *Life in the Medieval Cloister*, p. 118.
10 Idungus of Prüfung, 'A Dialogue Between Two Monks', III, 45, in *Cistercians and Cluniacs: the Case for Citeaux [A Dialogue between Two Monks; an Argument on Four Questions]*, ed. and trans. J. O'Sullivan and J. Leahey, Cistercian Fathers Series, 33 (Kalamazoo, 1977), pp. 19–141 (pp. 134–5).
11 William of St Thierry, *The Golden Epistle: a Letter to the Brethren at Mont Dieu*, trans. T. Berkeley, Cistercian Fathers Series, 12 (Kalamazoo, 1971), I, 29 (pp. 48–9).

from within, there were external controls to deter the brethren from straying and ensure that all misdemeanours were punished. Senior monks would patrol the monastery as the eyes and ears of the convent. Any errors were reported at the daily chapter meeting which was attended by the whole community and presided over by the abbot. Here, the monks were invited to confess their wrongs and atone for their sins. Offenders who did not volunteer this information were accused but were urged to regard this as an act of compassion since their accuser, like 'the razor of God', sought to remove their 'unsightly hair' so that they would appear 'more pleasing' in His presence.[12] Similarly, whatever punishment the abbot meted out was to be considered an act of love and essential to the spiritual progression of the monks.

Most offences were minor transgressions such as lateness, laziness, breaches of silence, and gluttony. These 'light' crimes were generally punished by fasting, flogging or the withdrawal of privileges. More serious offences included murder, apostasy and disregard of the basic monastic vows of charity, poverty and obedience.[13] They called for a harsher sentence which might include temporary removal to another house in the hope that this would induce a change of heart and, crucially, prevent the canker from spreading within the community. In 1218 a Cistercian monk of Foigny (Laon) who had disputed his abbot's sermons and was considered an agitator was sent away to an abbey in the Low Countries.[14] Imprisonment was not uncommon and was usually reserved for grave offences and for the unrepentant. A number of houses had their own prison cells where miscreants were separated from the rest of the brethren. There were seemingly two such cells at the Yorkshire abbey of Fountains which were uncovered in the abbot's chambers when the site was excavated in the nineteenth century. In one of the cells a former occupant had scrawled the words *Vale libertas* ('Farewell freedom').[15] Not everywhere had formal prison cells, and troublemakers might be incarcerated in the infirmary or another designated spot. At Esholt Priory (Yorkshire) a sixteenth-century nun of the house who was pregnant was imprisoned for two years in a room within the nuns' dormitory.[16] In serious cases incarceration was for life, and for the communal good the offender was 'turned out as a

---

[12] Stephen of Sawley, 'Mirror for Novices', in Stephen of Sawley, *Treatises*, ed. B. Lackner, trans. J. F. O'Sullivan, Cistercian Fathers Series, 36 (Kalamazoo, 1984), pp. 102–3.

[13] See 'Institutes of the General Chapter', nos 66 and 67, *NLT*, pp. 484–6. For a useful discussion of discipline in the cloister, see Cassidy-Welch, *Monastic Spaces*, pp. 116–26, and *Twelfth-Century Statutes*, pp. 39–40.

[14] Cassidy-Welch, *Monastic Spaces*, p. 123; Canivez, *Statuta*, I, 494 (1218: 47).

[15] Coppack, *Fountains Abbey*, pp. 99–100.

[16] H. E. Bell, 'Esholt Priory', *Yorkshire Archaeological Journal* 33 (1938), 5–33 (pp. 28–9); C. Cross and N. Vickers, *Monks, Friars and Nuns in Sixteenth-Century Yorkshire*, Yorkshire Archaeological Society Record Series, 150 (1995), p. 565.

diseased sheep is turned out from the flock, as a gangrenous limb is cut off from the body'.[17] In 1226 a monk of Jouy who had attempted to kill his abbot with a razor was imprisoned for life.[18] Permanent removal was to be considered a last resort and the abbot was urged to use all means at his disposal to effect remorse and induce repentance. As Bernard of Clairvaux advised:

> Do all that charity requires of you to save the brother, spare neither kindness, wholesome advice, rebukes in private, exhortations in public and if necessary sharp words and sharp floggings, but above all, what is usually more efficacious than anything in these cases do you and the brethren pray for him. [19]

If, and only if, all efforts failed might the abbot wash his hands of the offender and know that he would not be held accountable for the monk's waywardness on the Day of Judgement. By continually refusing to reform, the miscreant placed himself outside monastic discipline and was responsible for his own fate.

The devolution of power

Although the abbot had overall charge of the internal and external administration of the monastery, he was helped by a team of senior monks (obedientiaries) who were entrusted with the care of various offices. The cellarer, for example, looked after the community's supplies, whilst the sacrist maintained the church and vestments and was responsible for timekeeping; the guestmaster (or hosteller) was in charge of the hospice and ensured that visitors were received appropriately, whereas the infirmarer took care of the sick and elderly. The appointment of obedientiaries – and the so called 'obedientiary system' – was fundamental to western monastic administration and was not exclusive to the Cistercians. It had its origins in the Rule of St Benedict which named only a few domestic posts, for Benedict intended that most tasks would be shared amongst the brethren and rotated on a weekly basis. This was to prevent hostilities arising and to make sure that each member of the community pulled his weight. The number and nature of these posts evolved over the years to meet the monastery's changing needs. For instance, economic developments and the growing complexity of monastic administration led to the creation of new posts and the subdivision of offices. In many cases the obedientiary became less involved with the execution of the tasks

---

17 *Letters of St Bernard of Clairvaux*, no. 103 (p. 150).
18 Cassidy-Welch, *Monastic Spaces*, p. 123; Canivez, *Statuta*, II, 53 (1226: 25).
19 *Letters of St Bernard of Clairvaux*, no. 103 (p. 150).

and more of a manager, who oversaw the running of the office and was concerned with its finances.[20]

The twelfth-century Cistercian customs elaborate on the domestic offices cited in Benedict's Rule and name ten posts (prior, subprior, novicemaster, sacrist, precentor, infirmarer, cellarer, refectorer, guestmaster and porter). They provide a comprehensive guide to the nature of the obedientiaries' duties and any concessions they should receive on account of their work.[21] Thus, the cellarer might leave the refectory and dormitory whenever he needed and could speak with lay brothers, his assistant and guests within the monastery; like other officials, he was exempt from various claustral duties if necessarily detained by his office.[22] The 'obedientiary system' remained the chief and most effective way of managing the monastery throughout the Middle Ages, although it was modified over time and varied not only from order to order but from house to house. For instance in Cistercian abbeys the porter distributed alms and exercised charity on behalf of the community yet in Benedictine houses this was the duty of a monk almoner and the porter's office was often occupied by a layman.[23] The division of administration in this way was an efficient means of devolving power. Moreover, it equipped obedientiaries with important skills that would stand them in good stead if they were later appointed to the abbacy. Although it was prestigious to hold an office, the work could be demanding and stressful. Matthew of Rievaulx, who was precentor of the Yorkshire abbey in the late twelfth/early thirteenth centuries, attributed his ill-health and insomnia to the strains of his duties. Matthew claimed that he would never have accepted office had he known what was involved.[24]

Although significant powers were conferred on the abbot and senior monks, there were checks on their authority. They, like all members of the Order, were subject to the General Chapter and the Father Immediate or his delegate who conducted an annual visitation of the house.

---

[20] For a brief overview see J. Kerr, *Monastic Hospitality: the Benedictines in England c. 1070–1250* (Woodbridge, 2007), pp. 52–5.

[21] This does not include duties which were rotated on a weekly basis such as the weekly invitator, the reader in the refectory and the kitchen helpers.

[22] The cellarer's duties are detailed in chapter 117 of the *Usages*; for concessions accorded to him see, for example, *Ecclesiastica Officia*, chapter 74: 10–12 (p. 218); chapter 80: 7–8 (p. 232); chapter 81: 8 (p. 234); chapter 82: 6–7 (p. 236).

[23] See Kerr, *Monastic Hospitality*, pp. 78–9, 108.

[24] Cassidy-Welch, *Monastic Spaces*, pp. 161–2.

External administration

The General Chapter[25]

> Let all the abbots of our Order, having set aside every excuse, assemble yearly for the Cistercian General Chapter.[26]

Each September, around Holy Cross Day (14 September), all heads of Cistercian houses were required to gather at Cîteaux to attend the annual General Chapter. This ran over five days and was presided over by the abbot of Cîteaux. Initially, the Chapter comprised simply the abbot and monks of Cîteaux who were joined by the abbots of the four eldest daughter houses. As the Order grew and expanded across Europe, this became a large international gathering of Cistercian abbots and was no longer attended by the monks of Cîteaux. All abbots were obliged to be present at the meeting unless prevented by severe illness. Yet absenteeism was not uncommon, especially by those living in distant parts for whom the journey could be long, arduous and expensive. The round trip might take some abbots several months to complete. The General Chapter acknowledged their difficulty and conceded that abbots living in remote areas need not come to the assembly every year. From c. 1180 abbots travelling from Scotland were required to attend only once every four years, and from 1190 the concession was extended to the Irish houses. Further dispensations were granted throughout the thirteenth and fourteenth centuries. For example, from the early thirteenth century abbots in Sicily were to attend once every four years, those in Norway and Greece every five years, while for abbots living in Syria and Cyprus it was just one year in seven.[27] Still, absenteeism remained a problem and was exacerbated by war and schism which impeded and in some cases prevented travel to the meeting.[28]

The format of the meeting[29]

The General Chapter was effectively a macrocosm of the daily chapter meeting that was held in every monastery – business was discussed, prayers were said and disciplinary action was taken. Delegates generally arrived at Cîteaux the day before the Chapter formally began. Each day

---

[25] See the *Carta Caritatis Prior*, *NLT*, p. 446; *Carta Caritatis Posterior, ibid.*, pp. 501–2; for discussion, see *Twelfth-Century Statutes*, pp. 37–9 and Williams, *Cistercians in the Early Middle Ages*, pp. 33–41.

[26] *Carta Caritatis Posterior, NLT*, p. 501.

[27] *Twelfth-Century Statutes*, pp. 38, 39. Waddell explains that this concession was repeated in the codifications of 1202, 1237 and 1257, as well as in the 1289 *Libellus antiquarum definitionum*.

[28] The problems encountered by English Cistercian abbots attending Chapter are discussed in Janet Burton, 'The Monastic World', in *England and Europe in the Reign of Henry III*, ed. B. K. U. Weiler and I. W. Rowlands (Aldershot, 2002), pp. 121–36 (pp. 127–31).

[29] For a summary see *Twelfth-Century Statutes*, pp. 37–8; Williams, *Cistercians in the Early Middle Ages*, p. 33.

proceedings began after Mass, when the abbots assembled in Cîteaux's chapterhouse; three hundred could be accommodated there in the late twelfth century.[30] The meeting opened with a reading of the martyrology (a book listing the martyrs and saints in order of their anniversaries) and a chapter from the Rule of St Benedict, except on the first day when the *Carta Caritatis* was read. During the course of the assembly disciplinary matters were dealt with at the Chapter of Faults and business was discussed. The Chapter might, for instance, consider requests from would-be founders, from houses seeking affiliation and from Cistercian abbeys asking for various concessions. In 1191 the abbot of Heiligenkreuz (Austria) sought permission to celebrate Mass in the monastery's infirmary whilst in 1222 the Scottish houses were given consent to celebrate the feast of the Blessed Bridget.[31] Although there was a pattern to the daily agenda, each day had its own special format. On the first day a summary was given of legislation that had been issued the previous year and letters were read out which had been received since the last assembly. The next day punishment was meted out to abbots who had failed to attend the meeting and had no valid excuse. The Chapter discussed visitations which had not been undertaken during the year and then appointed definitors, who were responsible for drawing up the statutes and effectively formed an 'executive committee'.[32] Initially four definitors were chosen but this rose to twenty-five.[33] On the third day delegates prayed for members of the community who had died during the year and on the fourth day a general chapter of lay brothers was held in conjunction with the General Chapter proper. Prayers for rulers and protectors were said on the final day and the meeting concluded with the promulgation of the statutes which each abbot read out to his community when he returned home.[34]

The composition of the General Chapter and the nature of its record-keeping evolved throughout the Middle Ages. Dissatisfaction with and resistance to the abbot of Cîteaux's supremacy in the thirteenth century, especially from the abbots of the four eldest daughters and primarily the abbot of Clairvaux, led to papal intervention and was resolved in 1265 by Clement IV with the papal bull *Parvus Fons*. This bull modified the structure of the General Chapter and shared power equally amongst the abbots of Cîteaux and those of the four senior houses. Further, it curbed the powers of the Father Immediate and indeed of anyone

---

[30] Kinder, *Cistercian Europe*, p. 53.
[31] *Twelfth-Century Statutes*, p. 227 (1191: 35); Canivez, *Statuta*, I, 18 (1222: 24).
[32] Kinder, *Cistercian Europe*, p. 53.
[33] For the evolution of the *definitorium* and a summary of its work, see Kinder, *Cistercian Europe*, p. 53; Lekai, *Cistercians: Ideals and Reality*, pp. 70–2; *Twelfth-Century Statutes*, pp. 16–18.
[34] At least, the abbot read out the general definitions, i.e. statutes, pertaining to the Order *per se* rather than to individuals: *Twelfth-Century Statutes*, p. 15.

who was conducting a visitation; from then on, for example, the visitor generally needed authorisation from the General Chapter to depose an abbot.[35] The thirteenth century saw significant changes to record-keeping with the codification of the Order's key legal documents in 1202 – the 'Book of Definitions' (*Liber Definitionum*). This was periodically updated and expanded. Thus, in 1316, the 'Book of Old Definitions' replaced all previous publications. The compilation of the 'New Definitions' in 1350 introduced significant changes, particularly of a financial nature; this stood as the Order's legal handbook for the rest of the Middle Ages.[36]

Financial aid

The General Chapter required financial aid from its abbeys to help with running costs. Payments were first introduced c. 1235 as voluntary contributions, but soon became a form of taxation, to defray the expense of administration and also to help the Chapter through financial difficulties.[37] The fourteenth-century 'Tax Book' of the Order, the *Secundum Registrum*,[38] reveals that there were four categories of assessment; the choice of which to levy depended on how much money the Chapter required. Thus, *moderata* were collected when c. 9,000 *livres tournois*[39] (*l. t.*) were needed, *mediocris* when c. 12,000 *l. t.* were required, *duplex* to double the *moderata* and *excessiva* to double the *mediocris*.[40] It was generally expected that abbots would bring their contributions with them to the General Chapter meeting at Cîteaux or to an agreed collection point, such as the Cistercian *studium* in Paris, the markets at Provins and Troyes (Champagne) or at Bruges, where the abbots of Ter Doest and Ter Duinen received these payments on the Chapter's behalf.[41] There is evidence that Abbot Johannes Crabbe (1459–83) of Ter Doest took care of the banking between the English and Scottish abbeys and the General Chapter.[42] Houses often struggled to meet these fiscal demands,

35 P. King, *Western Monasticism: a History of the Monastic Movement in the Latin Church*, Cistercian Studies Series, 185 (Kalamazoo, 1999), p. 236; Kinder, *Cistercian Europe*, p. 53.

36 Freeman, *Narratives of a New Order*, p. 155; Kinder, *Cistercian Europe*, pp. 53–4.

37 See Peter King's discussion in *The Tax Book of the Cistercian Order*, ed. Arne O. Johnsen and H. Peter King (Oslo/Bergen/Tronsø, 1979), pp. 23–4.

38 Johnsen and King, *Tax Book*, pp. 27–8. According to King, disagreement over what precisely each community owed and the desire for a system of fixed quotas apparently led to the compilation of this book. Whilst the text was composed in the mid-fourteenth century it seems to have relied on earlier lists.

39 i.e. the Tours pound – a monetary unit used in medieval France.

40 Johnsen and King, *Tax Book*, pp. 28–9.

41 For collection in Paris see, David Ditchburn, 'Saints and Silver: Scotland and Europe in the Age of Alexander II', in *The Reign of Alexander II, 1214–49*, ed. Richard D. Oram (Leiden, 2004), pp. 179–210 (p. 183); for the fairs of Provins and Troyes see Canivez, *Statuta*, II, 426–7 (1257: 7); for Bruges, see Thomas Coomans, 'From Flanders to Scotland: the Choir Stalls of Melrose Abbey in the Fifteenth Century', in Kinder, *Perspectives for an Architecture of Solitude*, pp. 235–52 (p. 250).

42 See Coomans, 'From Flanders to Scotland', p. 250.

particularly in tumultuous times when finances were tight. They might be granted dispensation on account of their circumstances. When the Scottish abbeys were unable to pay their dues in 1346, in the aftermath of Edward III's invasion of Scotland and his victory at Neville's Cross, the abbot of Cîteaux granted them a reprieve and did not send a representative to demand money.[43]

It was not just the General Chapter that imposed payments on abbeys. They might be subject to exactions from their mother houses. In the late twelfth century monasteries in the Clairvaux affiliation were expected to contribute to the cost of a hospice in Dijon, which accommodated abbots travelling to the annual assembly.[44] Houses might also face heavy demands from secular and ecclesiastical authorities, irrespective of any fiscal exemptions they enjoyed. The General Chapter often intervened, fearing that the payment of such sums would set a precedent. This was the case in 1193 when the abbot of La Charité (Besançon) paid a livestock taxation to a certain count.[45] The Cistercians in England and Wales suffered considerably in 1200 and 1210 when King John (1199–1216) imposed a hefty exaction to cover the costs of war. Fountains, the premier Cistercian abbey in the kingdom, was crushed by the £800 payment levied, and had to disband, temporarily until it was once more solvent.[46] It was not simply financial aid that was demanded. In 1310 the monks of Kirkstall Abbey, Yorkshire, had to provide Edward II (1307–27) with victuals for his Scottish campaign.[47]

Visitation[48]

> Let the abbot of the senior church visit once a year all the monasteries he has founded personally or through one of his fellow abbots.[49]

The annual visitation of each house by its Father Immediate or his deputy was an effective means of maintaining and implementing uniformity of practice. It was also a way to provide guidance and support. All houses were subject to annual scrutiny, even Cîteaux which was visited by an abbot of one of its elder daughters.[50] Additional visitations were occasion-

---

43 Peter King, *The Finances of the Cistercian Order in the Fourteenth Century*, Cistercian Studies Series, 85 (Kalamazoo, 1985), p. 143.

44 *Twelfth-Century Statutes*, p. 277 (1193: 58–9), p. 345 (1195: 76). Clairvaux initially demanded sums from its houses but the General Chapter ruled that these should instead be freewill offerings.

45 *Twelfth-Century Statutes*, p. 278 (1193: 62).

46 B. Jennings, *Yorkshire Monasteries: Cloister, Land and People* (Otley, 1999), p. 89.

47 G. D. Barnes, *Kirkstall Abbey 1147–1539: an Historical Study*, Publications of the Thoresby Society, 58 (Leeds, 1984), p. 63.

48 For overviews, see *Twelfth-Century Statutes*, p. 41 and Williams, *Cistercians in the Early Middle Ages*, pp. 41–3.

49 *Carta Caritatis Posterior*, NLT, p. 501.

50 'Institutes of the General Chapter', no. 39, *NLT*, p. 471.

ally initiated by the General Chapter to investigate reports of abuse and to implement reform. In 1275–77, for example, allegations of disorderly behaviour in the Hungarian abbeys prompted the General Chapter to instigate a visitation of the abbeys there.[51] These visitations stood in place of any by an external authority since the Cistercians were exempt from episcopal visitation and monitored their own houses.

Provision for the annual visitation was set out in the *Carta Caritatis Prior*[52] (c. 1119) and modified in the *Carta Caritatis Posterior*[53] of the mid-twelfth century which allowed the Father Immediate to delegate visitation to a fellow abbot if he was unable to carry it out in person; later he might appoint two of his own monks to deputise for him, although their powers were constrained. By the late twelfth century a detailed exposition of the form that visitation should take had been incorporated within the Institutes. This was the *Forma Visitationis*, c. 1180. It underlined the mutual duties of the visitor and the visited. The former was urged to exercise diligence and caution when correcting abuses and restoring concord. Moreover, he was to 'draw the souls of the brethren to a greater reverence for their own abbot and to the Grace and mutual love of Christ'. The visitor was to be just and reasonable and not to be taken in by tittle-tattle or vendettas. The brethren for their part were to welcome the visitor and embrace his corrections.[54] During the course of the visitation enquiries were made about the celebration of the liturgy and monastic observance: Was silence preserved and the customary diet followed? Did the community have a copy of the Order's statutes? The visitor was to consider if there were underage novices, if hospitality and charity were exercised appropriately and whether the obedientiaries administered their posts responsibly. Not least, he was to examine the financial state of the house. The fifteenth-century register of Hailes Abbey (Gloucestershire) lists a number of questions that the visitor should ask and sheds light on the kinds of abuses that the Order was keen to stamp out at this time and which were perhaps most common. Disruption, malice and conspiracies against the abbot were to be reprimanded and, when assessing the general state of monastic observance, the visitor was to be particularly concerned with incidents of sodomy, sorcery and other 'superstitious arts'. He was also to check that women were kept out of the cloister, that there were no falcons or hawks and that the community had fulfilled its financial obligations to Cîteaux.[55]

---

51 See Williams, *Cistercians in the Early Middle Ages*, p. 43.
52 *Carta Caritatis Prior*, *NLT*, p. 445. On the dating of versions of the *Carta* see above, pp. 29–32.
53 *Carta Caritatis Posterior*, *NLT*, p. 501.
54 *Forma Visitationis*, *NLT*, pp. 470–1; see also *Twelfth-Century Statutes*, pp. 564–5.
55 Harper-Bill, 'Cistercian Visitation', 104. This part of the register seems to have been compiled in the late fifteenth century but includes earlier documents: *ibid.*, 103–4.

Visitation was intended to ensure compliance and to correct excesses, but it was to be a constructive process that would strengthen the community. Accordingly, the visitor was to act with 'paternal charity' and was liable to be punished if he abused his position. The brethren were warned that they should not resist the visitor but accept his criticisms. Yet hostility was not uncommon and in some cases visitors were faced with open rebellion. The abbot of Herrevad, a monastery whose location is now in Sweden but which was under Danish rule in the Middle Ages, was confronted with a revolt in 1191 from his daughter house of Løgum in Denmark. Dissension was stirred up by Germanus, a monk of Løgum, and endorsed by the abbot of the house; they were supported by the cantor and a lay brother of Herrevad. The rebels were duly punished by the General Chapter. Whereas Germanus was sent to Esrum Abbey and the lay brother to Søro, the abbot and cantor were instructed to appear before the abbot of Cîteaux to receive their sentence and were threatened with deposition should they refuse.[56] When Stephen of Lexington conducted a reforming visitation of the Irish houses in 1228 he met with vehement resistance, particularly at Mellifont, Maigue (Monasteranenagh) and Suir (Inislounaght) where he was physically attacked.[57] Maigue was a hotbed of revolt and put up a feisty resistance. The brethren fortified the abbey and mounted a siege, 'turning the monastery, the cloister as well as the church into a fortress against God'. They built a tower above the high altar to serve as a keep and grazed cattle in the cloister. Each monk and lay brother armed himself, although some of the older monks left the monastery lest they were implicated in this rebellion. Stephen was shocked at what he saw and claimed that the community had 'drunk from the chalice of Babylon'. He duly excommunicated the offenders who were later reconciled to the Order.[58] By the mid-thirteenth century the General Chapter considered hostility to visitation a significant problem and in 1268 took measures to suppress this.[59]

The neglect of visitation

It was not always easy for abbots to visit each of their daughter houses every year, especially if they had several dependencies (Clairvaux had over eighty) or if they were far away. In 1259 it was alleged that the abbot

---

[56] *Twelfth-Century Statutes*, pp. 229–30 (1191: 41); see also Williams, *Cistercians in the Early Middle Ages*, p. 42; France, *Cistercians in Scandinavia*, p. 132.

[57] B. O'Dwyer, *The Conspiracy of Mellifont 1216–1231*, Medieval Irish History Series, 2 (Dublin, 1970), pp. 22–3. The problem with the Irish houses is discussed below, pp. 97–9.

[58] Stephen of Lexington, *Letters from Ireland 1228–9*, ed. and trans. B. O'Dwyer, Cistercian Fathers Series, 28 (Kalamazoo, 1982), ep. 89 (pp. 188–91, especially p. 188); O'Dwyer, *Conspiracy of Mellifont*, pp. 23–4.

[59] Williams, *Cistercians in the Early Middle Ages*, p. 42; Canivez, *Statuta*, III, 60 (1268: 6).

of Bellevaux, Burgundy, had not visited his daughter house of Depheni in Greece for ten years.[60] By the thirteenth century the abbot of Fountains (Yorkshire) was struggling to visit in person his Norwegian daughter house of Lyse. First he neglected to visit the abbey and then sent two monks as his deputies but they exceeded their powers and all three were duly punished by the General Chapter. In 1213 the paternity of Lyse was transferred to a Scandinavian house – the Swedish abbey of Alvastra. This was short-lived for the journey across Sweden to Norway was even more problematic than from England and the abbot of Alvastra found it difficult to fulfil his duties; in 1235 custody of Lyse was restored to Fountains.[61]

During the Hundred Years War, which began in 1337, travel between the Continent and Britain was both difficult and dangerous and the abbot of Clairvaux often delegated visitation of his houses in England and Wales to abbots living there. In the fourteenth century Irish political antagonism presented similar problems for Welsh abbots who had dependencies in Ireland and they too might appoint deputies to carry out the visitations in their stead. In 1346 the abbot of Tracton (Cork) visited Tintern Parva (Wexford) for the abbot of Tintern (Monmouthshire), while in 1363 the abbot of Dunbrody (Wexford) acted as deputy for the abbot of Whitland (Carmarthenshire) at Tracton.[62] Visitation could be problematic for mother houses who suddenly found themselves on the opposite side of the border from their dependencies as a consequence of war. But, as Emilia Jamroziak has recently argued, this was not always the case and abbeys might continue to maintain strong links across the divide. Holm Cultram, which, as discussed above, was founded by Henry, son of David I of Scotland, in 1150 as a daughter house of Melrose in an area that was under Scottish control, found itself under English rule from 1157 and on the other side of the border to its mother house. Yet this was not initially a problem and as Jamroziak demonstrates visitation continued and monks from Melrose were appointed to office at Holm Cultram. Similarly, the Danish abbey of Esrum sent monastic officials to its daughter house of Kołbacz (Pomerania) for over thirty years after this area came under German rule in 1220.[63]

Whilst distance, war or multiple duties might deter or prevent abbots from carrying out visitation, the statutes reveal that often there was no such excuse for neglect. In 1198 the General Chapter reprimanded the

60 Williams, *Cistercians in the Early Middle Ages*, p. 42.
61 France, *Cistercians in Scandinavia*, pp. 320–2.
62 D. H. Williams, 'The Welsh Cistercians and Ireland', *Cistercian Studies* 15 (1980), 17–23 (p. 21).
63 E. Jamroziak, 'Holm Cultram Abbey: a Story of Success?', *Northern History* 45 (2008), 27–36; E. Jamroziak, 'Cistercian Identities on the Northern Peripheries of Medieval Europe from the Twelfth to the late Fourteenth Century', in Müller and Stöber, *Self-Representation of Medieval Religious Communities*, pp. 209–19.

abbot of Tarouca (Portugal) who had failed to visit either of his two daughter houses for three years, even though they were relatively close; one was even in the same diocese.[64]

Female houses

Female houses were similarly placed under the auspices of a Father Immediate, either at the time of their foundation like Tart (Burgundy), which was founded in 1132 by Cîteaux,[65] or when they were later incorporated within the Order. In 1250 the General Chapter placed the newly established nunnery of Marham (Norfolk) under the care of the abbot of Waverley (Surrey), who had been involved in the foundation.[66] The nuns of Kerkom sought incorporation under Villers Abbey (Brabant) and Abbot Walter (1214–21) duly organised for their transferral to La Ramée, where they joined with a community of holy women from Nivelles.[67] The Father Immediate was responsible for conducting an annual visitation of the nunnery or sending a deputy in his place. But he was also required to provide for the nuns' spiritual needs since women were not permitted to be ordained and were therefore dependent on male priests to celebrate Mass and hear their confessions. In the late thirteenth century the monks of Kołbacz (Pomerania) travelled either by water or by horse to tend the spiritual needs of the nuns of Szczecin.[68] At first abbots mostly used their own monks, but pressure on numbers might require them to look elsewhere and engage secular priests who were then affiliated to the Order. These spiritual advisors often resided within the precinct but were not generally permitted to hear the nuns' confessions. This was initially the prerogative of the Father Immediate or his deputies. While most nunneries would have had one spiritual advisor, larger houses might have two or three; in 1418 there were three chaplains at the Swedish house of Gudhem.[69] The services of outsiders, that is, of priests who were not Cistercians, could be expensive and the cost was seemingly borne by the nuns themselves. In 1422 the abbess of Vårfruberga, Sweden, sought papal dispensation to engage a Cistercian monk of Julita as the nunnery's chap-

---

[64] *Twelfth-Century Statutes*, p. 413 (1198: 32). The problems encountered by English Cistercian abbots in conducting visitations are discussed in Burton, 'The Monastic World', pp. 126–7.

[65] For a summary of Tart's foundations, see Kinder, *Cistercian Europe*, p. 34; Tart subsequently founded eighteen daughter houses and whilst the abbess of Tart conducted the annual visitations of these nunneries, she did so as a delegate of the abbot of Cîteaux. On the foundation of Tart see above, p. 28.

[66] Canivez, *Statuta*, II, 355 (1250: 43) and 364 (1251: 26). See also *Annales monasterii de Waverleia*, in *Annales Monastici*, ed. H. R. Luard, 5 vols, RS 36 (1864–69), II, 344–5.

[67] *Ida the Gentle of Léau, Cistercian Nun of La Ramée*, trans. M. Cawley, Guadalupe Translations (Lafayette, 1998), pp. x–xi. For further discussion of Abbot Walter see M. Cawley, 'Four Abbots of the Golden Age of Villers', *Cistercian Studies Quarterly* 27 (1992), 300–27 (pp. 314–19).

[68] Williams, *Cistercians in the Early Middle Ages*, p. 407.

[69] *Ibid.*, pp. 406–7; France, *Cistercians in Scandinavia*, p. 181.

lain since she could not afford a secular priest.[70] A variety of men might be appointed as spiritual advisors to these nuns. In 1276 the archbishop of York, Walter Giffard, recommended that the Cistercian nunneries in his archdiocese should engage either members of the Friars Minor or Friars Preacher as their confessors since these men 'shone in the church as the brightness of the firmament'.[71] Walter's sentiments were shared by his successors; in 1306 the nuns of Rosedale were advised to choose two friars as their confessors.[72] The nuns of Hampole (Yorkshire) received spiritual counsel from the hermit and mystic Richard Rolle (d. 1349), who also composed spiritual directives for them. Richard's cell was near the priory and he was buried in the nuns' courtyard. The sisters wrote Rolle's biography some thirty years after his death.[73]

Hagiographical works frequently allude to the strong bonds that developed between nuns and their confessors who were privy to the holy sisters' secrets and could testify to their devotion. The 'Life' of Ida of Louvain, a nun of Roosendaal in the late thirteenth century, was allegedly compiled from accounts written by her confessor, Hugo, who was a Cistercian monk and with whom Ida was joined in a 'firm bond of fidelity'. Ida believed that Hugo had been sent to her from God and had a vision of him before his arrival at the house. [74]

The family network

> They are welded together by such firm bands of charity that their society is as 'terrible as an army with banners'.[75]

The Cistercian network of filiation, as we have seen, was the mechanism for expansion across Europe and a way to foster cohesion and unity. It gave to individual abbeys a strong sense of identity both within the Order and within their own affiliation. The familial relationships were depicted visually as a family tree, with the various affiliations shown as branches. This imagery recurs in Cistercian literature to describe the growth of the Order and its familial relationships. The Book of Henryków records how the house was founded c. 1220 by Lubiąż (Silesia), which planted 'the

---

[70] France, *Cistercians in Scandinavia*, p. 181.
[71] J. Nichols, 'The Organisation of the English Cistercian Nunneries', *Cîteaux: Commentarii Cistercienses* 30 (1979), 23–40 (pp. 34–5).
[72] *The Register of William Greenfield, Lord Archbishop of York 1306–1315*, III, ed. W. Brown and A. H. Thompson, Surtees Society, 151 (1936), pp. 10–11.
[73] Jonathan Hughes, 'Rolle, Richard (1305x10–1349)', *ODNB*, vol. 47, pp. 619–22.
[74] 'The Life of Ida the Eager of Louvain', Book 3: 19a–20e, trans. M. Cawley, forthcoming. We are indebted to Father Martinus Cawley for providing copies of the new translation and introduction to his forthcoming edition of Ida's 'Life'.
[75] Walter Daniel, *Life of Aelred of Rievaulx*, p. 11.

flower of Divine Service at Henryków'.[76] The thirteenth-century foundation history of Fountains Abbey similarly evokes this imagery of planting and fruition to describe the foundation of its first daughter house at Newminster (1138) – 'holy seed sprouted in the soil and, being cast as it were in the lap of fertile earth, grew to a great plant, and from a few grains there sprang a plentiful harvest'.[77]

The network of affiliations not only brought cohesion and promoted unity but might serve as a conduit to disseminate knowledge, materials and manpower.[78] The latter was particularly important in a monastery's early years when the mother house could supply it with experienced personnel. In chapter 3 it was noted that ideas about architecture and design might be spread across Europe via the Cistercian network or, more specifically, by a particular affiliation. Other examples of this cultural exchange include the use of Caroline rather than Visigothic script in Galicia which D'Emilio argues should be attributed to the White Monks.[79] The Order quite literally spread its seeds. The *reinette grise* apple was seemingly passed across Europe by the Morimond branch of the family tree which took it from France to Poland via Camp, Thuringia, Saxony and Silesia. It is likely that the Warden pear actually originated in Burgundy and was brought to the south of England by the Cistercians.[80]

Whilst the family network could – and was intended to – foster unity within the Order, it might, conversely, lead to fragmentation if an affiliation challenged the General Chapter's authority. A notable example is the so-called Conspiracy of Mellifont which confronted the General Chapter in the thirteenth century and prompted it to take extreme action.

Disunity and fragmentation: the Conspiracy of Mellifont[81]

> Dissipation, dilapidation of property, conspiracies, rebellions and frequent machinations of death.[82]

---

[76] Górecki, *Henryków Book*, p. 90 (book 1: 1).
[77] *Memorials of Fountains*, I, 58–9, trans. A. W. Oxford, *The Ruins of Fountains Abbey* (London, 1910), appendix 1, pp. 127–230 (p. 187).
[78] For discussion of how Cistercian communities created 'a corporate past' and a shared identity, see J. Burton, 'Constructing a Corporate Identity: the *Historia Fundationis* of the Cistercian Abbeys of Byland and Jervaulx', in Müller and Stöber, *Self-Representation of Medieval Religious Communities*, pp. 327–40, and Jamroziak, 'Cistercian Identities'.
[79] J. D'Emilio, 'The Cistercians and the Romanesque Churches of Galicia: Compostela or Clairvaux?', in Kinder, *Perspectives for an Architecture of Solitude*, pp. 313–27 (p. 316).
[80] A. A. King, *Cîteaux and her Elder Daughters* (London, 1954), p. 355.
[81] For a comprehensive analysis see O'Dwyer, *Conspiracy of Mellifont*; for a summary of the events see Stalley, *Cistercian Monasteries of Ireland*, pp. 17–20.
[82] The abbot of Cîteaux in a letter to the pope regarding the Irish houses, cited in Stalley, *Cistercian Monasteries of Ireland*, p. 18.

Unity and cohesion became increasingly difficult to maintain as the Order expanded throughout Europe. This was compounded by war, schism and rising nationalism. In the thirteenth century the General Chapter was faced with a serious problem from Mellifont and her affiliated houses in Ireland. This lasted for over a decade and was initially regarded by the Chapter as a case for reform; but the gravity of the situation soon became apparent.

Mellifont (1142) was a daughter house of Clairvaux and, as noted in chapter 2, it was the first Cistercian house founded in Ireland. Mellifont spawned a large family and by the end of the twelfth century there were twenty-three houses in its affiliation. The General Chapter was first made aware of problems with Mellifont and its daughter houses in 1216, when there were reports of misconduct. A visitation was duly conducted to implement reform and several Irish abbots were deposed. There was a violent retaliation and the enormity of the problem became clear. The General Chapter now saw this as a conspiracy of one branch of the family against the Order, fuelled by sentiments of cultural difference. However, this needs to be seen in context, for Ireland was at this time in a state of turmoil following the Anglo-Norman invasion and the consequent 'Anglo-Normanisation' of the country. Foreign personnel replaced native officeholders in the church, the invaders took over land and they founded religious houses to consolidate their expansion; Cistercian examples include the abbeys of Grey and Inch in County Down.[83] This backdrop affected how the Irish monks perceived and reacted to the General Chapter's attempts at reform. Whereas the Chapter saw a need to restore unity to the Order by breaking up a rebellious faction, the Irish regarded its actions as an attack on their cultural identity and a continuation of the erosion of native life begun by the Anglo-Norman invaders. After all, by replacing Irish personnel with outsiders the General Chapter employed similar tactics to the conquerors; not least, it enlisted the help of Anglo-Norman abbeys such as Tintern Parva and Bective.[84]

The General Chapter had initially hoped to resolve its Irish problem through visitation but when this failed more radical measures were taken. It believed that as the situation stemmed from national sentiment it could be remedied by weakening the Irish composition of the houses and breaking up the Mellifont affiliation. Native abbots were duly replaced with outsiders from England, Ireland and Wales, native recruitment was restricted and rebels were sent away. One example is Prior Patrick of Maigue who was removed to Margam in Wales. A number of Mellifont's dependencies were removed from its authority and assigned to abbeys in

---

[83] For a summary of the Anglo-Norman invasion see Stalley, *Cistercian Monasteries of Ireland*, p. 16.
[84] Stalley, *Cistercian Monasteries of Ireland*, p. 37.

England and Wales. Jerpoint, for instance, was placed under the auspices of Fountains, in Yorkshire, while Fermoy and Suir were affiliated to the Lancashire abbey of Furness. Another area of concern was language. From the General Chapter's perspective a commonality of language was essential to the regularity of the Order. It was vital that visitors were able to communicate with the brethren when they carried out their investigations and that everyone could understand official mandates and legislation. The fact that Mellifont and her daughters used Irish rather than Latin or French was therefore problematic and was of particular concern to Stephen of Lexington who, as abbot of Stanley, conducted a rigorous visitation of the Irish houses in 1228.[85] Stephen ruled that only French or Latin should be used lest visitors wasted their time 'building a tower of Babel in the confusion of languages'. Further, he stipulated that all recruits should be able to make their confessions in one of these two languages.[86] For the native Irish, however, this was a further attack on their culture and linguistic identity and was perceived as a clear case of the imposition, from above, of policies designed to destroy native tradition.[87] Far from restoring unity and cohesion, the General Chapter's actions polarised the Irish Cistercians and deepened the gulf between them and their counterparts in Britain and Europe. Outsiders who were imposed on the Irish were resented and threatened. A monk of Clairvaux who replaced the abbot of Mellifont fled to France after just one year, amidst fears that he would be killed. In 1230 the foreign abbot of Fermoy was murdered in his monastery whilst an Anglo-Norman monk who replaced the deposed abbot of Baltinglass was attacked by the native community and had to assert his position with the help of an armed guard.[88] The intensity of the Mellifont conspiracy subsided after c. 1230, although there were occasional flare ups. In 1274, some fifty years after the rebellion had arisen, houses that had been removed from Mellifont's affiliation were restored.

There were other cases of resistance to the General Chapter's reforming efforts, particularly in the later Middle Ages when ties were weakened as a consequence of war and the papal schism of 1378–1417 which divided Western Christendom and split the Order.[89] France and thus Cîteaux

---

[85] For Stephen's letters recounting details of his visitation of the Irish houses, see Stephen of Lexington, *Letters*. Shortly after his return from Ireland Stephen was made abbot of Savigny and in 1243 he was elevated to the abbacy of Clairvaux.

[86] Stephen of Lexington, *Letters*, ep. 42 (pp. 91–2) and 99 (p. 210).

[87] O'Dwyer, *Conspiracy of Mellifont*, pp. 28–9.

[88] Stalley, *Cistercian Monasteries of Ireland*, pp. 18, 20; O'Dwyer, *Conspiracy of Mellifont*, p. 21; Stephen of Lexington, *Letters*, ep. 272 (pp. 65–9).

[89] Other orders were similarly affected. The Carthusians, for example, had one chapter headed by the Austrian house of Seitz and another by La Grande Chartreuse; each passed different acts and accordingly there was opportunity for houses to follow their own practices and indeed to adopt the customs of their fellow religious in the country; see, for example, J. Kerr, 'Balmerino Abbey: Cistercians on the East Coast of Fife', in *Life on the Edge: the Cistercian Abbey of Balmerino, Fife*, ed. T. N. Kinder,

supported the Avignon papacy, as did Spain and Scotland. Others, including England, Flanders, the Germanic and Italian States, turned to Rome where Boniface forbade Cistercians in countries loyal to him to have any contact with Cîteaux. He encouraged them to elect their own head of the Order and to hold national assemblies in place of the General Chapter, which would issue their own legislation. Warfare meant that even houses which supported Avignon might find it difficult to maintain contact with Cîteaux. Indeed, during the Hundred Years War the General Chapter had to relocate on several occasions – in 1360 it met at Dijon.[90]

Conditions in the fourteenth and fifteenth centuries thus led to the breakdown in central authority and a weakening of the General Chapter's position.[91] There was a tendency for houses to follow the customs and practices of their country unchecked. This set a precedent. Custom became practice and in some cases was staunchly defended in the face of reform. In the sixteenth century the Scottish Cistercians of Melrose, Newbattle and Balmerino vehemently opposed the reforms of Abbot Simon of Chaâlis who visited the kingdom in 1531. They considered his reforms as novelties and stood by their practices, claiming that they were simply following the example of their predecessors who had been holy and observant men.[92] The General Chapter's hold was weakened also by ecclesiastical and secular powers. For example, in the mid-fifteenth century the king of Aragon and the papacy countermanded the Chapter and permitted the Spanish monks of Poblet and Santa Creus to wear white scapulars.[93] In 1483 Richard III of England gave the abbot of Stratford Langthorne (London) authority over the Cistercian houses in his kingdom and declared that he would not permit interference from the abbot of Cîteaux or any others.[94] The later Middle Ages thus saw a fragmentation of the Order and a weakening of ties. However, as Kinder argues, this was not detrimental to the Order, since the emergence of congregations organised along national lines was perhaps the best way for this large organisation to function efficiently and may even have ensured its survival.[95]

Cîteaux: Commentarii Cistercienses 59 (2008), 37–60 (p. 56 note 85). For extensive discussion of the order see E. Margaret Thompson, *The Carthusian Order in England* (London, 1930).

90 L. J. Lekai, *The White Monks: a History of the Cistercian Order* (Okauchee, 1953), p. 68; Leroux-Dhuys, *Cistercian Abbeys*, p. 123.

91 Lekai, *Cistercians: Ideals and Reality*, pp. 93–4.

92 J. Campbell, *Balmerino and its Abbey* (rev. edn Edinburgh, 1899), pp. 227–30. The abbot was received by James in September 1531: see *Letters of James V*, collected and calendared R. K. Hannay, ed. D. Hay (Edinburgh, 1954), p. 202; Canivez, *Statuta*, VI, 702, 704 (1531: 49 and 53).

93 Cited by King, *Cîteaux and her Elder Daughters*, p. 51.

94 *Ibid.*, p. 64, note 4.

95 Kinder, *Cistercian Europe*, p. 37.

Demise and reform

Political and economic developments of the fourteenth and fifteenth centuries had a significant impact on the administrative structure of the Order but the subsequent centuries had a more profound effect, leading to the demise and in some cases the extinction of Cistercian life. This varied from country to country. In Catholic lands such as Spain, Hungary, Portugal and Poland, the Order flourished although in a baroque fashion.[96] Conversely, Luther's Reformation in Germany (1517), the Dissolution of the religious houses in England and Wales (1536–40) and Cromwell's conquest of Ireland (1649–50) brought an end to Cistercian practice in these countries.[97] In France the Cistercians were dealt a devastating blow by the Wars of Religion (1562–98) but the severity of the impact differed from region to region. In some areas the Order was extinguished, yet elsewhere it was reformed from the late sixteenth century, most notably with the emergence of the Cistercians of the Strict Observance in the early seventeenth century. This was a purely French affiliation and was distinct from the Cistercians of the Common Observance whose main foothold was in Germany and Eastern Europe. But it was a bitter split that divided these two branches of the Order.[98] The Cistercians of the Strict Observance sought to return to the rudiments of the Rule of St Benedict and observed a strictly vegetarian diet; hence they were known as the Abstinents. Under the direction of Armand-Jean-le Bouthillier de Rancé, abbot of La Trappe from 1663, the Cistercians of the Strict Observance rose to prominence and gained in popularity, despite their ascetic lifestyle.[99] The Revolution destroyed all religious life in France but some communities relocated. La Trappe brought the Cistercians of the Strict Observance to Switzerland, to the former Carthusian house of La Val Sainte, and following the defeat of Napoleon in 1815 they spread not only throughout Europe but across the globe and indeed to every continent. These monks were commonly known as the Trappists since each house had 'La Trappe' in its title but in 1892 they were officially named the Cistercian Order of Strict Observance. In 1898 the Trappists bought Cîteaux and settled a community there. The other branch of the Order, the former monks of the Common Observance, is now known

---

[96] Kinder, *Cistercian Europe*, p. 38; Leroux-Dhuys, *Cistercian Abbeys*, pp. 128–31; King, *Western Monasticism*, p. 211, writes: 'Baroque monasticism … was a feature of Catholic Europe from the Rhine to the borders of Russia.'

[97] For an extensive discussion, see King, *Western Monasticism*, pp. 384–93 and Lekai, *Cistercians: Ideals and Reality*, pp. 117–25.

[98] Kinder, *Cistercian Europe*, p. 39; King, *Western Monasticism*, p. 301; Lekai, *Cistercians: Ideals and Reality*, pp. 138–52.

[99] See King, *Western Monasticism*, pp. 302–3.

as the Cistercian Order and is organised essentially according to national congregations. There is subsequently a greater diversity in practice in the twenty-first century, with some of the houses exercising a more pastoral role. Today these two branches form a global organisation.[100]

---

[100] Kinder, *Cistercian Europe*, pp. 49–50; King, *Western Monasticism*, pp. 325–32; Lekai, *Cistercians: Ideals and Reality*, pp. 179–206.

CHAPTER FIVE

Ora et labora: Daily Life in the Cloister

Humility and chastity make the proper monk.[1]

A framework for living

Claustral life was highly organised and structured around the liturgical Office (*opus Dei*) celebrated in the church. The day began at daybreak with Lauds and ended with Compline at sunset. In accordance with the Rule of St Benedict the monks spent a part of each day engaged in physical labour and meditative reading (*lectio divina*); there was a daily chapter meeting and time allocated to eating, sleeping and matters relating to health and hygiene. But how precisely they spent their time varied, depending on the occasion as well as on the status and responsibilities of each monk. For example, there was a weekly Maundy, routine bloodletting and the occasional arrival of visitors. On feast days there was no manual work but an extended liturgy and extra time accorded to reading, whereas at harvest the entire community toiled in the fields and celebrated the Office while working. Elderly and infirm members of the community were released or excused from the daily round, and office-bearers might be exempted from certain communal activities on account of their duties.

Liturgical and daily life was codified in the Rule of St Benedict. These guidelines were elaborated on in the Cistercians' own prescriptive texts, chiefly the twelfth-century customs (the *Ecclesiastica Officia/Usages*), the Charter of Charity (*Carta Caritatis*) and statutes issued by the General Chapter. These detailed documents brought coherence and unity to Cistercian practice. They left few stones unturned and provided instruction on weighty matters such as the format of the liturgy, as well as guidance on more practical concerns that included shaving, bathing and how to deal with anyone who had a nosebleed during the Mass.[2] Still, there was scope for abbots to exercise discretion and practices might fluctuate not only from house to house but from one abbacy to another. Moreover, the official stance did not remain static, for the General Chapter periodi-

---

[1]   Walter Daniel, 'Letter to Maurice', in *Life of Aelred*, p. 76.
[2]   See, for example, *Ecclesiastica Officia*, chapter 84 (p. 244); chapter 89: 1–41 (pp. 252–3).

cally revised its position by introducing new prescriptions and modifying others to accommodate the demands and needs of the time.

This chapter explores daily life in the monastery and considers how the monks spent their time, the conditions under which they lived and how these affected relationships and the mood of the cloister.

A threefold division: the opus Dei, *manual labour* (labora) *and* lectio divina

> Paradise is among us here, in spiritual exercise, simple prayer and holy meditation.[3]

In accordance with the Rule of St Benedict the monk's day was threefold, with time spent on liturgical duties, contemplative reading and manual work. At the time of Cîteaux's origins in the late eleventh century, manual work was effectively a thing of the past and had been abandoned in favour of a more elaborate liturgy. The Cistercians stripped liturgical practice of its accretions and sought to reinstate manual labour as an integral part of daily life. This marked a return to St Benedict's tenets and was also an important act of humility. Not least, it was of practical importance given the amount of work that was required to keep the monasteries running. However, the performance of the 'Work of God' remained at the heart of the monastic life.

The liturgical round

The monastic day was shaped by the seven Canonical Hours (Offices) of Lauds, Prime, Terce, Sext, None, Vespers and Compline. An eighth Office of Vigils was celebrated at night, in accordance with Psalm 119.162, 'At midnight I rose to give thanks to thee.' When precisely each Office was celebrated varied according to the time of year, for claustral life was regulated by the sun; it began at daybreak and finished at sunset. Each Office was celebrated in the monks' choir, in the east end of the church, and the brethren were placed according to their seniority within the community. The most senior were not necessarily the oldest but those who had been monks for the longest or who held a monastic office (obedience). Attendance at the Hours was mandatory although concessions might be made to the sick and also to obedientiaries if they were legitimately (and unavoidably) detained by their duties.

Each Canonical Hour followed a prescribed format which was set out in the *Usages* of the Order. It began with the Lord's Prayer and was

---

[3] Matthew of Rievaulx (fl. early thirteenth century), cited in Cassidy-Welch, *Monastic Spaces*, p. 65.

followed by hymns, psalms and chants. Singing was led by the precentor, assisted by the succentor, who kept a keen eye on the brethren to make sure that everyone was attentive. This was especially important during the night Office of Vigils when it was often a struggle for the monks and particularly the novices to stay awake. New recruits who were unused to the short nights and lack of sleep frequently found this the most testing aspect of their new regime. To encourage vigilance tales were circulated warning of the perils which befell habitual snoozers. A striking example described how one monk was violently awoken from his slumbers by the figure of the Crucified Christ, which descended from the image of the Cross in the abbey church to deliver him an almighty wallop across the cheek. Such was the force of the blow that the monk died three days later.[4] Other tales recounted how Mary would wander around the choir during the Office, a reminder to the monks that they were always under scrutiny and in the presence of the Divine.[5] There were other ways to safeguard the brethren from drowsiness. Michael Carter has recently suggested that an image of St Christopher in the south transept of Rievaulx Abbey (Yorkshire) may have had a similar purpose to the same image in the same place at Westminster Abbey which was intended to protect the monks from exhaustion. Its position in the south transept was important, for the brethren would have beheld the saint as they entered the choir for the night Office of Vigils.[6] Several of the monks had their own and indeed unique ways of keeping vigilant. One twelfth-century prior of Clairvaux allegedly fitted a hammer above his head in the choir and organised it in such a way that should he nod off the hammer would strike a blow to his head as it fell forwards.[7]

Mass was celebrated at least once a day, but twice on Sundays and feast days when the liturgy was extended. Special masses were gradually introduced to include masses for the Virgin, benefactors and the dead. Ordained members of the community celebrated private masses at side altars, usually during the period allocated to reading.[8] The Cistercians took communion once a week and also on feast days. This was more frequent than in Benedictine houses where it was generally once a month. Otherwise the liturgy of the White Monks was less elaborate than the

---

4   Caesarius of Heisterbach, *Dialogus Miraculorum*, Book 4, chapter 38, trans. H. von E. Scott and C. C. S. Bland, *The Dialogue on Miracles*, 2 vols (London, 1929), I, 234.
5   For example, see Goswin of Bossut, 'Life of Abundus', chapters 8, 11, 20, in Cawley, *Send Me God*, pp. 209–46 (pp. 221–3, 225–8, 243–4).
6   Carter, 'The Cistercians' Use of Devotional Images'.
7   Conrad of Eberbach, *Exordium Magnum*, IV, 26, cited in B. P. McGuire, 'An Introduction to the *Exordium Magnum Cisterciense*', *Cistercian Studies Quarterly* 27:4 (1992), 277–97 (p. 295). This was John who was prior of Clairvaux in the 1170s.
8   'Institutes of the General Chapter', no. 51, *NLT*, p. 477; *Ecclesiastica Officia*, chapter 59: 1–6 (pp. 180–2).

Benedictines' since they endeavoured to return to the basics of the Rule of St Benedict.[9]

Daily work

> We all work in common, we [choir monks], our lay brothers and our hired hands, each according to his own capability, and we all make our living in common by our labour.[10]

Physical labour was considered an important way to avoid boredom and sloth. This duly protected the brethren from the devil who was thought to prey on the indolent. In summer, two periods were allocated to work but in winter there was just one, since the days were shorter. The nature of tasks varied considerably and might range from whitewashing walls and greasing boots to gardening and chopping wood. At harvest time the monks (and similarly, the nuns[11]) would join the lay brothers and perhaps also hired helpers to toil in the fields. This was gruelling work, especially for those of noble upbringing who had little experience of such hard graft; their enthusiasm and diligence were therefore all the more worthy. Rainald, a twelfth-century monk of Clairvaux who had previously been a Benedictine, described the great admiration he had for his fellow brethren as he watched them labour in the fields. He noted that many of these men were of gentle birth and unused to such work yet threw themselves into the task, toiling in the heat for Christ. On one occasion Rainald had a vision in which he saw the Virgin Mary, her cousin Elizabeth and Mary Magdalene visit the monks as they worked in the fields.[12] Similar stories were recounted to remind the brethren that they were not alone, even when bringing in the harvest, and that their efforts were noted. Caesarius of Heisterbach (d. c. 1240) recorded how two saints, Mary and Anne, visited monks of his abbey while they laboured in the fields. The holy women wiped the workers' brows and sent a breeze to cool them.[13] Abundus, a thirteenth-century monk of Villers (Brabant), had a similar experience. He saw the Virgin, accompanied by Mary Magdalene, fan

9 For further discussion of Cistercian liturgy and the texts, see J. Kerr, 'An Essay on Cistercian Liturgy', The Cistercians in Yorkshire Project: cistercians.shef.ac.uk/cistercian_life/spirituality/Liturgy/Cistercian_liturgy.pdf (accessed December 2010).
10 Idungus of Prüfung, 'A Dialogue between Two Monks', II, 52 (p. 94).
11 See for example the thirteenth-century 'Life' of Ida of Nivelles: at harvest half the community of La Ramée went with the prioress for eight days to Kerkom grange (the former abbey site), to gather in the crops: Goswin of Bossut, 'Life of Ida of Nivelles', chapter 20, in Cawley, *Send Me God*, pp. 60–2.
12 M. Casey, 'Herbert of Clairvaux's Book of Wonderful Happenings', *Cistercian Studies Quarterly* 25: 1 (1993), 37–64 (p. 49).
13 Caesarius of Heisterbach, *Dialogus Miraculorum*, Book 1, chapter 17, Scott and Bland, *Dialogue on Miracles*, I, 25–6.

each of the monk-workers with her sleeve and wipe away their sweat, to relieve them from their 'dogged labour'.[14]

Whereas the diligent would be rewarded for their exertions, shirkers would likely be punished for their laziness. The monks of Heisterbach (Germany) were reminded of this when their former sacrist, Isenbard, appeared in a vision to one of the brethren. The monk saw Isenbard crowned in Paradise but noticed a spot on his foot which was a mark of the sacrist's unwillingness to work in the monastery; his sloth had not gone unnoticed and nor, they were reminded, would theirs.[15] The monk's participation in manual labour was an exercise in humility and integral to his spiritual advancement, but it was also important for the community that each member contributed to the workload and pulled his weight. Herbert of Clairvaux described one monk, 'B', as a burden to his community since he would doze at Vigils and was lazy when it came to work.[16] There was no room in the monastery for sluggards.

The Cistercians' attitude to manual labour was quite different to that of their Benedictine contemporaries. Peter the Venerable, abbot of Cluny (1122–56), remarked on what he considered their rather idiosyncratic behaviour. Peter thought it improper that monks should be 'begrimed in dirt and bent down with rustic labours'. But he was amazed that the White Monks were actually able to graft, given their meagre diet, which at this time was much more frugal than that of the Cluniacs.[17] The Cistercians had no such reservations about the importance of physical work. This marked a return to the original ethos of the Rule but also, and crucially, they had before them the image of Christ as the gardener, who was the embodiment of humility.

Lectio divina

> A cloister without a bookcase [*armarium*] is like a fortress without weapons.[18]

Lectio divina, a slow, contemplative reading, was an essential part of monastic observance which encouraged introspection and furthered one's understanding of and progression to God. This was a communal activity in so far as the brethren sat together to read and meditate. But it was a solo journey which brought self-knowledge as well as enlightenment. *Lectio divina* was fourfold. The monk first read the text slowly and care-

---

[14] Goswin of Bossut, 'Life of Abundus', chapter 14, in Cawley, *Send Me God*, p. 234.
[15] Caesarius of Heisterbach, *Dialogus Miraculorum*, Book 2, chapter 11, Scott and Bland, *Dialogue on Miracles*, II, 245–6.
[16] Casey, 'Herbert of Clairvaux's Book of Wonderful Happenings', 44.
[17] PL, 189, cols 112ff (*Petrus Venerabilis, Epistolarum libri sex* [28]).
[18] 'Claustrum sine armario, castrum sine armamento', cited in Leroux-Dhuys, *Cistercian Abbeys*, p. 357.

fully and then searched for a deeper understanding of the words through meditation. Thereafter he prayed to discover what was good and bad, and finally he raised his heart to God through contemplation.

Stephen of Sawley (Stephen of Easton), who died in 1252, compiled a treatise advising novices on how best to approach *lectio divina*. He recommended that they begin with four basic works, namely the Cistercian customs (*Usages*) and antiphonary, Gregory the Great's *Dialogues* and the *Lives of the Fathers*. Once these core texts had been mastered they could study and memorise the Old and New Testaments to 'indulge in more solid food'. Stephen was emphatic that the Scriptures should not be read simply to acquire knowledge but should be used as a mirror which would reveal what was corrupt, aid correction and, importantly, show what was beautiful. The novice could then advance to other works which included the Rule of St Benedict, Cassian and Jerome, as well as contemporary writers such as Aelred of Rievaulx and Gilbert of Hoyland.[19] It was essential that the monks were not distracted in the cloister but remained focused on their reading. For this reason silence was mandatory and carvings and decorations were prohibited, since they would likely divert the eye. Bernard of Clairvaux alluded to this in his *Apologia*, c. 1125, in which he decried against fanciful images – 'filthy monkeys and fierce lions, fearful centaurs, harpies and striped tigers' – which drew one's attention away from the Word of God.[20] Aelred of Rievaulx was similarly critical of these frivolous 'amusements' that ran counter to monastic poverty.[21] The monks sat one behind the other to prevent them from communicating and hoods were worn down, lest anyone was tempted to take a nap under the cover of his cowl.[22] Although there was no talking in the cloister during the *lectio divina* there would have been an audible hum from the monks reading aloud, for at this time silent reading was uncommon and was in fact discouraged, since it was thought that reading out the words helped to focus the mind.

An austere existence: living in the cloister

> Our food is scanty, our garments rough; our drink is from the stream and our sleep upon our book. Under our tired limbs there is a hard mat; when sleep is sweetest we must rise at a bell's bidding.[23]

---

[19]   Stephen of Sawley, 'A Mirror for Novices', chapters 15–16 (pp. 106–8).
[20]   *St Bernard's Apologia to Abbot William*, p. 66.
[21]   Aelred of Rievaulx, *The Mirror of Charity*, trans. E. Connor, Cistercian Fathers Series, 17 (Kalamazoo, 1990), Book II, chapter 24 (pp. 212–13); PL, 195, col. 572.
[22]   *Ecclesiastica Officia*, chapter 71: 5, 8 (p. 212).
[23]   Aelred of Rievaulx, *Mirror of Charity*, Book II, chapter 17 (p. 194); PL, 195, cols 562–3.

The early Cistercians advocated a back-to-basics policy. The various indulgences and relaxations that had crept in over the years and become an accepted part of monastic life were stripped away and a much simpler regime was observed. The White Monks therefore forbade meat and prohibited furs and fine cloths. Moreover, they dispensed with the post-Vigils nap which meant that, unlike the Benedictines, the Cistercians did not return to bed after Vigils but stayed up to pray until Lauds at daybreak.[24] They did not, however, promote asceticism for its own sake but sought to exercise indifference and subjugate the senses to free the spirit. As William of St Thierry remarked, monks should mortify but not break their bodies. Accordingly, food was not to be savoured but regarded as a fuel; sleep was to refresh rather than indulge the body, while bedding and clothing were simply functional and were not for vanity or comfort.[25]

The severity of Cistercian life was well known and widely acknowledged. Whereas the harsh conditions deterred some from taking the white habit, recruits who experienced this austerity at first hand might be prompted to reconsider their suitability and perhaps abandon the cloister altogether. Waldef (d. 1159), who had been prior of the Augustinian house at Kirkham before joining the White Monks, was well used to self-discipline yet he was sorely tested by Cistercian asceticism and considered returning to his old priory. But he drew strength from God and persevered.[26] Waldef was later appointed abbot of Melrose, the premier Cistercian abbey in Scotland. Waldef was never formally canonised but his cult was popularly celebrated and the monastic community at Melrose campaigned for his canonisation; indeed Abbot Patrick of Melrose (1206–7) commissioned Jocelin of Furness to write Waldef's 'Life'.[27] The rigours of Cistercian life might cause families to worry for their kin who had taken the habit, particularly those of a frail disposition or who had little experience of such austerity. A striking testimony to this is Bernard of Clairvaux's letter to Geoffrey of Peronne, a young man of Flanders who had recently entered the Order. Geoffrey's family was evidently distressed at his decision to join the White Monks. His relatives grieved at their loss but were also concerned that Geoffrey would not be able to cope with such a demanding regime, given his rather delicate constitution. Bernard was quick to offer reassurance and showed remarkable empathy with their plight. He promised to look after Geoffrey as a father, mother, brother and sister, and assured them that they were not losing a son but gaining

[24] See William of Malmesbury's remarks in his *Gesta Regum*, I, 581–3.
[25] William of St Thierry, *The Golden Epistle*, I: 32–4 (pp. 52–6). See above, p. 34, for Bernard of Clairvaux's letter to his nephew who left the Order to join the Cluniacs.
[26] G. J. McFadden, 'An edition and translation of the 'Life' of Waldef, Abbot of Melrose, by Jocelin of Furness', Ph.D. thesis, University of Columbia (1952), pp. 240, 312.
[27] Derek Baker, 'Waldef (*c.*1095–1159)', *ODNB*, vol. 56, pp. 765–6. See below, pp. 131–2.

a family; they would all be embraced by the Clairvaux community – 'We at Clairvaux or of Clairvaux will receive him as a brother and you as our parents.'[28]

The Cistercian Order acknowledged the difficulties most faced in adjusting to the new routine and granted concessions to novices, so that they were not immediately confronted with the full rigours of claustral life. They were exempted from some of the liturgical duties, served a more plentiful diet and often had heated quarters. Allowances were similarly made for the elderly and infirm who received a more nourishing diet, which included meat.[29] They enjoyed relatively comfortable accommodation in the infirmary where the rules of silence were relaxed and the liturgical round was less onerous. Special dispensation might be granted to individuals on account of their specific needs or circumstances. For instance, those who returned home late from a long journey were allowed to remain in bed when the others rose for Vigils. A monk of Hailes (Gloucestershire) was permitted to wear linen on account of his ailments.[30]

The following section explores the nature of the Cistercian diet and its impact on the monks' physical and mental well-being.

Cistercian fare

> Black bread and plain water, mere greens and vegetables are assuredly no very delectable fare: what does give great pleasure is when, for the love of Christ and the desire of interior delight, a well-disciplined stomach is able to satisfy itself with such fare and be thankful.[31]

The Cistercians' desire to return to the essentials of the Rule meant adhering to a simple and frugal vegetarian diet. Food was to satisfy the body without tantalising the taste-buds for the monks were not to be servants to their physical desires; they were to exercise self-restraint. Benedict prescribed that the community should eat just once a day in winter but twice in summer, given the longer working day. A light breakfast might be served to novices who were unused to the rigorous regime and also to the refectory helpers, to sustain them through service, since they ate only after the community had dined.[32]

Each monk received a daily allowance of drink and coarse bran bread.[33] A choice of two cereal or vegetable-based cooked dishes (*pulmenta*) was

---

28 *Letters of St Bernard of Clairvaux*, no. 112 (p. 169).
29 'Institutes of the General Chapter', no. 25, *NLT*, p. 466.
30 Harper-Bill, 'Cistercian Visitation', 112. This was in 1461.
31 William of St Thierry, *The Golden Epistle*, pp. 44–5.
32 *Ecclesiastica Officia*, chapter 73: 9 (p. 216); 'Institutes of the General Chapter', no. 52, *NLT*, p. 478.
33 'Early Capitula', no. 12, *NLT*, p. 409.

offered and a third of fruit or vegetables was served if and when available. More substantial fare was enjoyed on feasts and anniversaries when the monks received delicacies known as pittances. These might be morsels of egg, fish or cheese, or perhaps fine bread rather than the customary coarse-grained kind.[34] During Lent, animal fats and dairy were prohibited on all but a few named days.[35]

The monastic diet was rich in fruit, vegetables, fish and beans. But what precisely was eaten and drunk varied according to the region and the season. Rye bread, for example, was common where wheat was scarce, whilst more northerly countries relied on oats and barley or bere (a type of barley grown in Scotland).[36] Inland houses might depend on freshwater fish, whereas monasteries on the coast would rely on herring, cod and other saltwater fish. Excavations at the Danish abbey of Øm, which lay between two lakes, uncovered the bones of perch, tench, bream, pike, salmon and burbot.[37] Wine was the preferred drink in the continental houses and a number of abbeys established themselves as notable producers. Cîteaux, for example, owned fifteen vineyards, while Fontfroide had over twenty. It was the fifteenth-century monks of Eberbach in the Rhineland who helped to make this an internationally renowned wine-making region.[38] In northern countries such as England, ale and cider were popular and the monastery generally had a brewhouse within the precinct; the foundations of the brewhouse at Waverley Abbey (Surrey) survive to the west of the cloister. Some wine was produced in colder climes although much was imported. Melrose Abbey in the Scottish Borders planted vinestakes in sheltered corners of the orchard walls.[39] The Hampshire monastery of Beaulieu had almost eight hundred vinestakes c. 1270, over half of which were within the precinct. But the Beaulieu monks enjoyed a variety of homebrewed and imported beverages. They produced their own cider and mead (some of which was then sold) and imported wine from Gascony.[40] The monks of Quarr on the Isle of Wight imported wine from

[34] For an extensive analysis of pittances in the monastery see B. Harvey, 'Monastic Pittances in the Middle Ages', in *Food in Medieval England: Diet and Nutrition*, ed. C. M. Woolgar, D. Serjeantson and T. Waldron (Oxford, 2006), pp. 215–27.

[35] 'Institutes of the General Chapter', no. 25, *NLT*, p. 466.

[36] Oram's recent analysis of the estates of Balmerino Abbey in Fife, Scotland, demonstrates that there, as elsewhere in Scotland, there was 'an oats and bere dominated agricultural regime': R. Oram, 'A Fit and Ample Endowment? The Balmerino Estate, 1228–1603', in Kinder, *Life on the Edge*, 61–80 (pp. 66–7).

[37] France, *Cistercians in Scandinavia*, p. 281.

[38] Williams, *Cistercians in the Early Middle Ages*, pp. 336–42; Leroux-Dhuys, *Cistercian Abbeys*, pp. 105–6.

[39] C. J. Bond, 'Production and Consumption of Food and Drink in the Medieval Monastery', in Keevil et al., *Monastic Archaeology*, pp. 54–87 (p. 69).

[40] Bond, 'Production and Consumption of Food', pp. 67–9; *Account Book of Beaulieu*, pp. 40, 170–1, 200–1.

northern France and Gascony; the Øm community occasionally enjoyed German ale instead of the rather inferior Danish brew.[41] Whilst regional differences in diet were inevitable and generally acceptable, deviations occasionally led to controversy. In 1533 the Scottish monks of Melrose, Balmerino and Newbattle objected to continental reforms imposed on them by Abbot Simon of Chaâlis, following his earlier visitation of their houses. The monks vehemently defended differences in their diet, arguing that the conditions in Scotland required them to modify the rules since they had less grain, oil, nuts and wine than their European counterparts.[42]

Where possible food was home grown or produced by the community. Monasteries might sell a surplus of goods and purchase additional supplies to supplement their own or to make up a dearth if the harvest had failed, animals had been lost to disease or the crop yield had been poor. In the late thirteenth century, the monks of Beaulieu bought all the eggs they needed for pittances even though they kept poultry; this amounted to over 1700 eggs.[43]

The monks' diet was shaped also by social and economic developments. In the later Middle Ages exotic foods were made available through trade with the East. Communities might purchase such delicacies as cumin, pepper, figs and dates, although these luxury items were perhaps more likely to appear on the abbot's table than in the refectory. Trade links brought rice and pepper to Scandinavia. James France explains that in 1315 the monks of Søro (Denmark) were served an occasional treat of rice, spiced fish and dishes prepared with pepper.[44] Sixteenth-century records for Whalley Abbey (Lancashire) reveal that dates, figs and sugar were purchased in 1520 when the community spent a striking two thirds of its annual expenditure on food and drink.[45] By the later Middle Ages a number of abbots had acquired the status of great lords and entertained lavishly. According to the Welsh bard Tudur Aled, Abbot Dafydd ab Owain[46] was a fulsome host whose table heaved with venison, wild game and seafood, as well as oranges, grapes and wines from Germany and Burgundy.[47] Abbot Greenwell of Fountains (1442–71) was equally profligate and offered guests a sumptuous spread of partridges, oysters, quails and venison, in addition to figs and walnuts.[48]

[41]   S. F. Hockey, *Quarr Abbey and its Lands 1132–1633* (Leicester, 1970), p. 132; France, *Cistercians in Scandinavia*, p. 410.
[42]   Campbell, *Balmerino and its Abbey*, pp. 227–30; *Letters of James V*, pp. 210–11, 286–7.
[43]   Bond, 'Production and Consumption of Food', p. 77; *Account Book of Beaulieu*, p. 309.
[44]   France, *Cistercians in Scandinavia*, pp. 409–10.
[45]   Lekai, *Cistercians: Ideals and Reality*, p. 371.
[46]   Dafydd was abbot of Strata Marcella, Strata Florida and finally, of Aberconwy c. 1485–1513.
[47]   See Robinson, *Cistercians in Wales*, pp. 163, 215–20.
[48]   For example, see *Memorials of the Abbey of St Mary of Fountains*, III, ed. J. T. Fowler, Surtees Society 130 (1918), pp. 14, 19, 25, 49, 50, 51, 56, 61.

One of the most significant developments was the sanctioning of meat-eating within the precinct. The Order initially stood out strongly against this, despite contemporary pressure – John of Salisbury (d. 1180) memorably dismissed the Cistercians' refusal to serve meat to guests as 'foreign to all civility, not to say humanity'.[49] From the late twelfth century a number of abbots defied the Order and served meat,[50] perhaps in response to their patrons, benefactors and guests who, like John, may have anticipated a meaty repast when they visited. This was seemingly the case at Schönthal (Baden-Württemberg) in 1194, when the General Chapter reprimanded lay brothers of the house for serving meat in the abbey guesthouse to a prince and his wife who were visiting the community. As the abbot of Schönthal regularly ate in the guesthouse and had not intervened, he was also deemed culpable and punished.[51] In the fourteenth century the Order revised its stance and moved with the times. In 1335 it was ruled that meat might be served in the infirmary and also at the abbot's table, a concession that would have benefited the monks as well as guests since the brethren were permitted to dine at the abbot's table occasionally, to enjoy a respite from the refectory fare.[52] More significant change came a century later. In 1439 the General Chapter conceded that each monk might eat meat once or twice a week, provided that this was not in the refectory and that there was a rota system, whereby at least two thirds of the community always observed the regular diet in the refectory. By the end of the century most Cistercians would have eaten meat two or three times a week in a special room known as the misericord.[53]

Documentary sources and excavation offer an insight into the kinds of meats that were served in the monastery in the later Middle Ages and in some cases indicate how they were cooked. However, it is not always clear if these meats were eaten by the monks themselves or served to visitors and the wider community. Analysis of animal bones at Kirkstall Abbey, Yorkshire, indicates that beef – cows and oxen – was most commonly eaten there, and that the meat was not roasted but tenderised by stewing suggests that the animals were generally butchered when they were too old to work.[54] Excavations at Fountains Abbey uncovered beef, pork, venison and mutton bones, whilst animal remains at Øm included oxen,

---

[49] John of Salisbury, *Ioannis Saresberiensis Episcopi Carnotensis Policratici*, ed. C. Webb, 2 vols (Oxford, 1909), II, 326.

[50] See Harvey, 'Monastic Pittances', p. 221.

[51] *Twelfth-Century Statutes*, 1194: 33 (p. 294).

[52] Canivez, *Statuta*, III, 423–5 (1335: 22). The following year Benedict XII sanctioned meat-eating by Benedictines on four days a week; see Harvey, 'Monastic Pittances', p. 221.

[53] Lekai, *Cistercians: Ideals and Reality*, p. 370; see above, p. 74, for the location of the misericord.

[54] Bond, 'Production and Consumption of Food', pp. 80–1.

sheep, roe deer, wild boar and European red deer; an inventory from the abbey reveals that smoked goose was enjoyed in 1534.[55]

Diet, morale and physical well-being

> Our order banishes from our dining room confections concocted of expensive and aromatic spices which delight our taste and smell. They are entirely unsuitable for monks except, perhaps, for those who are ill in the infirmary.[56]

St Benedict was well aware that the gruelling diet might affect the brethren's physical and mental well-being and made provision for the monks to dine occasionally at the abbot's table, to enjoy tastier and heartier fare. Later, as we have seen, this would have included meat. Yet for many in the cloister the austerity of the diet remained one of the most challenging aspects of monastic life. In the words of one twelfth-century monk, the tasteless food 'cleaved' to his mouth 'more bitter than wormwood'.[57] The number of stories that Caesarius of Heisterbach records concerning the brethren's struggles with the meagre diet is an indication of how significant this was. They include the account of a cleric who entered Clairvaux as a novice and was almost driven to despair with the loathsome food, particularly the barley bread. This soon changed, for the novice had a wondrous vision in which he beheld Christ dipping a morsel of the bread into the wound in His side. Thereafter the barley bread tasted as sweet as honey to the novice who ate it with relish.[58] News of the novice's experience would have offered consolation to others who were similarly tested by the diet and perhaps encouraged them to have patience and to persist with the monastic fare. Some, however, were less tolerant and feigned illness in the hope that this would secure for them the better dishes and more comfortable accommodation accorded to the sick. Bernard of Clairvaux (d. 1153) struck out against the 'cowardice' of these 'hale and hearty' detractors, who enjoyed fine food and idle chatter whilst their fellow brethren remained in the cloister 'wallowing in blood and gore'.[59] But the fact that they sought respite in this way underlines just what an impact the diet might have on palates and morale, especially of those who had been brought up on refined food and were unused to the coarseness as well as the frugality of monastic fare.

---

[55] Coppack, *Fountains Abbey*, p. 141; France, *Cistercians in Scandinavia*, p. 411.
[56] Idungus of Prüfung, 'A Dialogue between Two Monks', III, 22 (p. 112).
[57] Walter Daniel, *Life of Aelred*, p. 30.
[58] Caesarius of Heisterbach, *Dialogus Miraculorum*, Book 4, chapter 80, Scott and Bland, *Dialogue on Miracles*, I, 283.
[59] *St Bernard's Apologia to Abbot William*, pp. 57–8.

The austere diet might have consequences also for the monks' physical well-being. Bernard of Clairvaux claimed that 'because we are monks we all have stomach problems and take a little wine'.[60] His words suggest that ill health was an accepted part of the monastic state; it went with the territory. Bernard himself suffered serious infirmity as a direct consequence of his punishing regime. Years of asceticism caused extreme gastric problems and Bernard became so weak through fasting that he eventually had to absent himself from the choir – rather paradoxical since he claimed to eat frugally lest a full stomach prevented him from standing to pray.[61] Aelred of Rievaulx (d. 1167) was similarly dogged by long-standing health problems which are vividly described by his chaplain and biographer, Walter Daniel. Walter conveys the agony caused by colic and urinary stones which were the size of beans, and explains that Aelred's health deteriorated significantly during the last year of his life. The elderly abbot found it difficult to breathe and suffered from fever and a terrible cough that 'racked his breast'. Walter presents a poignant image of the feeble old abbot sitting hunched over a mat by the fire and rubbing his limbs, in the hope that the heat might bring some relief.[62]

Few, however, practised such excessive asceticism. Nor were they expected to do so. Each person had to act according to his own constitution and for most this meant exercising control and indifference rather than extremism, which could be injurious. Caesarius of Heisterbach cautioned against 'indiscreet fervor' by recounting the fate of Baldwin, a knight who entered the monastery of Riddagshausen, outside Brunswick. During his novitiate and after his profession Baldwin defied his superiors to pursue an overly rigorous regime – he kept vigil when the others slept and worked when they rested. There were serious repercussions. Baldwin's actions weakened his brain and he subsequently hanged himself from a bell rope. He was rescued by another monk but never fully recovered his senses.[63] Bernard of Clairvaux sought to prevent such calamities and warned that anyone who followed a less restrictive regime than his brethren should not push himself too much since this might break the body and the spirit. Similarly, those who observed rigorous austerity were not to belittle the others; it was a case of each to his own.[64] The degree of asceticism practised within the monastery depended also on the attitude

60 *Ibid.*, p. 56.
61 Bernard of Clairvaux, sermon 66 on the *Song of Songs*, cited in Lekai, *Cistercians: Ideals and Reality*, p. 368; *Vita Prima*, Book 1 (William of St Thierry), PL, 185, cols 249–52; Cawley, *Bernard of Clairvaux: Early Biographies*, chapter 8 (pp. 37–9).
62 Walter Daniel, *Life of Aelred*, pp. 49, 34, 55, 80.
63 Caesarius of Heisterbach, *Dialogus Miraculorum*, Book 4, chapter 45, Scott and Bland, *Dialogue on Miracles*, I, 242.
64 *St Bernard's Apologia to Abbot William*, p. 68.

of the individual abbot. At Aulne, Simon (d. 1229) the lay brother was permitted to fast three or four days a week, yet, at the neighbouring sister house of Villers (Brabant) fasting was prohibited. There, Simon's counterpart, Arnulf (d. 1228), instead exercised frugality and would forego his pittances; he also wore a hair-shirt and engaged in self-flagellation.[65]

The Cistercian diet therefore varied and was affected by regional conditions as well as social and economic developments. Moreover, it evolved over the years. The Cistercians of the later Middle Ages largely had a richer and more diverse diet than their twelfth-century predecessors. An increased number of pittances from the thirteenth century introduced new foods and variety to the refectory, while the regularisation of meat-eating meant that this was no longer the prerogative of the sick; each monk could legitimately indulge in the occasional fleshy repast. But it was not simply a case that standards had slipped or that ideals had been diluted. Expectations had changed, both within and outside the cloister. The Cistercians of the later Middle Ages were probably less tolerant of the traditional monastic fare than their forbearers, while outsiders may have been unwilling to embrace the frugal hospitality exercised by the early Cistercians.[66] The Order thus reacted and responded to the times, to accommodate a changing world.

The mentality of the cloister

> *Accidie* is a depression born from a troubled mind; or a sense of weariness and excessive bitterness of heart by which spiritual happiness is cast out and the judgement is overthrown by a headlong fall into despair. It is called *accidie* as if it were an acid which makes all spiritual exercises bitter and insipid to us.[67]

Claustral life was somewhat of a paradox. Although the monks adhered to a rigorous regime they might suffer from boredom or listlessness described as *accidie*. The brethren lived in a community and were constantly surrounded by others yet communication was restricted and the focus was on introspection. Accordingly, there was potential for loneliness and a sense of isolation, despite the physical presence of others.

---

[65] Newman, preface to Cawley, *Send Me God*, pp. xl–xli; Cawley, *ibid.*, pp. 3, 13; 'The Life of Arnulf, lay brother of Villers', Book 1, chapters 8 and 9, in Cawley, *ibid.*, pp. 125–205 (pp. 142–3).

[66] For discussion of the standard of food and drink in religious houses and changing expectations, see C. Harper-Bill, 'The Labourer is Worthy of his Hire? Complaints about Diet in Late Medieval English Monasteries', in *The Church in Pre-Reformation Society*, ed. C. M. Barron and C. Harper-Bill (Woodbridge, 1985), pp. 95–107.

[67] Caesarius of Heisterbach, *Dialogus Miraculorum*, Book 4, chapter 27, Scott and Bland, *Dialogue on Miracles*, I, 223–4.

Conversely, the monks might suffer from a lack of privacy or even a feeling of claustrophobia.

This final section looks more closely at the conditions of claustral life, the significance of friendship and various concerns that might trouble the brethren, to gain some insight into the monks' mental outlook.

The silence of the cloister

> The silence of the deep of the night reigns even in the middle of the day … The only sound that can be heard is the sound of the brethren at work or singing their Office in praise of God.[68]

As a place of contemplation the cloister was subject to strict rules regarding silence. Essential conversation might be carried out in the small parlour on the eastern range but otherwise there was to be no talking and necessary communication was made using signs. The silence of the cloister was not, however, absolute. A number of noises were part and parcel of daily life and were indeed integral to it. For instance, the peal of bells and the striking of clappers called the brethren to their tasks. There was the murmur of monks reading aloud or singing, of obedientiaries going about their duties and perhaps of workmen and animals in the outer court. There were times and places when the regulations were relaxed and others when the silence of the cloister was not to be compromised. No communication was permitted in either the dormitory or the warming house, and the preservation of silence from Compline until Prime was strictly enforced, even when guests were present.[69] Whilst talking in the refectory was prohibited – the monks were to feast their ears on the words of an edificatory reading as they nourished their bodies – they might use signs to convey essential information but were warned to exercise restraint.[70]

Still, there was opportunity for appropriate conversation and the monks of the community could draw great strength from the encouragement, empathy and advice of their fellow brethren. This was particularly important for novices who received support and counsel from their master (or mistress) or a senior member of the community. According to

---

[68] *Vita Prima*, Book 1 (William of St Thierry), chapter 7, in *St Bernard of Clairvaux, The Story of his Life as Recorded in the 'Vita Prima Bernardi' by certain of his Contemporaries, William of St Thierry, Arnold of Bonnevaux, Geoffrey and Philip of Clairvaux, and Odo of Deuil*, trans. G. Webb and A. Walker (London, 1960), p. 59.

[69] For example, see William of Malmesbury's remarks in the *Gesta Regum*, I, 582–3 – he noted that the Cistercians kept the strictest silence after Compline when even the cellarer and guestmaster ministered to visitors in silence.

[70] For a useful discussion of monastic sign language and the significance of silence, see S. G. Bruce, *Silence and Sign Language in Medieval Monasticism: the Cluniac Tradition c. 900–c. 1200*, Cambridge Studies in Medieval Life and Thought, fourth series, 68 (Cambridge, 2007).

Goswin of Bossut, Abundus (d. 1239), a monk of Villers, consoled one of the novices 'like a prudent physician', whilst at La Ramée Ida of Nivelles forged a strong relationship with a visiting nun of Florival, whom she mentored each day. This was Beatrice of Nazareth, who had been sent to La Ramée by her abbess, c. 1216, to learn the art of penmanship, so that she could return to her own community and copy books for the church.[71] On the afternoons of major feasts the restrictions on talking were seemingly relaxed and the brethren might pair off with friends to share their thoughts and feelings or to recount memories of their past.[72] It was perhaps on these occasions that Goswin interviewed his friend, Abundus, to collect material for his 'Life', and that Wimund, an old monk of Byland (Yorkshire) who had previously been a bishop, a pirate and an adventurer, related his 'most audacious acts as well as his merited misfortunes' to his fellow brethren.[73] Not everyone could engage in these periods of conversation for the community might be divided by language, especially if the monastery was in a border region. When Ida of Nivelles first entered Kerkom (c. 1214), which was in a Dutch-speaking area, she was unable to converse with the other sisters for she spoke only French. Ida felt rather isolated, and as her biographer explains, this prompted her to turn inwards to God. Ida did, however, seek other ways to communicate and sought to console one nun who was often downcast by sitting beside her, in the hope that her physical presence would lift the girl's mood.[74]

The rules regarding silence were not always adhered to. John of Forde (d. 1240), who was abbot of the Dorset house, described in a sermon his distress when some of the brethren would yawn, wander idly or gossip while their companions were engaged in reading and prayer – 'It makes me sigh because the man who gathers sparingly will also drink sparingly.'[75]

The observation of silence was less stringently imposed outside the cloister. For consolation the sick in the infirmary were permitted to talk together a little and travelling companions might speak with each other whilst on their journey. These concessions were not to be abused and the brethren were expected to exercise restraint; they were to shun gossip and

71 Goswin of Bossut, 'Life of Abundus', chapter 18, in Cawley, *Send Me God*, pp. 240–1; extracts from the 'Life' of Beatrice of Nazareth, trans. Cawley, in *ibid.*, appendix III, pp. 106–9, 116.
72 Newman, in Cawley, *Send Me God*, p. xvi.
73 Goswin of Bossut, 'Life of Abundus' (prologue), in Cawley, *Send Me God*, p. 209; *The History of William of Newburgh*, trans. J. Stevenson (Llanerch facsimile, Felinfach, 1996), pp. 430–2.
74 Goswin of Bossut, 'Life of Ida of Nivelles', chapter 2, in Cawley, *Send Me God*, pp. 34–5. See above (p. 63) for Cawley's suggestion that Ida was sent specifically to Kerkom so that she could become bilingual and translate for the nuns when they relocated.
75 John of Forde, sermon 91 on the Song of Songs, trans. Sister W. Beckett, in *Sermons on the Final Verses of the Song of Songs*, 7 vols, Cistercian Fathers Series, 29, 39, 43–7 (Kalamazoo, 1977–84), VI, 97–109 (p. 103).

talk of appropriate matters. Other orders had a more relaxed attitude to silence in the cloister. The Cluniacs allowed their monks to chat each day after the chapter meeting. According to the twelfth-century Cistercian Idung, this was a serious mistake for these periods turned into rowdy and often argumentative sessions. Idung compared the Cluniac cloister to a tavern full of drunks.[76]

The fellowship of the cloister

In these deserts of ours we have the solitude without lacking the consolation of sweet and holy companionship.[77]

Although communication was restricted within the monastery, the brethren were united in fellowship and strengthened by communal living – alone, the monk was vulnerable to the devil, whereas the community as a body could better withstand his wiles. Aelred of Rievaulx (d. 1167) regarded friendship as a foretaste of heaven which could help each monk advance on his spiritual journey. The brethren might benefit immensely from the guidance and support of other members of the community and draw comfort from their physical presence, and from being part of a corporate body. Alice (d. 1250), a thirteenth-century nun of La Cambre (Belgium), greatly missed the company of her fellow sisters when she contracted leprosy and was moved from the dormitory to an isolated hut. Alice had entered the convent at a young age and was accustomed to the communal living arrangements. She was unused to being alone and felt lonely and afraid sleeping in the solitary dark hut.[78] For some, however, the constant presence of others could be trying and they might seek a private corner to be alone and unobserved. A striking example relates to Ida of Léau, a thirteenth-century nun of La Ramée. Ida's ecstatic fits would startle her fellow sisters and she yearned to find a quiet place on her own where she could be free to succumb to her emotions and to 'flex her limbs' without shocking the others.[79] In the later Middle Ages attitudes to privacy changed in the monastery as they did in society at large. A number of abbots and some senior officials now had their own private

[76] Idungus of Prüfung, 'A Dialogue between Two Monks', I, 23 (pp. 36–7).
[77] Guerric of Igny, fourth sermon for Advent, cited in C. Walker Bynum, 'The Cistercian Conception of Community', in her *Jesus as Mother: Studies in the Spirituality of the Middle Ages* (Berkeley/Los Angeles/London, 1982), pp. 59–89 (p. 65).
[78] *Alice the Leper: Life of Alice of Schaerbeek by Arnold II of Villers* (?), trans. M. Cawley (Lafayette, 2000), pp. 9–10, 12–13.
[79] Cawley, *Ida the Gentle of Léau*, 48a (p. 50).

chamber or suite of rooms, and the dormitory and infirmary might be partitioned to provide separate cubicles for the brethren.[80]

Companionship within the cloister had several purposes. It provided comfort and consolation. It was instructive. Bynum argues that for the Cistercians the coenobitic life afforded an opportunity for each monk to learn from the others and advance spiritually, as well as emotionally.[81] But crucially, companionship offered protection from the devil. This dual purpose is clearly seen in the care of the sick and the dying who were assigned a companion to sit with them and read 'for recreation and solace'.[82] The brethren might take it in turns to sit with their ailing brother – or sister – so that he or she was never left alone to fall prey to the devil. It was for this reason that the corpse was not left unattended from when it was brought into the church until the burial. The community organised shifts to keep constant vigil and ensure that the psalmody was not broken.[83]

The cloister was not, however, immune to divisions. Tensions might arise between individuals: in 1261 the monks of Hailes (Gloucestershire) were reprimanded for bullying a member of their convent whilst in 1433 a monk of Combe (Warwickshire) fled to Waverley Abbey on account of 'the malice of his rivals'.[84] Or, factions might rip the entire community apart. Rifts of this kind were sometimes sparked off by an abbatial appointment. This was the cause of a bitter row at Fountains Abbey in the early fifteenth century, when the Yorkshire community was divided over the appointment of a successor to Abbot Robert (1383–1410). The monks set up rival camps, and slander and violence ensued as the argument escalated and was brought to the attention of the Council of Constance (1414–18) and to Parliament.[85]

Few disputes were this serious but occasional disagreements were an inevitable consequence of communal living and did not undermine the strong sense of community that prevailed and cemented the monks together. The departure of brethren who left to colonise a daughter house or to take up office in another abbey could have a devastating impact. Yet this was not uncommon, especially in the second half of the twelfth century when Cistercian expansion was at its height. Their departure could be traumatic, both for those who were wrenched from their home

[80] For further discussion see D. Bell, 'Chambers, Cells and Cubicles: the Cistercian General Chapter and the Development of the Private Room', in Kinder, *Perspectives for an Architecture of Solitude*, pp. 187–98.

[81] Bynum, 'The Cistercian Conception of Community', in her *Jesus as Mother*, pp. 59–89.

[82] Cawley, 'The Life of Ida the Eager of Louvain', Book 3: 4a.

[83] *Ecclesiastica Officia*, chapter 94: 45 (p. 272); chapter 96 (pp. 276–8).

[84] Harper-Bill, 'Cistercian Visitation', 107.

[85] E. F. Jacob, 'The Disputed Election at Fountains 1410–1416', in *Medieval Studies Presented to Rose Graham*, ed. V. Ruffer and A. J. Taylor (Oxford, 1950), pp. 78–97.

and for those who were left behind in a broken community. Several surviving letters convey the anguish of Clairvaux monks who were posted to another monastery and the distress of their abbot at the sad but necessary loss of his monks.[86] The chronicle of Hailes includes a particularly emotive account of the scene at Beaulieu Abbey (Hampshire) in 1246, on the departure of the group of monks who were to settle Hailes. The chronicle describes the community's final meal together in the refectory where 'the sound of weeping was more often heard than rejoicing'; those who remained at Beaulieu 'wept like Rachel for her children'.[87]

Relocation sometimes required the monks to move to a new and perhaps distant country, with an alien language, culture and climate. Philip of Kirkstead resigned from the abbacy at Hovedøya, Norway, after just seven years on account of the 'intemperate climate'; he returned to his Lincolnshire community and resumed his previous office as prior.[88] The colonising community might encounter local hostility. The nine monks of Clairvaux whom St Bernard sent to settle at Mellifont in Ireland had been reluctant to leave their home community; they were desperate to return since the natives were unwilling to embrace Cistercian practice and it was impossible for the men to implement unity. The group returned to France exasperated; only one could be persuaded to go back and few others would join him. Mellifont therefore had to rely on local recruitment.[89]

The refusal of the Clairvaux monks to go to Ireland is interesting but it is likely that in most cases the brethren had little choice but to go where their abbot sent them, regardless of how they felt at being uprooted from their home. However, they generally departed with the promise that they could return to their own monastery to die and that they would be buried in familiar surroundings, within the heart of their community. Bernard of Clairvaux was emphatic that his monks should be able to come home to end their lives, and was incredulous when his own brother, Abbot Guy of Pontigny, prevented one Clairvaux monk from returning from Normandy. The monk had taken ill and Bernard wanted him 'to die in his own little nest' at Clairvaux, as he had requested. But Guy was seemingly more concerned about the administration of the Norman house than the welfare of the monk and intervened. Bernard was appalled and vowed that Guy himself would be denied the privilege of burial at Clairvaux.[90] The number of examples of monks retiring to their home

---

[86] *Letters of St Bernard of Clairvaux*, no. 74 (p. 106).
[87] Cited in Winkless, *Hailes Abbey*, p. 8.
[88] France, *Cistercians in Scandinavia*, p. 88.
[89] J. Luddy, *Mellifont Abbey* (Waterford, 1938), pp. 21–7; *Letters of St Bernard of Clairvaux*, nos 384–5 (pp. 452–5).
[90] Casey, 'Herbert of Clairvaux's Book of Wonderful Happenings', 60–1.

community to die in the house where they had made their profession underlines the strong affinity that brethren had with their monastery and its location. It was clearly important for them to be buried in familiar surroundings amongst those with whom they had lived. The Cistercian rituals and ceremonies associated with death and burial reinforced links between the living and the dead, and tell us much about the Cistercian attitude towards death.

Death

> Be quiet, my brothers, be quiet! What are you saying? In reality, I say to you, I go to God trembling and worried, like someone who has never done anything worthy.... I am afraid and I tremble.[91]

The bonds between the living and the deceased continued beyond the grave. Whether alive or dead the monks remained united as members of the community and as part of the Cistercian family. Former brethren were remembered in the monks' prayers[92] and burial within the precinct meant that they were a physical presence within the monastery, particularly if buried at the heart of communal life in the church, chapterhouse or cloister.[93] Not infrequently the dead were invoked as intercessors, to assist, mediate or alleviate sickness. The Melrose Chronicle describes how one elderly monk of the house who was blind prayed for relief at the shrine of his former friend, who was renowned for his sanctity. Help was immediate. A clear bright light passed through the middle of 'the locked closets' of the monk's eyes and he was able to return to the cloister unassisted.[94] Following the death of Ida of Nivelles in 1231, various members of her community at La Ramée – and also outsiders – sought her assistance. They included nuns who suffered from deafness and catarrh, as well as a lay brother and a serving boy in the guesthouse.[95] It was not uncommon for the community to receive a visitation from departed brethren who came to offer encouragement or advice. Caesarius of Heisterbach recounted the experience of a nine-year-old nun of Mount St Saviour who received a warning from her former friend, with whom she

91 Stephen Harding's deathbed words to the monks of Cîteaux, reported by Conrad of Eberbach, *Le Grand Exorde de Cîteaux, ou, Recit des debuts de l'Ordre cistercien*, trans. Anthelmette Piebourg, intro. B. P. McGuire, Cîteaux: Commentarii Cistercienses, *Studia et documenta*, 7 (Turnhout, 1998), pp. xxiv–v; Conrad of Eberbach, *Exordium Magnum*, I, 31 (p. 60).
92 See, for example, *Ecclesiastica Officia*, chapter 98: 36–57 (pp. 286–7).
93 For a useful discussion of the ties between the living and the dead and ways in which the monks could aid the progress of their deceased brethren, see Cassidy-Welch, *Monastic Spaces*, pp. 223–41.
94 'The Chronicle of Melrose', in *The Church Historians of England*, IV, part 1, ed. and trans. J. Stevenson (London, 1854), pp. 77–242 (p. 95).
95 Goswin of Bossut, 'Life of Ida of Nivelles', chapter 35, in Cawley, *Send Me God*, pp. 96–9.

used to whisper in choir. The deceased revisited the scene of her sin and appeared in her old place in the choir, where she urged her terrified friend to mend her ways.[96] Bernard, a former monk of Villers, appeared to the monk Abundus (d. 1239) to tell him of the great joys he had experienced as a reward for the martyrdom he had suffered in the cloister, and which awaited everyone who persisted in their monastic vocation.[97]

The dead were thus a link to the unknown and the otherwise inaccessible. The community often took advantage of these visitations to find out more about what awaited them in the life hereafter and to enquire about the fate of former brethren and kin. They might even make a pact with the living to return to them when dead, to pass on this precious information. When it was Ida of Nivelles's turn to sit with an eleven-year-old sister of La Ramée who was dying, she asked the girl to visit her within seven days of her death to tell of her experience. In the event, she returned on the twenty-eighth day and explained that this time had been spent in Purgatory, to atone for past sins. Ida was eager to know about her own family and friends and also asked about her personal progress.[98] A monk and a lay brother of Stratford Langthorne were so curious to learn more about what awaited them that they drew up a formal agreement stating that whoever died first should return to inform the other of what lay ahead. The monk, Alexander, predeceased his friend and within thirty days appeared to him and was duly quizzed about the life hereafter. A year later Alexander reappeared as a marvellous bright light and a 'ravishing smell' for he was now in Paradise. The lay brother, Roger, again questioned him and was particularly anxious to know who was with Alexander in Paradise; he not only asked about the saints but about people he had known, including former members of the community. Alexander explained that the ascent to Paradise was a slow one but consoled his friend that he would eventually join him there.[99]

These exchanges between the living and the dead offer an insight into the concerns and anxieties that the brethren had about death and not just about their own fate, but that of family and friends who had not taken the habit and were not therefore guaranteed the reward reserved for the cloistered. The monks sought reassurance from the dead and were both curious and anxious about what lay ahead, hardly surprising given that their life was focused on earning and preparing for salvation. When Stephen Harding, the third abbot of Cîteaux, lay on his deathbed in 1134,

---

[96] Caesarius of Heisterbach, *Dialogus Miraculorum*, Book 12, chapter 36, Scott and Bland, *Dialogue on Miracles*, II, 323–5.
[97] Goswin of Bossut, 'Life of Abundus', chapter 15, in Cawley, *Send Me God*, pp. 235–6.
[98] Goswin of Bossut, 'Life of Ida of Nivelles', chapter 10, in *ibid.*, pp. 45–7.
[99] C. Holdsworth, 'Eleven Visions connected with the Cistercian Monastery of Stratford Langthorne', *Cîteaux: Commentarii Cistercienses* 13 (1962), 185–204 (pp. 197–201).

he allegedly expressed his great fear to the brethren and claimed that he went to God 'trembling and worried, like someone who has never done anything worthy'.[100] For some, fears of inadequacy led to despondency and despair which might drive them to consider suicide. One lay brother who had given up all hope of salvation threw himself into a fish pond, whilst a nun who was suddenly afflicted with doubts threw herself into the River Moselle.[101]

The monastic life was challenging if rewarding but demanded both discipline and persistence. Throughout the Middle Ages the goals of Cistercian life remained constant, although the conditions under which the brethren lived changed over time and also from region to region, for the monks did not live in a vacuum; they were affected by developments in the world around. The same phenomenon may be perceived in the Cistercians' spirituality – their interior life – as well as in the economic activities which were an important manifestation of the Order's interaction with the outside world. These are the subject of the chapters that follow.

[100] Cited by Conrad d'Eberbach, *Le Grand Exorde de Cîteaux*, trans. Piebourg, pp. xxiv–v; and see Conrad of Eberbach, *Exordium Magnum*, I, 31 (p. 60). See above, p. 122, note 91.
[101] Caesarius of Heisterbach, *Dialogus Miraculorum*, Book 4, chapters 40–1, Scott and Bland, *Dialogue on Miracles*, I, 237–40.

1 Sénanque Abbey, Provence

2 Fountains Abbey, Yorkshire, from the west

3 Lay brothers' dormitory, Clairvaux Abbey, Aube

4 Detail from Licence to Margaret Clifford, widow, to grant the advowson
of the church of Belton, in Axholme, to the prioress and convent
of Esholt, Yorkshire; letters patent Richard III, 1485;
West Yorkshire Archive Service, Leeds, WYL1530

CHAPTER SIX

'Angels of God': Cistercian Spirituality

In truth I tell you, that if that son of perdition, Judas, who sold and betrayed the Lord, had sat in this school of Christ and had been a member of this Order, through penitence he would have obtained pardon.[1]

Monastic spirituality encompasses many aspects of claustral life. The *opus Dei* and *lectio divina*, which essentially structured the conventual day and gave it both rhythm and meaning, were discussed in the previous chapter. Here Cistercian spirituality is explored more closely through considering the attitude of the White Monks towards saints and relics – an area of current research interest – and the nature and significance of mysticism to the Order. Before doing so it is useful to outline briefly several key religious developments at this time, to set the Cistercians in their wider context.

McGinn describes the twelfth century as 'a new departure' in the history of Latin Christianity that gave rise to the 'richest development of the monastic mystical tradition in the West'.[2] It saw a burgeoning interest in the humanity of Christ which from the late eleventh century focused on Jesus the man and later encompassed Jesus the boy, Jesus the baby and Mary the mother, who was duly accorded a prominent role in religious and liturgical life.[3] Mary was particularly associated with the new religious orders whose churches were largely dedicated to her.[4] Devotion to Christ and His presence in the Eucharist led in the thirteenth

---

[1] *Exordium Magnum*, II, 5 (p. 101; our translation). This passage is discussed in B. McGuire, 'Written Sources and Cistercian Inspiration in Caesarius of Heisterbach', *Analecta Cisterciensia* 35 (1979), 227–82 (p. 277); 'A Lost Exemplum Collection Found: the *Liber Visionum et Miraculorum* Compiled under Prior John of Clairvaux (1171–79)', *Analecta Cisterciensia* 37 (1981), 1–63 (p. 43); and 'Taking Responsibility: Medieval Cistercian Abbots as their Brother's Keepers', *Commentarii Cistercienses* 39 (1988), 249–68 (p. 258).

[2] B. McGinn, *The Growth of Mysticism, the Presence of God: a History of Western Christian Mysticism II* (New York, 1994), pp. xiii, 149. Bynum, *Jesus as Mother*, p. 17, writes of 'an outburst of mystical theology' in the twelfth century.

[3] See, for example, Bynum, *Jesus as Mother*, pp. 16–17; M. Rubin, *Mother of God: a History of the Virgin Mary* (London, 2010), pp. 129–30, 133, 154.

[4] For the growing cult of the Blessed Virgin at this time see R. and C. Brooke, *Popular Religion in the Middle Ages: Western Europe 1000–1300* (London, 1984), pp. 31–3; for an overview of Marian devotion in the Church in this period, see L. Gambero, *Mary in the Middle Ages: the Blessed Virgin Mary in the Thought of Medieval Latin Theologians* (Milan, 2000), pp. 105–8, and, most recently, Rubin, *Mother of God*, pp. 121–57, who discusses Cistercian devotion to Mary on pp. 149–57.

century to a surge in devotion to the Eucharist and to an intense desire
for communion, especially amongst women, who played a significant
part in thirteenth-century mysticism.[5] The humanity of Christ and the
Virgin held a special place for the Cistercians and was strongly associated
with St Bernard and his companions.[6] The White Monks thus stood at
the helm of religious developments, and, as is discussed throughout this
chapter, duly affected the course they would take.

The Cistercians, saints and cults

The Cistercians' concern to pare the liturgy and rid it of accretions meant
that they commemorated a number of saints but accorded feast days to
few. The earliest extant calendar of the Order dates from c. 1130, during
Stephen Harding's abbacy, and lists more than a hundred saints who
were commemorated and fifty-seven who had feasts.[7] Over time additional saints were added to the Cistercian calendar. In the thirteenth
century, for example, twenty-nine new feasts were introduced and six
were raised in rank.[8] Following the canonisation of Bernard of Clairvaux
in 1174, the Order introduced its own saints. Although records of papal
canonisation are known for only three Cistercians – St Bernard of Clairvaux (d. 1153, canonised 1174), William of Bourges (d. 1209, canonised
1219)[9] and Robert of Molesme (d. 1111, canonised 1222) – many more
were celebrated as saints and approved by the General Chapter.[10] They
include Aelred of Rievaulx (d. 1167), whose cult was observed locally

---

5   In her discussion of female mystics of Helfta, Bynum suggests that mystical devotion enabled these
    women to take on the role of preacher/mediator and to exercise priestly duties and power: C. Walker
    Bynum, 'Women Mystics in the Thirteenth Century', in her *Jesus as Mother*, pp. 170–262; see also
    C. Boudreau, 'With Desire Have I Desired: Ida of Nivelles's Love for the Eucharist', in *Hidden
    Springs: Cistercian Monastic Women*, 2 vols, ed. J. A. Nichols and L. T Shank, Cistercian Studies
    Series, 113 (Kalamazoo, 1995), I, 323–44.
6   For extensive discussion of Cistercian devotion to the humanity of Christ see M. Dutton, 'Intimacy
    and Initiation: the Humanity of Christ in Cistercian Spirituality', in *Erudition at God's Service:
    Studies in Medieval Cistercian History*, 11, ed. J. R. Sommerfeldt (Kalamazoo, 1987), pp. 33–70 and M.
    Dutton, 'The Face and the Feet of God: the Humanity of Christ in Bernard of Clairvaux and Aelred
    of Rievaulx', in *Bernardus Magister: Papers Celebrating the Nonacentenary of the Birth of Bernard of
    Clairvaux*, ed. John R. Sommerfeldt, Cistercian Studies Series, 135 (Kalamazoo, 1992), pp. 203–23;
    and see below, pp. 140–1.
7   K. Koch, 'Vollstandiges brevier aus der schreibstube des HL Stephen', *Analecta Cisterciensia* 2 (1946),
    146–7.
8   A. A. King, *Liturgies of the Religious Orders* (London, 1956), pp. 73, 114.
9   The feast of William of Bourges was promulgated by the General Chapter immediately after his
    papal canonisation and in 1261 his name was added to the Cistercian litany of saints. William entered
    Pontigny as a monk and was made abbot of Chaâlis in 1187 where he presided until 1200, when he
    was elevated to the see of Bourges: J. France, *The Cistercians in Medieval Art* (Stroud, 1998), p. 62;
    Canivez, *Statuta*, I, 485 (1218: 3); *ibid.*, II, 447–8 (1261: 12).
10 Williams, *Cistercians in the Early Middle Ages*, p. 64.

and promulgated by the Order in 1476.[11] Whilst the Cistercian calendar changed over time there were national, local and individual differences. For instance, from 1187 abbeys in Poitiers were permitted to celebrate the Feast of St Hilary as a feast of twelve lessons, in recognition of the saint's importance in that diocese; elsewhere in the Order Hilary's feast was simply commemorated. Similarly, although the Feast of St Julian of Le Mans was commemorated by the Cistercian Order as a whole from 1193 it was celebrated as an actual feast only by Cistercian monasteries in the diocese of Le Mans.[12] But it was with Mary that the Cistercians and individuals within the Order had a special association.

Marian devotion

> With every fibre of our being, every feeling of our hearts, with all the affections of our minds and with all the ardour of our souls, let us honour Mary because such is the will of God, who would have us obtain everything through her hands. Such, I say, is the will of God who intends it for our benefit.[13]

Mary held a prominent position amongst the Cistercians and each of their abbeys was dedicated to her under the title of the Assumption – 'Queen of Heaven and Earth'. This was after the example of Molesme from which the founding fathers of the Order had originated and thus the dedication represented a link with the first Cistercians. Later, Mary was named patron of the Order (1281).[14] Mary was accorded a special place in Cistercian liturgy. From 1152 she was commemorated in the daily Office and by the end of the twelfth century seven feast days were celebrated in her honour. In 1185 the 'Little Office of Our Lady' was approved as a community prayer and from 1220 a votive Mass to Mary was celebrated on Saturdays. From the thirteenth century the *Salve Regina*, which is in many ways a hallmark of the Order, was sung at the end of Compline to bring the liturgical day to a close.

The Cistercians' strong Marian associations were represented in imagery, iconography and devotional writings as well as in visions. From 1335 the General Chapter ruled that the official seal of every monastery should bear the Virgin's image.[15] She was commonly shown seated and holding the Christ Child, as seen on a mid-fifteenth-century conven-

---

[11]   David N. Bell, 'Ailred of Rievaulx (1110–1167)', *ODNB*, vol. 1, pp. 491–3.
[12]   *Twelfth-Century Statutes*, 1187: 9 (p. 146); 1193: 13 (p. 261).
[13]   Bernard of Clairvaux, 'Sermon for the Nativity of the Blessed Virgin', cited in *Bernard of Clairvaux: a Saint in Word and Image*, ed. K. Pennington (Huntingdon, 1994), p. 239.
[14]   'Institutes of the General Chapter', no. 18, *NLT*, pp. 332, 463; 'Early Capitula', no. 9, *ibid.*, pp. 408–9.
[15]   Canivez, *Statuta*, III, 411 (1335: 2).

tual seal from Cirta Abbey (Romania).[16] Another popular image depicted Mary protecting members of the Order beneath her mantle, the so-called 'Schutzmantel'. This seemingly had its origins in a vision recounted by Caesarius of Heisterbach (d. c. 1240) which told how a Cistercian monk fell into an ecstasy and viewed 'the glories of heaven'. There he saw the angels, apostles, confessors, martyrs, patriarchs and prophets grouped according to their order but was anxious since he could not see any Cistercians amongst them. His concerns were alleviated when the Virgin opened her gown to reveal a host of monks, nuns and lay brothers from his own Order. Mary explained that the Cistercians were so precious to her that she protected them in her own bosom.[17] Until 1316 only images of Christ were permitted in Cistercian churches yet even before this date a number of houses had images of Mary, and the earliest surviving sculpture of her dates from the mid-thirteenth century. Others are known to have predated this and include an ivory image of the Virgin from Zwettl (Austria) which was shown on feast days.[18] Interestingly, the first known recorded Marian rosary is Cistercian in origin and is from an early fourteenth-century manuscript belonging to the nunnery of St Thomas, Trier.[19]

Whilst Mary held a special place within the Order at large, a number of individuals showed her particular affection. Adam of Lexington, a thirteenth-century monk of Melrose (Scotland), allegedly held Mary in such esteem he would spend the winter nights before her altar in the abbey church, where he played the lute and sang songs in her honour.[20] Those who were especially devoted to Mary might be rewarded with a vision of her. Adam's contemporary and namesake at Melrose, the pious Adam of Yorkshire, on one occasion saw the Virgin as the all-embracing Church arrayed in pure white. Adam was so filled with joy that he fell to his knees, waved his arms and beat the ground in ecstasy. Unbeknown to Adam he was being watched by another monk of Melrose who wondered at the cause of his brother's jubilation and later asked Adam the reason for his joy. The monk was puzzled that he had not seen Mary, given that he was standing

---

[16] *Catalogue of Seals in the National Museum of Wales*, vol. 2, *Ecclesiastical, Monastic and Collegiate Seals with a Supplement Concerning* Wales, ed. D. Williams (Cardiff, 1998), p. 1.

[17] Caesarius of Heisterbach, *Dialogus Miraculorum*, Book 7, chapter 64, Scott and Bland, *Dialogue on Miracles*, I, 546.

[18] C. Kratzke, '*De Laudibus Virginis Matris*: the Untold Story of a Standing Infant Jesus, a Venerating Monk and a Moveable Madonna from Dargun Abbey', in Kinder, *Perspectives for an Architecture of Solitude*, pp. 269–81 (pp. 269–70).

[19] Annette Kehnel and Mirjam Mencej, 'Representing Eternity: Circular Movement in the Cloister, Round Dancing, Winding-Staircases and Dancing Angels', in Müller and Stöber, *Self-Representation of Medieval Religious Communities*, pp. 67–90 (p. 84).

[20] 'Chronicle of Melrose', p. 96.

close by, but Adam explained that she only showed herself to her intimates who had served her assiduously for many years.[21]

Bernard of Clairvaux was renowned for his devotion to the Virgin and his celebration of her mystery. He did much to propagate Mary's cult in the twelfth century, although he vehemently opposed the doctrine of her Immaculate Conception.[22] Bernard stressed Mary's humility and virginity and wrote four homilies in her honour.[23] He was buried at Mary's altar in the abbey church of Clairvaux[24] and his devotion to the Virgin was commemorated in Dante's *Divine Comedy*:

> And from Heaven's Queen, whom fervent I adore,
> All gracious aid befriend us;
> for that I am her faithful Bernard.[25]

In the Middle Ages Bernard was considered to have been the author of a popular tract known as the *Quis dabit* and by its longer title, the *Liber de passione Christi et doloribus et planctibus Matris eius* ('the book of the passion of Christ and the pains and lamentations of his mother').[26] In this striking text Mary narrates the Passion of Christ and describes the intensity of her grief to Bernard of Clairvaux, who wishes to share in her pain and suffering. Modern scholarship has argued that *Quis dabit* was in fact the work of the Cistercian Oglerius de Tridino (d. 1214), monk and later abbot of Locedio, near Milan, who composed the tract before 1205. It was part of a series of thirteen meditations on episodes in Mary's life (the *Tractatus in laudibus Sancte Dei Genetricis*) but circulated independently

[21] 'Chronicle of Melrose', pp. 95–6. According to the chronicle Adam was a monk of the house during the abbacy of Adam of Harcarres (d. 1245).

[22] E. Rozanne Elder, 'Shadows on the Marian Wall: the Cistercians and the Development of Marian Doctrine', in *Truth as Gift: Studies in Medieval Cistercian History in Honor of John R. Sommerfeldt*, ed. M. Dutton, D. M. LaCorte and P. Lockey, Cistercian Studies Series, 204 (Kalamazoo, 2005), pp. 537–74 (p. 538).

[23] For a useful an overview of Bernard's devotion to Mary, see Gambero, *Mary in the Middle Ages*, pp. 131–41 and Rubin, *Mother of God*, pp. 174–6; for other Cistercians (Amadeus of Lausanne, Aelred of Rievaulx, Isaac of Stella and Alan of Lille), see Gambero, *Mary in the Middle Ages*, pp. 155–61, 162–9, 170–6, 185–91; and Rubin, *Mother of God*, pp. 153–4 (Adam of Perseigne) and pp. 154–7 (Helinard of Froidmont).

[24] Alan of Auxerre's *Vita Bernardi*, chapter 31, in PL, 185, col. 524, cited in Gambero, *Mary in the Middle Ages*, p. 132.

[25] *Paradiso*: canto 31, lines 100–2: see *Dante – The Divine Comedy*, trans. C. H. Sisson, intro. and notes D. H. Higgins (London/Sydney, 1981), p. 489.

[26] We are indebted to Dr William Marx for drawing this important text to our attention and for generously providing copies of his publications on the work. For a modern edition of this text see C. W. Marx, 'The *Quis dabit* of Oglerius de Tridino, Monk and Abbot of Locedio', *Journal of Medieval Latin* 4 (1994), 118–29; for extensive discussion from which this section is drawn see C. W. Marx, 'The Middle English Verse *Lamentation of Mary to Saint Bernard* and the *Quis dabit*', in *Studies in the Vernon Manuscript*, ed. D. Pearsall (Cambridge, 1990), pp. 137–57, and 'The Edge of Orthodoxy: the Virgin Mary, St Bernard and the *Quis dabit*', in *Fact and Fiction from the Middle Ages to Modern Times, Essays Presented to Hans Sauer on the Occasion of his 65th Birthday*, Part II, ed. R. Bauer and U. Krischke (Frankfurt am Main, 2011).

and may have been composed separately.[27] According to Marx, *Quis dabit* was something of 'a best seller' in the Middle Ages and was perhaps the most influential medieval work composed by the Order.[28]

A number of Cistercian writers dedicated their work to the Virgin who was at the heart of the Order's mystical theology,[29] and, as is discussed in the second part of this chapter, the Cistercians celebrated her spiritual motherhood which was closely associated with their devotion to the person of Christ. Odo of Morimond, for instance, was known for his sermons on Mary's suffering at the foot of the Cross,[30] whilst Aelred of Rievaulx's treatise 'On Jesus at the age of twelve', compiled c. 1153×57, considers Mary's feelings during the boy Jesus's three-day absence and her elation when she was finally reunited with her son in the temple at Jerusalem (Luke 20.40–50); Aelred then invites Mary to embrace Jesus:

> Hold him fast, dearest Lady, hold fast him whom you love, cast yourself upon his neck, embrace him, kiss him and make up for his absence during three days.[31]

Mary was not just remembered by the monks but was an active presence in Cistercian monasteries. It was believed that she would frequent their houses and bestow her blessing on the brethren. A number of tales recounted sightings of the Virgin in the choir or dormitory to remind monks that they were always under scrutiny and should be ever mindful of their conduct. Goswin of Bossut's 'Life' of Abundus, a thirteenth-century monk of Villers, describes how one Candlemass, Abundus saw the Virgin in the choir of his church. He watched as Mary presented her infant son to each of the monks and noted that she remained longest with those who had shown her the greatest charity and service. On another occasion Abundus saw Mary incense the choir but pass over the lazy and indolent.[32] The message was clear. Caesarius of Heisterbach devoted an entire book of his *Dialogue on Miracles* to visions of the Virgin, a reflection of her significance to the Order.[33] Several of these allude to Mary's nightly circuits of the dormitory and describe how she would wander amongst the sleeping monks and bestow her blessing. It was thus important that the brethren conducted themselves appropriately even when asleep, lest they offended their heavenly visitor. It was alleged that one

---

[27] Marx, 'The Edge of Orthodoxy'.
[28] *Ibid.*
[29] Williams, *Cistercians in the Early Middle Ages*, p. 104.
[30] Lekai, *Cistercians: Ideals and Reality*, p. 234.
[31] 'On Jesus at the Age of Twelve', trans. T. Berkeley, in *Aelred of Rievaulx, Treatises and Pastoral Prayer*, Cistercian Fathers Series, 2 (Kalamazoo, 1971, repr. 1995), pp. 1–40 (pp. 11–12).
[32] Goswin of Bossut, 'Life of Abundus', chapter 11, in Cawley, *Send Me God*, p. 227; *ibid.*, chapter 20, p. 243.
[33] Caesarius of Heisterbach, *Dialogus Miraculorum*, Book 7.

monk who was not fully clothed caused the Virgin to avert her eyes and withhold her blessing.[34] Conversely Mary's intervention in the dormitory of Cheminon (Marne) was cited to illustrate the renown of the abbot of the house who had thrown off his frock during the heat of the night. A monk of Cheminon claimed to have seen the Virgin draw up the abbot's garment. Her response was not, however, seen as the correction of an abuse; rather it was regarded as an act of compassion since Mary feared such a worthy member of the Order would suffer from the night air.[35]

Devotion to the saints

> In 1229 the abbey of St Edward at Balmerino was erected by King Alexander [II] and his mother, Ermengarde, and a community was sent there from Melrose with Dom Alan as their abbot on the day of St Lucy the Virgin [13 December].[36]

Whilst Mary was pre-eminent amongst the Cistercians, other saints were favoured both by individuals and houses. A monk of Clairvaux was allegedly so attached to St John the Baptist that on one occasion when he was thinking of the saint during Lauds a flame was seen rising from his head. His fellow brethren interpreted this as a sign of the monk's burning affection for John.[37] Not infrequently houses sought the General Chapter's permission to include in their liturgy a local saint or one who had a special association with their monastery. In 1253 Buildwas Abbey (Shropshire) asked to celebrate the feast of St Winifred as a major feast of twelve lessons and requested that this concession be extended to its daughter house of Basingwerk (Wales), which was a centre of Winifred's cult.[38] Members of the community might invoke the help of a resident saint or write hagiographical works to commemorate the holy one's life and perhaps to support his or her papal canonisation. This was seemingly the primary intention of the 'Life' of St Waldef (d. 1159) by Jocelin of Furness (fl. 1199–1214), which was commissioned by Abbot Patrick of Melrose c. 1206/7, but it is not known

---

34 Caesarius of Heisterbach, *Dialogus Miraculorum*, Book 7, chapter 14, Scott and Bland, *Dialogue on Miracles*, I, 471–2.

35 Joinville, 'The Life of St Louis', chapter 3: 120–1, in *Joinville and Villehardouin: Chronicles of the Crusades*, trans. and intro. C. Smith (London, 2008), pp. 137–336 (p. 176).

36 *Scotichronicon by Walter Bower*, ed. Simon Taylor, Donald E. R. Watt and Brian Scott (Aberdeen/Glasgow, 1990), pp. 142–3.

37 Caesarius of Heisterbach, *Dialogus Miraculorum*, Book 8, chapter 49, Scott and Bland, *Dialogue on Miracles*, II, 48–9.

38 Canivez, *Statuta*, II, 394 (1253: 24); 'House of Cistercian Monks: Abbey of Buildwas', in *The Victoria County Histories: a History of the County of Shropshire*, 2, ed. A. T. Gayton and R. B. Pugh (London, 1973), pp. 50–9; David Thomas, 'Saint Winifred's Well and Chapel, Holywell', *Journal of the Historical Society of the Church in Wales* 8 (1958), 15–31. We are grateful to Dr Kathryn Hurlock for drawing this to our attention.

if the work was ever actually submitted to the abbot.[39] A notable corpus of hagiographical works associated with the Flemish abbey of Villers and thought to have been written by Goswin of Bossut, a monk of the house, includes the lives of Abundus, a monk of Villers, Arnulf, a lay brother of the abbey, and Ida, a nun of La Ramée.[40] The writing of hagiography might involve Cistercian authors in political and ecclesiastical affairs whether to promote their own or their patron's cause. Aelred of Rievaulx composed his 'Life of St Edward the Confessor' c. 1161×63, at the request of his kinsman, Abbot Laurence of Westminster.[41] This work can be seen as a continuation of Aelred's efforts to reconcile the king and pope – the abbot had been instrumental in persuading Henry II (1154–89) to recognise Alexander III as pope several years previously – and to unite the Saxon and Norman houses. For Aelred the historical facts of Edward's life were of less importance than the portrayal of the Saxon king as a devotee of the papacy and a model of humility and chastity to be held up to Henry II, who was descended from the Confessor and was of Saxon and Norman stock; in him the two lines met. Aelred makes this explicit in his prologue to the work in which he invokes the king to emulate his worthy predecessor:

> The justice of such a great king deserves imitation and it is impressive to see his self-restraint in the midst of so much wealth and luxury. Physical descent from his saintly stock is the particular boast of our King Henry. We believe that he promised that you would be the consoler of all England, for we have come to understand that in his prophetic parable at the end of his life he was designating you, the corner stone at which the two walls, the English and Norman nation, have come together, to our great delight … be sure to imitate his holiness.[42]

Whereas Aelred may have been promoting his own cause, Jocelin of Furness seems to have been concerned to advance that of his patrons in his lives of St Patrick and St Kentigern. The former was commissioned by the bishop of Down, the archbishop of Armagh and John de Courcy (d. c. 1219), the new Anglo-Norman lord of Ulaid (Down and Antrim). Birkett has

---

[39] See Helen Birkett's recent analysis of this and Jocelin's other 'Lives': H. Birkett, *The Saints' Lives of Jocelin of Furness: Hagiography, Patronage and Ecclesiastical Politics* (York, 2010), especially pp. 201–25.

[40] These three lives have recently been translated by Father Cawley in *Send Me God*.

[41] *The Life of St Edward, King and Confessor by Blessed Aelred, Abbot of Rievaulx*, trans. J. Bertram (Guildford, 1990; repr. Southampton, 1997); PL, 195, cols 737–90.

[42] Aelred of Rievaulx, *Life of St Edward*, p. 16. See also Dutton's discussion of the *Vita*: M. L. Dutton, 'Aelred, Historian: Two Portraits in Plantagenet Myth', *Cistercian Studies Quarterly* 28 (1993), 112–43, especially 116–23. For Aelred's other historical and hagiographical works, including his 'Life' of St Ninian, commissioned by the bishop of Whithorn, see *Aelred of Rievaulx, The Lives of the Northern Saints*, trans. J. P. Freeland, ed., intro. and notes M. L. Dutton, Cistercian Fathers Series, 71 (Kalamazoo, 2006) and R. Sharpe, *A Handlist of the Latin Writers of Great Britain and Ireland before 1540*, Publications of the Journal of Medieval Latin, 1 (Turnhout, 1997), pp. 28–30, 916.

recently argued that Jocelin's ecclesiastical patrons required him to rewrite an earlier work of Patrick and to shape this to represent their concerns. Accordingly he was to boost Down's claim to be the burial spot of St Patrick and to champion the primacy of Armagh, recently threatened by the establishment of a new archbishopric in Dublin.[43] His 'Life' of St Kentigern was equally purposeful. It was commissioned by the former abbot of Melrose, Bishop Jocelin of Glasgow, between 1175 and 1199, and Birkett holds that the 'Life' was part of 'a wider programme of regeneration' intended to bolster Glasgow's independence as well as that of the Scottish Church and the Church at large.[44] Through writing hagiography the Cistercians might therefore be embroiled in the world of politics.

Although all Cistercian houses were dedicated to Mary a small number of abbeys had a double dedication. In most cases this stemmed from the monastery's or the site's pre-Cistercian history. Houses that had belonged to another order might retain an earlier dedication. Thus Savigny and Aunay in Normandy, which had previously been part of the Savigniac congregation, were consecrated to the Holy Trinity as well as to Mary, whilst the former Benedictine hermitage of Monte Favale in Italy was dedicated to Mary and St Benedict.[45] Hovedøya in Norway was consecrated to Mary and St Edmund the Martyr since there had been an earlier church on the site dedicated to the former English king.[46] In some cases the reason for the choice of dedicatee is not clear – and even puzzling. A striking example is the Scottish abbey of Balmerino that was dedicated to St Edward the Confessor as well as to Mary. Balmerino may in fact have been the first monastery consecrated to this English royal saint. Hammond has recently discussed possible personal and political motives for this rather unusual dedication and the seeming decline of Edward's importance to the community following the death of the abbey's founder, Queen Ermengarde, in 1233.[47]

Cults and relics

According to the *Exordium Magnum* of Conrad of Eberbach (d. 1221), in the wake of Bernard of Clairvaux's funeral, reports that his corpse was working miracles at the monastery drew crowds of visitors to the abbey. The abbot of Cîteaux was deeply concerned for he feared that monastic observance at Clairvaux would be severely impeded if these numbers

[43] See Birkett, *Saints' Lives of Jocelin*, especially pp. 141–70.
[44] *Ibid.*, especially pp. 171–99.
[45] Williams, *Cistercians in the Early Middle Ages*, p. 22.
[46] France, *Cistercians in Scandinavia*, p. 87.
[47] See above, p. 131. Whereas Edward began as the chief dedicatee, he took second place to the Virgin following the death of William the Lion's widow, Ermengarde, and thereafter was effectively dropped from the title: M. Hammond, 'Queen Ermengarde and the Abbey of St Edmund, Balmerino', in Kinder, *Life on the Edge*, pp. 11–36.

continued. He thus ordered Bernard to cease working miracles and the dead man, allegedly, obeyed.[48] Caesarius of Heisterbach told a similar tale about a simple lay brother of Eberbach whose miraculous powers attracted hordes of folk to the abbey, hoping to be cured. His abbot was anxious that the community should not be disrupted and duly instructed the lay brother to stop working wonders; his gift was immediately withdrawn.[49] The Cistercians did not encourage public veneration of their relics, at least not initially, lest this impeded claustral life. Nor did they sanction pilgrimage by members of the Order for this was effectively considered a breach of their vow of stability. There was also a danger that brethren would use pilgrimage as a pretext to wander out of the cloister. Both Bernard of Clairvaux and William of Chaâlis wrote against brethren going on pilgrimage, and transgressors were usually punished by the General Chapter; in 1236 the abbots of Cherlieu and Gard were admonished for spending six days at Canterbury to visit Becket's shrine.[50] But the Order was not against relics *per se*; rather, it feared the consequences that the ingress of outsiders and egress of its members would have on monastic observance. Far from eschewing relics a number of houses owned and venerated these holy objects. Whereas Aelred of Rievaulx nursed a life-long devotion to St Cuthbert at Durham,[51] Bernard of Clairvaux was buried with a relic of St Jude from the Holy Land. In the 1170s Henry II received a relic of St Bernard's finger bone from the then abbot of Clairvaux as a mark of gratitude for his donation of lead to roof the abbey church.[52] Some monasteries observed the cult of a resident saint such as Robert of Newminster (d. 1159), the founding abbot of this Northumbrian house who was buried in the abbey church there.[53] Although Robert was never formally canonised his cult was celebrated by the community, and miracles reputed to have been worked by him were

---

[48] Conrad of Eberbach, *Exordium Magnum*, II, 20 (pp. 96–9), cited in A. Bredero, *Bernard of Clairvaux: Between Cult and History* (Edinburgh, 1996), p. 69.

[49] Caesarius of Heisterbach, *Dialogus Miraculorum*, Book 10, chapter 5, Scott and Bland, *Dialogue on Miracles*, II, 175–6.

[50] Williams, *Cistercians in the Early Middle Ages*, pp. 333, 334; Canivez, *Statuta*, II, 159 (1236: 30). It seems that the abbots went to Canterbury under the pretext of pilgrimage and spent their time wandering throughout the province in a rather unseemly way; and it was this which caused the Chapter concern.

[51] See A. Lawrence-Mathers, *Manuscripts in Northumbria in the Eleventh and Twelfth Centuries* (Cambridge, 2003), pp. 236–51, especially pp. 240–1. We are indebted to Dr Sally Crumplin for drawing this to our attention.

[52] N. Vincent, *The Holy Blood: King Henry III and the Westminster Blood Relic* (Cambridge, 2001), p. 139 and note 9; A. Gajewski, 'Burial, Cult and Construction at the Abbey Church of Clairvaux (Clairvaux II)', *Cîteaux: Commentarii Cistercienses* 56 (2005), 47–85 (pp. 76–7). Gajewski discusses Clairvaux 'as a place of cult' and considers how the shrines of Bernard and Malachy in particular helped promote Bernard's ideal of a reformed church.

[53] Robert, like Aelred of Rievaulx, was initially buried in the chapterhouse but was then moved to the abbey church.

recorded in his 'Life'. One monk of Newminster claimed to have twice invoked and received the holy man's help. On the first occasion he was cured of fevers at Robert's shrine and on the second saved from certain injury after falling from a ladder. The latter incident occurred when the monk was whitewashing the dormitory. His ladder slipped and as he tumbled towards the stone step of the nightstair he cried out to Robert; quite miraculously the monk suffered no harm upon landing and was convinced that the saint had cushioned his fall.[54]

Although the abbots of Cîteaux and Eberbach discouraged pilgrimage to their houses there is evidence that later some communities supported and even promoted pilgrimage to their monasteries. This could be prestigious and lucrative and was particularly advantageous during times of hardship when financial aid was needed. In early fifteenth-century Wales, Tintern and Basingwerk turned to the pilgrim trade to raise funds to carry out necessary repairs following destruction caused by the Owain Glyn Dŵr revolt. Tintern encouraged pilgrimage to its galilee chapel, to see a miracle-working statue of Mary, and Basingwerk to St Winifrid's Well, which lay some two kilometres from the abbey and therefore posed less of a threat to monastic observance.[55] The well had belonged to the Benedictine abbey of St Werburgh, Chester, from the late eleventh century but in 1240 it was gifted to the Cistercians of Basingwerk by Dafydd ap Llywelyn and the Cistercian abbey retained it until the Dissolution.[56] Disruption to claustral life was also lessened if the relics were housed in a chapel at the monastery gate rather than in the church. An image of the Virgin was kept in the chapel at the gate at Merevale Abbey (Warwickshire) and was evidently popular, for in 1351 there were allegedly so many pilgrims they were almost crushed to death.[57] Another way to minimise disruption was to restrict access to the relic. Instead of having the object on permanent display it was brought out occasionally for visitors to see. The thirteenth-century 'Life' of Ida of Louvain, who was a nun of Roosendaal (Flanders), describes how a reliquary containing a chip of the lance-head that pierced Christ's side was brought out from time to time for public veneration and would emit a fine odour.[58]

[54] W. Watkins, 'The Life of St Robert of Newminster', *Downside Review* 58 (1939), 137–49 (pp. 147–8). Leyser explains that the two surviving lives are seemingly abbreviations of an original which is no longer extant and comprised two books – the life and posthumous miracles: Henrietta Leyser, 'Robert [St Robert] (d. 1159)', *ODNB*, vol. 47, pp. 92–3.

[55] Williams, *Welsh Cistercians*, pp. 55, 147–8. Indulgences were granted to pilgrims visiting the image of Mary at Tintern in 1414 and to those visiting St Winifred's Well in 1427; see *Calendar of Entries in the Papal Registers relating to Great Britain and Ireland: Papal Letters*, ed. W. H. Bliss, C. Johnson, J. A. Twemlow and M. J. Haren (London, 1893– in progress), V, 507–8; VI, 452; VII, 503. We are indebted to Dr Kathryn Hurlock for these references.

[56] Bond, 'Monastic Water Management in Great Britain', p. 100.

[57] R. Midmer, *English Medieval Monasteries* (London, 1979), p. 218.

[58] Cawley, 'Life of Ida the Eager of Louvain', Book 3: 24a.

The promotion of a cult and the encouragement of pilgrimage often meant renegotiating rules regarding the admittance of outsiders, particularly women, and might require the community to undertake construction work to house the relic in suitable surroundings. Monasteries might secure special permission to allow access to women at given times. Pope Alexander IV (1254–61) granted a dispensation to Pontigny to permit English women to enter the abbey precinct on the feast of the translation of the relics of St Edmund of Abingdon, a former archbishop of Canterbury.[59] The Yorkshire abbey of Meaux received licence from the General Chapter, c. 1339, granting men and women of honest character the right to enter the abbey church to view the miracle-working crucifix in the lay brothers' choir. But the community was warned that no women other than the patron's wife and daughter were permitted to go inside the dormitory, cloister or any of the other buildings; an infringement of this ruling would result in the entire privilege being withdrawn.[60] It was important that the relic was housed in a fitting place which was accessible to outsiders. Lindy Grant demonstrates that from the late twelfth century communities often extended the east end of the presbytery to form an ambulatory or apse to accommodate such relics. Examples include Clairvaux, where St Bernard was interred, and Savigny, which housed the relics of its early abbots.[61] Stalley suggests that it is likely that rebuilding in the abbey church at Holy Cross (Ireland), c. 1420, was primarily intended to accommodate the monastery's relics which included a piece – or pieces – of the True Cross; the shrine was built into the fabric in the south transept.[62] At Hailes (Gloucestershire) the east end of the abbey church was reconstructed to build a shrine for a portion of the Holy Blood that was given to the community by its patron, Edmund of Cornwall (d. 1300), and which made the abbey one of the most important pilgrim sites in the country. The Cistercians may not in general have been keen promoters of cults and relics but, as Vincent argues, it was fitting that one of their abbeys had a portion of the Holy Blood, given the Order's celebration of the humanity of Christ. In the later Middle Ages Hailes was well prepared for the pilgrim trade. A sixteenth-century visitor explained that pilgrims who had come to the abbey to venerate the Holy Blood could read about the history of the relic on a table outside the chapel where the holy object was kept.[63]

59 N. Shead, 'Four Scottish Indulgences at Sens', *Innes Review* 58 (2007), 210–16 (p. 210).
60 *Chron. Melsa*, III, 35–6; for further discussion of this example and access for women, see J. Kerr, 'Cistercian Hospitality in the Later Middle Ages', in *Monasteries and Society in the British Isles in the Later Middle Ages*, ed. J. Burton and K. Stöber (Woodbridge, 2008), pp. 25–39 (pp. 25, 32–3).
61 Grant, *Architecture and Society in Normandy*, pp. 154–5.
62 Stalley, *Cistercian Monasteries of Ireland*, pp. 115–17.
63 Winkless, *Hailes Abbey*, p. 57.

It was uncommon for a Cistercian abbey to be a major pilgrim centre but Hailes was not exceptional.[64] In the mid-thirteenth century the shrine of St Edmund of Abingdon (Edmund Rich) made Pontigny one of the most important Cistercian pilgrim sites in Europe. Edmund had stayed at Pontigny shortly before his death in 1240 and his body was brought there for burial. The following year the General Chapter spearheaded the campaign for Edmund's canonisation and in December 1246 Innocent IV pronounced him a saint. The formal translation of Edmund's holy remains was witnessed in the summer of 1247 by the king of France (Louis IX) who was accompanied by many prelates and dignitaries.[65] A number of pilgrims duly visited the shrine, particularly from England. They included Richard of Cornwall in 1247 and his brother, Henry III, who stopped off at the abbey in 1254 on his way to meet Louis IX. Henry had previously shown his support for the cult by sending a chasuble and chalice to Pontigny for the first celebration of the feast; he also granted money to maintain four candles around the saint's shrine.[66]

Relics from the Holy Land took on a new significance during the Crusades, especially in the thirteenth century, and several Cistercian houses acquired these holy objects from their founder or patron. Vale Royal (Cheshire), for example, was given a fragment of the Holy Cross by its founder, Edward I (1272–1307), who had reputedly taken this himself and worn it in the Holy Land.[67] Přemysl Otaker II (d. 1276), the founder of Zlatá Koruna (Crown of Gold) in southern Bohemia, presented his abbey with a spoke from the Crown of Thorns which he had allegedly received from Louis IX of France. The abbey was initially called 'Santa Corona Spinea' to commemorate its possession of this relic, but was later renamed.[68] As previously noted a portion of the Holy Blood given to Hailes by Edmund of Cornwall made this a leading centre of pilgrimage. Edmund was the son of the abbey's founder, Richard of Cornwall (d. 1272), and according to the chronicle of the house[69] Edmund had brought back the blood from Germany c. 1268 and deliberated over what he should do with it. Following his decision to go on crusade in the

---

[64] Vincent, *The Holy Blood*, p. 139 and see below for Pontigny and Hailes.

[65] C. H. Lawrence, 'Abingdon, Edmund of [St Edmund of Abingdon, Edmund Rich] (*c.* 1174–1240)', *ODNB*, vol. 1, pp. 103–6.

[66] Shead, 'Four Scottish Indulgences at Sens', 210.

[67] Denton, 'From the Foundation of Vale Royal Abbey', p. 125; *The Ledger Book of Vale Royal Abbey*, ed. J. Brownbill, Record Series of Lancashire and Cheshire, 68 (1914), no. 8 (pp. 9–10).

[68] Leroux-Dhuys, *Cistercian Abbeys*, p. 390; Zlatá Koruna Monastery website: www.zlatakoruna.cz/index.php?nid=1657&lid=EN&oid=204215 (accessed December 2010).

[69] This account is preserved in BL Cotton Cleopatra D. iii, fol. 73r, which dates to c. 1300; see Vincent, *The Holy Blood*, p. 137, note 2 and p. 140; and see M. N. Blount, 'A Critical Edition of the Annals of Hailes (MS Cotton Cleopatra D. iii, ff. 33–59v) with an Examination of their Sources', MA thesis, Manchester, 1974. A later version of the chronicle, post 1360, in BL MS Harley 3725, fols 13v–15r, is printed in Dugdale, *Monasticon*, V, 686–7.

spring of 1271 Edmund decided to divide the relic between his own foundation of Bonshommes Canons at Ashridge (London) and his father's Cistercian house at Hailes.[70] However, as Vincent stresses, for a cult to be successful it needed to be nurtured. The Hailes community actively promoted pilgrimage to the Holy Blood through the legend of its pedigree which Vincent has discussed in some detail. Suffice it to say this blended the real with the imaginary and alleged that the relic had passed to Charlemagne from the Roman Emperors and was given to Edmund by the 'lord of Doilaunde' who was guardian of 'Trivelensis' Castle (Trifels Castle, south of Mainz), where Edmund had played as a boy. The Hailes Blood accordingly enjoyed a more distinguished and credible pedigree than the Holy Blood of Westminster and enabled Edmund to evoke and perpetuate his father's connections with the Holy Roman Empire and with Charlemagne.[71]

Costly building work was undertaken at Hailes to construct a suitable shrine and at a ceremony in September 1270 Edmund formally handed over the relic to the abbots of Hailes and Winchcombe, who placed the phial in its new shrine behind the high altar.[72] Although the rebuilding of the east end was expensive the community recouped these costs from the large number of pilgrims who travelled to the shrine.[73] The popularity of the cult is attested to by Chaucer (d. 1400), who mentions the Holy Blood of Hailes in his 'Pardoner's Tale', and by the 'Life' of the mystic Margery Kempe (d. 1417), who visited the shrine on her return from pilgrimage in the Holy Land.[74] Writing c. 1515, Richard Pynson, a printer, claimed that a baker from Stone was able to support his family from the profits he made selling bread to pilgrims to Hailes Abbey between Whitsun and Corpus Christi.[75] Hailes remained one of the most attractive pilgrim sites in Britain until the Dissolution in the sixteenth century when the phial was taken to London and the contents pronounced to be

---

[70] In the event Edmund was called back from crusade owing to the murder of his older brother; Edmund duly became his father's sole heir: Vincent, *The Holy Blood*, p. 151.

[71] Vincent, *The Holy Blood*, pp. 72 and 137–53. Vincent maintains that previous suggestions that the blood was given to Edmund in the 1260s by the patriarch of Jerusalem are wrong, for whilst Urban IV reputedly supported the legend's acquisition from Germany and had in fact served as patriarch, his endorsement of the relic was given during his papacy: *ibid.*, p. 77.

[72] J. G. Coad, *Hailes Abbey*, English Heritage Guide, 2nd edn (London, 1993), pp. 22, 150.

[73] Winkless, *Hailes Abbey*, pp. 21–2.

[74] See Vincent, *The Holy Blood*, p. 197; Geoffrey Chaucer, 'The Pardoner's Tale', lines 651–2, in *The Riverside Chaucer*, ed. Larry Dean Benson, 3rd edn (Oxford 1987, repr. 2008), pp. 193–202 (p. 198); *The Book of Margery Kempe*, trans. B. A. Windeatt (Harmondsworth, 1985, rev. 1994), chapter 5, p. 148.

[75] Vincent, *The Holy Blood*, p. 197; J. C. T. Oates, 'Richard Pynson and the Holy Blood of Hayles', *The Library*, fifth series, 13 (1958), 266–77.

clarified honey with saffron. There had previously been allegations that the monks simply topped up the phial with duck blood.[76]

Both the Cistercian General Chapter and the papacy supported the promotion of the cult of the Holy Blood of Hailes. In 1275 the Chapter conceded that Hailes might hold an annual ceremony in honour of its relic and accorded this all the solemnities usually reserved for major church festivals.[77] Three years later Pope John XXI allegedly agreed that the community might engage two priests to serve the shrine who could offer penance and confession to pilgrims. By the end of the fifteenth century pilgrims were offered up to twenty-two days' remission of enjoined penances,[78] and everyone who visited on the feast of Corpus Christi was granted a further relaxation of seven years and two hundred and eighty days.[79] The Hailes example shows how together a community, its patron and the Order hosted, supported and promoted a cult which became a major pilgrim attraction.

In their efforts to promote a cult – and perhaps to claim a saint as their own – the Cistercians might manipulate his or her legend. Geens has argued that this was apparently the case at San Galgano, near Sienna, where a Cistercian abbey was founded in the early thirteenth century on the site formerly occupied by the hermit saint Galganus (d. 1181). The monastery possessed Galganus's head and in the late thirteenth century the monks commissioned a reliquary for this which depicted the saint's legend. Geens considers how the Cistercians reworked Galganus's legend visually on this reliquary and in written form in sixteenth- and seventeenth-century lives of the saint, to promote the hermit as one of their own. The later lives, for instance, claim that Galganus entered Paradise as a Cistercian. They describe how three Cistercian abbots who were returning from the General Chapter came upon Galganus's corpse at the time of his funeral and asked to clothe him in a Cistercian habit since this, they alleged, had been Galganus's wish during his life. Geens suggests that the same point is depicted visually on the earlier reliquary which focuses on the funeral scene and shows Galganus's corpse wearing a long-sleeved garment that is generally associated with the Cistercians; he is clothed in the same garb when entering Paradise and taking his place amongst the saints.[80] Geens thus argues that the monks of San Galgano

---

[76] Coad, *Hailes Abbey*, p. 22; Colin Platt, *The Abbeys and Priories of Medieval England* (London, 1984), p. 78; L. Butler and C. Given-Wilson, *Medieval Monasteries of Great Britain* (London, 1979), p. 258.

[77] Vincent, *The Holy Blood*, p. 137, citing Canivez, *Statuta*, III, 149 (1275: 69).

[78] Enjoined penance was imposed by a priest during the confessional process.

[79] Vincent, *The Holy Blood*, p. 138.

[80] F. Geens, 'Galganus and the Cistercians: Relics, Reliquaries, and the Image of a Saint', in *Images, Relics, and Devotional Practices in Medieval and Renaissance Italy*, Medieval and Renaissance Texts and Studies, 296, ed. S. J. Cornelison and S. B. Montgomery (Tempe, AZ, 2005), pp. 55–76.

gave Galganus's legend a Cistercian gloss to promote both his cult and the relic they possessed, but also, and importantly, to depict the saint as one of their own.

The Cistercians and mysticism

> ... enter I beg, the house of Simon the Pharisee and watch with how loving, how gentle, how pleasant, how merciful a face He looks upon the sinful woman prostrate on the ground. Watch what compassion He gives her those most holy feet to wash with tears of repentance, to dry with the hair which had hitherto been the tool of pride and wantonness, gently to kiss with her lips defiled by the filth of so many sins.[81]

A definition of mysticism is somewhat elusive and, as Gilson notes, it might be thought of 'in an endless variety of ways'.[82] Here it is understood as the 'contemplative experience of God', a temporary fusion of a human soul with the Divine which provides a brief but real experience of the Divine.[83] It is a foretaste of the heavenly bliss that awaits the soul in eternity. Thus Bernard of Clairvaux writes in sermon 52 on the Song of Songs:

> ... What do you think she [the soul] will receive there [in Heaven], when now [on earth] she is favoured with an intimacy so great as to feel herself embraced by the arms of God, cherished on the breast of God, guarded by the care and zeal of God lest she be roused from her sleep by anyone till she wakes of her own accord?[84]

Cistercian mysticism centred on devotion to the humanity of Christ which, as mentioned above, had been increasing in popularity from the late eleventh century. This was developed on three levels. First was the historical, which was the story of the Gospels and involved remembering Christ's life. Second was the allegorical level whereby Jesus was understood metaphorically through human images and mostly as the lover and the bridegroom; its 'story' was the Song of Songs. Third was the moral level which involved union with God in the flesh through consumption of Jesus in the Eucharist.[85]

---

[81] Aelred of Rievaulx, 'On Jesus at the Age of Twelve', trans. Berkeley, p. 33.
[82] Gilson, *Mystical Theology*, p. 119.
[83] See William of St Thierry, *The Golden Epistle*, p. 92, note 3 and McGinn, *The Growth of Mysticism*; Gilson, *Mystical Theology*, pp. 80, 89, 111. For an outline of Bernard of Clairvaux's theology on the soul's transition to perfection, see *ibid.*, pp. 99–118.
[84] Sermon 52: 2, in *Bernard of Clairvaux, Sermons on the Song of Songs*, trans. K. Walsh and I. Edmonds, 4 vols, Cistercian Fathers Series, 4, 7, 31, 40 (Kalamazoo, 1971–81), II, 49–57 (p. 51).
[85] See Dutton, 'Intimacy and Initiation', pp. 63–4.

Through meditation on the compassion and sufferings of Christ and by remembering[86] the Mysteries, it was held that the soul was moved to a more fervent love of God and prepared for divine union. This personal experience of 'God's abundant sweetness' (William of St Thierry) was actively sought[87] and was the consummation of one's earthly devotion to God which would only be perfectly realised after the resurrection of the body.[88] As previously noted, the Cistercians drew on human metaphors of love to describe the soul's intimate relationship with God. The soul, as the Bride, was wedded through love (*caritas*) to the Word (Christ) in a spiritual marriage.[89] Whilst Bernard of Clairvaux inspired the first Cistercian meditations on the humanity of Christ, Aelred of Rievaulx was one of the first actually to practise meditation on His life.[90] As Dutton explains, he alone 'lingers' on episodes in Christ's adult life; others pass from the Nativity to the Passion.[91] Aelred's treatise, 'On Jesus at the age of twelve', considers the historical, allegorical and moral meanings of the boy Jesus's three-day absence before Mary found him in the temple at Jerusalem. Aelred wonders how and where Jesus spent this time, who fed and clothed him and why he was seemingly unconcerned about his mother's grief. Aelred's allegorical interpretation equates Christ's physical growth with humanity's spiritual development:

> he advanced and grew up according to the flesh, in order that we who in spirit are little children, or rather almost nothing, might be born spiritually and, passing through the successive ages of the spiritual life grow up and advance. Thus His bodily progress is our spiritual progress and what we are told he did at each stage of his life is reproduced in us spiritually according to the various degrees of progress.[92]

Whereas Bernard of Clairvaux and others held that Jesus was separate and distinct from God and that to know Christ was a step towards knowing God, for Aelred they were one and the same and as Dutton explains, to kiss the feet of Christ was to behold the face of God.[93]

[86] Dutton (*ibid.*, pp. 60–2) underlines that Cistercian devotion to the humanity of Christ was intimate rather than imitative; the monks sought to act like Christ rather than to walk in his shoes.
[87] *Ibid.*, p. 57.
[88] Gilson, *Mystical Theology*, p. 89; J. Sommerfeldt, *Aelred of Rievaulx – Pursuing Personal Happiness* (Mahwah, 2005), p. 127.
[89] For further discussion see, for example, Brooke and Brooke, *Popular Religion*, pp. 141–5.
[90] *Ibid.*, p. 142.
[91] Dutton, 'Intimacy and Initiation', p. 42.
[92] Aelred of Rievaulx, 'On Jesus at the Age of Twelve', trans. Berkeley, p. 15.
[93] This is extensively discussed by Dutton in 'The Face and the Feet of God'.

Mystical writing

> What takes place between God and me I can feel but not express;
> when with you, on the contrary, I try to speak in a way that you will
> understand ... it is great and sublime, the virtue of humility which
> obtains the reality of what cannot be expressed, which alone teaches
> what cannot be taught.[94]

For Bernard of Clairvaux literature and mysticism were effectively insepa-
rable since he held that writing was inspired by a personal knowledge of
God. Words were not therefore for self-aggrandisement but a means to
glorify God and to affect the reader to a greater love and understanding
of the Divinity. Bernard thus declared it his intent to 'move hearts' rather
than to 'explain words' whilst Aelred of Rievaulx (d. 1167) hoped that his
works would offer 'seeds for meditation'. For Leclercq this 'detachment'
distinguished spiritual writing from other literature.[95] Gilson argues that
for the Cistercians the Song of Songs was 'the initiation *par excellence* into
the mystical life'.[96] But they were not the first or only ones to employ the
language of love and to offer an allegorical interpretation of this book.
The Victorines, for instance, similarly drew on bridal imagery and the
mystery of Redemption.[97] Still Bernard and his fellow Cistercians did
much to promote this imagery and fully developed the idea of spiritual
marriage, most notably with a collection of over two hundred and fifty
sermons on the Song of Songs. This was begun by St Bernard (d. 1153)
who wrote the first eighty-six sermons – 'his mystical masterpiece'[98] –
and continued by Gilbert of Hoyland (d. 1172) who compiled the next
forty-eight. John of Forde (d. 1214) wrote over one hundred and twenty
sermons to complete the collection.[99]

Aelred of Rievaulx shared his fellow Cistercians' ideas on humanity's
salvation through the love of Christ, but the role he accorded friendship
in the path to Divine union and his understanding of God as friendship
were distinctive, and, for McGinn, friendship was one of the most significant of the Cistercians' contributions to twelfth-century mysticism.[100]

---

94 Bernard of Clairvaux, final sermon on the Canticles, trans. in J. Leclercq, *The Love of Learning and the Desire for God: a Study of Monastic Culture* (New York, 1961; repr. 1982), pp. 268–9.
95 *Ibid.*, pp. 260–1, 264, 265. For McGinn, *The Growth of Mysticism*, p. 224, the emphasis on personal experience and on 'the book of life' distinguishes St Bernard and his companions and marks a significant contribution to twelfth-century mysticism.
96 Gilson, *Mystical Theology*, p. 70.
97 See Elder, 'Shadows on the Marian Wall', pp. 537–74 (pp. 556–62) for traditionalist Benedictines and for the 'liturgical and intellectual evolution' of Marian devotion at Canterbury where the feast of the conception of the Blessed Virgin was restored c. 1129.
98 McGinn, *The Growth of Mysticism*, p. 165.
99 Bernard of Clairvaux, *Sermons on the Song of Songs*; Gilbert of Hoyland, *Sermons on the Song of Songs*, ed. and trans. L. C. Braceland, 3 vols, Cistercian Fathers Series, 17, 20, 26 (Kalamazoo, 1978–9); John of Ford, *Sermons on the Final Verses of the Song of Songs*.
100 McGinn, *The Growth of Mysticism*, pp. 309–23, especially p. 317.

This doctrine is most fully worked out in Aelred's treatise 'On spiritual friendship', composed c. 1164×67, and set out as a Ciceronian dialogue.[101] Whilst Aelred drew on the Ancients, Patristic Fathers and the Bible, he surpassed his sources to produce an 'innovative theological exposition of human friendship' which showed how this could effect union with Christ on earth and lead to beatitude in the life hereafter.[102]

Devotion to the person of Christ prepared the soul for mystical union which might manifest itself in a sublime experience, a foretaste of eternal bliss. The following section considers the nature of these ecstasies and the rather ambiguous attitude to enraptured individuals whose eccentric and even shocking conduct might disrupt monastic observance and shake the community.

Mystical experiences

> Abundus was in this spiritual refectory, being fattened on the marrow of supreme sweetness and reading from the Book of Life a lesson containing the fullest and the best.[103]

When Abundus, a monk of Villers (Flanders), was about twenty-five years of age he yearned for a heavenly experience and prayed assiduously for this revelation. Fourteen days later, between Christmas and Epiphany, Abundus's devotion was rewarded. Whilst he was praying in the church around the hour of Terce 'the heavens opened before him' and Abundus was flooded with grace. He was transported to a state of ecstasy and beheld a glimpse of the Trinity; this wondrous sight filled Abundus with overwhelming joy and heavenly bliss. On this occasion and on others Abundus was so satiated by the spiritual fare he was unable to eat for several days. Whereas his brethren at Villers dined in the refectory, Abundus, 'drunk on Grace', feasted in his 'spiritual refectory' in the chapterhouse.[104] Abundus's experience incorporates a number of elements that recur in accounts of other ecstatic experiences, notably how the monk was nourished and even inebriated with spiritual joy which removed any need of or desire for food and drink. In some cases this prompted revulsion of physical fare. The 'Life' of Ida of Louvain, a thirteenth-century nun of Roosendaal (Flanders), records how 'bodily foods all became vile to her' on days when she received the sacrament. If Ida was forced to

---

[101] Aelred of Rievaulx, *Spiritual Friendship*, trans. L. C. Braceland, ed. and intro. M. Dutton, Cistercian Fathers Series, 5 (Collegeville, 2010), p. 22.
[102] See Dutton, intro. to *Spiritual Friendship*, pp. 25–6.
[103] Goswin of Bossut, 'Life of Abundus', chapter 6, in Cawley, *Send Me God*, p. 220.
[104] Goswin of Bossut, 'Life of Abundus', chapters 6 and 7, in Cawley, *Send Me God*, pp. 216–21.

swallow food at these times she would resist and experience 'tedium in doing so'.[105]

Ida, like a number of holy women at this time, was prone to ecstatic trances triggered by the Eucharist, often at its elevation.[106] At times Ida was affected by the sheer proximity of the Host, and, filled with spiritual delights, would swoon and collapse to the ground in its very presence.[107] The intensity of this heavenly experience wrought striking physical changes. Ida's eyes would glow like sunbeams while the ardour of love which inflamed her soul would cause her entire body to swell up and burst out of her clothing; sometimes she would have to remove her belt and garters to accommodate her expanding girth.[108] Ida of Nivelles (d. 1231), a nun of La Ramée (Flanders), was similarly affected by the Eucharist and reputedly trembled whenever she passed the reserved sacrament that was kept in the pyx.[109] Her near contemporary at La Ramée, Ida of Léau,[110] would keel over at the very sight of the Host and fall into ecstatic trances after receiving the Eucharist. On these occasions the nun was allegedly so 'full of God'[111] that she seemed to lose control over her body and entered an almost vegetative state – she was unable to stand, eat, speak or move and was immobilised, 'like someone dead'.[112]

This inability to control one's bodily functions might seem at odds with conventual life which taught its adherents to exercise mastery over their physical needs and desires. But these incidents should perhaps be understood as a shutting down of the body rather than a lack of discipline. The sublime spiritual experience effectively transported the soul beyond the mortal realm; as the 'Life' of Ida of Louvain writes, the 'bodily senses went dormant' or 'dozed off' while the mind was 'piloted by the Holy Spirit' and the contemplative gaze began 'to penetrate the hidden recesses of the heavenly mysteries'.[113]

Although this ecstatic behaviour was largely recognised as divinely inspired and prompted by a spiritual experience, it could nonetheless pose problems for communities who battled to deal with what was 'at

---

[105] Cawley, 'Life of Ida the Eager of Louvain', Book 3: 3c.
[106] Note that in Cistercian houses the Host was elevated at Mass pre-1210, earlier than in the Church *per se*: C. O'Dell, 'Ida of Léau: Woman of Desire', in Nichols and Shank, *Hidden Springs*, I, 415–43 (pp. 431–2), citing Canivez, *Statuta*, I, 369–75 (1214: 16).
[107] Cawley, 'Life of Ida the Eager of Louvain', Book 3: 9b.
[108] Cawley, 'Life of Ida the Eager of Louvain', e.g. Book 3: 9b and 21abc.
[109] Goswin of Bossut, 'Life of Ida of Nivelles', in Cawley, *Send Me God*, pp. 80–1. For further discussion see M. Cawley, 'Ida of Nivelles: Cistercian Nun', in Nichols and Shank, *Hidden Springs*, I, 305–21; Boudreau, 'With Desire Have I Desired', *ibid.*, pp. 323–44.
[110] This is old Gorsleeuw, near to modern Gors-Opleeuw. Cawley suggests that Ida entered La Ramée c. 1245 and died c. 1263; see his forthcoming edition of the 'Life' and also O'Dell, 'Ida of Léau'.
[111] See for example, Cawley, *Ida the Gentle of Léau*, 26a (p. 27).
[112] For example, *ibid.*, 26b, 30b, 31b, 49b and c (pp. 27, 31–2, 37–8, 51).
[113] Cawley, 'The Life of Ida the Eager of Louvain', Book 2: 11ab and 40a.

once spiritual and yet seemingly wanton'[114] – and was invariably disruptive to communal observance. The enraptured might erupt into hysterical laughter or cry out aloud, breaking the silence in the refectory or the church; or they might swoon before the high altar and bring the Mass to a standstill. This disorderly and at times shocking behaviour was difficult to tolerate and in 1261 the General Chapter ruled that those who were unable to receive the chalice in a fitting manner should be excluded from Communion.[115] Thus, even though the nuns of La Ramée regarded Ida of Léau as privy to divine knowledge, her extreme reaction to the Eucharist compelled them to ban her from receiving the sacrament in public.[116]

Not infrequently the community was split in its attitude to these mystics. At Roosendaal there were some who believed that Ida of Louvain's rapturous behaviour was prompted by her 'yearnings of vainglory'. Her biographer dismisses their 'malice' as the work of the devil but the account is an important reminder that for many this eccentricity was both perplexing and intolerable.[117] The brethren at Villers (Flanders) were similarly divided over their opinion of Arnulf (d. 1228), a lay brother of the house, who would break out into hysterical laughter and tap his feet on the ground, almost in a dance. Arnulf's biographer, Goswin of Bossut, explains that it was thought that this had started when Arnulf had a personal experience of the Trinity and recurred whenever the lay brother was flooded with grace, for example, if he heard a sermon on something joyous. Conversely, Arnulf fell into a gloom if he heard of the Passion or Hell. At times Arnulf's joy was so intense and his need to be in the church so great that he simply ran out of the chapter meeting. This was not only a serious breach of conduct but would invariably have disrupted proceedings and could not be condoned. According to Goswin, while some at Villers accepted that Arnulf was moved by spiritual reasons others regarded his jubilant laughter 'in an evil light'.[118]

Communal life could be equally problematic for the recipients of these ecstasies who might feel inhibited, constrained and unable to submit wholly to the experience in the presence of their brethren. Ida of Léau was acutely aware that her companions at La Ramée found her behaviour shocking and would therefore seek out a private corner where she could freely succumb to her ecstasies:

> She wished to be enclosed in solitude, in a place where she could be louder and more ardent in the groans and sobs her lamenting mind

---

[114] 'Life of Arnulf', Book 2: 7, in Cawley, *Send Me God*, p. 167.
[115] See O'Dell, 'Ida of Léau', p. 433.
[116] Cawley, *Ida the Gentle of Léau*, 19b–20a (pp. 19–20).
[117] Cawley, 'The Life of Ida the Eager of Louvain', Book 2: 32a to 33c.
[118] 'Life of Arnulf', Book 2, chapter 7, in Cawley, *Send Me God*, p. 168.

would offer to her Spouse and in the sighs of her vehement soul, a place where she could flex her limbs without shocking anyone, where she could conduct herself as her heart's desire might suggest.[119]

As previously noted, thirteenth-century mysticism was associated primarily with women who were particularly known for their devotion to the Eucharist and also to the Christ Child.[120] The two were often conflated. Once, at Mass, Ida of Nivelles saw the infant Jesus in a priest's arms instead of the Host.[121] The women might experience a very personal and direct encounter with Christ. A striking example concerns Ida of Léau. One Vigils, on a feast of Our Lady, Ida reputedly saw Mary while standing in the choir and watched as she carried the Christ Child in her arms with 'reverence and warm heartedness'. Mary then held out the child to Ida who took Him, 'lover to lover, bride to groom, maid to man'. But this presented Ida with a problem for it was her turn to sing a versicle in the choir and according to the rules of the Order she was required to wear the sleeves of her cowl down while singing. Ida feared that the infant would fall if she dropped her arms but was reluctant to defy the rules and dutifully lowered her arms. As she did so the infant clung to her neck and no harm was done. After Ida had finished singing she reputedly sat down with the child on her lap, a maternal and intimate image.[122]

Whilst many of the thirteenth-century female mystics were beguines, a number were Cistercian or influenced by the Order. Examples include Beatrice of Nazareth (d. 1268), a Cistercian nun of Florival (Bloemendaal) in Flanders, who was latterly the founding prioress of Nazareth (1237– 68).[123] Beatrice is best known for her treatise on the Seven Manners of Love[124] – or perhaps more correctly, 'experiences' of love[125] – which describes various stages in the mystical growth process and the soul's journey from exile on earth to its homeland in heaven.[126] Beatrice stands

---

[119]   Cawley, *Ida the Gentle of Léau*, 48a (p. 50).
[120]   See for example Boudreau, 'With Desire Have I Desired', and Bynum, *Jesus as Mother*, pp. 18, 162, 170–4, 184–5, 247–62 .
[121]   Cawley, intro. to 'The Life of Ida the Eager of Louvain'.
[122]   Cawley, *Ida the Gentle of Léau*, 37 (pp. 38–9).
[123]   From Florival Beatrice moved to Maagdendaal and finally settled at Nazareth; her father had founded both of these convents: M. A. Sullivan, 'An Introduction to the *Vita Beatrici*', *Hidden Springs*, I, 345–50 (pp. 345–6). For further discussion of Beatrice see, for example, R. de Ganck, *Beatrice of Nazareth in her Context*, 2 vols, Cistercian Studies Series, 121–2 (Kalamazoo, c. 1991); J. Kroll and B. S. Bachrach, *The Mystic Mind: the Psychology of Medieval Mystics and Ascetics* (New York/ Abingdon, 2005), pp. 146–60.
[124]   This is translated, for example, by R. de Ganck in his *Life of Beatrice of Nazareth*, Cistercian Fathers Series, 50 (Kalamazoo, 1991), pp. 289–331. See too E. Petroff's translation in her *Medieval Women's Visionary Literature* (Oxford, 1986), pp. 200–6.
[125]   See R. Bradley, 'Love and Knowledge in *Seven Manners of Loving*', *Hidden Springs*, I, 361–76 (p. 368).
[126]   Sullivan, '*Vita Beatrici*'; Bradley, 'Love and Knowledge'.

at the fountainhead of Flemish vernacular spirituality and is seen as a bridge between the Latin theologians such as St Bernard and vernacular mystics who include Eckhart.[127] Beatrice's own 'Life' was written by a confessor at Nazareth some five to ten years after her death and from notes she had kept in a journal.[128] It reveals the ecstatic highs and also the lows she experienced during her life and suggests that Beatrice initially placed great emphasis on asceticism and bodily mortification but later sought divine union, chiefly through prayer and contemplation.[129]

Elisabeth of Spalbeek (fl. 1246–1304) was seemingly a beguine but had links to the Cistercian Order and likely ended her life in their convent at Herkenrode, Liège, perhaps as a nun.[130] Moreover, her 'Life' was written by Abbot Philip of Clairvaux (1262–73), following his visit to the holy woman in 1266/67. Philip had apparently been struck by reports of Elisabeth's reception of the stigmata and visited her when he was at the nearby convent of Herkenrode. He subsequently wrote Elisabeth's biography – or rather, a *probatio* – to show that she merited canonisation and to verify her miracles and stigmata which he had himself seen.[131] Elisabeth's form of imitating Christ brought a new meaning to affective piety for she did not simply empathise with Him, imagining His pains and compassion, but physically played out the Passion, taking on the role of Jesus as well as of His persecutors. Moreover, each Friday Elisabeth would receive the stigmata and was probably the first known case since St Francis (d. 1226).[132] These re-enactments were performed before an audience and were evidently quite a spectacle. They were physical, highly emotional and often violent – on one occasion Elisabeth attempted to gouge out her eyes. But for Philip of Clairvaux and others these 'mesmerising performances' were 'a powerful sign of God's Grace'.[133]

---

[127] Sullivan, '*Vita Beatrici*', p. 355.

[128] *Ibid.*, pp. 345–6.

[129] Kroll and Bachrach, *The Mystic Mind*, pp. 146–60.

[130] See J. N. Brown, *Three Women of Liège: a Critical Edition of and Commentary on the Middle English Lives of Elizabeth of Spalbeek, Christina Mirabilis and Marie d'Oignies* (Turnhout, 2008), p. 2; J. Njus, 'The Politics of Mysticism: Elisabeth of Spalbeek and her Context', *Church History* 77 (2008), 285–317 (pp. 291, 296–7). Although Elisabeth is traditionally thought of as being a beguine, Brown suggests that her way of life was perhaps more similar to an anchoress – indeed she had a cell attached to the church at Spalbeek.

[131] Brown, *Three Women of Liège*, especially pp. 5, 191–2, 196–7; Njus, 'The Politics of Mysticism', 292.

[132] See Brown, *Three Women of Liège*, pp. 2, 191–217; K. Silen, 'Elisabeth of Spalbeek: Dancing the Passion', in *Women's Work: Making Dance in Europe before 1800*, ed. L. M. Brooks (Madison, Wisconsin, 2007), pp. 207–27; S. Rodgers and J. E. Ziegler, 'Elizabeth of Spalbeek's Trance Dance of Faith: a Performance Theory Interpretation from Anthropological and Art Historical Perspectives', *Performance and Transformation – New Approaches to Late Medieval Spirituality*, ed. M. Sydam and J. Ziegler (New York, 1999), pp. 299–355.

[133] Njus, 'The Politics of Mysticism', 286.

Doubts, fears and crises of faith

Daily life in the cloister was structured around private and corporate devotion, and spirituality was, of course, the basis and rationale of monastic life. Yet the monks and nuns were susceptible to doubts, fears and crises of faith. Gerald of Wales (d. c. 1220) claimed that he knew of two Cistercians who had turned to Judaism and fled 'to the synagogue of Satan'. One had been a monk of Garendon in Leicestershire.[134] More common were feelings of uncertainty about salvation and concerns as to whether one was worthy of heaven. One lay brother of the Order allegedly threw himself into a fish pond as he had given up all hope of salvation, whilst a nun who was suddenly afflicted with doubts attempted to drown herself in the River Moselle.[135]

Chapter five discussed how visits from the dead who could testify to the heavenly rewards of the devout might allay the brethren's fears of the afterlife and encourage them to persevere in claustral life. Stories recounting the fate of reprobates and apostates were similarly circulated as incentives to listeners to adhere to the rules and as warnings to would-be detractors. They include the tale of Walter, an illiterate lay brother of Melrose Abbey, Scotland, who was tempted by the devil to study and learn the Old Law. This led him to doubt his own faith and to consider becoming a Jew. Walter said nothing to anyone else of his uncertainties and for seven years he lived at Melrose 'under the habit of religion'. Walter was later prompted to reconsider when he experienced a horrific vision. This showed him the rewards of the faithful and the fate of non-believers; fearing the latter Walter decided to reconfirm his faith. Walter remained at Melrose until his death and reputedly wrote eloquent verse in the vernacular.[136]

Exempla, *moralia* and visitations from the dead were all effective ways of bolstering the brethren and assuaging their doubts. But the support and encouragement they received from other members of the community were perhaps most significant in fortifying the monks and helping them progress on their heavenly journey.

---

134 Gerald of Wales, *Speculum Ecclesiae*, in *Giraldi Cambrensis Opera*, ed. J. S. Brewer, J. F. Dimock and G. F. Warner, 8 vols, RS 21 (London, 1861–91), IV, 139–40.
135 Caesarius of Heisterbach, *Dialogus Miraculorum*, Book 2, chapter 6, and Book 4, chapter 40, Scott and Bland, *Dialogue on Miracles*, II, 240–1; I, 237–9.
136 McFadden, 'An Edition and Translation of the Life of Waldef', pp. 170–6 (trans. pp. 322–8).

CHAPTER SEVEN

Conversi, granges and the Cistercian economy

Monks of our Order should derive their means of subsistence from the work of their hands, from farming, and from animal husbandry. Accordingly we too are permitted to own for our own use streams and lakes, forests, vineyards, meadows, land distant from populated places, and animals other than those which more ordinarily provoke curiosity and show vanity rather than serve any useful purpose – such as deer, cranes and others of this sort. In order to operate, cultivate, and administer all these, whether close at hand or at a distance – though not farther off than a one-day journey – we may have granges, which are to be managed by lay brothers.[1]

The monastery's survival depended on the development of a sound economy to support the community's needs. The Cistercians are typically regarded as great accumulators of land and able agriculturalists who were efficient if at times aggressive in exploiting their holdings. Even those who were critical of the Order's practices acknowledged its effectiveness. The satirical account of the Cistercians by Walter Map (d. c. 1210) describes how they would secure a plot of valueless land from a rich donor 'by much feigning of innocence and long importunity, putting in God at every other word' and duly convert this into a productive unit:

> The wood is cut down, stubbed up and levelled into a plain, bushes give place to barley, willows to wheat, withies to vines. ... and so all the whole earth is full of their possessions; and though the gospel does not permit them to take thought for the morrow, they have such a reserve of wealth accruing from their care that they could enter the ark in the same spirit of security as Noah who had nothing left outside to look to.[2]

The picture painted by Walter and other critics of the Order has coloured the historical reputation of the Cistercians as pioneers – somewhat ruthlessly – growing rich through acquisitiveness and the extension of cultivable land.[3] Research suggests, however, that the situation was rather more

---

[1]   'Institutes of the General Chapter', no. 5, *NLT*, p. 459.
[2]   Walter Map, *De Nugis Curialium: Courtiers' Trifles*, ed. and trans. M. R. James, rev. edn C. N. L. Brooke and R. A. B. Mynors, OMT (Oxford, 1983), pp. 75, 87.
[3]   See also Archbishop John Pecham's letter to Edward I, 1284, on behalf of Bishop Aniane of St Asaph, objecting to the proposed transfer of Cistercian monks from Aberconwy (Bangor) to Maenan (St

complex. The early Cistercians may have transformed the landscape by bringing wasteland into cultivation, clearing forests and draining marshland; and likewise monks who acquired desolate border lands or expanded into northern England where areas were still barren after the 'Harrying of the North'.[4] Elsewhere there was often little unsettled land available and communities had to adapt their economic practices according to the local environment. It is therefore important to understand each house in its context and, as Oram urges, to acknowledge the Order's 'flexibility in approach', for there was a variety of ways in which monasteries reacted with their landscape.[5] Thus, whilst Berman has shown that in southern France the Cistercians developed a successful economy through reorganising settled holdings and managing these efficiently, recent analysis of the Galician monastery of Santa Mariá de Montederramo (Orense) suggests that this abbey was as much a distributor as an accumulator of land, and accrued power chiefly though engaging in local networks and participating in an exchange of goods and services with the community.[6] Further, although the Cistercian economy was land based, monasteries drew income from tolls and engaged in the market. Houses sold their surplus to purchase products they could not provide for themselves and also produced for profit. A notable example is the export of wool, chiefly associated with the Cistercians in Yorkshire. These and other aspects of the Order's economy are discussed later in the chapter to assess the nature and distinctiveness of the Cistercian economy. Before doing so it is important to consider the identity and role of the lay brethren (*conversi*) who were the backbone of the Order's economic structure from the twelfth century until their demise in the late thirteenth century.

Asaph), cited in J. S. Donnelly, 'Changes in the Grange Economy of English and Welsh Abbeys 1300–1540', *Traditio* 10 (1954), 399–458 (p. 409): 'For where they plant their foot they destroy villages, take away tithes and curtail by their privileges the power of the prelacy.'

4   For further discussion see, for instance, C. Berman, *Medieval Agriculture, the Southern French Countryside and the Early Cistercians. A Study of Forty-three Monasteries*, Transactions of the American Philosophical Society, new series 76: 5 (Philadelphia, 1986), especially pp. 11–30; and R. Oram, 'Holy Frontiersmen: Twelfth- and Early Thirteenth-century Monastic Colonisation and Socio-economic Change in Poland and Scotland', in *Britain and Poland-Lithuania: Contact and Comparison from the Middle Ages to 1795*, ed. R. Unger (Leiden, 2008), pp. 103–21. The evidence for the Yorkshire Cistercians is complex, as historians have been divided as to the nature and extent of Domesday 'waste' and its relationship to the 'Harrying'; see Burton, *Monastic Order in Yorkshire*, especially pp. 216–76, and R. A. Donkin, 'Settlement and Depopulation on Cistercian Estates during the Twelfth and Thirteenth Centuries, especially in Yorkshire', *Bulletin of the Institute of Historical Research* 33 (1960), 141–65, and 'The Cistercian Grange in England in the 12th and 13th Centuries, with special reference to Yorkshire', *Studia Monastica* 6 (1964), 95–144.

5   Oram, 'Holy Frontiersmen', especially p. 120.

6   Berman, *Medieval Agriculture*; E. Pascua, 'Vassals and Allies in Conflict: Relations between Santa Maria de Montederramo and Local Galician Society in the Thirteenth Century', in *Beyond the Market: Transactions, Property and Social Networks in Monastic Galicia, 1200–1300*, ed. R. Pastor (Leiden, 2002), pp. 25–106. See below, pp. 166–77.

The lay brothers

> Having spurned this world's riches, behold! The new soldiers of Christ, poor with the poor Christ, began discussing by what planning, by what device, by what management they would be able to support themselves in this life, as well as their guests who came, both rich and poor, whom the Rule commands to welcome as Christ. It was then that they enacted a definition to receive, with their bishop's permission, bearded lay brothers, and to treat them as themselves in life and death – except that they may not become monks – and also hired hands; for without the assistance of these they did not understand how they could fully observe the precepts of the Rule day and night.[7]

The decision to introduce a lay brotherhood was made when the Order was expanding, within twenty years of the foundation of Cîteaux. It became apparent that systemised help was necessary to enable the monasteries to exploit their holdings directly and free up the monks for their liturgical duties. The Cistercians were not the first to engage lay brothers, but they were the first to make these men an integral part of the Order and to draw up a comprehensive customary for their organisation. This was the *Usus Conversorum*, and although the date of its compilation is not known Waddell speculates that the earliest version must have been put together in the 1120s and modified over the years. He believes that the text we now have is a remnant of a larger and longer treatise; hence the focus on the *conversi*'s pastoral duties, that is animal husbandry, and an almost absence of agricultural work.[8]

The lay brothers took vows of obedience and were required to carry out some liturgical duties, but their day was focused on the workplace rather than the cloister and most of their devotions were celebrated there. They were responsible for managing the land, tending livestock, engaging in industrial activities and conducting business on behalf of the monastery, thereby shielding the monks (or nuns) from secular affairs. The distinction in function between the two groups was underlined by official legislation which forbade lay brothers to be literate – or at least anyone who was literate was not to exercise this skill and was forbidden to read from books lest this led to errors and heresies.[9] The lay brothers were also

---

[7] 'The First Cistercians', from the *Exordium Parvum*, NLT, p. 435.
[8] *Cistercian Lay-Brothers: Twelfth-Century Usages with Related Texts*, ed. C. Waddell, Cîteaux: Commentarii Cistercienses, Studia et documenta, 10 (Brecht, 2000), pp. 51–78 (Latin edition), pp. 164–95 (English translation); for the dating of the customary see *ibid.*, pp. 20–1. Berman, however, argues for a later date – c. 1160 – and holds that the fact it concentrates on pastoral work is because at this time the lay brethren were not involved in agricultural work: see C. Berman, 'Distinguishing between the Humble Cistercian Lay Brother and Sister, and the Converted Knight in Southern France', in Jamroziak and Burton, *Religious and Laity in Western Europe*, pp. 278–9.
[9] *Usus Conversorum*, chapter 9, in Waddell, *Cistercian Lay Brothers*, p. 182.

set apart from the monks by their appearance. They wore work clothes and boots rather than habits, and were not tonsured but had fringes and beards.[10] Moreover, as noted in chapter 3, the two groups occupied different parts of the precinct with the *conversi* having a dormitory and refectory on the western range and choir stalls in the nave of the church, which were divided from the monks' choir by the rood screen.

The lay brothers effectively formed a separate community which ran in tandem but parallel to the choir monks, and indeed the one was not to be seen as a stepping stone to the other: far from it. Early legislation stipulated that anyone who entered the Order as a lay brother should remain as such and was not to become a monk.[11] There were, however, exceptions such as the lay sister of Yesse, near Groningen, who was in 1425 permitted to become a choir nun of the house providing that she learnt Latin.[12] Despite the differences – and even barriers – that separated the monks and the lay brothers there is evidence that in some cases they forged close bonds. A notable example is the friendship that developed between Simon (d. 1229), a renowned lay brother and visionary of Aulne who was duly beatified, and Conrad, a monk of the abbey who was subsequently abbot of Villers (1209–14), Clairvaux and Cîteaux, and was ultimately made a cardinal. Friendship between the two was cemented when they were caught up in a storm while travelling together on abbey business. Conrad retained a high regard for Simon, and, as abbot of Villers, he was sympathetic to Simon's contemporary, Arnulf the wagoneer.[13] Another example is the relationship between Alexander, a monk of Stratford Langthorne, and a lay brother of the house, whose pact is described in chapter 5.[14] There was clearly some opportunity for monks and lay brothers to mingle and for friendships to be formed, although this was perhaps less common amongst choir monks than monastic office holders who had greater occasion to travel on business with the *conversi* and to work alongside them when exercising their administrative duties.

[10] See Constable's discussion on the significance of beards and tonsures in his introduction to *Apologiae Duae: Gozechini Epistola ad Walcherum: Burchardi, ut Videtur, Abbatis Bellevallis Apologia de Barbis*, Corpus Christianorum, Continuatio Mediaevalis, 62, ed. R. B. C. Huygens (Turnhout, 1985), pp. 47–130, especially pp. 126–30.

[11] 'Early Capitula', no. 22, *NLT*, p. 412.

[12] G. de Moor, 'Cistercian Laybrothers and Laysisters in Frisia and Holland', *Cistercian Studies Quarterly* 27:4 (1992), 329–39 (pp. 335, 332); Canivez, *Statuta*, IV, 298–9 (1425: 73). Although James France, *Cistercians in Scandinavia*, pp. 120, 145–6, infers from the Øm chronicle that Abbot Thorkil (1199–1216) had been a lay brother of the house before he became a monk, it seems that the use of *conversus* here refers to Thorkil's entry as an adult convert; Janet Burton notes a similarly ambiguous use of *conversus* in the Byland chronicle (Burton, *Foundation History of Byland and Jervaulx*, pp. xxix, 11; *Monastic Order in Yorkshire*, p. 156). The passage in question appears in chapter 36 of the chronicle, see *Exordium Monasterii Carae Insulae*, chapter 36 (p. 193).

[13] Cawley, *Send Me God*, pp. 3; 14; and Goswin of Bossut, 'Life of Arnulf', p. 139.

[14] See above, p. 123.

Still, in many cases the two groups would have remained separate and segregated with little opportunity for interaction.

On the same lines as the male *conversi*, lay sisters were introduced into some houses to assist with the daily running of the monastery. They are less well recorded than their male counterparts, and the prescriptive texts of the Order do not legislate about them in the same way as for the *conversi*. However, there are some glimpses in the documentary records of their presence and their activities. Fifteenth- and sixteenth-century records from the convent of Leeuwenhorst (Holland), for instance, reveal that there the lay sisters were drawn primarily from the middle ranks of society whereas the nuns were from the higher ranks. The number of lay sisters engaged varied considerably. Whereas at Leeuwenhorst there were never more than nine lay sisters to serve a community of thirty nuns – and only one or two in the late sixteenth century – at Loosduinen the lay sisters outnumbered the nuns in the mid-sixteenth century. In some cases these lay sisters were attached to male houses where they might tend to nuns who stayed overnight at the monastery or help with important tasks such as the Maundy of children and the collection of rents.[15]

Who were the lay brothers?

> For book he had his conscience, for teacher the Holy Spirit; and reading in the book of experience he grew day by day in the knowledge of holy things, having even the spirit of revelation.[16]

The question of who precisely joined Cistercian abbeys as lay brothers is not always easy to determine, although it is likely that they were frequently recruited from the neighbourhood. This was seemingly the case in southern France where most of the identifiable *conversi* – and also the monks – came from the locality; Berman suggests that their experience and knowledge of the area contributed significantly to the Cistercians' success in exploiting the landscape and in entering and negotiating the land market.[17] In Scandinavia and other places where monasteries were settled by a foreign monastic community, the divisions between monks and *conversi* would have been heightened by nationality.[18]

Berman has recently argued that the very term *conversus* seems to have undergone a change in meaning in accordance with changes in Cistercian economic practice. In traditional Benedictine parlance a *conversus* meant an adult recruit to the monastic life, as opposed to a child oblate. Berman

---

[15]   de Moor, 'Cistercian Laybrothers and Laysisters', 334–5, 338.
[16]   This describes Sinnulph, a twelfth-century lay brother of Fountains: *Memorials of Fountains*, I, 118.
[17]   Berman, *Medieval Agriculture*, p. 35.
[18]   See France, *Cistercians in Scandinavia*, p. 148, for the situation in Denmark.

maintains that within a Cistercian context *conversi* initially referred to adult converts to the lay brotherhood, who were often members of the knightly classes and thus men of standing, but the term was gradually applied to agricultural labourers; in between the term might refer to peasants who worked in a pastoral capacity, whether as shepherds, cowherds, millers or smiths.[19] She would thus posit that initially the lay brothers were brought in to carry out pastoral duties but as the economic situation changed they took on agricultural work. In some cases the lay brothers were peasants whose lands had been acquired by the abbey.[20] James France suggests that the group of men from Ørslev Vestre (Denmark) who joined Sorø as lay brothers in the mid-thirteenth century were probably peasants who had been evicted from their lands by the monastery. A few were men of means such as Oluf Kviter, who joined the Danish abbey of Øm as a lay brother and became master of its grange at Tåning; Olaf granted the monastery his property at Hagetued which included woods, a house, animals and land.[21] Peasants who gave up their lands to the abbey and enrolled as lay brothers did not necessarily do so against their will but acted voluntarily, believing that *conversi* status offered better labour conditions as well as salvation. The benefits were not insignificant and, as Berman explains, in return for transferring their lands to the monastery they could continue to work in the same capacity as before whilst receiving security in this life and the next. The attraction of life as a *conversus* would have been heightened in periods of economic boom, when land was in short supply – and the twelfth century was such a time. Berman cites the example of a lay brother who entered the southern French abbey of Valmagne in 1161 and settled in a shepherd's hut where he made cheese.[22] Noell similarly underlines the appeal of the lay brotherhood and how this drew not only the rural peasantry but the bourgeoisie and the emerging urban proletariat. He argues that the *conversi* esteemed and guarded the privileges they considered their due and that later, when they felt that these benefits were being thwarted by the monastic hierarchy, they openly resisted.[23]

In 1188 the General Chapter ruled that from then on nobles should not become lay brothers but must join the Order as monks.[24] This would suggest that from at least the late twelfth century lay brothers and monks were distinguished by standing. However, it was rather more complex

---

19 Berman, 'Distinguishing between the Humble Cistercian Lay Brother and Sister'.
20 See below, pp. 169–70, for the eviction of peasant communities.
21 France, *Cistercians in Scandinavia*, pp. 147, 270.
22 Berman, 'Distinguishing between the Humble Cistercian Lay Brother and Sister', p. 277.
23 B. Noell, 'Expectation and Unrest among Cistercian Lay Brothers in the Twelfth and Thirteenth Centuries', *Journal of Medieval History* 32 (2006), 253–74.
24 *Twelfth-Century Statutes*, p. 151 (1188: 5).

than that, for the nobility continued to enrol as lay brothers, albeit in smaller numbers[25] – and there is reputedly an instance of a royal *conversus*.[26] Further, it was not uncommon for members of the same family to join as both monks and lay brothers. Examples include Bernard, a lay brother of Gimont, Gascony, whose father and uncle were monks of the house; and a cantor of the Danish monastery of Løgum whose brother was a lay brother of the abbey.[27] In these and other cases literacy was perhaps the key factor which determined whether the recruit entered as a monk or *conversus*, but they highlight the diversity of backgrounds and means of the men who became Cistercian lay brothers. The *conversi* were not simply humble peasants but might be substantial landholders or members of the knightly ranks. Moreover, they came with quite differing life experience: one recruit had previously been an acrobat and allegedly showed his devotion to Mary by secretly performing moves in her honour.[28] Evidence from the Dutch houses from the late thirteenth century to the fifteenth century reveals that occasionally monastery servants became lay brothers and sisters of the house, although this may not have been widespread. Examples include a husband and wife who were servants of the convent at Leeuwenhorst; and a 'reliable and devoted servant' of Warmond who after twenty-five years of service to the house took vows to become a lay brother there. He is described as being of noble birth.[29]

Some of the lay brethren were relatively powerful figures before they joined the Order and others rose to prominence through their work for the monastery and the prestige that this accorded them. Their expertise and skill might lead to their being engaged, temporarily, by secular and ecclesiastical powers, frequently as almoners. But they might serve as envoys, artisans or advise on construction work.[30]

By the mid-late twelfth century a sense of monastic superiority had developed and the lay brothers were often considered an inferior community. They might be marginalised and accorded fewer rights and privileges.

[25] Kinder, *Cistercian Europe*, p. 308, notes that in the twelfth and thirteenth centuries about fifty knights became lay brothers at Himmerod.
[26] According to Alberic of Trois Fontaine, Alexander (d. 1229) was a son of the king of Scots and died as a lay brother of Foigny in 1229; Alberic also refers to Alexander's sister, Matilda of Lappion, who died in 1220, see *Early Sources of Scottish History 500 to 1286*, collected and trans. A. O. Anderson, 2 vols (Edinburgh 1922, repr. Stamford, 1990), II, 444, 470. The identity of this Alexander is, however, problematic and as Richard Oram explains (personal communication) there are problems with the chronology; whilst there could be a link via Alexander I's illegitimate children, little is now known about that line's descent.
[27] Berman, 'Distinguishing between the Humble Cistercian Lay Brother and Sister', pp. 274–5; France, *Cistercians in Scandinavia*, p. 148.
[28] See Rubin, *Mother of God*, p. 128.
[29] de Moor, 'Cistercian Laybrothers and Laysisters', 333, 336.
[30] See Williams, *Cistercians in the Early Middle Ages*, p. 86.

For instance the *conversi* were not permitted to participate in the election of abbots, they might be subjected to more severe punishments than the choir monks and have poorer facilities at their disposal.[31] This differentiation seemingly prompted the *conversi*-led rebellions and acts of resistance that are documented both in the General Chapter's statutes and in local records. However, as Cassidy-Welch notes, it is often unclear whether these were serious or minor offences, rumblings or full-scale revolts.[32] One of the earliest known cases of a *conversi*-rebellion took place c. 1168 at Schönau, near Heidelberg. It centred on boots. At Schönau it had been customary for both the monks and the lay brothers to receive new boots each year until one abbot withheld this boon from the *conversi* since he found them 'delighting in this rash arrogance'. The lay brothers were angered at their loss and the fact that the monks continued to receive their boots. They duly retaliated and significantly struck out at the monks whose boots they destroyed when the monks were celebrating the Office in church.[33] Several incidents of *conversi* violence were sparked off by the prohibition of ale on the abbey granges, and some resulted in brutality and even bloodshed. When in 1206 the abbot of Margam, Wales, banned ale at the abbey's granges the lay brothers attacked him as well as their cellarer; they then barricaded themselves inside the monks' dormitory and refused to give the brethren any food.[34] Noell has recently suggested that these outbreaks of violence were not simply caused by the *conversi* feeling oppressed but that their main concern – and the chief motive behind these actions – was to prevent their ambitions from being frustrated by the monastic hierarchy.[35]

What did they do?
Just as the identity of the lay brothers varied, so the work that they carried out both within the precinct and on the monastery's holdings was diverse. The *conversi* are typically associated with pastoral and agricultural work. They laboured alongside hired workers to develop and manage the granges and tend the abbey's livestock; they might carry out industrial work such as metallurgy, and negotiate with merchants and traders.[36] Many would have brought with them knowledge and experience that they could then use on the monastery's behalf. The lay brother

[31] For further discussion see Noell, 'Expectation and Unrest' and Cassidy-Welch, *Monastic Spaces*, pp. 167–93.
[32] Cassidy-Welch, *Monastic Spaces*, pp. 180–4.
[33] This is reported by Conrad of Eberbach in his *Exordium Magnum*, IV, 10, cited in Noell, 'Expectation and Unrest', 271.
[34] Canivez, *Statuta*, I, 324 (1206: 23).
[35] Noell, 'Expectation and Unrest'.
[36] See below, pp. 177–86, for further discussion.

of Pipewell Abbey (Nottinghamshire) who in 1278 painted glass windows for Rockingham Castle is likely to have been a glazier before he joined the community.[37] The necrology of the fifteenth-century Dutch monastery at Warmond lists seventy lay brothers who belonged to the abbey or to one of its affiliated houses and sheds light on the various jobs that they carried out in the later Middle Ages. It describes *conversi* who were cooks, carpenters, brewers and cowherds; who made cloth for the community, tended the orchards and bees, went to market and acted as porters. One lay brother allegedly had a good knowledge of medicine which he used to serve the community well. The list reveals that some of these men had been lay brothers for many years. One had reputedly looked after the monastery's guests for over sixty years.[38]

Although the monks and lay brothers were generally differentiated by function, the boundaries were not absolute. A few *conversi* undertook skilful artistic work and carried out tasks more frequently associated with monks. They include a lay brother of Løgum (Denmark) who copied the *Aurora*[39] of Peter of Riga, and Ulrich, a fifteenth-century *conversus* of Maulbronn, who was responsible for the vault and wall paintings in the nave of his church. Ulrich's pictures brought colour to the abbey and included the Adoration of the Magi and a depiction of Maulbronn's founder, Walter, being received into the house as a lay brother.[40]

The *conversi* were to act as a link between the monastery and the outside world, and by negotiating on the monks' behalf they helped to shield them from the disruption of external affairs. Their role as mediators is usually thought of in terms of managing the estates, carrying messages and trading at market. Yet they sometimes exercised a more pastoral role that involved counselling the laity and even influencing recruitment to the Order. This is not perhaps surprising given that the lay brothers were more mobile and more accessible to the outside world than the choir monks and had greater opportunity to mix with the public. A well-known example of a *conversus* advising the laity is Sinnulph, a twelfth-century lay brother of Fountains Abbey (Yorkshire), who was responsible for counselling the knight Ralph Haget to take the Cistercian habit c. 1170. According to the thirteenth-century foundation history of Fountains, Ralph had been discontent with his military life and actively

---

[37] R. Marks, *Stained Glass in England During the Middle Ages* (London, 1993), p. 40. Marks notes that in the thirteenth century most glass painters in England were laymen; the *conversus* of Pipewell is thus something of an exception.

[38] de Moor, 'Cistercian Laybrothers and Laysisters', 336–7.

[39] A versification of parts of the Bible.

[40] France, *Cistercians in Scandinavia*, p. 148; Anstett, *Maulbronn Monastery*, pp. 13, 32. The Gothic revamp of the building in the late fifteenth century was overseen by another lay brother, Berthold, who was a master builder.

sought out Sinnulph to pray with him and discuss his decision to become a monk of Fountains. Following his meetings with the lay brother Ralph decided to enter Fountains and later presided as abbot of the house.[41] There are other examples of lay brothers being approached by members of the public for advice and spiritual support. Simon (d. 1229), a visionary and grangemaster of Aulne (Flanders), was known for his prophecies and duly visited by the laity who were eager to hear his visions. But there were seemingly restrictions on Simon's powers on account of his lay-brother status and concern as to what was deemed appropriate behaviour for one of his standing, for his biographer was keen to underline that Simon never attempted to interpret his visions; he was a receptacle and simply conveyed the information to which he was privy.[42] Simon's counterpart at Villers, Arnulf (d. 1228), was a wagoneer and was similarly sought out by the laity who in some cases were sent to him by his abbot, William of Brussels (1221–37). According to Arnulf's 'Life', compiled by a monk of Villers, Abbot William sent noblemen to the grange where Arnulf was based that they might consult with him. The 'Life' reveals that in his capacity as wagoneer Arnulf distributed alms and visited the abbey's 'welfare clients' to whom he offered words of consolation as well as food. His rather liberal generosity was a matter of concern to some members of the community who believed in the need to economise, and Arnulf was duly removed to another grange.[43]

Change and demise

The lay brotherhood was primarily a workforce that was engaged to facilitate the direct exploitation of Cistercian lands and to spare the monks from secular affairs. But as we have seen, the *conversi*'s role was much more diverse. Further, their function and status changed as the world around them evolved. A shift in attitude to the management of property and the growing tendency to lease out lands had a particularly marked impact on their role and position and led to a significant decline in their numbers, although it is often difficult to know exactly how many lay brothers there were at any given time and to what extent this varied from house to house. This fall in *conversi* numbers was often reflected in the architectural arrangements. At Øm (Denmark), for example, the nave

---

[41] *Memorials of Fountains*, I, 117–20, 123. Ralph presided over the abbey from 1190 to 1203. Prior to this he was abbot of Kirkstall, now in Leeds. The fact that the Haget family had links with Fountains no doubt influenced Ralph's decision to choose Fountains; for the Hagets as benefactors of Fountains see J. Wardrop, *Fountains Abbey and its Benefactors, 1132–1300*, Cistercian Studies Series, 91 (Kalamazoo, 1987), p. 207.

[42] On Simon see Cawley, intro. to *Send Me God*, pp. 17–18.

[43] Goswin of Bossut, 'Life of Arnulf'; see, for example, Books 2: 1, 2 and 3, in Cawley, *Send Me God*, pp. 153–9. The phrase 'welfare client' is Newman's (*ibid.*, p. xl).

of the church, consecrated in 1257, had only one bay, whilst there were just two in the new nave at Vitskøl (Denmark) in 1287. The fact that the Vitskøl bays did not join up with the western range suggests that there were not enough lay brothers to make this worthwhile.[44]

The mid-thirteenth century was effectively the highpoint of *conversi* power but the end of the century saw their demise in most places, although the pace of change varied from country to country. In Germany, for instance, the lay brothers remained the stalwart of the Cistercian economy until the mid-fourteenth century.[45] According to Donnelly, Boniface VIII's bull of 1302 struck the critical blow to the lay brotherhood.[46] This extended the Order's exemption from tithes to all lands from which they had not previously been collected, no matter the method of cultivation, and precipitated the wide-scale leasing out of granges and lands.[47] The impact on the number and role of the *conversi* was profound and lay brothers in Flanders complained that they were effectively 'redundant' as a consequence.[48] Most of the *conversi* were unable to oppose these changes but a few actively sought to defend their prerogatives against the leasing out of lands. They included the lay brothers of Ter Doest, Flanders, who in 1308 were led by their fellow *conversus* William of Saeftingen to mount a resistance. William was a prominent figure within the locality having risen to power following the Battle of Courtrai in 1302 where he fought alongside the local Flemish nobility to defeat Philip the Fair's troops. The lay brothers' rebellion resulted in bloodshed and during the fracas William killed the cellarer of Ter Doest and wounded the abbot. Yet William suffered little damage to his reputation or his position within the community as a consequence. Indeed, on account of his standing in the locality William received the protection of the citizens of Bruges and after completing a pilgrimage to Jerusalem he was absolved by the Church. William duly returned to Ter Doest and assumed a position of responsibility.[49]

The decline in the number of *conversi* was exacerbated by the Black Death in the mid-fourteenth century. From this time onwards it was no longer the case that lay brothers outnumbered monks by two or even three to one. By the end of the Middle Ages there was merely a handful of *conversi*. Figures for the Yorkshire abbey of Meaux illustrate the severity of

---

[44] France, *Cistercians in Scandinavia*, pp. 155–6.
[45] Noell, 'Expectation and Unrest', 273–4.
[46] J. Donnelly, *The Decline of the Medieval Cistercian Laybrotherhood* (New York, 1949), pp. 55–60; Noell, 'Expectation and Unrest', 274.
[47] This is discussed further below, pp. 175–7.
[48] Cassidy-Welch, *Monastic Spaces*, p. 179; Noell, 'Expectation and Unrest', especially 273–4.
[49] William was promoted to head either a grange of the abbey or one of its urban centres: Noell, 'Expectation and Unrest', 274.

this decline. Whereas there had been some ninety lay brothers at Meaux in the mid-thirteenth century (as compared to sixty monks), there were only seven a century later and after the Black Death none remained.[50]

The focus of this discussion now turns from the lay brothers to the Cistercian economy in general. What made this distinctive and to what extent were houses affected by regional practice?

The Cistercian economy

The Cistercians' commitment to self-sufficiency and to rural living meant that they developed extensive precincts to help sustain their communities. These were generally larger than the precincts of other orders and although most encompassed twenty or thirty acres some were considerably bigger. In Yorkshire, Rievaulx's precinct was over ninety acres and Byland's more than one hundred acres. Various industrial and agricultural tasks were carried out within the confines of the precinct such as brewing, forging, tanning and bee-keeping. But facilities differed depending on the community's needs and resources as well as its areas of expertise. For instance, it is known that there was a 'highly productive' brick and floor-tile workshop at Pilis, Hungary, whilst excavations at Bordesley Abbey (Worcestershire) revealed evidence of an industrial complex in the eastern part of the precinct.[51]

The precinct alone could not sustain the community. To ensure its growth and survival each house had to develop a portfolio of holdings and rights. This included land for arable and pasture; woodland which afforded pannage,[52] fuel and building materials; minerals, fishing and urban property. The latter, as we shall see, was especially important to facilitate trade. Certain forms of revenue were forbidden. Early Cistercian legislation prohibited the acquisition of spiritualities (churches and tithes), vills or villeins as well as the rents from mills, ovens and other such assets.[53] The White Monks were to exploit their lands directly and live off the sweat from their own brows.

The Cistercians' rejection of tithes, their creation of a largely rural economy and their efficient exploitation of the land through grange farming are all regarded as defining features of the Order's economy. But just how distinctive was it, given that from as early as the twelfth century

---

[50] Kinder, *Cistercian Europe*, p. 310.

[51] For Pilis see, Szabó, *Woodland and Forests in Medieval Hungry*, p. 115; for Bordesley see the various essays in Astill, *A Medieval Industrial Complex*. The industrial complex at Bordesley functioned from the late twelfth century until the late fourteenth.

[52] This was the right to pasture pigs in woodland or forest where they could eat fallen nuts, acorns etc.

[53] See for example the *Early Capitula*, no. 23, *NLT*, p. 412 and 'Institutes of the General Chapter', no. 9, *NLT*, p. 460. For further discussion of these sources see above, p. 35 and note 47.

houses were acquiring tithes and other forbidden forms of income; that
there was a shift from demesne farming to the leasing out of lands from
the thirteenth century; and that, although in some places the White
Monks transformed the landscape through clearance and drainage, in
most cases they took over cultivated lands and assimilated the established socio-economic pattern?[54] In other words, did the Cistercians have
a specific economic agenda and, if so, when was this formulated?

It is generally agreed that the Cistercians' economic policy was developed gradually during the first decades of the twelfth century as the
White Monks became a constituted Order, but that practices varied
as communities responded to their surroundings and, where necessary,
assimilated the local socio-economic structure.[55] Recent research has
thus emphasised the diversity of the Order's economic practices. Typically Cistercian components were often combined with uncharacteristic
or even prohibited elements as the monks adapted to their environs.[56]
An example is the thirteenth-century foundation of Henryków (Silesia).
According to Górecki, the Henryków community adopted the regional
economic model and fused this with Cistercian features such as the use
of lay brothers and the reorganisation of lands into granges. The result
was an 'eclectic' mix of peoples, spaces and amenities associated with
the monastery that was characteristic of the area.[57] Monasteries might be
compelled to exercise different practices in different places. In some areas
they started with a blank canvas and were free to exploit the land as they
wished, yet elsewhere were constrained by the socio-economic pattern *in
situ* and might take on existing units or accept revenues that were based
on rents, trade and renders of tenants. As such the Cistercians were as
much participants in, as developers of, the local economy.[58] For Bouchard
the variety of economic practices adopted by the twelfth-century Cistercians in Burgundy actually facilitated the growth of the Order there and
supported its success.[59]

The Cistercian economy is explored more closely by considering how
communities expanded their holdings and rights, of what these comprised

---

[54] See for example Oram, 'Holy Frontiersmen'; Pascua, 'Vassals and Allies', and Berman, *Medieval
Agriculture*, especially pp. 11–30; Berman notes that where there was assarting this was generally
carried out by local peasantry rather than the Cistercians: *ibid.*, p. 37.

[55] The debate about the date at which we can speak of a Cistercian Order was discussed in chapter 2,
above, pp. 29–35. For further discussion see Burton, *Monastic Order in Yorkshire*, pp. 216–43, especially pp. 217–19, and C. Bouchard, 'Cistercian Ideals versus Reality: 1134 Reconsidered', *Cîteaux:
Commentarii Cistercienses* 39 (1988), 217–31.

[56] See Oram, 'Holy Frontiersmen', and Berman, *Medieval Agriculture*.

[57] P. Górecki, *A Local Society in Transition: the Henryków Book and Related Documents* (Toronto, 2002),
pp. 82–3.

[58] Oram, 'Holy Frontiersmen', p. 111.

[59] C. Brittain Bouchard, *Holy Entrepreneurs: Cistercians, Knights and Economic Exchange in Twelfth-
Century Burgundy* (Ithaca, 1991), especially p. 187.

and how they were exploited; of further interest is the extent to which practices changed both over time and from region to region.

The acquisition and exploitation of lands

It was the task of the founding abbot and his successors to build on the monastery's endowment and acquire a variety of interests to support a growing community. Stone and timber were needed for building work, particularly in the early days when the precinct was under construction, although maintenance, repairs and rebuilding were ongoing. A supply of fuel was essential, as were arable, pasture and other important assets such as minerals and fisheries. In some instances the acquisition of holdings was both rapid and extensive. By 1146, less then fifteen years after its foundation, the Yorkshire abbey of Fountains had secured a significant number of interests in its vicinity and further afield. By the end of the century Fountains had created over thirty granges – a quite remarkable number – and amassed assets within Yorkshire, Cumberland, Lancashire and Lincolnshire.[60] This was not the case everywhere. Whilst there was sometimes an explosion of acquisitions, there might instead be a slow and steady accumulation. Conversely, some houses encountered difficulties and found their hopes of expansion impeded or crushed. In severe circumstances this might lead to the closure of the monastery and perhaps its conversion into a grange. In 1227 the struggling abbey of Kilkenny, Ireland, was merged with Duiske (Graignamanagh) and in 1253 its former site was made into a grange of the abbey.[61] Houses generally concentrated their holdings around the immediate vicinity of the monastery but some had scattered possessions and might have significant interests remote from the abbey.[62]

There were various ways in which monasteries expanded their holdings and rights. A number were acquired through benefaction, often in return for spiritual reward but not infrequently for material gain or because of family or tenurial connections. Recruits might bring with them a substantial endowment when they joined the community or the monastery might actively solicit lands through coercion, purchase or exchange.

[60] Wardrop, *Fountains Abbey*, pp. 54–6.
[61] G. Carver, *Norman Splendour: Duiske Abbey, Graignamanagh* (Belfast, 1979), pp. 45–6. Carver notes that the process of conversion was 'elaborate'.
[62] Examples include Rievaulx and Fountains: see Burton, *Monastic Order in Yorkshire*, p. 222; and Melrose, see below, pp. 168–9.

Benefaction: donation, coercion and sale

> I leave and commend my soul to God and the Blessed Mary and all
> his saints, and my body to be buried in the monastery of Roche [south
> Yorkshire], in the chapel of the Blessed Mary, before her image, situ-
> ated in the southern part of the church of the said monastery ... Also,
> I leave to Roche one white vestment so that one monk of the abbey
> will celebrate for my soul for a week and have a penny each day, that
> another will celebrate for a second week and so on, that each in turn
> in the monastery shall celebrate and pray for my soul for the space of
> seven years complete.[63]

In chapter two we examined some of the reasons that inspired men and
women across Europe to become founders and patrons of the Cistercian
Order. Here, we shall look more closely at benefaction and consider from
whom the monasteries received grants of lands and the donors' motives
for giving.

Men and women of all ranks made donations to the Cistercians. They
ranged from great magnates to humble artisans such as Robert, the local
glazier of Ingerthorpe who became a benefactor of Fountains Abbey.[64]
Most, however, were drawn from the local knightly ranks, a group that
encompassed a diversity of individuals of varying fortunes and degrees
of influence. This was as true of a modest foundation like Balmerino
Abbey in Fife as of the large Yorkshire houses of Fountains and Rievaulx.[65]
Wardrop has shown that the knightly families accounted for about 60%
of Fountains's assets in the twelfth and thirteenth centuries and a striking
80% of its lands.[66]

Benefactors might be inspired by spiritual or worldly motives – and
often by both. The reason for giving is not always stated explicitly but
the most commonly cited motive is a concern for salvation. The donor
requested spiritual benefits in return for his or her grant in the hope that
these would hasten the soul's journey to heaven; in effect this was a way
to purchase Paradise and invest in one's spiritual welfare. What precisely
was received in return for the gift varied but prayers or masses for the
soul were most usual. Donors might request a burial spot within the

---

[63] From the will of Matilda of York, countess of Cambridge, 26 August 1446, who died shortly after
making this will: *Testamenta Eboracensia Part II: A Selection of Wills from the Registry at York*, ed. J.
Raine, Surtees Society, 30 (1855), no. 97 (pp. 118–24); Aveling, *History of Roche*, pp. 58–9.

[64] Wardrop, *Fountains Abbey*, pp. 120, 137–47.

[65] See Berman, *Medieval Agriculture*, pp. 34–5; Oram, 'A Fit and Ample Endowment?', 78; Jamroziak,
Rievaulx Abbey and its Social Context, pp. 93–110. See also L. Rasmussen, 'Monastic Benefactors
in England and Denmark: Their Social Background and Distribution', in Jamroziak and Burton,
Religious and Laity in Western Europe, pp. 77–92 (p. 83).

[66] Wardrop, *Fountains Abbey*, pp. 171–212.

monastery, reception into the fraternity of the house[67] or the chance to take the habit shortly before death (*ad succurrendum*), which was thought to significantly better one's chances of salvation. The charters recording these grants were probably penned and formulated by the monastery but might nonetheless reflect the donors' sentiments or aspirations. Indeed we should not underestimate the value of spiritual benefits at this time. The twelfth century saw a growing concern with the soul's transition through Purgatory and with how those on earth might influence its passage. This strengthened belief in the power of intercession as an effective way to speed the soul's journey heavenwards and increased demand for the monks' prayers and masses.[68] Burial within the monastery precinct – and particularly in the church – was an opportunity to be physically and eternally present within a sacred environment, and was highly valued as a consequence. The General Chapter initially prohibited burial to outsiders other than guests who died during their stay, but reviewed its stance in the mid-twelfth century, at first permitting burial to prelates and sovereigns and then to patrons. In 1217 the privilege was extended to all laity, providing that they had secured the permission of their parish priests. In effect this was an official endorsement of what was already commonplace – and moreover had been for some years.[69] The relative popularity of lay burial within Cistercian precincts is indicated by the number of charters requesting interment as well as by the physical remains of medieval tombs and the excavation of monastic cemeteries. The latter can also shed light on the Cistercians' burial practices and their attitude to the burial of women and children. Excavations at Stratford Langthorne (London) from 1973 to 1994 uncovered over 1300 graves and skeletons; it is the largest study of Cistercian skeletons in Europe to date.[70] Analysis was far from conclusive, particularly given the paucity of comparative evidence from other Cistercian houses, but the study suggested that burial patterns there were fairly typical of a medieval burial ground and may have been influenced significantly by regional practice.[71]

The holier the monks the more efficacious their prayers were deemed to be, the more powerful their monastery walls and the greater the strength

---

[67] See, for example, Jamroziak, *Rievaulx Abbey and its Social Context*, pp. 208–9.

[68] The key discussion of this is J. Le Goff, *The Birth of Purgatory*, trans. A. Goldhammer (Chicago, 1984).

[69] Canivez, *Statuta*, I, 47 (1152: 10); 68 (1157: 63); 465 (1217: 3). In 1322 the Chapter ruled that anyone who had helped with the construction of the church might be buried within the precinct: B. Barber, S. Chenu, T. Dyson and B. White, *The Cistercian Abbey of Stratford Langthorne, Essex*, Museum of London Archaeology Service Monograph, 18 (London, 2004), pp. 114–15. For lay burial in the Yorkshire houses see Cassidy-Welch, *Monastic Spaces*, pp. 232–6; for the Danish houses see McGuire, *Cistercians in Denmark*, pp. 174–5.

[70] 667 graves were uncovered and 647 skeletons. For a detailed analysis of the excavations and for what follows see Barber, Chenu, Dyson and White, *Cistercian Abbey of Stratford Langthorne*.

[71] *Ibid.*, especially p. 116.

of their habit in securing salvation. The Cistercians' lofty reputation and their international renown, particularly in the mid-twelfth century which was a golden age for the Order, would have made the White Monks' services especially attractive to would-be donors who were looking for the best return for their investment. The initiative to give frequently came from benefactors who wished to make provision for their souls. But communities were often proactive and vigorously promoted their services to attract donations. This was the case at Revesby Abbey (Lincolnshire) during the anarchic years of Stephen's reign (1135–54), when Aelred was abbot of the house. According to Walter Daniel's biography of Aelred, the abbot successfully turned the turbulence and uncertainty of the times to Revesby's advantage. He persuaded knights whose lands were in dispute to transfer their holdings to the monastery, arguing that this way they were guaranteed a return. Aelred pointed out that should they continue to fight for their lands they would likely lose them and have nothing in return. If on the other hand they granted their holdings to the monastery they would receive spiritual benefits for their generosity.[72] The fact that Revesby was enriched by these gifts is not only a testimony to Aelred's powers of persuasion but suggests that his words struck a chord; these men clearly believed in the potency of the monks' prayers and the need to invest in their souls.

Although the donor's spiritual welfare is frequently the reason given for his or her grant this might mask or coexist with more worldly and material concerns. Benefaction could confer prestige and help to consolidate or enhance one's social standing. It was also a way to raise cash whether this was needed to repay debts or to finance a costly undertaking such as pilgrimage or crusade. When Roger de Mowbray (d. 1188), founder of Byland Abbey and a generous benefactor to a number of religious houses, required money in the 1170s to fund his pilgrimage to the Holy Land he looked to the Cistercians, and particularly to the monks of Fountains, as a source of cash. From 1174 to 1176 Roger sold Fountains lands and rights amounting to the considerable sum of £450.[73] Roger's other money-making schemes included his sale of woodland to the Cistercians of Combe (Warwickshire) to repay his debts to Jewish moneylenders.[74] Burton suggests that Roger's need for money at this time was most probably the consequence of his involvement in the failed

---

[72] Walter Daniel, *Life of Aelred*, pp. 28–9; J. Burton, 'The Estates and Economy of Rievaulx Abbey', *Cîteaux: Commentarii Cistercienses* 49 (1998), 29–93 (p. 33). Aelred was abbot of Revesby from 1143 until 1147 when he was elevated to the abbacy of Rievaulx.

[73] J. Burton, '*Fundator Noster*: Roger de Mowbray as Founder and Patron of Monasteries', in Jamroziak and Burton, *Religious and Laity in Western Europe*, pp. 23–39, especially pp. 36–7; Wardrop, *Fountains Abbey*, p. 137; Jennings, *Yorkshire Monasteries*, pp. 79–80.

[74] H. Thomas, 'Mowbray, Sir Roger (I), de', *ODNB*, 39, pp. 588–90; Burton, '*Fundator Noster*', p. 36.

rebellion of the Young King, 1173–74. Roger's reputation suffered as a result of his treachery but he also lost lands and some of his estates were confiscated. Having been a generous benefactor to Fountains and other houses when he had the means, Roger now found himself in need. But he clearly recognised the Cistercians as a source of ready cash and a mutually beneficial arrangement was duly negotiated: Roger had a buyer for his lands and could raise the funds he needed, whilst the monastery had an opportunity to expand its interests in an important area. It was not just the great and the powerful who might broker a deal of this kind. Pascua's analysis of the Galician monastery of Santa Mariá de Montederramo (Orense) in the thirteenth century reveals how the abbey would buy land from locals who had fallen on hard times and were in need of cash. The monks often allowed the individual to remain on the land and receive the usufruct on the understanding that the property would pass to the community upon his or her death. Pascua argues that in this way the monastery gave the illusion of aid but was in fact the main beneficiary, reaping both short- and long-term advantages. The community secured the holding for the future but in the meantime had someone to manage the property who would be loyal to the house, as one who was in the community's debt. In this and in other ways the Galician abbey participated in the local system of communal exchange.[75] There are similar examples from across Europe. Jamroziak demonstrates how in Pomerania and Neumark the Cistercians were able to capitalise on the turbulence and uncertainty caused by fighting amongst the ducal houses in the thirteenth and fourteenth centuries. They acquired lands from laity who were forced to sell in these tumultuous times, purchasing the holdings for life-long rents.[76] In twelfth-century Burgundy the Cistercians engaged in complex economic transactions, especially with their knightly neighbours, that involved the mortgaging and leasing of lands, pawning and the exchange of gifts.[77]

In addition to gifts from benefactors, monasteries might secure significant grants from recruits or their families who donated lands and goods to the community upon entering the house. When Roger de Mowbray's former cook, Serlo, became a lay brother at Byland (Yorkshire) he granted the abbey his lands in Ellington together with ten cows, ten oxen, six mares and their foals.[78] Whilst Serlo's gift was a boon to Byland's economy,

---

[75] See for example, Pascua, 'Vassals and Allies', pp. 82–8.
[76] Emilia Jamroziak, 'Border Communities between Violence and Opportunities: Scotland and Pomerania Compared', in Unger, *Britain and Poland-Lithuania*, pp. 123–36 (p. 126).
[77] Bouchard, *Holy Entrepreneurs*.
[78] J. Burton, 'The Settlement of Disputes between Byland Abbey and Newburgh Priory', *Yorkshire Archaeological Journal* 55 (1983), 67–72 (p. 68); *Foundation History of Byland and Jervaulx*, pp. 49–50. Byland later granted ten bovates of land here to Jervaulx.

the arrival of wealthy recruits at Fountains in 1135 was regarded as a life-line to the struggling community which was at this time on the point of disbanding. Chief amongst the newcomers was Hugh, the former dean of York Minister, who brought with him money, furniture and a collection of books that formed the basis of the library at Fountains.[79] Details of this kind are not frequently recorded and it is therefore difficult to determine if entry grants were commonplace or if these are rather isolated cases. Certainly the concept of such gifts was problematic for there was a danger that they would be regarded as simony, a way of buying one's way into the community. Still, there was perhaps an expectation that recruits would make some kind of grant to the monastery, particularly nuns who were generally of the higher ranks and whose entrance gifts were effectively seen as their dowries; and they of course were Brides of Christ.[80] This is illustrated in a charter from Port Royal, west of Paris, which refers to the entry of a goldsmith's two daughters in 1266. The goldsmith was a bourgeois of Paris and made over his daughters' inheritance to the convent in their name when they joined the community. Port Royal duly acquired a vineyard, half the rents from a winepress near Meudon and the right to crush half of its vines there. The goldsmith effectively made the convent his heir and this is explicit in his charter which states 'if one makes a monastic house one's heir it is impossible to die without heirs'.[81] The document also highlights how the permanence of an institution gave security to the benefactor.

Discussion now turns from how the Cistercians acquired holdings to their management of the land and the grange system of farming.

An efficient economy: 'a new grange agriculture'[82]

The grange system of farming was at the heart of the Cistercian economy and became synonymous with the Order's successful exploitation of the land.[83] Through consolidating lands into single units which were administered from agricultural centres, staffed by lay brothers and, importantly,

---

[79] *Memorials of Fountains*, I, 52–3.
[80] See J. Burton, 'Looking for Medieval Nuns', in Burton and Stöber, *Monasteries and Society*, pp. 123–33 (pp. 114–15).
[81] *Cartulaire de l'abbaye de Porrois au diocèse de Paris plus connue sous son nom mystique, Port Royal*, ed. A. de Dion (Paris, 1903), no. 306, cited in Berman, *Women and Monasticism in Medieval Europe*, pp. 53–4.
[82] This phrase is used by Berman, *Medieval Agriculture*, p. 61.
[83] For further discussion see Berman, *Medieval Agriculture*, especially pp. 59–93; T. A. M. Bishop, 'Monastic Granges in Yorkshire', *English Historical Review* 51 (1936), 193–214; Burton, *Monastic Order in Yorkshire*, pp. 254–69; Donkin, 'The Cistercian Grange in England'; C. V. Graves, 'The Economic Activities of the Cistercians in Medieval England', *Analecta Cisterciensia* 13 (1957), 3–62; C. Platt, *The Monastic Grange in Medieval England: a Reassessment* (London, 1969).

exempt from tithes,[84] the Order established an efficient and profitable land-based economy, albeit one that forged important links with urban centres. The size, form and function of granges varied and, as we shall see, they supported a diversity of economic activities that included arable farming, animal husbandry and industrial work.

Granges were in theory to be located no more than a day's journey from the monastery (c. thirty kilometres) so that the *conversi* who worked these centres could easily return to their abbey on Sundays and feast days, when they were required to celebrate all liturgical offices. Frequently the granges were clustered around the abbey precinct with one or more serving as the monastery's home grange. The Yorkshire abbey of Fountains had three home granges: Haddockstones, Morker and Swanley. All three were accessible from the outer court of the monastery precinct and supplied the community at Fountains with its immediate needs. For instance fish was brought from Haddockstones which also provided the kitchener with fowl and pigs; grain from this grange was delivered to the granary and butter and cheese to the dairy.[85] By the early thirteenth century Bordesley (Worcestershire) had created some twenty granges within a thirty-five-kilometre radius of the abbey, but not infrequently these centres were rather remote from the monastery and much further than the permitted one-day's journey.[86] Øm's grange at Rosmos, Djursland, lay some eighty kilometres from the abbey and was a three-day journey away. However, the limestone quarry at Rosmos meant this was a valuable asset for the monastery and one that it would have been eager to keep.[87] As we shall see, communities frequently annexed or exchanged their outlying and isolated holdings to compact their estates and consolidate their property. This was not always the case, and Oram describes Melrose's 'unique' solution to managing its assets in central Ayrshire (Carrick, Kyle and Nithsdale), which lay over eighty kilometres from the abbey. Melrose wanted to retain these holdings despite their remoteness, since they provided important resources such as saltpans, minerals and salmon fishing as well as large tracts of pasture. Melrose accordingly established Mauchline as 'a super grange' to co-ordinate activities in the area and to oversee the other

---

[84] For further discussion of the Cistercians' exemption from tithes on the produce from lands they directly exploited, which was granted to the Order by Innocent II in 1132, see Berman, *Medieval Agriculture*, especially pp. 50–3, and Burton, *Monastic Order in Yorkshire*, pp. 264–5. For analysis of monastic tithes in general, see G. Constable, *Monastic Tithes from their Origins to the Twelfth Century* (Cambridge, 1964).

[85] *Memorials of Fountains*, I, 317.

[86] The Bordesley Abbey Project, www.reading.ac.uk/bordesley/Granges.htm (accessed December 2010).

[87] France, *Cistercians in Scandinavia*, p. 258.

granges; it effectively functioned as a cell of the house and was the key to efficient estate management in the area.[88]

There were various ways in which the Cistercians created their granges and in many cases this could be a long process involving discussions, negotiations and sales. The following section focuses on examples from southern France and Yorkshire to illustrate how the Cistercians compacted their estates, the activities they supported and how the function and management of these centres were affected by economic developments as well as by political affairs.

Compacting estates and creating granges

> Creating Cistercian granges involved a total reorganization of the land-tenure system – a change in the actual workings of the rural countryside which was as complete a transformation as any clearance of forest or drainage of swamp would have been.[89]

From her study of the Cistercian houses in southern France Berman has shown that there the White Monks were not so much pioneers as entrepreneurs whose successful reorganisation of fragmented estates into granges reshaped the landscape and laid the basis for an efficient economy. She argues that there is little evidence for the Cistercians in southern France reclaiming land through drainage or clearance. Rather, they acquired cultivated holdings which they consolidated into large estates – perhaps larger than parishes or vills – that were more economical to run. Further, by using their own domestic workforce – the *conversi* – and benefiting from the Order's exemption from tithes on produce from lands they themselves exploited, as well as from various tolls and taxes, the White Monks increased the productivity of their holdings and made these more profitable than when they had been under peasant cultivation. The income generated was often used to buy new lands and in this way the Cistercians expanded their demesne and established themselves as major landholders.[90] Berman argues that the improvement in agriculture in southern France was largely attributable to the Cistercians' 'managerial efficiency'. Their prowess and prudence, combined with the advantages the Order enjoyed – primarily its exemption from tithes – enabled the monks to ameliorate the land and profit from their industry.[91]

The creation of granges in southern France often involved the displacement of peasant communities. Indeed there and elsewhere the arrival

---

[88] R. Oram, 'The Estates and Possessions of the Abbey', in Fawcett and Oram, *Melrose Abbey*, pp. 209–71 (pp. 228–34).
[89] Berman, *Medieval Agriculture*, p. 53.
[90] For further discussion see *ibid.*, especially pp. 61–93.
[91] *Ibid.*, especially pp. 10, 43, 59–61, 87–93.

of the White Monks could mean upheaval for the local population.[92] In some cases they forcibly resisted expulsion. When Abbot Lambert of Kirkstall (c. 1190–93), displaced the local community at Accrington Park (Lancashire) to make a grange there, the natives retaliated by burning down the grange and murdering the three *conversi* who managed it.[93] The Cistercians gained a reputation for their ruthless expulsion of peasant communities and certainly there are known cases to support this indictment;[94] but this was not ubiquitous. Nor was it perhaps typical, for research suggests that not infrequently the Cistercians invited the local peasantry to join the lay brotherhood or as hired workers; they might be allowed to remain on the land for the rest of their lives or be moved to a new tenancy by their former lord.[95] Or, as in Galicia, the monastery might form relationships and alliances with the local community and engage in social transactions.[96]

The establishment of grange farming was not everywhere the same. Burton's analysis of the Yorkshire monasteries reveals that there the programme of creating granges was marked by its ambitious scale – by 1215 the eight Yorkshire abbeys had collectively established over eighty granges – as well as by the speed with which it was initiated, although not necessarily completed. Indeed the actual creation of a grange could take considerably longer than the records would suggest, and what was described as a grange was often a grange in the making. Burton considers the example of grange-formation at Meaux Abbey to show that whereas charters and bulls might refer to a 'grange' within several years of land being acquired, evidence from the monastery's chronicle indicates that it might take many more years to secure the lands fully.[97] In contrast to southern France, there is evidence for assarting (clearing land) in Yorkshire, but, as in the Midi, the creation of these granges might involve the removal or absorption of the local peasantry.[98]

---

92 See Berman, *Medieval Agriculture*, pp. 31, 59–60; but, as Berman argues, the White Monks brought benefits also: *ibid.*, pp. 119–20.
93 Clark, *The Foundation of Kirkstall Abbey*, pp. 184–5.
94 See below, note 98.
95 R. Wright, '"Casting Down the Altars and Levelling Everything before the Ploughshare?" The Expansion and Evolution of the Grange Estates of Kirkstall Abbey', in *Thirteenth Century England IX: Proceedings of the Durham Conference 2001*, ed. M. Prestwich, R. Britnell and R. Frame (Woodbridge, 2003), pp. 187–200; Berman, *Medieval Agriculture*, pp. 47–59; Burton, *Monastic Order in Yorkshire*, pp. 255–6.
96 See Pascua, 'Vassals and Allies' and R. Pastor, 'Social Mobility and the Personal Networks of "Low-intermediate Social Groups": Relations between Communities of Peasants and *Foreros* and the Monastery of Oseira in the Thirteenth Century', in Pastor, *Beyond the Market*, pp. 245–318.
97 Burton, *Monastic Order in Yorkshire*, pp. 254–64, especially pp. 255–62.
98 Examples include the depopulation of the vills at Cayton, Herleshow and Thorpe Underwood by Fountains Abbey and of Melsa by the monks of Meaux: see Coppack, *Fountains Abbey*, p. 105; Williams, *Cistercians in the Early Middle Ages*, p. 278; Burton, *Monastic Order in Yorkshire*, p. 255.

Communities that relocated sometimes converted their former abbey site into a grange.[99] But the process of establishing a grange was often lengthy and complicated. It was invariably the result of a series of negotiations and transactions as the community endeavoured to compact its holdings in a specific area, generally one where it already had extensive interests. Byland's consolidation of its holdings in Upper Nidderdale, Yorkshire, illustrates this process. Byland acquired significant interests in this region from its founder, Roger de Mowbray, which included pasture, minerals and timber for construction work. Roger used the area for hunting and his gifts came with restrictions since he was concerned to protect the game. For instance he forbade arable farming, stipulated that the Cistercians should chain up any ferocious guard dogs and prohibited Byland's shepherds from poaching game. Later in the century Roger's financial problems and his need for ready cash presented Byland with an opportunity to extend its interests in Nidderdale and to develop its grange economy there. Roger mortgaged lands in Nidderdale to the community for an annual rent and on the understanding that ownership of the lands would pass to the monastery should he fail to repay the remaining money within ten years. In the event no additional cash was paid and Byland secured the holdings. In this way Byland was able to establish a series of granges in Nidderdale to co-ordinate sheep rearing, arable and dairy farming.[100] It could take time for the monastery to secure dominance in the area and to buy out its neighbours. Accordingly the Cistercians might find themselves working alongside their lay neighbours in the interim; as Burton explains, it was not always possible for the White Monks to cultivate their lands in isolation.[101]

Once lands and rights had been acquired and the grange had been created there were often problems in managing and defending the estate. Communities might be threatened with repossession by the donors' heirs. These challenges could be costly as well as time consuming and could result in extensive legal proceedings.[102] The monastery sometimes faced resistance from neighbouring laity or other religious communities who had rival claims in the area and sought to restrict the Cistercians' rights

---

99 Examples include La Ramée's grange at Kerkom, Kirkstall's grange at Barnoldswick and Byland's at Old Byland.

100 Cistercians in Yorkshire: cistercians.shef.ac.uk/byland/lands/lands2.php (accessed December 2010); *A History of Nidderdale*, ed. B. Jennings, 3rd edn (Huddersfield, 1992), pp. 38–39, 42; and see Burton's discussion of Roger de Mowbray and the community's lands in Nidderdale, in *The Cartulary of Byland Abbey*, ed. J. Burton, Surtees Society, 208 (Woodbridge, 2004), especially pp. lvi–lix and 248–58.

101 Burton, *Monastic Order in Yorkshire*, p. 261.

102 See, for example, McGuire, *Cistercians in Denmark*, pp. 172–4, for Sorø's tussle to retain lands at Søtrop which lay to the north-west of the monastery; the abbey was engaged in conflict for over thirty years.

– or to limit the vehemence with which they pursued them. Whereas the monks of Esrum (Denmark) faced opposition from the locals of Halland who objected to the monks' right to fell trees in the area,[103] Melrose Abbey's attempts to maximise its interests in Wedale brought it into conflict with others who had rights within this area of the royal forest from the late twelfth century. They included the Morville family, who were royal constables and hereditary foresters, and the bishop of St Andrews who in 1268 excommunicated the abbot and several members of the community, alleging that they had attacked his house in Wedale and killed a clerk there.[104] Disputes between or amongst Cistercian houses were not unknown and whilst the General Chapter endeavoured to resolve these conflicts, severe cases might be referred to secular or ecclesiastical powers. The lands of Fountains Abbey in Craven, Yorkshire, were at the heart of a lengthy and bitter disagreement between the Yorkshire monastery and Furness Abbey, Lancashire. The dispute was resolved in 1211 and a treaty was drawn up but concord was temporary. Conflict resurfaced in the fourteenth century when Furness questioned the validity of the agreement, claiming that as the abbot of Furness at the time had been a monk of Fountains his actions were biased. An enquiry was duly launched and various representatives from the Order were called upon to resolve the matter. Their lack of agreement meant that the case was handed over to the bishop of Carlisle and the Exchequer who found in Fountains's favour.[105] In Ireland an altercation between Duiske and Jerpoint lasted over one hundred and fifty years. It centred on Jerpoint's former daughter house of Kilkenny which was united with Duiske in 1227. Its site was subsequently made into a grange of Duiske which duly acquired about 4000 acres of good tillage, a significant boost to its landed holdings. Some fifty years later Jerpoint contested Duiske's right to the grange. In 1288 an agreement was reached whereby Duiske effectively bought off Jerpoint, which was in financial straits at the time. Duiske agreed to take over Jerpoint's debts to the sum of 1000 marks and to spend an additional 300 marks on its lands. This was not the end of the matter and negotiations continued. In 1290 the abbot of Jerpoint agreed that for £10,000 he would not challenge Duiske's ownership, but it was not until 1362 that Jerpoint finally yielded and gave up its claim to the land.[106]

Aside from problems concerning management and ownership, granges were susceptible to trespass, thieving and ambush. The Cistercians in Pomerania and Neumark suffered attacks and even kidnapping from

[103] McGuire, *Cistercians in Denmark*, p. 86.
[104] Oram, 'The Estates and Possessions', pp. 214–16.
[105] Wardrop, *Fountains Abbey*, p. 123.
[106] Carver, *Norman Splendour*, pp. 46–8.

their neighbours during the turbulence of the thirteenth and fourteenth centuries. Jamroziak demonstrates that as the religious houses remained relatively wealthy and stable during these tumultuous times they were a source of resentment to their lay neighbours who destroyed monastic property and were violent towards members of the communities. Most attacks were made on the granges, which were not only easier to target but, importantly, were the source and a visible sign of the monks' economic strength.[107]

Granges in border areas were particularly vulnerable during times of warfare when invading armies might plunder them for their own benefit or destroy them to cripple the monastery. Fighting between England and Scotland wrought considerable damage on Melrose's estates and those of its daughter house, Holm Cultram, which lay across the divide in Cumbria.[108] In 1235 Holm Cultram took measures to safeguard its property and resources from Scottish attack and secured permission from Henry III to billet servants armed with bows on its granges. The situation intensified from the late thirteenth century. In c. 1315–16 Holm Cultram suffered so much damage to its abbey and estates the community was forced to disband and take refuge with the monks of Tintern (Monmouthshire) until its buildings had been restored and its lands were once more productive.[109] Edward II's advance into southern Scotland in August 1307 caused devastation to Melrose's grange at Dunscore (Nithsdale), provoking the two monk keepers to complain to the king. Edward duly agreed to compensate Melrose for the destruction caused by his men and awarded the community 6s 8d.[110] On occasion troops were billeted at Cistercian granges. In December 1256 Prince Llywelyn ap Gruffudd and his army stayed at Strata Florida's grange at Morfa Mawr (Ceredigion), whilst in 1263 Henry III's troops sought shelter at the abbey's grange of Abermiwl (Powys) where they were duly killed by the Welsh.[111]

The function

The granges in southern France were used largely for cereal production and for pasturing animals in winter.[112] In Yorkshire, the moorland granges belonging to Byland and Rievaulx were primarily for sheep farming whereas Fountains's Nidderdale granges focused on dairy farming, especially from the mid-fourteenth century when there was a shift away

---

[107] Jamroziak, 'Border Communities', pp. 126–7.
[108] For further discussion see Jamroziak, 'Holm Cultram'.
[109] Jamroziak, 'Border Communities', p. 129.
[110] Oram, 'The Estates and Possessions', p. 241; Oram, 'Holy Frontiersmen', pp. 119–120.
[111] Williams, *Welsh Cistercians*, pp. 28, 31, 146.
[112] Berman, *Medieval Agriculture*, pp. 93–4, 121.

from wool production.[113] Elsewhere granges specialised in other activities such as fishing, salt production or horse-breeding. Fountains, for example, had an important fish-farming centre at Cayton grange in Lower Nidderdale, and dammed the waters there to create a series of ponds.[114] The Italian community of Brondolo extracted salt at its grange in Chioggia, on the Adriatic, whilst the Danish abbey of Øm had a stud farm at Svestrup grange.[115] The grange might function as an industrial centre to co-ordinate mining, smelting or the production of tiles, and it was often used as a hospice by members of the community.[116] Oram has suggested that granges in Scotland may have served as staging posts to facilitate the movement of the monastery's goods and livestock, both for its own consumption and for the market.[117] Although granges might have a specialism they were generally multifunctional and supported various agricultural, industrial and also social activities. In 1457 Abbot Greenwell of Fountains received the duke of York at Swanley grange and on this occasion the pair dined on fish costing 2s 8d.[118] It was prudent and indeed important for the community to have a diversity of granges, to draw from different soils, climates and resources; in this way, the monastery could balance its assets.[119]

Just as the function of granges varied so too did their size and composition. Sorø's (Denmark) grange at Gudum was around four hundred and fifty acres but its grange at Vejleby, which was largely meadow and pasture, was almost seven hundred acres.[120] Strata Florida's grange at Mefenydd, Wales, supported sheep farming and was over 5000 acres.[121] The Yorkshire granges were typically some three hundred to four hundred acres but might be significantly larger; Fountains' grange at Bradley comprised over 4000 acres of pasture, arable, moorland and woodland and had a water-driven industrial complex.[122] In southern France some granges were the size of vills or parishes whereas others were modest complexes and simply consisted of a dwelling, a cellar and perhaps a mill.[123] Despite the variation in size and components, the Cistercian grange effectively comprised

[113] Burton, *Monastic Order in Yorkshire*, p. 263.
[114] J. McDonnell, *Inland Fisheries in Medieval Yorkshire 1066–1300*, Borthwick Papers 60 (York, 1981), p.16; for further discussion of Cayton grange see E. Dent, 'The Impact of Fountains Abbey on Nidderdale', BA dissertation, University College Ripon and York, 1995.
[115] Williams, *Cistercians in the Early Middle Ages*, p. 379; France, *Cistercians in Scandinavia*, p. 279.
[116] See below, pp. 178–9 for further discussion.
[117] Oram, 'Holy Frontiersmen', pp. 117–20; Oram, 'The Estates and Possessions', especially pp. 234–7.
[118] J. S. Fletcher, *The Cistercians in Yorkshire* (London, 1919), p. 154; *Memorials of Fountains*, III, 15.
[119] Berman, *Medieval Agriculture*, pp. 69–70.
[120] France, *Cistercians in Scandinavia*, p. 266.
[121] Williams, *Welsh Cistercians*, p. 193.
[122] Platt, *Monastic Grange*, p. 79; C. J. Bond, *Monastic Landscapes* (Stroud, 2004), p. 48; Coppack, *Fountains Abbey*, p. 111.
[123] Berman, *Medieval Agriculture*, p. 61.

fields, farms and buildings such as barns and granaries, a domestic range and workshops. The complex was often enclosed by a wall or in some cases by a moat or a ditch. Granges that had fisheries might have a smokehouse on site;[124] there would be forges on granges that practised metallurgy and those that supported sheep farming would have bercaries (sheep cotes).[125] Neath Abbey's grange at Monknash (Vale of Glamorgan) – 'the grange *par excellence* in Wales' – encompassed over eight hundred acres and included a large granary, a dovecot, a chapel and three mills.[126]

What precisely lay within the grange enclosure – and its overall size – was obviously closely related to the function of the grange as well as to the nature of the landscape and the community's wealth. But the composition and the management of the grange may also have been significantly affected by the number of lay brothers available to work it. Where manpower was in short supply the administration and the very form of the grange may have been quite different to what we now consider to be traditional. From the late thirteenth century socio-economic developments precipitated a change in Cistercian land-holding policy and altered the management and composition of these estates. There was a shift away from demesne farming and a number of granges were now leased out to secular tenants. Some were let out as single units but others were divided, subdivided or dismantled. The sheep cotes and cattle ranches might be abandoned and in some cases the large timber and stone buildings erected by the Cistercians were replaced with more modest structures.[127]

Later changes

The grange was the linch-pin of the Order's land-based economy until the thirteenth century when there was a reorganisation of estate management. Cistercian land-holding policy was transformed. From 1208 the General Chapter revised its stance regarding the direct exploitation of land, largely in response to the shortage of lay brothers and a lack of manpower. The dearth in numbers may have been caused or exacerbated by the General Chapter itself which was perhaps reluctant to take on more lay brothers in light of recent *conversi* hostilities. At first the Chapter permitted the leasing out of 'less useful' holdings and after some debate extended this to other lands in 1224.[128] There was subsequently a move away from demesne farming as lands and properties were increas-

---

[124] An example is Fountains's home grange of Haddockstones; see Coppack, *Fountains Abbey*, p. 115.

[125] This sheltered housing for sheep could be extensive and comprise pasture, pens and associated buildings. For further discussion see C. Dyer, 'Sheepcotes: Evidence for Medieval Sheep Farming', *Medieval Archaeology* 39 (1995), 136–64.

[126] Williams, *Welsh Cistercians*, p. 200.

[127] This was the case at Cowton grange, Yorkshire, in the fourteenth century; see Coppack, *Fountains Abbey*, pp. 117–18.

[128] Canivez, *Statuta*, I, 346 (1208: 5); II, 31 (1224: 10).

ingly let to lay tenants in return for payments in kind but sometimes also in cash; in some cases these tenants were abbey servants or lay brothers of the house.[129] Other lands were retained as demesne and farmed by lay keepers; generally the home grange was farmed as demesne.[130] This reorganisation of estate management was intended to improve efficiency and indeed it made sense for communities to lease out their remote or less valuable holdings.[131] But leasing was often an important way for monasteries to raise money to deal with rising debt and also to cope with the severe drop in the number of lay brothers following the Black Death in the fourteenth century.[132] The speed and extent to which leasing was carried out were not everywhere the same. Whereas Kirkstall Abbey (Yorkshire) started to lease out its lands in the late thirteenth century, Melrose (Scotland) began this only in the early fifteenth century. In Denmark it became increasingly common from the fourteenth century for rent-paying peasants to take over abandoned granges.[133] Nevertheless leasing was widespread from the thirteenth century and gathered pace in the later Middle Ages as holdings close to the monastery and even within the abbey precinct were leased.[134] In England and Wales the process was accelerated on the eve of the Dissolution with communities hoping either to raise money to stave off suppression or to provide financial security for individual members.[135] In Scotland the leasing out of lands ('feuing') intensified following the Reformation, as the monasteries struggled to raise cash to fund the Crown's heavy taxations.[136]

Surviving leases which detail the terms of tenancies are insightful and indicate that tenants were often subject to strict guidelines. In addition to paying rent in kind or in cash they might be required to carry out labour services. Tenants of Strata Florida (Ceredigion) were obliged to seek the monastery's permission if they wished to bring up the offspring of a great man.[137] The tenant was usually responsible for maintaining the property and was often liable for damages incurred, the loss of livestock and perhaps a failure to meet the set targets.[138] All this would be set out

---

129 For examples from Fountains Abbey see Platt, *Monastic Grange*, pp. 96–7 and *The Fountains Abbey Lease Book*, ed. D. J. H. Michelmore, Yorkshire Archaeological Society Record Series, 140 (1981), p. xxxvii and nos 235, 276.
130 They effectively became abbey servants: see Michelmore, *The Fountains Abbey Lease Book*, p. xxxvii.
131 Wardrop, *Fountains Abbey*, pp. 86–94.
132 For further discussion see Burton, 'The Estates and Economy of Rievaulx Abbey', 89–90; France, *Cistercians in Scandinavia*, pp. 270–3; Williams, *Welsh Cistercians*, pp. 279–83.
133 McGuire, *Cistercians in Denmark*, pp. 215–16.
134 See for example, Williams, *Welsh Cistercians*, p. 280.
135 *Ibid.*, pp. 77–9.
136 Oram, 'The Estates and Possessions', pp. 221, 266–70. This was allegedly to finance the College of Justice but in effect funded a lavish building programme.
137 Williams, *Welsh Cistercians*, p. 282.
138 Michelmore, *The Fountains Abbey Lease Book*, p. xlix.

in the lease. It was often important for the monastery to retain access rights to the leased holding, so that members of the community had somewhere to stay and a source of supplies when travelling in the area. Some tenants were expected to finance this hospitality, but it was not uncommon for the monastery simply to reserve the right to lodgings and provisions and accept responsibility for other costs. This was the case in 1558 when Abbot Donald and the monks of Coupar Angus (Perth) granted land in Galloraw to Robert Alexander and his wife, Margaret, and their heirs. The lease is very explicit and reveals that in addition to paying rent – in cash and in kind – and carrying out various services, Robert and Margaret were to make appropriate provision at Galloraw for members of the community and to put this at the brethren's disposal. The couple was required to build a large hall and chambers with well-appointed tables; there was to be a stable with straw, hay and oats and a cellar stocked with wine, drinks and foods that might be sold whenever needed to the abbot, convent and their servants, but also to other guests arriving on the seacoast of Angus.[139] Similar agreements were made with the abbey's tenants at Bogside and Boghall.[140]

It was not just economic developments that wrought a change to grange farming but prevailing political situations and conditions across Europe. With the onset of the Hundred Years War a number of Cistercian granges on the Gascon border were converted into military settlements known as bastides. Examples include Bonnefont's grange of Apas. The Cistercians acted in conjunction with the king of France to establish these fortified towns and in so doing the Order reintroduced peasant populations to areas from which it had previously driven them away.[141]

Industry and commerce

The Cistercians' drive for self-sufficiency required communities to support a range of industrial activities both within the monastery precincts and on their estates. For example they had tanneries to cure leather, they quarried for stone, dug peat and had saltworks.[142] Not every house was

---

[139] *Rental Book of the Cistercian Abbey of Cupar-Angus with the Breviary of the Register*, ed. C. Rogers, 2 vols, Grampian Club (London, 1879–80), II, no. 208 (pp. 167–9, at p. 168).

[140] *Ibid.*, II, no. 145 (pp. 135–6, at p. 136) and no. 220 (pp. 178–80, at p. 179).

[141] Berman, *Medieval Agriculture*, pp. 63, 71, 120. For further discussion see C. H. Berman, 'From Cistercian Granges to Cistercian Bastides: using the Order's Records to Date Landscape Transformation', in L. Pressouyre, *L'espace Cistercien*, Memoires de la section d'archéologie et d'histoire de l'art, 5 (Paris, 1994), pp. 204–15.

[142] In most cases salt was obtained from the sea rather than from rock and collected by evaporation. Communities often acquired saltpans on the coast such as Melrose's on the Clyde coast, in the west of Scotland, and Eldena's on the Baltic Coast. See Williams, *Cistercians in the Early Middle Ages*, pp. 375–8; Oram, 'The Estates and Possessions', pp. 243–5.

involved in every industry. Neighbouring monasteries or those within the same filiation might exchange goods and services, but often communities relied on the market to purchase or supplement their supplies. Houses also produced for the market. The Cistercian economy was not solely rural and monasteries established strong urban ties. This final section looks more closely at aspects of Cistercian industry and of the White Monks' involvement in the market.

Industrial activities

Evidence for the nature of industrial work associated with Cistercian sites comes from a variety of sources. They include documentary records, excavation and standing remains such as the thirteenth-century wooden forge at Maulbronn and the hammer-driven forge at Fontenay which had its origins in the twelfth-century mill.[143] Reference to the use of land is often disclosed in charters, lawsuits and chronicles. For instance the Sorø Donation Book, compiled c. 1440, details Archbishop Absalon's gift of Tuååker (Halland) to the community and reveals that the monks extracted iron there and collected salt.[144] Thomas Burton's chronicle of Meaux (Yorkshire), composed at the turn of the fifteenth century, records that smiths and pelterers worked at the abbey's North Grange as well as at Wawne, but were transferred to the monastery precinct by Abbot Michael (1235–39) who was also responsible for building a stone woolshed (*lanaria*) at Wawne.[145] Archaeological research has shed considerable light on the monks' industrial activities and suggests that the Cistercians were as quick to adopt and disseminate new technologies as they were architectural styles.[146] Excavations within the precinct at Bordesley Abbey (Worcester-shire) uncovered evidence for one of the earliest water-powered metal-working mills in England. From the various finds it has been possible to reconstruct some of the mill's machinery and thereby attain a better understanding of the technology employed. The finds also indicated that as well as metalworking, repairs were carried out, and that items manufactured at the forge were not simply for the abbey but supplied its granges and perhaps also the local markets.[147] Analysis of the iron-working landscape in and around Rievaulx suggests that the sixteenth-century community of this Yorkshire abbey was at the vanguard of one

[143] Anstett, *Maulbronn Abbey*, p. 70; Kinder, *Cistercian Europe*, p. 372. For further discussion see P. Benoît, 'La forge de l'abbaye de Fontenay', *Dossiers: histoire et archéologie* 107 (1986), 50–2.
[144] McGuire, *Cistercians in Denmark*, p. 86.
[145] *Chron. Melsa*, II, xiv, 63.
[146] See above, pp. 77–81.
[147] Bond, 'Monastic Water Management in Great Britain', p. 114; www.reading.ac.uk/bordesley/Water-mills.htm (accessed December 2010); see also the various articles in Astill, *A Medieval Industrial Complex*.

of the most significant technological advances in metallurgy, namely the shift from using small iron-smelting furnaces to the development of the blast furnace. Rievaulx was smelting and working iron from the twelfth century but on the eve of the Dissolution had constructed a proto-blast furnace at Laskill which lay several miles from the abbey. Smelt from Laskill was sent to Rievaulx's forge within the abbey precinct where it was worked. It is argued that Rievaulx's development of blast-furnace technology was halted by the suppression of the house in December 1538; it was over thirty years later that the first blast furnace in Yorkshire was constructed – at Rievaulx.[148]

Excavation has also revealed much about the manufacture and design of Cistercian tiles. Three tile kilns were uncovered at Meaux's North Grange, which lay about half a mile from the Yorkshire abbey. Two of the kilns were for making roof tiles but the third was for firing the distinctive decorative mosaic floor tiles that have been found at a number of northern houses belonging to the reformed orders, particularly the Cistercians, and are unique to the region.[149] Stopford explains that they are the northern houses' version of the earlier stone *opus sectile* pavements and tapestry design of southern Europe and are seemingly linked to the building campaigns in the region.[150] The Meaux chronicle reveals that the monastery was making these mosaic tiles during William Driffield's abbacy (1249–69) when the pavement was laid in the abbey's new church; some of these tiles were recovered *in situ* when the site was excavated.[151] A tilery within the precinct or on a grange was by no means a standard feature of Cistercian abbeys but Meaux was not unique and a number of Cistercian tileries are known across Europe. They include Yorkshire tileries associated with Byland, Fountains and Rievaulx.[152] French examples include Pontigny[153] and Chaâlis, whose tilery on its grange of Commelles, near

---

[148] R. W. Vernon, G. McDonnell and A. Schmidt, 'The Geophysical Evaluation of an Ironworking Complex: Rievaulx and Environs', *North Yorkshire Archaeological Prospection* 5 (1998), 181–201; R. W. Vernon, G. McDonnell and A. Schmidt, 'An Integrated Geophysical and Analytical Appraisal of Early Iron Working: Three Case Studies', *Journal of the Historical Metallurgy Society* 32: 2 (1998), 67–81; Archaeometallurgy: archmetals.org.uk/rievaulx.html (accessed December 2010).

[149] E. Eames, 'A Thirteenth-century Tile Kiln Site at North Grange, Meaux, Beverley, Yorkshire', *Medieval Archaeology* 5 (1961), 137–68.

[150] J. Stopford, *Medieval Floor Tiles of Northern England. Pattern and Purpose: Production between the 13th and 16th centuries* (Oxford, 2005), pp. 14–15, 24, 71.

[151] *Chron. Melsa*, II, 119; E. Eames, *English Tilers* (London, 1992) p. 302.

[152] Plain mosaic floor tiles were manufactured at these sites in the first half of the thirteenth century. For extensive discussion see Stopford, *Medieval Floor Tiles*, especially pp. 10–24 and 91–128.

[153] For further discussion see T. Kinder, 'Clay and what they did with it: Medieval Tiles and Bricks at Pontigny', in *Studies in Cistercian Art and Architecture*, 4, ed. M. Parsons Lillich, Cistercian Studies Series, 134 (Kalamazoo, 1993), pp. 15–44.

Senlis, is one of the few in the country to survive above ground. Remains include a chimney which appears to date to the thirteenth century.[154]

Although it is clear that the Cistercians were manufacturing tiles on their lands it is not always easy to determine if the work was carried out by monks, lay brothers or itinerant craftsmen. There are several isolated references to thirteenth-century monk tile-makers. One, a monk of Beaubec, made tiles for other Cistercian houses as well as for outsiders until the General Chapter intervened and put a stop to the latter.[155] Lay brothers may have assisted with tile production but specific reference to their involvement is scant. It is likely that in many cases the tiles were made by itinerant or mobile craftsmen who moved from one site to another and set up a kiln, but might remain in the one place for several years.[156] Tiles made from different clays but using the same methods and designs indicate that they were produced by the same workmen or workshop, and there has been considerable research into the activities and itineraries of the various tile workshops.[157] The thirteenth-century northern tiles, which include Meaux's, were seemingly made by 'the most prolific' workshop in Britain at this time which also produced tiles for York Minster.[158] In the late thirteenth century itinerant craftsmen from the Garonne valley workshop set up kilns at a number of religious and ecclesiastical sites in the area including Agen Cathedral and the Cistercian abbeys of Belleperche and Grandselve. Similarities between the Grandselve tiles and those at its Spanish daughter house of Santa Creus prompt Norton to suggest that one of the Garonne valley tilers was sent to Santa Creus to make its tiles; the fact these north-European style of inlaid tiles are the only ones of their kind in Spain would seem to support this hypothesis.[159] Elsewhere regional contacts were of greater importance than familial ties. In northern England interaction between the Cistercians and other reformed orders, especially the Augustinians, seemed to impact on the dissemination and distribution of these mosaic tiles; in some cases the houses shared the same patron or were joined on confraternity.[160]

[154] C. Norton, 'The Production and Distribution of Medieval Floor Tiles in France and England', in *Artistes, artisans et production artistique au moyen âge: Colloque international. Fabrication et consummation de l'oeuvre*, 3, ed. X. Barral I Altet (Paris, 1990), pp. 101–31 (p. 104); Williams, *Cistercians in the Early Middle Ages*, p. 220.
[155] Stopford, *Medieval Floor Tiles*, p. 22.
[156] C. Norton, 'Medieval Floor Tiles in Scotland', in *Medieval Art and Architecture in the Diocese of St Andrews*: British Archaeological Association Conference Transactions for 1986, 14, ed. J. Higgett (Leeds, 1994), pp. 137–73 (pp. 109–19). Eames, *English Tilers*, p. 30, infers that the lay brothers of Meaux worked the kilns at North Grange.
[157] Stopford, *Medieval Floor Tiles*, p. 12.
[158] Norton, 'Medieval Floor Tiles in Scotland', pp. 142–3.
[159] Norton, 'The Production and Distribution of Medieval Floor Tiles', pp. 116–18.
[160] Stopford, *Medieval Floor Tiles*, pp. 23–4, 71.

Monasteries that had no means to produce their own tiles might acquire or import them from another abbey or from a commercial tilery. Meaux may have shipped tiles across the Humber to its fellow Cistercians at Louth Park and the Augustinians at Thornton.[161] There was also an extensive trade in tiles with the Continent, especially in the later Middle Ages. Whereas the two-colour tiles found at Hovedøya in Norway, a country with no established tile industry, were perhaps imported from Artois, the plain glazed tiles found at the Scottish houses of Balmerino, Kinloss and Melrose were most probably imported from the Low Countries. Flanders monopolised the tile market in the later Middle Ages and tiles were imported from there 'in their thousands'. A number have been found at secular, ecclesiastical and monastic sites in Scotland which suggests that the Cistercians in Scotland were influenced by contemporary trends and patterns of trade.[162]

Across Europe the Cistercians were extensively involved in mining as well as metallurgy, and might play a leading role in its regional exploitation. From the late twelfth or early thirteenth century Newbattle and Culross were working mines in the Lothian and Forth Valley and were at the forefront of coal-mining in Scotland.[163] Culross was also significantly involved in the exportation of coal and engaged almost two hundred ships to transport its cargo.[164] Walkenreid Abbey in Lower Saxony exploited various copper mines and had several copper smelting works, whilst the monks of Sedlac, Bohemia, extracted silver from the mines at Kutná Hora which lay partly on their lands. It was alleged that a monk of Sedlac had discovered the silver there shortly before the community began mining in 1282.[165] Lead was a particularly important resource for monasteries, not just for manufacturing implements and tools, but for window tracery, covering roofs and making pipes. Strata Florida exploited lead as well as silver and zinc from its mines at Cwmystwyth which lay several miles from the abbey. This was not just for domestic use, for in 1451 lead from the abbey's mines was used to repair Cardigan Castle.[166] Fountains Abbey was similarly producing for the market. The Pipe Rolls of 1363 reveal that one hundred and sixty-eight pigs of lead from Fountains's mines in Nidderdale, Yorkshire, were dispatched via Hull to Windsor, to roof

[161] Norton, 'Medieval Floor Tiles in Scotland', p. 143. Carver, *Norman Splendour*, p. 35, suggests that the decorative floor tiles at Duiske – which were unique as some bore both shamrocks and the Norman fleur-de-lis – may have been shipped to the abbey from its mother house of Stanley, Wiltshire.
[162] Norton, 'Medieval Floor Tiles in Scotland', pp. 150–1. See Stopford, *Medieval Floor Tiles*, especially pp. 46–51, 71, 217–19, for the use of these tiles in the north of England.
[163] Oram, 'The Estates and Possessions', p. 234.
[164] Lekai, *White Monks*, p. 221.
[165] Williams, *Cistercians in the Early Middle Ages*, p. 372; Leroux-Dhuys, *Cistercian Abbeys*, p. 332.
[166] S. Timberlake, 'Archaeological and Circumstantial Evidence for Early Mining in Wales', *Bulletin of the Peak District Mines Historical Society* 12: 3 (1994), 133–43 (p. 142).

the castle; an additional twenty-four fothers were transported there in 1365. In the fifteenth century lead from the abbey's grange at Warsill was sent to York Minster.[167] Fountains's involvement in the lead market – its ambition, success and particularly the fact that the community enjoyed commercial privileges – was a threat to other traders. The Fellowship of Merchants at York feared for its monopoly and wrote to Abbot Huby (1495–1526) asking that Fountains cease trading. The abbot duly ignored this request and Fountains continued its commercial activities.[168]

The Cistercian economy may have been rural based with an emphasis on self-sufficiency but, as we have seen, produce was not solely for domestic use. Monasteries might sell their surplus. The monks of Beaulieu (Hampshire) sold over half of the honey produced in their workshops c. 1270, which amounted to some thirty gallons.[169] Moreover, communities that had holdings remote from the abbey might choose to sell whatever was produced there at local markets rather than to transport these goods to the monastery which could be onerous and time-consuming.[170] But communities also produced specifically for the market. To facilitate the exchange and sale of goods the Cistercians acquired holdings in towns and cities. They also secured commercial rights and freedoms from tolls which might provoke hostility from their competitors; indeed the monks of Eberbach who had shops in Cologne and Ulm were forced into closure by their competitors who resented their exemption from taxation.[171] The following section looks more closely at these urban ties.

The Cistercians and commerce

From a relatively early date Cistercian communities were selling produce at local markets or from retail outlets in urban centres. They included the monks of Rein who were trading from their shop in the town of Graz from the mid-twelfth century, where they sold wine and agricultural produce.[172] Some goods were sold on site although the General Chapter initially prohibited the sale of wine and beer 'on tap' (for immediate consumption) at abbeys and granges.[173] From the late twelfth century the intensity of the Order's commercial activities increased. This was a direct response to the growth of towns and the burgeoning of trade. The Cister-

---

167   Jennings, *History of Nidderdale*, pp. 63–4, 66, 77.
168   *A History of Lead Mining in the Pennines*, ed. A. Raistrick and B. Jennings (London, 1965), pp. 35–6.
169   Bond, 'Production and Consumption of Food', p. 70.
170   See, for example, Oram, 'The Estates and Possessions', pp. 263–6.
171   Lekai, *White Monks*, p. 222; Leroux-Dhuys, *Cistercian Abbeys*, p. 109; see also Berman, *Women and Monasticism*, pp. 9–10.
172   Lekai, *White Monks*, p. 216.
173   See for example, 'Institutes of the General Chapter', no. 54, *NLT*, p. 480; *Twelfth-Century Statutes*, pp. 99 (1182: 6), 132 (1186: 4); 199 (1190: 20); 267–8 (1199: 34).

cians now developed 'a new non-rural outlook' as communities across Europe forged ties with urban centres; for Berman this was 'a Cistercian economic innovation'. This process occurred at different times in different places and with differing degrees of intensity. In southern France the Cistercians had become increasingly involved in commercial activities by the late twelfth century, with monasteries acquiring urban properties and rights to facilitate the transportation and sale of their produce. These exemptions from tolls and taxations gave the monks a competitive edge and were highly prized. In fact the Cistercians in southern France received more grants of commercial rights from patrons than of land.[174] This commercialisation occurred later in Denmark where the landscape became 'less rural' from 1300. However, it was in the late fourteenth and early fifteenth centuries that the Danish Cistercians really made their presence felt in urban centres, acquiring holdings and also establishing contacts with townsfolk who duly appeared as witnesses in their charters and were welcomed into the monastic confraternities.[175] The Yorkshire Cistercians similarly responded to urban growth. They attended markets and fairs around the country and secured properties – or access to properties[176] – in leading commercial centres such as Boston (Lincolnshire), where the internationally renowned fair of St Botolph was held, and York, which was important for the export of wool.[177] The creation of the northern boroughs in England led to a significant rise in the number of markets and fairs in the north and some Cistercian houses began to hold their own. They include Meaux which from the late thirteenth century held two weekly markets as well as an annual fair at both Pocklington and Kingston-on-Hull; Jervaulx had a weekly market and two annual fairs at East Witton Manor.[178]

Across the border in Scotland there were similar developments. The monks of Melrose expanded their interests in both Scottish and English burghs and, like the Yorkshire monks, had property in Boston which gave them a base for St Botolph's fair. In the mid-thirteenth century Melrose acquired significant holdings in the port of Berwick which was at this time a thriving commercial centre and the principal outlet for the export of Scottish wool.[179] Melrose had commercial properties in Berwick as well as hospices where members of the community could stay when

---

[174] Berman, *Medieval Agriculture*, especially pp. 122–4.
[175] McGuire, *Cistercians in Denmark*, pp. 237–9.
[176] See for example the agreement between Jordan de Boston and the monks of Fountains in the late twelfth century, Wardrop, *Fountains Abbey*, pp. 113–14.
[177] See below, p. 185.
[178] Cassidy-Welch, *Monastic Spaces*, pp. 177–8.
[179] For further discussion of Berwick at this time and its importance for foreign trade, see W. Stevenson, 'The Monastic Presence: Berwick in the Twelfth and Thirteenth Centuries', in *The Scottish Medieval Town*, ed. M. Lynch, M. Spearman and G. Stell (Edinburgh, 1988), pp. 99–115, especially pp. 109–11.

conducting business; but it also rented out property to generate income. The monks of Melrose actively developed their interests in Berwick to gain a strong foothold in what was at this time the leading commercial centre in the country. Thus, although some of the Berwick properties were granted to the community most were purchased and a number were secured through buying up debts and mortgages from burgesses who were in financial straits. When Leith took over from Berwick as the primary exporter of Scottish wool and hides in the late fourteenth century, Melrose duly shifted its focus north and expanded its holdings in Leith and Edinburgh. By the fifteenth century Melrose was using Leith not only to export its products but to import goods.[180]

The example of Melrose shows how the Cistercians moved with the times and adapted their economy in response to changes in the market. Communities built up interests in key commercial centres, where they acquired properties for their own use but also to let out. The Hungarian abbeys of Pilis and Zirc seemingly relied on their secondary economies, deriving a significant amount of their income from tolls and rents.[181] Houses also tailored their production to the market. The Cistercians responded to continental demand for wool in the late twelfth century and significantly increased their production. This meant acquiring more pasture for grazing sheep as well as securing rights of passage and exemption from tolls to facilitate the transportation and export of wool. In the 1180s Count Philip of Flanders granted Melrose Abbey free passage throughout his country as well as freedom from all tolls.[182] Flanders was at this time the leading centre of cloth production in northern Europe. Henry III accorded similar privileges to the monks of Pipewell (Northamptonshire) in 1235, exempting the brethren from all tolls, passage and pontage[183] in his kingdom. These freedoms greatly reduced the costs of conveying and exporting the wool.[184] Although communities dealt with foreign merchants at markets and at ports, as well as on site, they might secure ships to trade overseas. It is known that Melrose either owned or hired a ship in the 1220s, and that Fountains had a ship licensed to carry wool in 1224.[185]

Fountains and its fellow Yorkshire houses were most associated with the wool industry. They monopolised the market in the twelfth and thir-

---

180 Oram, 'The Estates and Possessions', pp. 245–54, 265. The abbot of Melrose, for instance, had a significant house in the Cowgate, Edinburgh: *ibid.*, pp. 251–3.
181 Szabó, *Woodland and Forests in Medieval Hungary*, pp. 113, 115, 142. Pilis had property in Bratislava.
182 Stevenson, 'The Monastic Presence', p. 109; Oram, 'The Estates and Possessions', p. 263.
183 The toll levied to help pay for the building and maintenance of a bridge.
184 A. R. Bell, C. Brooks and P. R. Dryburgh, *The English Wool Market c. 1230–1327* (Cambridge, 2007), p. 81.
185 Oram, 'The Estates and Possessions', p. 264; Coppack, *Fountains Abbey*, p. 114.

teenth centuries, first with Flanders and later with the Italian merchants. The very fact that in 1193 they (and other northern houses) paid their share of Richard I's ransom in a year's wool clip underlines just how significant this was to the monasteries' economies.[186] The contemporary chronicler William of Newburgh remarked that this was the White Monks' chief means of subsistence.[187] English wool in general was considered to be of a high quality but Cistercian wool was particularly prized in the twelfth and thirteenth centuries, perhaps because of the monks' better breeding techniques but also as it was meticulously prepared and graded; Fountains, for example, graded its wool into six categories.[188] Fountains Abbey was the biggest producer of wool in Yorkshire and at one time in the country; at the turn of the fourteenth century it headed the list of wool producers supplying an Italian merchant with a total of seventy-six sacks for sale.[189] To facilitate their trade in wool the Yorkshire Cistercians acquired properties in key centres, chiefly Boston which, as we noted earlier, was integral to the export of wool to Flanders and Italy, and York, which was important for trade in wool and fishing. The monks of Byland had a wool house at Clifton which lay just outside the city of York and on the River Ouse. Clifton was an important base for the delivery of wool to Italian merchants and we know that in the late thirteenth and early fourteenth centuries Byland had contracts with merchants from Florence and Lucca; the community sold over two hundred bags of wool from Clifton during this period.[190] The wool industry in Yorkshire and indeed throughout the country was devastated by the sheep scab (murrain) in the late thirteenth century. The Cistercians lost a significant number of animals and this, together with the system of advance payments, led several houses into bankruptcy or near bankruptcy; some were forced temporarily to disband. Kirkstall dispersed in 1281 and Rievaulx in 1292.[191] Rievaulx, which had been one of the main wool producers in the country, was bankrupt in 1288 and 1297, and although the community did recover it was later hit hard by Scottish attacks on its lands as well as by the Black Death and the general economic slump.[192] Despite difficulties that arose from time to time there can be no doubt as to the importance of

---

[186] Burton, *Monastic Order in Yorkshire*, p. 270.
[187] *The History of William of Newburgh*, trans. Stevenson, p. 615.
[188] Bell, Brooks and Dryburgh, *The English Wool Market*, pp. 116, 134; *Memorials of Fountains*, III, xiv–xv.
[189] Francesco Balducci Pegolotti, *La Pratica della Mercatura*, ed. Allan Evans (Cambridge, Mass., 1936), p. 260. Each sack might hold about 150 kilograms of wool: Williams, *Welsh Cistercians*, p. 258.
[190] R. A. Donkin, *The Cistercians: Studies in the Geography of Medieval England and Wales*, Pontifical Institute of Medieval Studies (Toronto, 1978), pp. 142, 195.
[191] Bell, Brooks and Dryburgh, *The English Wool Market*, p. 70.
[192] E. Jamroziak, 'Rievaulx Abbey as a Wool Producer in the Thirteenth Century: Cistercians, Sheep and Big Debts', *Northern History* 40 (2003), 197–218.

the Cistercians in developing trade links. McGuire claims that the 'rich trading' in wax and hides between France and Denmark was cultivated by the Cistercians, and cites an exemption granted to the monks of Clairvaux by Valdemar II in 1230. This freed the community from tolls when buying skins and wax in Denmark and transporting them to France. The trade link that these French and Danish Cistercians nurtured endured; there is evidence that in the late fifteenth century Troyes was purchasing skins and wax from Denmark.[193]

Conclusion

> Give the Cluniacs today a tract of land covered with marvellous buildings, endow them with ample revenues and enrich the place with vast possessions: before you can turn round it will all be ruined and reduced to poverty. On the other hand, settle the Cistercians in some barren retreat which is hidden away in an overgrown forest: a year or two later you will find splendid churches there and fine monastic buildings, with a great amount of property and all the wealth you can imagine.[194]

Contemporaries were struck by the speed and the sheer scale of the Cistercians' acquisition of land and remarked on the successfulness of their rural economy. For some, however, the White Monks were overly zealous and even aggressive in their pursuit of property. According to the 'Life' of Wulfric of Haselbury, composed c. 1184 by a Cistercian, John of Forde,[195] although the hermit was a great admirer of the Order and championed its ascetic practices he questioned the Cistercians' policies of land acquisition and management. Wulfric believed that the monks exerted their rights rather too liberally on lands that had been made over to them and felt that they ought to be 'more mindful' of their responsibility to those committed to their lordship.[196] The Cistercians' critics caricatured their greediness for land and portrayed them as ruthless predators who resorted to coercion, trickery and if need be, violence.[197] Some claimed that the brethren would prey on the vulnerabilities of the dying, guaranteeing them salvation in return for their lands. Gerald of Wales (d. c.

193 McGuire, *Cistercians in Denmark*, pp. 125, 306 note 68.
194 Gerald of Wales, *Journey Through Wales*, ed. and trans. L. Thorpe (Harmondsworth, 1978), pp. 105–6.
195 At the time of writing the 'Life' John was prior of Forde (Dorset) but from 1191 to 1214 he presided as abbot of the house; see C. Holdsworth, 'Forde, John of (c.1150–1214)', *ODNB*, vol. 20, p. 350.
196 From John of Forde's 'Life of Wulfric' in Matarasso, *Cistercian World*, pp. 231–73 (pp. 253–4).
197 A particularly extreme example is the account of the massacre of a knight who refused the Cistercians' offer of prayers in return for his land; the White Monks allegedly resorted to deception and violence to secure his holdings which resulted in the slaughter of the knight and his family: see Walter Map, *De Nugis Curialium*, pp. 107–9; Gerald of Wales, *Speculum Ecclesiae*, in Gerald of Wales, *Giraldi Cambrensis Opera*, IV, 225–7. This was seemingly about the monks of Byland: Burton, *Monastic Order in Yorkshire*, p. 308.

1220), who was one of the Cistercians' harshest critics, alleged that several of the monks visited a wealthy lady of Ewyas Harold, Herefordshire, as she lay on her deathbed and refused to leave until she had received the tonsure and transferred her assets to the monastery.[198] Gerald and his fellow detractors were undoubtedly economical with the truth but their allegations were not wholly unfounded. In 1342 there was an investigation into the transfer of Cockerington manor to the monks of Louth Park (Lincolnshire) by a dying man – Henry le Vavasour. The fact that the abbot of Louth Park had sent a covered cart to bring Henry to the monastery to sign over his property and had witnessed the agreement was a cause of concern and prompted some to question the legitimacy of the conveyance. The abbot defended his actions and was adamant that Henry had himself initiated the transfer since he wished to augment worship in the house. Henry's widow, Constance, cast aspersions on this account. She claimed that her husband had not been in a sound state when making his will and that he had been brought to the abbey under false pretences, believing that he would be cured there. There were also suggestions that the abbot had forged the will. Others, however, came to the abbot's defence. An important witness was Henry's servant, Alice, who had tended him at the monastery and vouched that there had been no foul play.[199] The Cistercians' critics would have fed off incidents such as these, exaggerating and distorting the facts to indict the monks.

A key question throughout this chapter – and an important theme throughout the book – is the matter of the Cistercians' distinctiveness. Is it appropriate to speak of a Cistercian economy and what exactly does this mean? Detailed analysis of the evidence has underlined the flexibility of the Order. Its economy was Cistercian at the core but took on a regional gloss as communities responded to their environment. Ideals and practices were adapted to accommodate the different socio-economic milieus and importantly were modified in response to economic developments; the White Monks moved with the times. But, as Bouchard warns, the Order's competence and economic success did not signify a falling away from its spiritual ideals; the two were not incompatible and indeed could be mutually supportive.[200]

The Cistercian economy was influenced by contemporary demands and regional practice but the monks also brought about economic change

---

[198] See B. Golding, 'Gerald of Wales and the Cistercians', *Reading Medieval Studies* 21 (Reading, 1995), 5–30 (pp. 18–9).

[199] Patent Roll 19 Edward III (1345), 'Exemplification of depositions touching the making of a feoffment by Sir Henry le Vavasour', in *The Chronicle of Louth Park Abbey with an Appendix of Documents*, ed. E. Venables, trans. A. R. Maddison, Lincolnshire Record Society, 1 (1891), appendix 20 (pp. 57–61); Williams, *Cistercians in the Early Middle Ages*, p. 133.

[200] Bouchard, *Holy Entrepreneurs.*

whether as pioneers, entrepreneurs or disseminators of methods and techniques. Perhaps the Cistercians' most enduring legacy comes from their reorganisation of the land. Across Europe a number of Cistercian granges survive as working farms and the field patterns that the White Monks set down some eight hundred years ago have been preserved and indeed are used to this day.[201]

---

[201] For example, Ninevah Farm in north Yorkshire occupies the site of Fountains's former grange of Morker; Kinder notes that six of the eleven granges that Pontigny had created by the mid-twelfth century were still working farms with medieval buildings at the start of the twenty-first century: Kinder, 'Living in a Vale of Tears', p. 91.

CHAPTER EIGHT

'Lanterns shining in a dark place':
The Cistercians and the World

Shining through the mist like the morning star, the holy Cistercian Order fights in the Church militant by work and example. By the exercise of holy contemplation and the merit of innocent life, it fervently strives to scale the heights with Mary. It strives to conform itself to the work of the anxious Martha through the exercise of praiseworthy deeds and assiduous concern for pious works.[1]

The Cistercians may have preferred rural locations which were removed from the distractions of urban life, but as we have seen throughout this discussion their desert was more metaphoric than real. Cistercian sites were not isolated; nor were communities cut off from society. On the contrary the White Monks engaged with the world. They both influenced, and were influenced by, social, economic, political and spiritual developments. This might mean taking on regional practices and disseminating new styles and techniques of architecture and farming, or working with secular and ecclesiastical powers to champion reform or augment state building. Communities were at times hit by warfare, plague and famine; individual members served as diplomats and arbiters in local, national and international affairs. Some held public office. The Cistercians of San Galgano, Tuscany, acted as treasurers for Siena from the mid-thirteenth century until the early fourteenth century.[2] This interaction with society should not, however, be seen as an abandonment of the desert and a falling away from ideals. As Martha Newman has argued, the Cistercians engaged with the world from the outset. Indeed their involvement was fundamental to the Order's understanding of *caritas*: as monks and Christians the Cistercians had a duty to reform the world outside

---

[1] Pope Benedict XII, 1335, cited in France, *Cistercians in Medieval Art*, p. 50. The quotation in the chapter title is from Orderic Vitalis, *Ecclesiastical History*, IV, 325.

[2] F. Andrews, 'Living like the Laity? The Negotiations of Religious Status in the Cities of Late Medieval Italy', *Transactions of the Royal Historical Society*, sixth series, 20 (2010), 27–55; see also her 'Monastic Observance and Communal Life: Siena and the Employment of Religious', in *Pope, Church and Laity: Essays in Honour of Brenda M. Bolton*, ed. F. Andrews, C. Egger and C. Rousseau (Leiden, 2008), pp. 357–83.

the monastery and a responsibility for the spiritual welfare of others.[3] Far from being incompatible with Cistercian beliefs – or indeed with the tenets of Benedict's Rule – their ties with rulers, the papacy, ecclesiastics and laity augmented the Order's expansion throughout Western Christendom and supported its very survival.

The monastery was a place of contemplation but the precinct walls were not impenetrable and the Cistercians, like other religious communities, engaged with society from within the confines of their cloisters. The brethren sent out their prayers to assist individuals and support specific ventures such as war and the Crusades. They welcomed guests, buried outsiders and wrote letters of advice to men and women of all states. Sometimes they struggled to meet the demand. In a letter to the canon Oger, Bernard of Clairvaux explained that in summer he would rise early to deal with his correspondence yet he was still finding it difficult to keep apace with Oger's communications. He was also concerned that it was exhausting for the messengers to be conducting so many of their letters back and forth. Bernard thus asked Oger to slow down his replies and suggested he might devote more time to meditation.[4]

The Cistercians also engaged with the world by leaving the confines of the monastery. This might seem a flagrant breach of the vow of stability but monks were permitted to leave the cloister for legitimate reasons and with the growth of monastic administration this became increasingly common. As we noted in chapter 4, abbots were expected to attend the annual General Chapter at Cîteaux which might involve considerable travel and require them to be absent from their communities for several months. They were obliged to visit their daughter houses each year, and both they and the obedientiaries had occasion to leave the monastery from time to time to tend to business relating to the house. Whilst on their travels the monks might endeavour to win recruits to the Cistercian life. Whenever Bernard of Clairvaux journeyed through France he would stop off at Paris to address the schoolmen, both on his way out and on his return. In 1140 Geoffrey of Auxerre was amongst those whom the charismatic abbot 'netted in that catch' and was duly compelled to take the Cistercian habit.[5] From the mid-thirteenth century monks were permitted – and in some cases obliged – to leave the cloister to attend university and acquire the necessary training to equip them to oppose heresy. The Cistercians established *studia* in various university towns throughout Europe such as Paris, Toulouse, Montpellier and Oxford, so

3 Newman, *Boundaries of Charity*.
4 *Letters of St Bernard of Clairvaux*, no. 91 (p. 135).
5 *Vita Tertia* (Geoffrey of Auxerre, PL 185, cols 527–8), Book 3, chapter 9, in Cawley, *Bernard of Clairvaux: Early Biographies*, p. 72.

that members of the Order could study in appropriate surroundings.[6] In some places the Cistercians played a leading role in the very foundation of the university. In 1288 the abbot of Alcobaça was instrumental in lobbying for the establishment of a university at Lisbon which was founded two years later.[7]

This final section explores two key areas of the Cistercians' interaction with the world. The first focuses on their administration of charity which was largely dispensed from the monastery, while the second considers their involvement in one of the most significant events of the Middle Ages, the Crusades.

Charity

> O fount of gardens, paupers' open gate
> You cure the sick, disease alleviate.[8]

A poem written by a monk of Rievaulx in the early thirteenth century paid tribute to the charity exercised by his neighbouring Cistercians at Fountains who openly welcomed the poor and tended the sick.[9] His praise was perhaps inspired by Fountains's response to the famine of 1194 when the community set up a refuge camp at the gates of the monastery to shelter and tend the indigent.[10] Care of the poor was integral to monastic administration and was addressed by Benedict in chapter 53 of his Rule, which related to the reception of guests. Benedict urged communities to welcome outsiders but to show particular care to the poor in whom Christ was more truly received. This care of the needy followed the precepts of Matthew 25.35–45, and made the administration of charity and hospitality both a Christian and a monastic duty. Cistercian legislation elaborated on the Rule. The twelfth-century customs of

---

[6] For further discussion see, for example, P. Dautrey, 'Croissance et adaptation chez les Cisterciens au triezième siécle: les debuts du College des Bernardins de Paris', *Analecta Cisterciensia* 32 (1976), 122–215; Davis, 'The Church of the Collège Saint-Bernard', pp. 223–34; *The Early History of St John's College Oxford*, ed. W. H. Stevenson and H. E. Salter, Oxford Historical Society, new series, 1 (1939); C. H. Talbot, 'The English Cistercians and the Universities', *Studia Monastica* 4 (1962), 197–220; R. B. Dobson, 'The Religious Orders 1370–1540', in *The History of the University of Oxford II: Late Medieval Oxford*, ed. J. I. Catto and R. Evans (Oxford, 1992), pp. 539–79.

[7] *Charters of Foundation and Early Documents of the Universities of the Coimbra Group*, ed. J. J. Hermans and M. Nelissen, second revised edn (Leuven, 2005), p. 38. In 1308 the university relocated to Coimbra.

[8] Matthew of Rievaulx, 'Epistulare Carmen de Fontibus', lines 5–6, trans. A. Rigg, *A History of Anglo-Latin Literature 1066–1422* (Cambridge, 1992), p. 136. The entire poem, in Latin, is printed in A. Wilmart, 'Les mélanges de Matthieu préchantre de Rievaulx au debut du XIIIe siècle', *Revue Bénédictine* 52 (1940), 15–84.

[9] *Ibid.*

[10] *Memorials of Fountains*, I, 123.

the Order entrusted the monastic porter with the task of distributing alms at the gate; he was to keep a stash of bread at hand to distribute to wayfarers.[11] The porter exercised charity on behalf of the community thereby ensuring that this important duty was carried out and that it did not impinge on monastic devotions. As the organisation of the monastery became increasingly complex the porter's role, like that of the other obedientiaries, was developed and the precise nature of his tasks varied from house to house and over time. According to the late thirteenth-century account book of Beaulieu Abbey, Hampshire, the porter was to lodge thirteen poor folk every night but on feast days admit as many poor as there were monks. He also distributed the brethren's old clothes and shoes to the needy. On Maundy Thursday each of the poor received a penny from the Beaulieu community.[12]

Charity and almsgiving thus formed a basic component of Cistercian life and the mechanism for their practice was set down in the Order's legislative texts. But the extent and nature of care each community provided were affected by contemporary conditions. The Cistercians were discriminating in their almsgiving and sought to assist only the deserving poor. Accordingly they cut their charity during harvest when there was plenty of work available for the needy to earn their own crust.[13] In times of shortage and crises, however, they accepted greater responsibility for the indigent who evidently saw the monastery gate as a symbol of succour and a place to gather in times of need. Jocelin of Furness's 'Life' of Waldef, a former abbot of Melrose, describes how during a famine in the mid-twelfth century hordes of the hungry flocked to the Scottish house. They built shelters and erected tents in the fields and forests around the abbey, and such were their numbers the encampment extended for over two miles. Abbot Waldef and the cellarer of Melrose visited the folk and took a personal interest in their welfare. Struck with pity at their plight and concerned at the lack of supplies, the cellarer offered to slaughter the monastery's herds. The dearth of grain was remedied though God's assistance. Jocelin explained that when Waldef learned that there was only a two-week supply of grain at the abbey's barns of Gattonside and Eildon, he visited each in turn and there thrust his staff into the bin and prayed for help. Waldef's pleas were answered and for three months the grain stores were never depleted but managed to sustain all the needy. Jocelin compared this miracle with the multiplication of meal and oil at Sarepta

---

11   *Ecclesiastica Officia*, chapter 120: 20 (p. 334).
12   *Account Book of Beaulieu Abbey*, pp. 32, 219; C. H. Talbot, 'The Account Book of Beaulieu Abbey', *Cîteaux in de Nederlanden* 9 (1958), 189–210 (p. 195).
13   *Account Book of Beaulieu Abbey*, p. 174; Talbot, 'The Account Book of Beaulieu Abbey', 195.

(3 Kings 17) as well as the feeding of the children of Israel in the desert (Exodus 16).[14] Shortly thereafter a second famine afflicted the region and Melrose once more gave up its animals to be slaughtered. But this time the monks responded personally to the crisis and each offered to split his bread allowance to share with the poor. The brethren's sacrifice was augmented by divine intervention for it was reputed that the bread supply never ran out during this time of need.[15] There are similar tales for other Cistercian abbeys – and indeed for houses of other orders for this was by no means peculiar to the White Monks.[16] Caesarius of Heisterbach records that when famine devastated Siebengebirge, Germany, in 1190, some 1500 of the local poor found relief daily at his abbey. Abbot Gerard made sure that a large ox was cooked with vegetables each day and he personally distributed this amongst the needy who gathered at the monastery. As at Melrose this charitable work received heavenly assistance; it was said that the monastery's flour never ran out and that its bread quite miraculously expanded in the oven.[17]

The nature of charity exercised by Cistercian houses was influenced by specific members of the community who were especially devoted to almsgiving. They include Adam of Lexington, a renowned monk of Melrose in the thirteenth century, who would sit by the door of the abbey church, reciting the Psalter, with a basket of bread at hand for the poor.[18] It was also affected by benefactors who might make a grant to augment the community's care of the needy. During Henry III's reign Roger Bertram confirmed a grant of land in Aldworth to Newminster Abbey, Northumberland, from which one hundred of the poor were to receive two oatcakes and two herrings on St Katherine's Day.[19]

The abbey gate was the main focus of Cistercian charity and it was here that most of the community's alms were distributed. In 1124 the monks of Clairvaux allegedly fed and tended hundreds of the local poor at its gatehouse each day, while in the thirteenth century Villers Abbey (Brabant) distributed over 2000 loaves of bread every week at its gate.[20] But Cistercian charity extended beyond the monastery. Alms were dispensed from the abbey's granges which might also provide lodgings for the poor. In 1221 Wilin de Archis gave ten cartloads of turf to Furness

---

[14] McFadden, 'An Edition and Translation of the Life of Waldef', pp. 134–6 (trans. pp. 266–70).
[15] *Ibid.*, pp. 136–7 (trans. pp. 270–1).
[16] For Benedictine examples including Evesham, Abingdon and St Albans, see Knowles, *Monastic Order*, p. 485.
[17] Caesarius of Heisterbach, *Dialogus Miraculorum*, Book 4, chapter 65, Scott and Bland, *Dialogue on Miracles*, I, 265–6.
[18] 'Chronicle of Melrose', p. 96.
[19] *Newminster Chartulary*, ed. J. T. Fowler, Surtees Society, 66 (1878) p. 108.
[20] Leroux-Dhuys, *Cistercian Abbeys*, p. 34; Kinder, *Cistercian Europe*, p. 370.

Abbey (Lancashire) to warm the poor folk accommodated at the gate of its grange at Winterburn.[21] In chapter seven we noted that Arnulf, a lay brother of Villers, distributed alms from the abbey's grange at Chênoit, but that some members of the community objected to the extent of his generosity and regarded the lay brother's liberality as a liability. The abbot of Villers duly intervened. He removed Arnulf to another grange (Sart) and punished him with eleven days' major excommunication and forty days' lesser.[22] There were clearly limits to Cistercian charity, particularly in times of financial hardship and rising debt when philanthropic ideals might be superseded by a concern for prudent economic management.

Recent research has highlighted a link between the Cistercian nunneries in northern France in the thirteenth century and the care of lepers, as well as of the sick and poor more generally. Lester notes that these convents were often situated beside or within leper communities and small hospitals for the indigent, although the houses were not necessarily Cistercian from the outset. The nuns were regarded as active carers of the sick and needy, and not simply as guardians of relics that might cure them, as was the case in the twelfth century. Lester suggests that the nuns' provision for the indigent was 'a specific kind of female Cistercian piety' and became an integral part of their spiritual endeavours; it was perhaps regarded as a form of manual labour. This growing concern for lepers and the sick may have been connected to urban growth and although it was strongly associated with the Cistercian women, it was not exclusive to them; a similar role was adopted by Premonstratensian nuns as well as by the nuns of Fontevraud.[23]

Elsewhere Cistercian involvement in the world drew the brethren out of the cloister. An important example is the Order's involvement in the Crusades, the Holy Wars against the infidel which sought to defend the Faith and secure Jerusalem for Western Christendom.

The Cistercians and the Crusades

> An excellent whelp; a guardian of the House of God, ready to bark out loud against foes of the faith.[24]

---

[21] *Coucher Book of Furness*, II (iii), no. 42 (pp. 381–2).

[22] Cawley, *Send Me God*, p. 15; Goswin of Bossut, 'Life of Arnulf', Book 2, chapter 3, in *ibid.*, pp. 156–9. See above, p. 158.

[23] A. E. Lester, 'Cares Beyond the Walls: Cistercian Nuns and the Care of Lepers in Twelfth- and Thirteenth-Century Northern France', in Jamroziak and Burton, *Religious and Laity in Western Europe*, pp. 197–224.

[24] A description of Bernard of Clairvaux from the *Vita Prima*, Book 1 (William of St Thierry), chapter 1, in Cawley, *Bernard of Clairvaux: Early Biographies*, p. 4.

Cistercian involvement in the crusades is often associated with St Bernard of Clairvaux's preaching of the Second Crusade, which was called by his former monk Pope Eugenius III after the fall of Edessa to resurgent Muslims in December 1144.[25] It was thus a Cistercian enterprise of sorts and showed the White Monks working in tandem with the papacy to fight the heathen. Purkis has recently argued that Bernard and Eugenius together endeavoured to 'create a new vocabulary for crusading'. They took on an unprecedented role in the theological development of twelfth-century crusading to implement a very different understanding of the crusader badge. The Cross was no longer to be regarded as a sign of the Passion – this identification with Christ was reserved for monks. It was now to signify the indulgence secured by those who took up arms against the infidel. Indeed for Bernard the crusade was not simply to liberate the Church in the East but provided western Christians with an opportunity to expiate their sins and thereby secure salvation.[26]

Bernard's preaching mission took him through France, Flanders and the Rhineland. His charisma which compelled recruits to take the Cistercian habit now moved men to take up arms for God. Such was Bernard's magnetism that it was said that women hid their husbands from him and mothers their sons.[27] Bernard also encouraged rulers to commit to the Crusade, notably Louis VII of France and Conrad III of Germany. However, no Cistercian monk or lay brother was to join the Holy War and transgressors faced excommunication.[28] The Second Crusade thrust Bernard and the Cistercians generally onto the international stage and set them at the forefront of current affairs. Bernard was certainly uneasy about the nature and extent of his involvement and how this jarred with his life as a monk. He famously described himself as a chimera of the age, an allusion to his incongruous blend of monk, preacher and politician: 'I have kept the habit of a monk but I have long ago abandoned the life.'[29] But however reluctant or unsuited to the task he professed to be – the abbot compared himself to an ant pulling a cart – Bernard regarded it as his duty to undertake this work and as a matter of obedience. The

---

[25] For a useful outline of the events of the Second Crusade see Phillips's and Hoch's introduction to *The Second Crusade: Scope and Consequences*, ed. J. Phillips and M. Hoch (Manchester, 2001), especially pp. 2–12.

[26] W. J. Purkis, *Crusading Spirituality in the Holy Land and Iberia, c. 1095–1187* (Woodbridge, 2008), pp. 86–119, 181; R. Hiestand, 'The Papacy and the Second Crusade', in Phillips and Hoch, *The Second Crusade*, pp. 32–53 (p. 45).

[27] *Vita Prima*, PL, 185, col. 235.

[28] *Letters of St Bernard of Clairvaux*, no 396 (pp. 396–7).

[29] *Ibid.*, no. 326 (p. 402).

pope, after all, was God's representative on earth and as such was to be honoured and obeyed.[30]

Bernard's preaching of the Second Crusade was effective. It drummed up considerable support for the campaign and heightened expectations of victory. But the Crusade itself was a spectacular disaster that left Western Christendom stunned and demoralised. This had significant consequences for papal prestige as well as for the crusading idea; moreover, an explanation for God's failure to reward the crusaders was needed. Various reasons were given and scapegoats made. Blame was attributed to the devil, to the people of Europe as well as to the crusaders themselves whose hearts, it was said, had clearly not been pure. For Bernard the outcome was to be understood as God's will and he was reassured that those who had participated in the campaign would ultimately be strengthened.[31]

Following the failure of the Second Crusade and subsequent criticism of Bernard some members of the Order voiced their concern at future participation in the campaigns. Yet the Cistercians' alliance with the pope continued, distinguishing their involvement with the papacy from that of other religious orders.[32] The General Chapter as a body and individual monks, as well as former brethren who had been elevated to ecclesiastical office, endorsed and actively supported the papacy's campaign to fight for Christendom. Notable participants include Archbishop Baldwin of Canterbury, former abbot of Forde (Dorset), who in 1188 preached the Third Crusade throughout Wales to incite men to take the Cross and as a prelude to his own departure for the Holy Land. Gerald of Wales accompanied Baldwin on his preaching mission and has left a vivid and lively account of their journey.[33] Some fifty years later Odo of Châteauroux, who was at that time abbot of either Grandselve or Ourscamp, was made Louis IX's legate and in this capacity accompanied the king on his crusade to Damietta (1248–54).[34]

The papacy accorded the Cistercians a prominent role in its campaigns against the Cathar heretics in the south of France. This culminated in the Albigensian Crusade (1209–29), one of the most brutal endeavours

---

[30] J. R. Sommerfeldt, *Bernard of Clairvaux on the Spirituality of Relationship* (Mahwah, 2004), pp. 114–23; Iben Fonnesberg-Schmidt, *The Popes and the Baltic Crusades 1147–1254* (Leiden, 2007), p. 41.
[31] See Phillips's and Hoch's introduction to *The Second Crusade*, p. 12; Fonnesberg-Schmidt, *The Popes and the Baltic Crusades*, p. 36; B. Bolton, 'The Cistercians and the Aftermath of the Second Crusade', in *The Second Crusade and the Cistercians*, ed. M. Gervers (New York, 1992), pp. 131–40 (p. 135). For further discussion of the nature and impact of the Second Crusade see the other essays in this collection.
[32] See Fonnesberg-Schmidt, *The Popes and the Baltic Crusades*, pp. 42, 51; Bolton, 'Cistercians and the Aftermath of the Second Crusade', pp. 136–9, outlines deliberations over a new crusade in 1150.
[33] Gerald of Wales, *Itinerarium Cambriae*, in Gerald of Wales, *Giraldi Cambrensis Opera*, VII; trans. L. Thorpe, *The Journey Through Wales/The Description of Wales*, pp. 74–209. Baldwin died at Acre in 1190.
[34] France, *Cistercians in Medieval Art*, pp. 187–8.

of the Middle Ages. Cistercian involvement in the Languedoc stemmed back to 1145 when Bernard of Clairvaux embarked on a preaching mission to the Midi to convert the heretics there. From the late twelfth century the papacy drew increasingly on the Order's support for its legatine missions to the Languedoc but the nature of its participation was taken to a new level by men such as Henry de Marcy, abbot of Clairvaux (1177–79), and Arnold Amaury, abbot of Cîteaux (1201–12) and later archbishop of Narbonne, who not only preached against the heretics but led armies against them.[35] In 1178 Abbot Henry was sent to Toulouse to preach against the Cathar heresy, following Count Raymond V's request to the General Chapter for help. At the Third Lateran Council of 1179 Henry was made cardinal bishop of Albano and was entrusted with a mission against the Albigensians; he was assisted by the former abbot of Pontigny.[36] Under Innocent III (1198–1216) these legations against the Cathars became ever more Cistercian in character as the papacy sought not only to stamp out heresy but to reform the Church in Languedoc so that it could assist with the mission.[37] The most prominent – and notorious – participant was Arnold Amaury, abbot of Cîteaux, who as former abbot of Grandselve was no stranger to the region. In 1204 Innocent III made Arnold his legate and put him in charge of a mission against the Albigensians; in 1209, the crusaders gathered under Arnold's leadership, following Innocent's proclamation of the Crusade, and in 1212 he led an army of knights from France to Spain for the Battle of Las Navas de Tolosa. Arnold enlisted the help of his fellow Cistercian abbots to assist in these campaigns.[38] The Albigensian Crusade resulted in the massacre of thousands, and Arnold's methods of dealing with the heretics were regarded by some as unduly severe. One contemporary Cistercian, who was a supporter of the Crusade, has left an account of Arnold's alleged response at the Fall of Béziers in 1209. On hearing from his soldiers that they could hardly differentiate between Catholics and heretics, Arnold is reputed to have instructed the men to kill everyone, for God would be able to tell his own.[39] Arnold's harsh reaction stemmed from a real and profound fear of the spread of heresy and a concern that should any of the Cathars be spared – and even if they recanted – they would

---

[35] Kienzle, *Cistercians, Heresy and Crusade*, pp. 204–8.
[36] King, *Cîteaux and her Elder Daughters*, p. 254; E. Graham-Leigh, *The Southern French Nobility and the Albigensian Crusade* (Woodbridge, 2005), esp. pp. 75–6; France, *Cistercians in Medieval Art*, p. 64.
[37] Graham-Leigh, *Southern French Nobility*, pp. 75–7.
[38] *Ibid.*, pp. 2, 75–6. For extensive discussion of Arnold's involvement see Kienzle, *Cistercians, Heresy and Crusade*, especially pp. 136–61.
[39] Caesarius of Heisterbach, *Dialogus Miraculorum*, Book 5, chapter 21, Scott and Bland, *Dialogue on Miracles*, I, 343–7 (pp. 345–6).

later return to their ways, 'like dogs to their vomit' (2 Peter 2.22), and continue to threaten the Church.[40] In the thirteenth century the papacy relied largely on the mendicant friars to preach both against heresy and in support of the crusades, but it was the Cistercians who had created a model for public preaching.[41]

The White Monks also supported the campaigns against the heathens from within their cloisters. The General Chapter pre-empted Innocent III's endeavours to make liturgical support a permanent component of the crusades and from the late twelfth century extended its liturgy to accommodate corporate prayers, processions and masses in support of the holy wars. Every Cistercian house – male and female – was to offer prayers for the crusaders, as set down in the Order's statutes. Additional statutes were promulgated to augment this liturgical assistance. For example, in the mid-thirteenth century the General Chapter ruled that all houses in France should offer prayers and make weekly processions for the success of Louis IX's crusade. In 1269 Louis asked female communities in his kingdom to pray for the crusaders before they left for the Holy Land and to celebrate anniversary masses for anyone who died on crusade.[42] There was a strong belief in the potency of the nuns' prayers – and in the prayers of pious women *per se*. In thirteenth-century Champagne crusading families founded Cistercian nunneries in part to function as powerhouses of prayer to support the military campaigns. Through prayer as well as through liturgical devotion and ministering to the indigent, the nuns practised a penitential piety whereby they shared in the suffering and sacrifice of the crusaders and evoked that of Christ. Lester argues that this form of *imitatio Christi* enabled them to contribute to the crusades from the home front. She refers to the Cistercian nun and leper Alice of Schaerbeek as a distinctive example of this correlation. Alice had suffered the loss of her right eye as a consequence of leprosy and in 1247 passed on the spiritual benefits she had gained from this affliction to Louis IX, to support his crusade in Damietta. The female kin of crusaders might enter Cistercian convents founded or patronised by their relatives to provide active support for the holy wars. Returning crusaders requested burial in these foundations and secured the nuns' prayers for their soul, and some chose to mark their departure for the Holy Land with a ritual at their Cistercian foundation or even took their formal leave from the house. In 1270 Guy of Dampierre set off for Louis IX's crusade from the Cistercian convent that his mother had founded at Flines, Flanders.[43]

---

[40]   Graham-Leigh, *Southern French Nobility*, p. 40.
[41]   Kienzle, *Cistercians, Heresy and Crusade*, especially p. 210.
[42]   A. E. Lester, 'A Shared Imitation: Cistercian Convents and Crusader Families in Thirteenth-Century Champagne', *Journal of Medieval History* 35 (2009), 353–70 (pp. 366–7).
[43]   *Ibid.*, 365, 370.

The Cistercians' endorsement and active support of these military campaigns might seem surprising and at odds with the ethos of monastic life. But their own life in the cloister was conceived of in terms of a battle against the devil and for St Bernard his monastery at Clairvaux was the heavenly Jerusalem and 'the fortress of God'.[44] This military imagery is vividly evoked in Bernard's letter to Henry I in 1131, in which he tells the king of his plans to found an abbey in northern England (Rievaulx) as 'an outpost of my Lord' that he would 'occupy' with his 'army', namely monks from Clairvaux.[45] More striking is a passage in the *Apologia* in which Bernard condemns monks who profess to be ill to secure a respite from claustral life in the comfort of the infirmary. Bernard decries the cowardice of these 'brave warriors' who abandon their 'comrades' to 'wallow in blood and gore' and behave as if the war had been won when the enemy continues to attack the monastery with spears and arrows.[46] The campaigns against the heathens and the heretics were regarded as a continuation of this battle against evil, which not only justified but necessitated the monks' active involvement and required them to look beyond the 'domestic vineyard' of the monastery to 'the Lord's vineyard', of which they were a part.[47] Preaching and persuasion might be preferable to arms but the use of the sword was warranted and even called for to safeguard the Faith. Indeed Bernard was a strong proponent of the Knights Templar, the fighting monks who were responsible for securing the pilgrim routes to Jerusalem and protecting the Crusader States. Bernard contributed to the composition of the Templar rule and c. 1130 wrote a quite remarkable tract, 'In Praise of the New Knighthood' (*De laude novae militiae*), in which he compared the Templars' apostolic spirituality to that espoused by the new religious orders.[48] He held the Templars up as a mirror to the secular knights and encouraged them to join the Templar ranks. For Bernard these warrior monks fused the spiritual and the military and fought a twofold battle. They killed the infidel for Christ thus exercising 'malicide' rather than committing homicide,

---

[44] For discussion of Clairvaux as the heavenly Jerusalem see Bredero, *Bernard of Clairvaux: Between Cult and History*, pp. 266–75.

[45] *Letters of St Bernard of Clairvaux*, no. 95 (pp. 141–2). See above, p. 38.

[46] *St Bernard's Apologia to Abbot William*, pp. 57–8.

[47] Bernard evokes this imagery in sermon 65 on the Song of Songs; for extensive discussion of this motif see Kienzle, *Cistercians, Heresy and Crusade*, pp. 8–9, 78–80, 85–90.

[48] *The Rule of the Templars. The French Text of the Rule of the Order of the Knights Templar*, trans. J. Upton-Ward (Woodbridge, 1992); *De laude novae militiae*, in *Sancti Bernardi Opera*, ed. J. Leclercq, H. M. Rochais and C. H. Talbot, 8 vols (Rome, 1957–77), III, 207–39; trans Conrad Greenia, *The Works of Bernard of Clairvaux: Volume Seven, Treatises III*, Cistercian Studies Series 19 (Kalamazoo, 1977).

and had no fear of death since for them 'to live is Christ and to die is gain' (Philippians 1.21).[49]

'The sweetness of the vine'[50]

> The duty of a monk is not to preach but to pray. He ought to be one for whom towns are a prison and the wilderness a paradise.[51]

The Cistercian cloister brought together solitary and communal living. It provided an opportunity for each monk to pursue his inner journey to salvation and draw on the support of his brethren. This accorded practical benefits such as sharing the household tasks and administrative duties as well as developing a sound economic structure. But most important, it helped the monk stand strong in the face of evil; as a body the brethren could better withstand the wiles of the devil. Just as the monks helped and supported each other within the cloister so they had a responsibility for those outside the monastery in 'the Lord's vineyard' and for the state of the world *per se*. The battle against evil and concern for society might, as we have seen, require them to look far beyond the confines of the monastery to distant lands. For some it meant leaving the cloister altogether to take up ecclesiastical or even papal office. Bernard of Clairvaux considered this was a step too far and he eschewed episcopal promotion but a number of Cistercians made this transition and, however reluctantly, left 'the paradise of the cloister' to assume office.[52]

The Cistercians therefore had an obligation to the world but they were also dependent on it, for the ties that bound them were mutually beneficial. Earlier chapters noted how the support of the papacy, rulers, patrons and benefactors was instrumental to the expansion of the Order and to the survival of individual communities, as well as to the growth of a successful economy. Not least, through their links with society monasteries could draw in new recruits and thereby secure the continuance of Cistercian life. These ties were therefore instrumental to the development of the Order and the fulfilment of Cistercian ideals. But just as each abbot had to balance his role as head of an institution with his spir-

---

49 *De laude novae militiae*, III: 4. For further discussion see, for example, M. Bulst-Thiele, 'The Influence of St Bernard of Clairvaux on the Formation of the Order of the Knights Templar', in Gervers, *The Second Crusade*, pp. 57–65; A. Grabois, '*Militia* and *Malitia*: the Bernardine Vision of Chivalry', in *ibid.*, pp. 49–56; Purkis, *Crusading Spirituality*, esp. pp. 60, 84, 101, 108.

50 From Peter de Celle's letter to Pope Alexander III, asking that Abbot Henry de Marcy not be raised to the see of Toulouse but allowed to remain at Clairvaux, cited in *Peter de Celle, Selected Works*, trans. H. Feiss, Cistercian Studies Series, 100 (Kalamazoo, 1987), p. 4.

51 *Letters of St Bernard of Clairvaux*, no. 393 (p. 465).

52 The quotation is from Peter de Celle's letter to Pope Alexander III regarding Henry de Marcy, see above, note 50.

itual life as a monk, so communities – and the Order as a whole – had to control the nature and extent of external links lest these endangered rather than enhanced monastic observance. At times it was difficult to strike the balance. Bernard of Clairvaux feared that his involvement in secular affairs had pulled him too far from the cloister and that he had lost his monastic identity. Yet properly managed the Cistercians' external ties could help them survive and flourish in a changing world.

Glossary

ABACUS: the uppermost part of a CAPITAL or column, often square.

ABBOT: superior who presides over the monastery and is responsible for the internal and external administration of the house. The head of a priory is a PRIOR.

AMBULATORY: polygonal or semicircular aisle or passageway, often around the east end of the CHOIR.

APSE: polygonal, semicircular or rectangular end of a building.

BEGUINE: holy woman leading a religious life but who had not taken vows.

BENEDICT OF NURSIA (ST): considered the founder of western monasticism, his rule (RULE OF ST BENEDICT) for the monks of Monte Cassino, compiled c. 480–550, became and remains the blueprint for monastic observance in the West.

BENEDICTINE: monk who lives according to the RULE OF ST BENEDICT and pledges stability to his monastery and the way of life. The Benedictines dominated monastic observance in the West until the late eleventh century and the emergence of the new religious orders such as the CARTHUSIANS and CISTERCIANS.

BREVIARY: service book containing prayers and offices.

CALEFACTORY: the warming house, often located on the south CLAUSTRAL range; it was one of the few places in the monastery that was heated.

CANONICAL HOURS: the liturgical offices that structured the monastic day.

CAPITAL: carved or sculpted top of a column.

CARTHUSIANS: contemplative order founded by St Bruno in 1084 at La Grande Chartreuse, near Grenoble. Carthusian monasticism combines communal and solitary living – the monks live in private cells arranged around the cloister where they sleep, work, pray and eat most of their meals, alone.

CARTULARY: manuscript containing a collection of charters pertaining to lands, rights and legal transactions.

CELLARER: an important monastic official (OBEDIENTIARY) who had charge of the monastery's provisions.

CHARTER OF CHARITY (*Carta Caritatis*): pioneering Cistercian document that set down the constitutional framework of the Order.

CHOIR: area in the east end of the church occupied by the monks' stalls.

CISTERCIAN ORDER: one of the most important religious orders to emerge from the eleventh-century reform movement and renowned for its commitment to observing a simpler interpretation of the RULE OF ST BENEDICT. The Cistercians were characterised by their habits of undyed wool, their emphasis on MANUAL LABOUR, the familial arrangement of houses and the introduction of LAY BROTHERS as an integral part of the community.

CLAUSTRAL: pertaining to the cloister or to monastic life.

CLOISTER: the heart of the monks' home; an open quadrangle (garth) surrounded by covered walkways or arcades (ranges) which house the domestic offices.

COENOBITIC: refers to monks living in a community and not as solitaries.

COLLATIONS: daily reading from John Cassian's *Collationes Patrum* (*Conferences*) and other edifying texts which took place before COMPLINE.

COMPLINE: the CANONICAL HOUR which brought the monks' day to a close.

CONVENTUAL: relating to the monastic community.

CONVERSUS: see LAY BROTHER

CUSTOMARY/CUSTUMAL/BOOK OF CUSTOMS: directory of customs relating to liturgical observance and also to the daily administration and organisation of the monastery.

DAUGHTER HOUSE: the monastery founded by another was known as its daughter house.

EARLY GOTHIC: style of architecture thought to have originated in north-east France, with Abbot Suger's rebuilding of St Denis, Paris, c. 1135. Characterised by its use of rib vaults, lancet windows, moulded piers and three-storey elevations, it created buildings that were loftier and lighter than those built in the ROMANESQUE style.

ECCLESIASTICA OFFICIA: detailed instructions for the performance of the CANONICAL HOURS and the administration of Cistercian houses; compiled in the twelfth century.

EREMITIC: living a solitary life as a hermit.

EXORDIUM CISTERCII ('The Beginning of Cîteaux'): brief historical foundation narrative describing the origins of Cîteaux, but a retrospective account that reworks the Cistercian story. The date and authorship of this text and also the *EXORDIUM PARVUM* have generated considerable debate.

EXORDIUM MAGNUM ('The Great Beginning'): completed in the

early thirteenth century by Conrad, a monk of Clairvaux and later abbot of Eberbach (d. 1221), this six-part work recounts the early history of the Order, tells of St Bernard and his successors and of the remarkable experiences of certain members of the Order. It fuses history, hagiography and the miraculous to incite contemporary Cistercians to revive the lofty standards of their predecessors.

EXORDIUM PARVUM ('The Little Beginning'): foundation narrative that tells the story of the early Cistercians and includes various letters relating to their origins as well as early institutes; this reworking of the Cistercians' origins is regarded as a justification and defence of the Order.

FATHER IMMEDIATE: abbot of the MOTHER HOUSE; he was expected to conduct an annual VISITATION of his DAUGHTER HOUSE and to offer the community advice and support.

GALILEE: see NARTHAX

GENERAL CHAPTER: annual general meeting attended by the heads of houses. The Cistercians were the first to make this an integral part of their administrative structure; the assembly met each September at Cîteaux, Burgundy.

GRANGE: agricultural centre from which the community co-ordinated farming and industrial work.

HABIT: regulation garb worn by the monk.

HAGIOGRAPHY: writings on saints and venerated persons.

HORARIUM: daily timetable in the monastery that was structured around the CANONICAL HOURS.

LAUDS: CANONICAL HOUR celebrated at dawn.

LAY BROTHER (*CONVERSUS*): the term initially described an adult convert to the religious life but later referred to men who took vows and were received as members of the community but were chiefly responsible for agricultural and industrial work. They effectively formed a separate community within the monastery. Lay sisters were females who occupied a similar role.

LECTIO DIVINA: 'divine reading'. Contemplative reading through which the monk sought communion with God. This formed part of the monastic day according to the RULE OF ST BENEDICT.

MANUAL LABOUR: an act of humility and an integral part of the monastic day according to the RULE OF ST BENEDICT. The monks might, for example, work in the gardens, grease boots or chop wood. Two periods were accorded to manual work in summer but just one in winter.

MARTYROLOGY: book listing the martyrs and saints in order of their anniversaries.

MATINS: CANONICAL HOUR celebrated before PRIME and now known as LAUDS.

MISERICORD: a room in the monastery where the monks were permitted to eat meat once this had been formally sanctioned; initially meat was prohibited to all but the sick. No meat was to be eaten in the refectory.

MOTHER HOUSE: the monastery which sent a colony of monks to settle a new foundation became its mother house; its abbot (FATHER IMMEDIATE) conducted an annual visitation of the new monastery and advised the community.

NARTHAX: small porch at the west end of the church, also known as the 'Galilee' or 'Paradise'.

NAVE: main body of the church in the western part of the building; in Cistercian churches this was usually occupied by the LAY BROTHERS.

NIGHTSTAIRS: staircase connecting the monks' dormitory with their CHOIR in the eastern part of the church and providing covered access for the night office of VIGILS.

NOCTURNS: see VIGILS

NONE(S): CANONICAL HOUR sung at the ninth hour.

NOVICE: probationary member of the monastery who received instruction and guidance from his NOVICEMASTER until he made his profession and was received as a full member of the monastic community.

NOVICEMASTER: monastic official (OBEDIENTIARY) who had charge of the novices and prepared them for monastic life.

NOVITIATE: probationary period required of a newcomer before he was fully received as a monk. The length of time varied but was traditionally a year.

OBEDIENTIARY: monastic office-holder, such as the CELLARER, sacrist and porter, entrusted with administrative duties.

OPUS DEI: 'the work of God'. This refers to the daily round of prayer in the monastery.

PRESBYTERY: eastern part of the church occupied by the monks' CHOIR and the high altar.

PRIEST: ordained member of the clergy who has the right to celebrate and administer the holy rites. During the Middle Ages it became increasingly common for monks to be ordained into the priesthood.

PRIOR: the head of a priory but second in command in an abbey.

PRIME: CANONICAL HOUR celebrated at daylight.

PULPITUM: screen with a central doorway dividing the east of the church from the nave in the west.

PYX: vessel in which the elements (bread and wine) are brought to the altar and in which the host is reserved.

REFECTORY (FRATER): the monks' dining room.

REREDORTER: the toilet block often accessed from the dormitory.

RETROCHOIR: area immediately behind the monks' CHOIR; this was occupied by the sick and infirm who observed a more relaxed regime than the others.

ROMANESQUE: architectural style characterised by its round arches, columns and piers and thick stone walls. It is associated especially with the eleventh and twelfth centuries.

ROOD SCREEN: screen separating the nave of the church (west) from the presbytery (east) and named after the Cross or Rood of Christ above it.

RULE OF ST BENEDICT: compiled by ST BENEDICT OF NURSIA, c. 480–550, to regulate the life of his monks at Monte Cassino. From the ninth century his 'little rule for beginners' became the cornerstone of western monasticism.

SEXT: CANONICAL HOUR originally celebrated at the sixth hour of the day.

SEYNEY: the process of bloodletting that was common in the Middle Ages to prevent ill-health and also to cure sickness. Monks were routinely bled in groups to prevent illness.

STATUTES: regulations issued to the monastic community to correct and reform, generally following the VISITATION of the house; also the regulations (*capitula*) promulgated by the GENERAL CHAPTER following its annual meeting.

TERCE: third CANONICAL HOUR, celebrated mid-morning.

TONSURE: rite of shaving the crown of the head, in imitation of Christ's Crown of Thorns; this was symbolic of both clerical and monastic status.

USUS CONVERSORUM: twelfth-century regulations drawn up for liturgical and daily practices of the Cistercian LAY BROTHERS. This was the first comprehensive legislation specifically for lay brethren.

VERSICLE: short liturgical verse sung or recited.

VESPERS: CANONICAL HOUR celebrated at the approach of dusk and named after Hesperus, the evening star.

VIGILS: night office (NOCTURNS) traditionally celebrated at midnight in accordance with Psalm 119.162 ('At midnight I rose to give thanks to Thee'). This is now referred to as MATINS. In the later Middle Ages MATINS and LAUDS were together known as Vigils.

VISITATION: formal inspection of the monastery by the bishop, his deputy or a member of the Order, to correct abuse and offer advice.

Bibliography

Printed primary sources

The Account Book of Beaulieu Abbey, ed. S. F. Hockey, Camden fourth series, 16 (London, 1975)

The Acts of the Welsh Rulers 1120–1283, ed. Huw Pryce with the assistance of Charles Insley (Cardiff, 2005)

AELRED OF RIEVAULX, *Treatises and Pastoral Prayer*, ed. M. Pennington, Cistercian Fathers Series, 2 (Kalamazoo, 1971, repr. 1995)

—— *De spiritali amicitia*, in *Aelredi Rievallensis, Opera Omnia*, I, *Opera Ascetica*, ed. A. Hoste and C. H. Talbot, Corpus Christianorum Continuatio Mediaevalis, 1 (Turnhout, 1971), 279–350; trans. M. E. Laker, *On Spiritual Friendship*, Cistercian Fathers Series, 5 (Kalamazoo, 1977); trans. L. C. Braceland, ed. and intro. M. Dutton, *Spiritual Friendship*, Cistercian Fathers Series, 5 (Collegeville, 2010)

—— *Speculum caritatis*, in *Aelredi Rievallensis, Opera Omnia*, I, 3–161; trans. E. Connor, *The Mirror of Charity*, Cistercian Fathers Series, 17 (Kalamazoo, 1990)

—— *The Life of St Edward, King and Confessor*, trans. J. Bertram (Guildford, 1990, repr. Southampton, 1997)

—— *The Liturgical Sermons: the First Clairvaux Collection*, trans. T. Berkeley and M. B. Pennington, Cistercian Fathers Series, 58 (Kalamazoo, 2001)

—— *Aelred of Rievaulx, The Lives of the Northern Saints*, trans. J. P. Freeland, ed., intro. and notes M. L. Dutton, Cistercian Fathers Series, 71 (Kalamazoo, 2006)

Alice the Leper The Life of Alice of Schaerbeek by Arnold II of Villers (?), trans. M. Cawley, Guadalupe Translations (Lafayette, 2000)

Annales monasterii de Waverleia, in *Annales Monastici*, ed. H. R. Luard, 5 vols, RS, 36 (1864–69), II, 127–411

Apologiae Duae: Gozechini Epistola ad Walcherum: Burchardi, ut Videtur, Abbatis Bellevallis Apologia de Barbis, Corpus Christianorum, Continuatio Mediaevalis, 62, ed. R. B. C. Huygens (Turnhout, 1985)

BERNARD OF CLAIRVAUX, *Sancti Bernardi Opera*, ed. J. Leclercq, H. M. Rochais and C. H. Talbot, 8 vols (Rome, 1957–77)

—— *St Bernard of Clairvaux, The Story of his Life as Recorded in the 'Vita Prima' by certain of his Contemporaries, William of St Thierry, Arnold of Bonnevaux, Geoffrey and Philip of Clairvaux, and Odo of Deuil*, trans. G. Webb and A. Walker (London, 1960)

—— *St Bernard's Apologia to Abbot William*, trans. M. Casey, intro. J. Leclercq (Kalamazoo, 1970)

—— *On the Song of Songs*, trans. K. Walsh and I. M. Edmonds, 4 vols, Cistercian Fathers Series, 4, 7, 31, 40 (Kalamazoo, 1971–81)

—— *De laude novae militiae*, in *Sancti Bernardi Opera*, III, 207–39; trans. Conrad Greenia, *The Works of Bernard of Clairvaux: Volume Seven, Treatises III*, Cistercian Studies Series, 19 (Kalamazoo, 1977)

—— *The Letters of St Bernard of Clairvaux*, trans. B. S. James (London, 1953); repr. with new intro. and bibliography B. Kienzle (Stroud, 1998)

Bernard of Clairvaux: Early Biographies, trans. M. Cawley, Guadalupe Translations (Lafayette, 2000)

CAESARIUS OF HEISTERBACH, *Dialogus Miraculorum*, ed. J. Strange, 2 vols (Cologne/Brussels/Bonn, 1851); trans. H. von E. Scott and C. C. S. Bland, *The Dialogue on Miracles*, 2 vols (London, 1929)

Calendar of Entries in the Papal Registers relating to Great Britain and Ireland: Papal Letters, ed. W. H. Bliss and J. A. Twemlow (London, 1893–)

Carta Caritatis Posterior, *NLT*, pp. 381–8 (trans. pp. 500–5)

Carta Caritatis Prior, *NLT*, pp. 274–82 (trans. pp. 440–50)

Cartulaire de l'abbaye de Porrois au diocèse de Paris plus connue sous son nom mystique, Port Royal, ed. A. de Dion (Paris, 1903)

Cartularium Abbathiae de Rievalle, ed. J. C. Atkinson, Surtees Society, 83 (1889)

The Cartulary of Byland Abbey, ed. J. Burton, Surtees Society, 208 (Woodbridge, 2004)

Charters of Foundation and Early Documents of the Universities of the Coimbra Group, ed. J. J. Hermans and M. Nelissen, second rev. edn (Leuven, 2005)

Chartes et documents concernant l'abbaye de Cîteaux 1098–1182, ed. J. Marilier, Bibliotheca Cisterciensis, 1 (Rome, 1961)

CHAUCER, GEOFFREY, 'The Pardoner's Tale', in *The Riverside Chaucer*, ed. Larry Dean Benson, third edn (Oxford 1987, repr. 2008), pp. 193–202

Chronica Monasterii de Melsa, a fundatione usque ad annum 1396, auctore Thoma de Burton, abbate. Accedit continuatio ad annum 1406 a monacho quodam ipsius domus, ed. E. A. Bond, 3 vols, RS, 43 (London, 1866–68)

The Chronicle of Louth Park Abbey with an Appendix of Documents, ed. E. Venables, trans. A. R. Maddison, Lincolnshire Record Society, 1 (1891)

'The Chronicle of Melrose', in *The Church Historians of England*, IV, part 1, ed. and trans. J. Stevenson (London, 1854), pp. 77–242; repr. in *Medieval Chronicles of Scotland: the Chronicles of Melrose and Holyrood* (Llanerch facsimile, Felinfach, 1988), pp. 7–124

Cistercian Lay Brothers: Twelfth Century Usages with Related Texts, ed. C. Waddell, Cîteaux: Commentarii Cistercienses, Studia et documenta, 10 (Brecht, 2000)

The Cistercian World: Monastic Writings of the Twelfth Century, ed. P. Matarasso (Harmondsworth, 1993)

CONRAD OF EBERBACH, *Exordium Magnum Cisterciense sive Narratio de Initio Cisterciensis Ordinis*, ed. B. Greisser, Corpus Christianorum Continuatio Mediaevalis, 138 (Turnhout, 1994); trans. as *Le Grand Exorde de Cîteaux, ou Recit des debuts de l'Ordre cistercien. Traduit du latin par Anthelmette Piebourg*, intro. B. P. McGuire, Cîteaux: Commentarii Cistercienses, Studia et documenta, 7 (Turnhout, 1998)

The Coucher Book of Furness Abbey, ed. J. C. Atkinson and J. Brownbill, Chetham Society, 3 vols (1886–88)

DANTE ALIGHIERI, *The Divine Comedy*, trans. C. H. Sisson, intro. and notes D. H. Higgins (London/Sydney, 1981)

Decrees of the Ecumenical Councils, I, ed. N. P. Tanner (Georgetown, 1990)

Early Sources of Scottish History 500 to 1286, 2 vols, collected and trans. A. O. Anderson (Edinburgh 1922, repr. Stamford, 1990)

Les Ecclesiastica Officia Cisterciens du xiième siècle, ed. D. Choisselet and P. Vernet (Reiningue, 1989); trans. *The Ancient Usages of the Cistercian Order [Ecclesiastica Officia]*, Guadalupe Translations (Lafayette, 1998)

English Historical Documents, 1189–1327, ed. H. Rothwell (London, 1975)

Exordium Monasterii Carae Insulae, in *Scriptores Minores Historiae Danicae*, 2, ed. M. Cl. Gertz (Copenhagen, 1970), pp. 153–264

The Foundation History of the Abbeys of Byland and Jervaulx, ed. and trans. Janet Burton, Borthwick Texts and Studies, 35 (York, 2006)

The Foundation of Kirkstall Abbey, ed. and trans. E. Clark, *Miscellanea*, Publications of the Thoresby Society, 4 (Leeds, 1895)

The Fountains Abbey Lease Book, ed. D. J. H. Michelmore, Yorkshire Archaeological Society Record Series, 140 (Leeds, 1981)

GEOFFREY 'GROSSUS', *Vita B. Bernardi Tironiensis*, PL, 172, cols 1362–1446, trans. Bernard Beck, *Saint Bernard de Tiron, l'ermite, le moine et le monde* (Cormeilles-le-Royal, 1998)

GERALD OF WALES, *Giraldi Cambrensis Opera*, ed. J. S. Brewer, J. F. Dimock and G. F. Warner, 8 vols, RS, 21 (London, 1861–91)

—— *The Journey Through Wales/The Description of Wales*, ed. and trans. L. Thorpe (Harmondsworth, 1978)

—— *The Autobiography of Giraldus Cambrensis*, ed. and trans. H. E. Butler, intro. C. H. Williams, guide to reading J. Gillingham (Woodbridge, 2005)

GILBERT FOLIOT, *The Letters and Charters of Gilbert Foliot*, ed. Z. N. Brooke, A. Morey and C. N. L. Brooke (Cambridge, 1967)

GILBERT OF HOYLAND, *Sermons on the Song of Songs*, ed. and trans. L. C. Braceland, 3 vols, Cistercian Fathers Series, 14, 20, 26 (Kalamazoo, 1978–79)

GOSWIN OF BOSSUT, 'The Life of Abundus', in *Send Me God: the Lives of Ida the Compassionate of Nivelles, Nun of La Ramée, Arnulf, Lay Brother of Villers, and Abundus, Monk of Villers, by Goswin of Bossut*, trans. and intro. M. Cawley, preface B. Newman (Turnhout, 2003; repr. as paperback, University Park, Pennsylvania, 2006), pp. 209–46

—— 'The Life of Arnulf, lay brother of Villers', in Cawley, *Send Me God*, pp. 125–205

—— 'The Life of Ida of Nivelles', in Cawley, *Send Me God*, pp. 2–99

Henryków Book, trans. P. Górecki, *A Local Society in Transition: the Henryków Book and Related Documents* (Toronto, 2002), pp. 91–202

Ida the Gentle of Léau, Cistercian Nun of La Ramée, trans. M. Cawley, Guadalupe Translations (Lafayette, 1998)

IDUNGUS, *Le moine Idung et ses deux ouvrages; 'Argumentum super quatuor questionibus' et 'Dialogus duorum monachorum'*, ed. R. B. C. Huygens (Spoleto, 1980); trans. J. F. O'Sullivan, 'A Dialogue between Two Monks', in *Cistercians and Cluniacs: The Case for Cîteaux [A Dialogue between Two Monks; an Argument on Four Questions]*, Cistercian Fathers Series, 33 (Kalamazoo, 1977), pp. 3–141

JOHN OF FORDE, 'Sermons on the Song of Songs', trans. Sister W. Beckett, in *Sermons on the Final Verses of the Song of Songs*, 7 vols, Cistercian Fathers Series, 29, 39, 43–7 (Kalamazoo, 1977–84), vol. VI

Bibliography

JOHN OF SALISBURY, *Ioannis Saresberiensis Episcopi Carnotensis Policratici*, ed. C. Webb, 2 vols (Oxford, 1909)

JOINVILLE, 'The Life of St Louis', in *Joinville and Villehardouin: Chronicles of the Crusades*, trans. and intro. C. Smith (London, 2008), pp. 137–336

The Ledger Book of Vale Royal Abbey, ed. J. Brownbill, Record Series of Lancashire and Cheshire, 68 (1914)

Letters of James V, collected and calendared R. K. Hannay, ed. D. Hay (Edinburgh, 1954)

'Liber Sancte Marie de Balmorinach', in *The Chartularies of Balmerino and Lindores*, Abbotsford Club, 22 (Edinburgh 1841)

The Life of Beatrice of Nazareth, trans R. de Ganck, Cistercian Fathers Series, 50 (Kalamazoo, 1991)

The Life of Ida the Eager of Louvain, trans. M. Cawley (forthcoming)

MARGERY KEMPE, *The Book of Margery Kempe*, trans. B. A. Windeatt (Harmondsworth, 1985, rev. 1994)

MATTHEW OF RIEVAULX, 'Les mélanges de Matthieu préchantre de Rievaulx au debut du XIIIe siècle', ed. A. Wilmart, *Revue Bénédictine* 52 (1940), 15–84

Memorials of the Abbey of St Mary of Fountains, I, ed. J. R. Walbran, Surtees Society, 42 (1863)

Memorials of the Abbey of St Mary of Fountains, III, ed. J. T. Fowler, Surtees Society, 130 (1918)

Narratio de fundatione Fontanis monasterii, in *Memorials of Fountains*, I, 1–129; trans. A. W. Oxford, *The Ruins of Fountains Abbey* (London, 1910), appendix 1 (pp. 127–230)

Narrative and Legislative Texts from Early Cîteaux, ed. and trans. C. Waddell, Cîteaux: Commentarii Cistercienses, Studia et documenta, 9 (Cîteaux, 1999)

Newminster Chartulary, ed. J. T. Fowler, Surtees Society, 66 (1878)

OGLERIUS DE TRIDINIO, 'The *Quis dabit* of Oglerius de Tridino, Monk and Abbot of Locedio', ed. C. W. Marx, *Journal of Medieval Latin* 4 (1994), 118–29

ORDERIC VITALIS, *The Ecclesiastical History of Orderic Vitalis*, ed. and trans. M. Chibnall, 6 vols, OMT (Oxford, 1969–80)

Patrologiae Cursus Completus, Series Latina, ed. J. P. Migne, 221 vols (Paris, 1844–64)

PEGOLOTTI (Francesco Balducci), *La Pratica della Mercatura*, ed. Allan Evans (Cambridge, Mass., 1936)

PETER DE CELLE, *Peter de Celle, Selected Works*, trans. H. Feiss, Cistercian Studies Series, 100 (Kalamazoo, 1987)

Philip of Clairvaux, 'The Middle English Life of Elizabeth of Spalbeek', in *Three Women of Liège*, ed. J. N. Brown (Turnhout, 2008), pp. 27–50

Records of the Monastery of Kinloss, ed. J. Stuart (Edinburgh, 1872)

The Register of William Greenfield, Lord Archbishop of York 1306–1315, III, ed. W. Brown and A. H. Thompson, Surtees Society, 151 (1936)

Registrum Epistolarum Fratris Johannis Peckham Archiepiscopi Cantuariensis, ed. C. T. Martin, 3 vols, RS, 77 (London, 1882–5)

Registrum Roberti Winchelsey, II, transcribed and ed. R. Graham, Canterbury and York Society, 52 (London, 1956)

Rental Book of the Cistercian Abbey of Cupar-Angus with the Breviary of the Register, ed. C. Rogers, 2 vols, Grampian Club (London, 1879–80)

212

Bibliography

The Rule of St Benedict, ed. and trans. D. O. Hunter Blair, fifth edn (Fort Augustus, 1948)

The Rule of the Templars. The French Text of the Rule of the Order of the Knights Templar, trans. J. Upton-Ward (Woodbridge, 1992)

Statuta Capitulorum Generalium Ordinis Cisterciensis ab Anno 1116 ad Annum 1786, ed. J. M. Canivez, 8 vols (Louvain, 1933–41)

STEPHEN OF LEXINGTON, *Registrum Epistolarum Abbatis Stephani de Lexinton*, ed. B. Griesser, *Analecta Sacri Ordinis Cisterciensis* 2 (1946), 1–118; ed. and trans. B. O'Dwyer, *Letters From Ireland 1228–9*, Cistercian Fathers Series, 28 (Kalamazoo, 1982)

STEPHEN OF SAWLEY, *Treatises*, ed. B. Lackner, trans. J. F. O'Sullivan, Cistercian Fathers Series, 36 (Kalamazoo, 1984)

Summae Cartae Caritatis, NLT, pp. 183–5 (trans. pp. 404–7)

The Tax Book of the Cistercian Order, ed. Arne O. Johnsen and H. Peter King (Oslo/Bergen/Tronsø, 1979)

Testamenta Eboracensia Part II: A Selection of Wills from the Registry at York, ed. J. Raine, Surtees Society, 30 (1855)

Twelfth-Century Statutes from the Cistercian General Chapter, Latin Text with English Notes and Commentary, ed. C. Waddell, Cîteaux: Commentarii Cistercienses, Studia et documenta, 12 (Brecht, 2002)

WALTER BOWER, *Scotichronicon by Walter Bower*, ed. Simon Taylor, Donald E. R. Watt and Brian Scott (Aberdeen/Glasgow, 1990)

WALTER DANIEL, *The Life of Aelred of Rievaulx*, ed. and trans. F. M. Powicke, NMT/OMT (London, 1950; repr. Oxford, 1978)

WALTER MAP, *De Nugis Curialium: Courtiers' Trifles*, ed. and trans. M. R. James, rev. edn C. N. L. Brooke and R. A. B. Mynors, OMT (Oxford, 1983)

WILLIAM OF MALMESBURY, *Gesta Regum Anglorum: the History of the English Kings*, ed. and trans. R. A. B. Mynors, R. M. Thomson and M. Winterbottom, 2 vols, OMT (Oxford, 1998–99)

WILLIAM OF NEWBURGH, *The History of William of Newburgh*, trans. J. Stevenson (Llanerch facsimile, Felinfach, 1996)

WILLIAM OF ST THIERRY, *The Golden Epistle: a Letter to the Brethren at Mont Dieu*, trans. T. Berkeley, Cistercian Fathers Series, 12 (Kalamazoo, 1971)

Secondary sources

ANDREWS, F., 'Monastic Observance and Communal Life: Siena and the Employment of Religious', in Andrews, Egger and Rousseau, *Pope, Church and Laity*, pp. 357–83

—— 'Living like the Laity? The Negotiations of Religious Status in the Cities of Late Medieval Italy', *Transactions of the Royal Historical Society*, sixth series, 20 (2010), 27–55

—— EGGER, C. and ROUSSEAU, C. (eds), *Pope, Church and Laity: Essays in Honour of Brenda M. Bolton* (Leiden, 2008)

ANSTETT, P. R., *Maulbronn Monastery*, second edn (Munich, 1995)

Bibliography

ASTILL, G. G. (ed.), *A Medieval Industrial Complex and its Landscape: the Metalworking, Watermills and Workshops of Bordesley Abbey* (York, 1993)
—— and WRIGHT, S. M., 'Perceiving Patronage in the Archaeological Record: Bordesley Abbey', in Carver, *In Search of Cult*, pp. 125–37
AUBERGER, J. -B., *L'Unanimité Cistercienne Primitive: myth ou realité?*, Cîteaux: Commentarii Cistercienses, Studia et documenta, 3 (Achel, 1986)
—— 'Chrysogonus Waddell, *Narrative and Legislative Texts from Early Cîteaux*', a review, *Cîteaux: Commentarii Cistercienses* 51 (2000), 193–7
AVELING, J. W., *The History of Roche Abbey from its Foundation to its Dissolution* (Worksop, 1870)
BAKER, D., 'The Genesis of English Cistercian Chronicles: the Foundation of Fountains Abbey I', *Analecta Cisterciensia* 25 (1969), 14–41
—— 'The Genesis of English Cistercian Chronicles: the Foundation of Fountains Abbey II', *Analecta Cisterciensia* 31 (1975), 179–212
BARBER, B. and THOMAS, C., *The London Charterhouse*, Museum of London Archaeological Service Monograph, 10 (London, 2002)
—— and CHENU, S., DYSON, T., and WHITE, B., *The Cistercian Abbey of Stratford Langthorne, Essex*, Museum of London Archaeological Service Monograph, 18 (London, 2004)
BARNES, G. D., *Kirkstall Abbey 1147–1539: an Historical Study*, Publications of the Thoresby Society, 58 (Leeds, 1985)
BARRAL I ALTET, X. (ed.) *Artistes, artisans et production artistique au moyen âge: Colloque international. Fabrication et consummation de l'oeuvre*, 3 (Paris, 1990)
BARRIÈRE, B., 'Les abbayes issues de l'érémitisme', in *Les Cisterciens de Languedoc*, pp. 72–105
BARRON, C. M. and HARPER-BILL, C. (eds), *The Church in Pre-Reformation Society* (Woodbridge, 1985)
BELL, A. R., BROOKS, C. and DRYBURGH, P. R., *The English Wool Market c. 1230–1327* (Cambridge, 2007)
BELL, D. N., 'The English Cistercians and the Practice of Medicine', *Cîteaux: Commentarii Cistercienses* 40 (1989), 139–74
—— (ed.), *Corpus of Mediaeval Library Catalogues, 3: The Libraries of the Cistercians, Gilbertines and Premonstratensians* (London, 1992)
—— 'The Siting and Size of Cistercian Infirmaries in England and Wales', in Lillich, *Studies in Cistercian Art and Architecture*, 5, pp. 211–38
—— 'Chambers, Cells and Cubicles: the Cistercian General Chapter and the Development of the Private Room', in Kinder, *Perspectives for an Architecture of Solitude*, pp. 187–98
BELL. H. E., 'Esholt Priory', *Yorkshire Archaeological Journal* 33 (1938), 5–33
BENOÎT, P., 'La forge de l'abbaye de Fontenay', *Dossiers: histoire et archéologie* 107 (1986), 50–2
BENSON, R. L. and CONSTABLE, G. (eds), *Renaissance and Renewal in the Twelfth Century* (Oxford, 1982)
BERMAN, C. H., *Medieval Agriculture, the Southern French Countryside, and the Early Cistercians. A Study of Forty-three Monasteries*, Transactions of the American Philosophical Society, new series, 76:5 (Philadelphia, 1986)

214

—— 'From Cistercian Granges to Cistercian Bastides: using the Order's Records to Date Landscape Transformation', in Pressouyre, *L'espace cistercien*, pp. 204–15

—— 'Cistercian Nuns and the Development of the Order: the Cistercian Abbey of Saint-Antoine-des-Champs outside Paris', in Elder, *The Joy of Learning and the Love of God*, pp. 121–56

—— *The Cistercian Evolution: the Invention of a Monastic Order in Twelfth-Century Europe* (Philadelphia, 2000)

—— (ed.), *Women and Monasticism in Medieval Europe: Sisters and Patrons of the Cistercian Reform* (Kalamazoo, 2002)

—— (ed.), *Medieval Religion: New Approaches* (New York/London, 2005)

—— 'Were there Twelfth-Century Cistercian Nuns?', in Berman, *Medieval Religion*, pp. 217–48

—— 'Distinguishing between the Humble Cistercian Lay Brother and Sister, and the Converted Knight in Southern France', in Jamroziak and Burton, *Religious and Laity in Western Europe*, pp. 263–83

—— 'Monastic Hospices in Southern France and Colleges in Montpellier, Toulouse, Paris, and Oxford: the Cistercian Urban Presence', *Revue d'Histoire Ecclésiastique* 102 (2007), 747–80

BETHELL, D., 'The Foundation of Fountains Abbey and the State of St Mary's, York, in 1132', *Journal of Ecclesiastical History* 17 (1966), 11–27

BINNS, A., *Dedications of Monastic Houses in England and Wales, 1066–1216* (Woodbridge, 1989)

BIRKETT, H., *The Saints' Lives of Jocelin of Furness. Hagiography, Patronage and Ecclesiastical Politics* (York, 2010)

BISHOP, T. A. M., 'Monastic Granges in Yorkshire', *English Historical Review* 51 (1936), 193–214

BLANKS, D., FRASSETTO, M. and LIVINGSTONE, A. (eds), *Medieval Monks and their World: Ideas and Realities, Studies in Honor of Richard E. Sullivan*, Brill's Series in Church History, 25 (Leiden, 2006)

BOLTON, B., 'The Cistercians and the Aftermath of the Second Crusade', in Gervers, *The Second Crusade*, pp. 131–40

BOND, C. J., 'Water Management in the Rural Monastery', in *The Archaeology of Rural Monasteries*, ed. R. Gilchrist and H. Mytum, British Archaeological Reports, British Series, 203 (Oxford, 1989), pp. 83–111

—— 'Monastic Water Management in Great Britain: a Review', in Keevil *et al.*, *Monastic Archaeology*, pp. 88–136

—— 'Production and Consumption of Food and Drink in the Medieval Monastery', in Keevil *et al.*, *Monastic Archaeology*, pp. 54–87

—— *Monastic Landscapes* (Stroud, 2004)

BONIS, A. and WABONT, M. (eds), *L'hydraulique monastique* (*Actes* of the colloquium *L'hydraulique monastique*, Royaumont, 1992) (Grâne, 1996)

—— *Monastic Landscapes* (Stroud, 2004)

BOSTOCK, T. and HOGG, S., *Vale Royal Abbey and the Cistercians 1277–1538* (Northwich, 1998)

BOUCHARD, C. Brittain, 'Cistercian Ideals versus Reality: 1134 Reconsidered', *Cîteaux: Commentarii Cistercienses* 39 (1988), 217–31

—— *Holy Entrepreneurs: Cistercians, Knights and Economic Exchange in Twelfth-Century Burgundy* (Ithaca, 1991)

—— '"Feudalism", Cluny and the Investiture Controversy', in Blanks *et al.*, *Medieval Monks and their World*, pp. 81–92

BOUDREAU, C., 'With Desire Have I Desired: Ida of Nivelles's Love for the Eucharist', in Nichols and Shank, *Hidden Springs*, I, 323–44

BOUTER, N. (ed.), *Unanimité et diversité Cistercienne: filiations – reseaux – relectures du XIIe au XVIIe siècle*. Actes de Quatrième Colloque International du C.E.R.C.O.R., Dijon, 23–25 Septembre 1998 (St Étienne, 2000)

BRACHMANN, H., FOSTER, E., KRATZKE, C. and REIMANN, H. (eds), *Das Zisterzienserkloster Dargun in Stammesgebeit der Zirzipanen* (Stuttgart, 2003)

BRADLEY, R., 'Love and Knowledge in *Seven Manners of Loving*', in Nichols and Shank, *Hidden Springs*, I, pp. 361–76

BREDERO, A., *Bernard of Clairvaux: Between Cult and History* (Edinburgh, 1996)

BROOKE, C., 'Princes and Kings as Patrons of Monasteries', in *Il Monachesimo e la Riforma Ecclesiastica 1049–1122*, Miscellanea del centro di studi medieovali, 6 (Milan, 1971), pp. 125–52

—— *The Age of the Cloister: the Story of Monastic Life in the Middle Ages* (Stroud, 2003)

—— and BROOKE, R., *Popular Religion in the Middle Ages: Western Europe 1000–1300* (London, 1984)

BROOKS, L. M. (ed.), *Women's Work: Making Dance in Europe before 1800* (Madison, Wisconsin, 2007)

BROWN, J. N. (ed.), *Three Women of Liège: a Critical Edition of and Commentary on the Middle English Lives of Elizabeth of Spalbeek, Christina Mirabilis and Marie d'Oignies*, Medieval Women: Texts and Studies, 23 (Turnhout, 2008)

BRUCE, S. G., *Silence and Sign Language in Medieval Monasticism: the Cluniac Tradition c. 900–c. 1200*, Cambridge Studies in Medieval Life and Thought, fourth series, 68 (Cambridge, 2007)

BULST-THIELE, M., 'The Influence of St Bernard of Clairvaux on the Formation of the Order of the Knights Templar', in Gervers, *The Second Crusade*, pp. 57–65

BURTON, J. E., *The Yorkshire Nunneries in the Twelfth and Thirteenth Centuries* (York, 1979)

—— 'Charters of Byland Abbey Relating to the Grange of Bleatarn, Westmorland', *Transactions of the Cumberland and Westmorland Antiquarian and Archaeological Society* 79 (1979), 29–50

—— 'The Settlement of Disputes between Byland Abbey and Newburgh Priory', *Yorkshire Archaeological Journal* 55 (1983), 67–72

—— 'The Foundation of the British Cistercian Houses', in Norton and Park, *Cistercian Art and Architecture*, pp. 24–39

—— *The Monastic and Religious Orders in Britain 1000–1300* (Cambridge, 1994)

—— 'The Estates and Economy of Rievaulx Abbey', *Cîteaux: Commentarii Cistercienses* 49 (1998), 29–93

—— *The Monastic Order in Yorkshire 1069–1215*, Cambridge Studies in Medieval Life and Thought, fourth series, 40 (Cambridge, 1999)

—— 'The Chariot of Aminadab and the Yorkshire Nunnery of Swine', in Horrox and Jones, *Pragmatic Utopias*, pp. 26–42

—— 'The Monastic World', in Weiler and Rowlands, *England and Europe in the Reign of Henry III*, pp. 121–36

—— 'Rievaulx Abbey: the Early Years', in Kinder, *Perspectives for an Architecture of Solitude*, pp. 47–53

—— '*Fundator Noster*: Roger de Mowbray as Founder and Patron of Monasteries', in Jamroziak and Burton, *Religious and Laity in Western Europe*, pp. 23–39

—— '*Homines sanctitatis eximiae religionis consummatae*: the Cistercians in England and Wales', *Archaeologia Cambrensis* 154 (2007 for 2005), 27–49

—— 'Past Models and Contemporary Concerns: the Foundation and Growth of the Cistercian Order', in Cooper and Gregory, *Revival and Resurgence*, pp. 27–45

—— 'Looking for Medieval Nuns', in Burton and Stöber, *Monasteries and Society*, pp. 123–33

—— 'English Monasteries and the Continent', in Dalton and White, *King Stephen's Reign*, pp. 98–114

—— 'Constructing a Corporate Identity: the *Historia Fundationis* of the Cistercian Abbeys of Byland and Jervaulx', in Müller and Stöber, *Self-Representation of Medieval Religious Communities*, pp. 327–40

—— '*Moniales* and *Ordo Cisterciensis* in Medieval England and Wales' in *Female 'vita religiosa' between Late Antiquity and the High Middle Ages. Structures, Developments and Spatial Contexts*, ed. G. Melville and A. Müller, Vita regularis Ordnungen und Deutungen religiosen Lebens im Mittelalter, 46 (Berlin, 2011), pp. 375–89

and STÖBER, K. (eds), *Monasteries and Society in the British Isles in the Later Middle Ages* (Woodbridge, 2008)

BUTLER, L., and GIVEN-WILSON, C., *Medieval Monasteries of Great Britain* (London, 1979)

BYNUM, C. Walker, *Jesus as Mother: Studies in the Spirituality of the Middle Ages* (Berkeley/Los Angeles/London, 1982)

CAMPBELL, J., *Balmerino and its Abbey* (Edinburgh, 1867, repr. 1899)

CANTOR, N. F., 'The Crisis of Western Monasticism, 1050–1130', *American Historical Review* 66 (1960), 47–67

CARTER, M., 'Late Medieval Relief Sculptures of the Annunciation to the Virgin from the Cistercian Abbeys of Rievaulx and Fountains', *Cîteaux: Commentarii Cistercienses* 60 (2009), 1–22

—— 'The Cistercians' Use of Devotional Images in Late Medieval England: Some Northern Evidence', paper given at the International Medieval Congress, Leeds, July 2010

—— 'Remembrance, Liturgy and Status in a Late Medieval English Cistercian Abbey: the Mourning Vestment of Abbot Robert Thorton of Jervaulx (1510–33)', *Textile History* 41 (2010), 3–18

CARVER, G., *Norman Splendour: Duiske Abbey, Graignamanagh* (Belfast, 1979)

CARVER, M. (ed.), *In Search of Cult: University of York Archaeological Papers* (Woodbridge, 1993)

CASEY, M., 'Herbert of Clairvaux's Book of Wonderful Happenings', *Cistercian Studies Quarterly* 25: 1 (1993), 37–64

CASSIDY-WELCH, M., *Monastic Spaces and their Meanings: Thirteenth-Century English Cistercian Monasteries* (Turnhout, 2001)

CATTO, J. I. and EVANS, R. (eds), *The History of the University of Oxford II: Late Medieval Oxford* (Oxford, 1992)

CAWLEY, M., 'Four Abbots of the Golden Age of Villers', *Cistercian Studies Quarterly* 27:4 (1992), 300–27

—— 'Ida of Nivelles: Cistercian Nun', in Nichols and Shank, *Hidden Springs*, I, 305–21

CLARKE, J., *The Benedictines in the Middle Ages* (Woodbridge, 2011)

COAD, J. G., *Hailes Abbey*, English Heritage Guide, second edn (London, 1993)

COLDSTREAM, N., 'Architecture from Beaulieu to the Dissolution', in Norton and Park, *Cistercian Art and Architecture*, pp. 139–59

—— 'The Mark of Eternity: the Cistercians as Builders', in Robinson, *Cistercian Abbeys of Britain*, pp. 35–51

CONNOR, E., 'The Abbey of Tart', in Elder, *The New Monastery*, pp. 211–18

CONSTABLE, G., *Monastic Tithes from their Origins to the Twelfth Century* (Cambridge, 1964)

—— 'Renewal and Reform in Religious Life', in Benson and Constable, *Renaissance and Renewal in the Twelfth Century*, pp. 37–67

—— *The Reformation of the Twelfth Century* (Cambridge, 1996)

COOMANS, T., 'Fontenay au-delà de Saint Bernard: à propos de deux publications récentes sur l'abbaye et son architecture', *Cîteaux: Commentarii Cistercienses* 54 (2003), 171–86

—— 'From Flanders to Scotland: the Choir Stalls of Melrose Abbey in the Fifteenth Century', in Kinder, *Perspectives for an Architecture of Solitude*, pp. 235–52

COOPER, K. and GREGORY. J. (eds), *Revival and Resurgence in Christian History*, Studies in Church History, 44 (Woodbridge, 2008)

COPPACK, G., *Fountains Abbey Yorkshire*, English Heritage Guide (London, 1993)

—— *The White Monks: the Cistercians in Britain 1128–1540* (Stroud, 1998)

—— *Fountains Abbey: the Cistercians in Northern England* (Stroud, 2003)

—— '"According to the Form of the Order"? The Earliest Cistercian Buildings in England and their Context', in Kinder, *Perspectives for an Architecture of Solitude*, pp. 35–45

—— 'The Water-driven Corn Mill at Fountains Abbey: a Major Cistercian Mill of the Twelfth and Thirteenth Centuries', in Lillich, *Studies in Cistercian Art and Architecture*, 5, pp. 270–96

—— and FERGUSSON, P., *Rievaulx Abbey* (London, 1994)

—— and GILYARD-BEER, R., 'Excavations at Fountains Abbey in N. Yorkshire, 1979–80: the Early Development of the Church', *Archaeologia* 108 (1986), 147–88

CORNELISON, S. J. and MONTGOMERY, S. B. (eds), *Images, Relics, and Devotional Practices in Medieval and Renaissance Italy*, Medieval and Renaissance Texts and Studies, 296, (Tempe, AZ, 2005)

COSS, P. R. and LLOYD, S. D. (eds), *Thirteenth Century England IV: Proceedings of the Newcastle Upon Tyne Conference 1991* (Woodbridge, 1992)

COWLEY, F. G., *The Monastic Order in South Wales 1066–1349* (Cardiff, 1977)

CRANE, E., *The Archaeology of Beekeeping* (London, 1983)

CROSS, C. and VICKERS, N., *Monks, Friars and Nuns in Sixteenth-Century Yorkshire*, Yorkshire Archaeological Society Record Series, 150 (1995)

CROUCH, D., *The Reign of Stephen 1135–1154* (London, 2000)

DALTON, P., *Conquest, Anarchy and Lordship: Yorkshire 1066–1154*, Cambridge Studies in Medieval Life and Thought, fourth series, 27 (1994)

—— and WHITE, G. J. (eds), *King Stephen's Reign (1135–1154)* (Woodbridge, 2008)

DAUTREY, P., 'Croissance et adaptation chez les Cisterciens au treizième siécle: les debuts du College des Bernardins de Paris', *Analecta Cisterciensia* 32 (1976), 122–215

DAVIS, M. T., 'The Church of the Collège Saint-Bernard', in Kinder, *Perspectives for an Architecture of Solitude*, pp. 223–34

de GANCK, R., *Beatrice of Nazareth in Her Context*, 2 vols, Cistercian Studies Series, 121–2 (Kalamazoo, c. 1991)

D'EMILIO, J., 'The Cistercians and the Romanesque Churches of Galicia: Compostela or Clairvaux?', in Kinder, *Perspectives for an Architecture of Solitude*, pp. 313–27

de MOOR, G., 'Cistercian Laybrothers and Laysisters in Frisia and Holland', *Cistercian Studies Quarterly* 27:4 (1992), 329–39

DENTON, J., 'From the Foundation of Vale Royal Abbey to the Statute of Carlisle: Edward I and Ecclesiastical Patronage', in Coss and Lloyd, *Thirteenth Century England IV*, pp. 123–37

DITCHBURN, D., 'Saints and Silver: Scotland and Europe in the Age of Alexander II', in Oram, *The Reign of Alexander II*, pp. 179–210

DOBSON, R. B., 'The Religious Orders 1370–1540', in Catto and Evans, *History of the University of Oxford II*, pp. 539–79

DONKIN, R. A., 'The Urban Property of the Cistercians in Mediaeval England', *Analecta Sacri Ordinis Cisterciensis* 15 (1959), 104–31

—— 'Settlement and Depopulation on Cistercian Estates during the Twelfth and Thirteenth Centuries, especially in Yorkshire', *Bulletin of the Institute of Historical Research* 33 (1960), 141–65

—— 'The Cistercian Grange in England in the 12th and 13th Centuries, with Special Reference to Yorkshire', *Studia Monastica* 6 (1964), 95–144

—— *The Cistercians: Studies in the Geography of Medieval England and Wales*, Pontifical Institute of Medieval Studies (Toronto, 1978)

DONNELLY, J. S., *The Decline of the Medieval Cistercian Laybrotherhood* (New York, 1949)

—— 'Changes in the Grange Economy of English and Welsh Abbeys 1300–1540', *Traditio* 10 (1954), 399–458

DUFIEF, A., 'Filiations des abbayes cisterciennes bretonnes', in Bouter, *Unanimité et diversité*, pp. 121–8

DUGDALE, W., *Monasticon Anglicanum*, ed. J. Caley, H. Ellis and B. Bandinel, 6 vols in 8 (London, 1817–30)

DUTTON, M. L., 'Intimacy and Initiation: the Humanity of Christ in Cistercian Spirituality', in Sommerfeldt, *Erudition at God's Service*, pp. 33–70

—— 'The Face and the Feet of God: the Humanity of Christ in Bernard of Clairvaux and Aelred of Rievaulx', in Sommerfeldt, *Bernardus Magister*, pp. 203–23

—— 'Aelred, Historian: Two portraits in Plantagenet Myth', *Cistercian Studies Quarterly* 28 (1993), 112–43

—— LaCORTE, D. M. and LOCKEY, P. (eds), *Truth as Gift: Studies in Medieval*

Cistercian History in Honor of John R. Sommerfeldt, Cistercian Studies Series, 204 (Kalamazoo, 2005)

DYER, C., 'Sheepcotes: Evidence for Medieval Sheepfarming', *Medieval Archaeology* 39 (1995), 136–64.

EAMES, E., 'A Thirteenth-century Tile Kiln Site at North Grange, Meaux, Beverley, Yorkshire', *Medieval Archaeology* 5 (1961), 137–68

—— *English Medieval Tiles* (London, 1985)

—— *English Tilers* (London, 1992)

ELDER, E. R. (ed.), *Goad and Nail: Studies in Medieval Cistercian History*, 10, Cistercian Studies Series, 84 (Kalamazoo, 1985)

—— (ed.), *The Joy of Learning and the Love of God: Studies in Honour of J. Leclercq*, Cistercian Studies Series, 160 (Kalamazoo, 1995)

—— (ed.), *The New Monastery: Texts and Studies on the Early Cistercians*, Cistercian Fathers Series, 60 (Kalamazoo, 1998)

—— 'Shadows on the Marian Wall: the Cistercians and the Development of Marian Doctrine', in Dutton *et al.*, *Truth as Gift*, pp. 537–74

FAWCETT, R. and ORAM, R., *Melrose Abbey* (Stroud, 2004)

FELTEN, F., 'Waren die Zisterzienser frauenfeindlich? Die Zisterzienser und die religiöse Frauenbewegung im 12. und frühen 13. Jahrhundert. Versuch einer Bestandsaufnahme der Forschung seit 1980', in Felten and Rosener, *Norm und Realität*, pp. 179–223

—— and ROSENER, W. (eds), *Norm und Realität: Kontinuität und Wandel der Zisterzienser im Mittelalter*, Vita regularis Ordnungen und Deutungen religiosen Lebens im Mittelalter, 42 (Berlin, 2009)

FERGUSSON, P., 'Early Cistercian Churches in Yorkshire and the Problem of the Cistercian Crossing Tower', *Journal of the Society of Architectural Historians* 29 (1970), 211–21

—— 'The First Architecture of the Cistercians in England and the Work of Abbot Adam of Meaux', *Journal of the British Archaeological Association* 136 (1983), 74–86

—— *Architecture of Solitude: Cistercian Abbeys in Twelfth-Century England* (Princeton, 1984)

—— 'The Twelfth-century Refectories at Rievaulx and Byland Abbeys', in Norton and Park, *Cistercian Art and Architecture*, pp. 160–80

—— '*Porta patens esto*. Notes on Early Cistercian Gatehouses in the North of England', in Fernie and Crossley, *Mediaeval Architecture*, pp. 47–60

—— *Roche Abbey*, English Heritage Guide (London, 1990, repr. 1999)

—— 'Aelred's Abbatial Residence at Rievaulx abbey', in Lillich, *Studies in Cistercian Art and Architecture*, 5, pp. 41–58

—— and HARRISON, S., 'The Rievaulx Abbey Chapter-house', *Antiquaries Journal* 74 (1994), 216–53

—— *Rievaulx Abbey: Community, Architecture and Memory* (New Haven, 1999)

FERNIE, E. and CROSSLEY, P. (eds), *Mediaeval Architecture and its Intellectual Context: Studies in Honour of Peter Kidson* (London, 1990)

FLETCHER, J. S., *The Cistercians in Yorkshire* (London, 1919)

FONNESBERG-SCHMIDT, I., *The Popes and the Baltic Crusades 1147–1254* (Leiden, 2007)

FRANCE, J., 'St Bernard, Eskil and the Danish Cistercians', *Cîteaux: Commentaria Cistercienses* 39 (1988), 232–48

—— *The Cistercians in Scandinavia*, Cistercian Studies Series, 131 (Kalamazoo, 1992)

—— 'Cistercian Foundation Narratives in Scandinavia in their Wider Context', *Cîteaux: Commentarii Cistercienses* 43 (1992), 119–60

—— 'The Coming of the Cistercians to Scandinavia – *ad exteras et barbaras regiones*', *Cîteaux: Commentaria Cistercienses* 48 (1997), 5–15

—— *The Cistercians in Medieval Art* (Stroud, 1998)

—— 'The Cistercians in Scandinavia', in Felten and Rosener, *Norm und Realität*, pp. 475–87

FREEMAN, E., *Narratives of a New Order: Cistercian Historical Writing in England, c. 1150–1220* (Turnhout, 2002)

—— 'Houses of a Peculiar Order: Cistercian Nunneries in Medieval England, with Special Attention to the Fifteenth and Sixteenth Centuries', *Cîteaux: Commentarii Cistercienses* 55 (2004), 245–87

GAJEWSKI, A., 'Burial, Cult and Construction at the Abbey Church of Clairvaux (Clairvaux II)', *Cîteaux: Commentarii Cistercienses* 56 (2005), 47–85

GAMBERO, L., *Mary in the Middle Ages: the Blessed Virgin Mary in the Thought of Medieval Latin Theologians* (Milan, 2000)

GEENS, F., 'Galganus and the Cistercians: Relics, Reliquaries, and the Image of a Saint', in Cornelison and Montgomery, *Images, Relics, and Devotional Practices*, pp. 55–76

GERLI, E. M. and ARMISTEAD, G. (eds), *Medieval Iberia: An Encyclopaedia* (London/New York, 2003)

GERVERS, M. (ed.), *The Second Crusade and the Cistercians* (New York, 1992)

GILCHRIST, R. and MYTUM, H. (eds), *The Archaeology of Rural Monasteries*, British Archaeological Reports, British Series, 203 (Oxford, 1989)

GILSON, E., *The Mystical Theology of St Bernard*, trans. A. H. C. Downes, Cistercian Studies Series, 120 (Kalamazoo, 1990)

GILYARD-BEER, R., 'Fountains Abbey: the Early Buildings, 1132–50', *Archaeological Journal* 125 (1968), 313–19

GOLDING, B., 'Gerald of Wales and the Cistercians', *Reading Medieval Studies* 21 (Reading, 1995), 5–30

GÓRECKI, P., *A Local Society in Transition: the Henryków Book and Related Documents* (Toronto, 2002)

GRABOIS, A., 'Militia and Malitia: the Bernardine Vision of Chivalry', in Gervers, *The Second Crusade*, pp. 49–56

GRAHAM-LEIGH, E., *The Southern French Nobility and the Albigensian Crusade* (Woodbridge, 2005)

GRANT, L., *Architecture and Society in Normandy 1120–1270* (New Haven/London, 2005)

GRAVES, C., 'The Economic Activities of the Cistercians in Medieval England', *Analecta Cisterciensia* 13 (1957), 3–62

GRÉLOIS, A., 'L'expansion cistercienne en France: la part des affiliations et des moniales', in Felten and Rosener, *Norm und Realität*, pp. 287–324

GRIFFITH-JONES, R. and PARK, D. (eds), *The Temple Church in London: History, Architecture, Art* (Woodbridge, 2010)

HALL, J., 'English Cistercian Gatehouse Chapels', *Cîteaux: Commentarii Cistercienses* 52 (2001), 61–91

—— 'East of the Cloister: Infirmaries, Abbots' Lodgings and Other Chambers', in Kinder, *Perspectives for an Architecture of Solitude*, pp. 199–211

HAMMOND, M., 'Queen Ermengarde and the Abbey of St Edmund, Balmerino', in Kinder, *Life on the Edge*, pp. 11–36

HARPER-BILL, C., 'Cistercian Visitation in the Late Middle Ages: the Case of Hailes Abbey', *Bulletin of the Institute of Historical Research* 53 (1980), 103–14

—— 'The Labourer is Worthy of his Hire? Complaints about Diet in Late Medieval English Monasteries', in Barron and Harper-Bill, *The Church in Pre-Reformation Society*, pp. 95–107

HARRISON, S., *Byland Abbey*, English Heritage Guide (London, 1995)

—— *Cleeve Abbey, Somerset*, English Heritage Guide (London, 2000)

—— '"I lift up mine eyes": a Re-evaluation of the Tower in Cistercian Architecture in Britain', in Kinder, *Perspectives for an Architecture of Solitude*, pp. 125–35

—— 'L'abbaye de Longuay: une évaluation architecturale', *Cîteaux: Commentarii Cistercienses* 58 (2007), 279–97

—— 'The Abbey Church of Fontenay: a Reassessment of the Evidence', forthcoming *Cîteaux: Commentarii Cistercienses*

HARVEY, B., *Living and Dying in England c. 1100–1540: the Monastic Experience* (Oxford, 1993)

—— 'Monastic Pittances in the Middle Ages', in Woolgar *et al.*, *Food in Medieval England*, pp. 215–27

HAYS, R. W., *The History of the Abbey of Aberconway 1186–1537* (Cardiff, 1963)

HICKS, L., *Religious Life in Normandy, 1050–1300: Space, Gender and Social Pressure* (Woodbridge, 2007)

HIESTAND, R., 'The Papacy and the Second Crusade', in Phillips and Hoch, *The Second Crusade*, pp. 32–53

HIGGETT, J. (ed.), *Medieval Art and Architecture in the Diocese of St Andrews*, British Archaeological Association Conference Transactions for 1986, 14 (Leeds, 1994)

HOCKEY, S. F., *Quarr Abbey and its Lands 1132–1633* (Leicester, 1970)

—— *Beaulieu: King John's Abbey* (Beaulieu, 1976)

HOLDSWORTH, C., 'Eleven Visions connected with the Cistercian Monastery of Stratford Langthorne', *Cîteaux: Commentarii Cistercienses* 13 (1962), 185–204

—— '*Narrative and Legislative Texts from Early Cîteaux*: a Review Article', *Cîteaux: Commentaria Cistercienses* 51 (2000), 157–66

HOPE, W. St John, 'Fountains Abbey', *Yorkshire Archaeological Journal* 15 (1898–99), 269–402

HORROX, R. and JONES, S. R. (eds), *Pragmatic Utopias: Ideals and Communities, 1200–1630* (Cambridge, 2001)

HUNT, N. (ed), *Cluniac Monasticism in the Central Middle Ages* (Hamden, CN/ London, 1971)

JACOB, E. F. 'The Disputed Election at Fountains 1410–1416', in Ruffer and Taylor, *Medieval Studies*, pp. 78–97

JAMROZIAK, E., 'Rievaulx Abbey as a Wool Producer in the Thirteenth Century: Cistercians, Sheep and Big Debts', *Northern History* 40 (2003), 197–218

—— *Rievaulx Abbey and its Social Context 1132–1300: Memory, Locality and Networks* (Turnhout, 2005)

—— 'St Mary Graces: a Cistercian House in later Medieval London', in Trio and de Smet, *The Use and Abuse of Sacred Places in Late Medieval Towns*, pp. 153–64

—— 'Holm Cultram Abbey: a Story of Success?', *Northern History* 45 (2008), 27–36

—— 'Border Communities between Violence and Opportunities: Scotland and Pomerania Compared', in Unger, *Britain and Poland-Lithuania*, pp. 123–36

—— 'Cistercian Identities on the Northern Peripheries of Medieval Europe from the Twelfth to the late Fourteenth Century', in Müller and Stöber, *Self-Representation of Medieval Religious Communities*, pp. 209–19

—— and BURTON, J. (eds), *Religious and Laity in Western Europe, 1000–1400: Interaction, Negotiation and Power*, Europa Sacra, vol. 2 (Turnhout, 2006)

JENNINGS, B. (ed.), *A History of Nidderdale*, third edn (Huddersfield, 1992)

—— *Yorkshire Monasteries: Cloister, Land and People* (Otley, 1999)

JORDAN, W. C., 'The Representation of Monastic–Lay Relations in the Canonization Records for Louis IX', in Jamroziak and Burton, *Religious and Laity in Western Europe*, pp. 225–40

—— 'The English Holy Men of Pontigny', *Cistercian Studies Quarterly* 44 (2009), 63–75

KEEVIL, G., ASTON, M. and HALL, T. (eds), *Monastic Archaeology* (Oxford, 2001)

KEHNEL, A. and MENCEJ, M., 'Representing Eternity: Circular Movement in the Cloister, Round Dancing, Winding-Staircases and Dancing Angels', in Müller and Stöber, *Self-Representation of Medieval Religious Communities*, pp. 67–90

KEMP, E., 'La presence cistercienne dans la Suisse médiévale', in Bouter, *Unanimité et diversité*, pp. 400–18

KERR, J., *Monastic Hospitality: the Benedictines in England c. 1070–1250* (Woodbridge, 2007)

—— 'Balmerino Abbey: Cistercians on the East Coast of Fife', in Kinder, *Life on the Edge*, 37–60

—— 'Cistercian Hospitality in the Later Middle Ages', in Burton and Stöber, *Monasteries and Society*, pp. 25–39

—— *Life in the Medieval Cloister* (London/New York, 2009)

—— 'The Symbolic Significance of Hospitality', in Müller and Stöber, *Self-Representation of Medieval Religious Communities*, pp. 125–42

KIENZLE, B., 'The Tract on the Conversion of Pons of Léras and the True Account of the Beginning of the Monastery at Sylvanès', *Cistercian Studies Quarterly* 30 (1995), 219–43

—— *Cistercians, Heresy and Crusade in Occitania, 1145–1299: Preaching in the Lord's Vineyard* (York, 2001)

KINDER, T. N., 'Aménagement d'une vallée de larmes: les Cisterciens et l'eau à Pontigny', in Bonis and Wabont, *L'hydraulique monastique*, pp. 383–95

—— 'Clay and what they did with it: Medieval Tiles and Bricks at Pontigny', in Lillich, *Studies in Cistercian Art and Architecture*, 4, pp. 15–44

—— 'Living in a Vale of Tears: Cistercians and Site Management in France: Pontigny and Fontfroide', in Keevil *et al.*, *Monastic Archaeology*, pp. 37–53

—— *Cistercian Europe: Architecture of Contemplation* (Grand Rapids/Cambridge/Kalamazoo, 2002)

—— (ed.), *Perspectives for an Architecture of Solitude: Essays on Cistercians, Art, and Architecture in Honour of Peter Fergusson* (Turnhout, 2004)

—— (ed.), *Life on the Edge: Balmerino Abbey, Fife, Cîteaux: Commentarii Cistercienses* 59 (2008)

KING, A. A., *Cîteaux and her Elder Daughters* (London, 1954)

—— *Liturgies of the Religious Orders* (London, 1956)

KING, E., *King Stephen* (London, 2010)

KING, P., *The Finances of the Cistercian Order in the Fourteenth Century*, Cistercian Studies Series, 85 (Kalamazoo, 1985)

—— *Western Monasticism: a History of the Monastic Movement in the Latin Church*, Cistercian Studies Series, 185 (Kalamazoo, 1999)

KLOCZOWSKI, J., 'Les Cisterciens en Europe du Centre-Est au moyen âge', in Bouter, *Unanimité et diversité*, pp. 421–39

KNOWLES, D., *The Monastic Order in England: a History of its Development from the Times of St Dunstan to the Fourth Lateran Council, 940–1216*, second edn (Cambridge, 1963)

—— BROOKE, C. N. L. and LONDON, V. C. M., *The Heads of Religious Houses in England and Wales, 1, 940–1216*, second edn (Cambridge, 2001)

—— and GRIMES, W. F., *Charterhouse: the Medieval Foundation in the Light of Recent Discoveries* (London, 1954)

—— and HADCOCK, R. N., *Mediaeval Religious Houses, England and Wales*, second edn (Harlow, 1971)

KOCH, K., 'Vollstandiges brevier aus der schreibstube des HL Stephen', *Analecta Cisterciensia* 2 (1946), 146–7

KROLL, J. and BACHRACH, B. S., *The Mystic Mind: the Psychology of Medieval Mystics and Ascetics* (New York/Abingdon, 2005)

KRATZKE, C., '*De Laudibus Virginis Matris*: the Untold Story of a Standing Infant Jesus, a Venerating Monk and a Moveable Madonna from Dargun Abbey', in Kinder, *Perspectives for an Architecture of Solitude*, pp. 269–81

LAWRENCE-MATHERS, A., *Manuscripts in Northumbria in the Eleventh and Twelfth Centuries* (Cambridge, 2003)

LECLERCQ, J., 'The Monastic Crisis of the Eleventh and Twelfth Centuries', in Hunt, *Cluniac Monasticism*, pp. 217–37

—— *The Love of Learning and the Desire for God: a Study of Monastic Culture* (New York, 1961; repr. 1982)

Le GOFF, J., *The Birth of Purgatory*, trans. A. Goldhammer (Chicago, 1984)

LEKAI, L. J., *The White Monks: a History of the Cistercian Order* (Okauchee, Wis., 1953)

—— *The Cistercians: Ideals and Reality* (Kent State, Ohio, 1977)

LEROUX-DHUYS, Jean-Francois, *Cistercian Abbeys: History and Architecture* (Paris, 1998)

Les Cisterciens de Languedoc XIIIᵉ–XIVᵉ siècle, Cahiers de Fanjeaux, 21 (Toulouse, 1986)

LESTER, A. E., 'Cares Beyond the Walls: Cistercian Nuns and the Care of Lepers in Twelfth- and Thirteenth-Century Northern France', in Jamroziak and Burton, *Religious and Laity in Western Europe*, pp. 197–224

—— 'A Shared Imitation: Cistercian Convents and Crusader Families in Thirteenth-Century Champagne', *Journal of Medieval History* 35 (2009), 353–70

LILLICH, M. Parsons (ed.), *Studies in Cistercian Art and Architecture*, 4, Cistercian Studies Series, 134 (Kalamazoo, 1993)

—— (ed.), *Studies in Cistercian Art and Architecture*, 5, Cistercian Studies Series, 167 (Kalamazoo, 1998)

LITTLE, L. K., *Religious Poverty and the Profit Economy in Medieval Europe* (London, 1978)

LOPRETE, K. A., *Adela of Blois: Countess and Lord (c. 1067–1137)* (Dublin, 2007)

LUDDY, J., *Mellifont Abbey* (Waterford, 1938)

LYNCH, M., SPEARMAN, M. and STELL, G., *The Scottish Medieval Town* (Edinburgh, 1988)

MARKS, R., *Stained Glass in England During the Middle Ages* (London, 1993)

MARX, C. W., 'The Middle English Verse *Lamentation of Mary to Saint Bernard* and the *Quis dabit*', in Pearsall, *Studies in the Vernon Manuscript*, pp. 137–57.

—— 'The Edge of Orthodoxy: the Virgin Mary, St Bernard and the *Quis dabit*', in *Fact and Fiction from the Middle Ages to Modern Times, Essays Presented to Hans Sauer on the Occasion of his 65th Birthday*, ed. R. Bauer and U. Krischke (Frankfurt am Main, 2011)

McDONNELL, J., *Inland Fisheries in Medieval Yorkshire 1066–1300*, Borthwick Papers, 60 (York, 1981)

McGINN, B., *The Growth of Mysticism, the Presence of God: a History of Western Christian Mysticism II* (New York, 1994)

McGUIRE, B. P., *Conflict and Continuity at Øm Abbey: a Cistercian Experience in Medieval Denmark* (Copenhagen, 1976)

—— 'Written Sources and Cistercian Inspiration in Caesarius of Heisterbach', *Analecta Cisterciensia* 35 (1979), 227–82

—— 'A Lost Exemplum Collection Found: the *Liber Visionum et Miraculorum* Compiled under Prior John of Clairvaux (1171–79)', *Analecta Cisterciensia* 37 (1981), 1–63

—— *The Cistercians in Denmark: their Attitudes, Roles and Functions in Medieval Society*, Cistercian Studies Series, 35 (Kalamazoo, 1982)

—— 'Why Scandinavia? Bernard, Eskil and Cistercian Expansion in the North', in Elder, *Goad and Nail*, pp. 251–81

—— 'Taking Responsibility: Medieval Cistercian Abbots as their Brother's Keepers', *Commentarii Cistercienses* 39 (1988), 249–68

—— 'Purgatory, the Communion of Saints and Medieval Change', *Viator* 20 (1989), 61–84

—— 'An Introduction to the *Exordium Magnum Cisterciense*', *Cistercian Studies Quarterly* 27:4 (1992), 277–97

—— 'Charity and Unanimity: the Invention of the Cistercian Order: a Review Article', *Cîteaux: Commentarii Cistercienses* 51 (2000), 285–97

—— *Friendship and Faith: Cistercian Men, Women, and their Stories, 1100–1250* (Aldershot, 2002)

MIDMER, R., *English Medieval Monasteries* (London, 1979)

MÜLLER, A., 'Presenting Identity in the Cloister', in Müller and Stöber, *Self-Representation of Medieval Religious Communities*, pp. 167–88

—— and STÖBER, K. (eds), *Self-Representation of Medieval Religious Communities: the British Isles in Context*, Vita regularis Ordnungen und Deutungen religiosen Lebens im Mittelalter, 40 (Berlin, 2009)

NEWMAN, M., *The Boundaries of Charity: Cistercian Culture and Ecclesiastical Reform 1098–1180* (Stanford, 1996)

NICHOL, D., *Thurstan, Archbishop of York 1114–1140* (York, 1964)

NICHOLS, J. A., 'The Organisation of the English Cistercian Nunneries', *Cîteaux: Commentarii Cistercienses* 30 (1979), 23–40

—— and SHANK, L. T. (eds), *Hidden Springs: Cistercian Monastic Women*, 2 vols, Cistercian Studies Series, 113 (Kalamazoo, 1995)

NJUS, J., 'The Politics of Mysticism: Elisabeth of Spalbeek and her Context', *Church History* 77 (2008), 285–317

NOELL, B., 'Expectation and Unrest among Cistercian Lay Brothers in the Twelfth and Thirteenth Centuries', *Journal of Medieval History* 32 (2006), 253–74

NORTON, C., 'Table of Cistercian Legislation on Art and Architecture', in Norton and Park, *Cistercian Art and Architecture*, pp. 315–93

—— 'Medieval Floor Tiles in Scotland', in Higgett, *Medieval Art and Architecture in the Diocese of St Andrews*, pp. 137–73

—— 'The Production and Distribution of Medieval Floor Tiles in France and England', in Barral i Altet, *Artistes, artisans et production artistique au moyen âge*, pp. 101–31

—— *St William of York* (York, 2006)

—— and PARK, D. (eds), *Cistercian Art and Architecture in the British Isles* (Cambridge, 1986)

OATES, J. C. T., 'Richard Pynson and the Holy Blood of Hayles', *The Library*, fifth series, 13 (1958), 266–77

O'DELL, C., 'Ida of Léau: Woman of Desire', in Nichols and Shank, *Hidden Springs*, 1, pp. 415–43

O'DWYER, B., *The Conspiracy of Mellifont 1216–1231*, Medieval Irish History Series, 2 (Dublin, 1970)

ORAM, R. D., 'The Estates and Possessions of the Abbey', in Fawcett and Oram, *Melrose Abbey*, pp. 209–71

—— (ed.), *The Reign of Alexander II, 1214–49* (Leiden, 2004)

—— 'A Fit and Ample Endowment? The Balmerino Estate, 1228–1603', in Kinder, *Life on the Edge*, 61–80

—— 'Holy Frontiersmen: Twelfth- and Early Thirteenth-century Monastic Colonisation and Socio-Economic Change in Poland and Scotland', in Unger, *Britain and Poland-Lithuania*, pp. 103–121

Oxford Dictionary of National Biography in Association with the British Academy, from the Earliest Times to the Year 2000, ed. H. D. G. Matthew and B. Harrison (Oxford, 2004)

PACAUT, M., *Les moines blancs: histoire de l'ordre de Cîteaux* (Saint-Armond-Cher, 1993)

PARISSE, M., 'La formation de la branche de Morimond', in Bouter, *Unanimité et diversité*, pp. 87–101

PASCUA, E., 'Vassals and Allies in Conflict: Relations between Santa Maria de

Montederramo and Local Galician Society in the Thirteenth Century', in Pastor, *Beyond the Market*, pp. 25–106

PASTOR, R. (ed.), *Beyond the Market: Transactions, Property and Social Networks in Monastic Galicia, 1200–1300* (Leiden, 2002)

—— 'Social Mobility and the Personal Network of "Low-intermediate Social Groups": Relations between Communities of Peasants and *Foreros* and the Monastery of Oseira in the Thirteenth Century', in Pastor, *Beyond the Market*, pp. 245–318

PEARSALL, D. (ed.), *Studies in the Vernon Manuscript* (Cambridge, 1990)

PENNINGTON, K. (ed.), *Bernard of Clairvaux: a Saint in Word and Image* (Huntingdon, 1994)

PEREIRA, P., *Abbey of Santa Maria: Alcobaça* (London, 2007)

PETROFF, E., *Medieval Women's Visionary Literature* (Oxford, 1986)

PHILLIPS, J. and HOCH, M. (eds), *The Second Crusade: Scope and Consequences* (Manchester, 2001)

PILAT, Z., 'Le réseau des cisterciens en Europe du Centre-Est du XIIe au XVe siècle', in Bouter, *Unanimité et diversité*, pp. 441–51

PLATT, C., *The Monastic Grange in Mediaeval England: a Reassessment* (London, 1969)

—— *The Abbeys and Priories of Mediaeval England* (London, 1984)

PRESSOUYRE, L. (ed.), *L'espace cistercien*, Memoires de la section d'archéologie et d'histoire de l'art, 5 (Paris, 1994)

PRESTWICH, M., BRITNELL, R. and FRAME, R. (eds), *Thirteenth Century England IX: Proceedings of the Durham Conference 2001* (Woodbridge, 2003)

PRYCE, H., 'Patrons and Patronage among the Cistercians in Wales', *Archaeologia Cambrensis* 154 (2007 for 2005), 81–95

PURKIS, W., *Crusading Spirituality in the Holy Land and Iberia, c. 1095–1187* (Woodbridge, 2008)

RAISTRICK, A. and JENNINGS, B. (eds), *A History of Lead Mining in the Pennines* (London, 1965)

RASMUSSEN, L., 'Monastic Benefactors in England and Denmark: their Social Background and Distribution', in Jamroziak and Burton, *Religious and Laity in Western Europe*, pp. 77–92

RIGG, A., *A History of Anglo-Latin Literature 1066–1422* (Cambridge, 1992)

ROBINSON, D. (ed.), *The Cistercian Abbeys of Britain: Far from the Concourse of Men* (London, 1998, repr. 2002)

—— *The Cistercians in Wales: Architecture and Archaeology 1130–1540*, Reports of the Research Committee of the Society of Antiquaries of London, 73 (London, 2006)

RODGERS, S. and ZIEGLER, J. E., 'Elizabeth of Spalbeek's Trance Dance of Faith: a Performance Theory Interpretation from Anthropological and Art Historical Perspectives', in Sydam and Ziegler, *Performance and Transformation*, pp. 299–355

RUBIN, M., *Mother of God: a History of the Virgin Mary* (London, 2010)

RUCQUOI, A., 'Les Cisterciens dans la peninsula ibérique', in Bouter, *Unanimité et diversité*, pp. 487–523

RUFFER, V. and TAYLOR, A. J. (eds), *Medieval Studies Presented to Rose Graham* (Oxford, 1950)

SHARPE, R. (ed.), *A Handlist of the Latin Writers of Great Britain and Ireland before 1540*, Publications of the Journal of Medieval Latin, 1 (Turnhout, 1997)

SHAW, H., 'Cistercian Abbots in the Service of British Monarchs 1135–1335', *Cîteaux: Commentarii Cistercienses* 58 (2007), 225–44

SHEAD, N., 'Four Scottish Indulgences at Sens', *Innes Review* 58 (2007), 210–16

SILEN, K., 'Elisabeth of Spalbeek: Dancing the Passion', in Brooks, *Women's Work*, pp. 207–27

SMITH, D. M. (ed.), *The Heads of Religious Houses in England and Wales 3, 1377–1540* (Cambridge, 2008)

—— and LONDON, V. C. M., *The Heads of Religious Houses in England and Wales 2, 1216–1377* (Cambridge, 2001)

SOMMERFELDT, J. R. (ed.), *Erudition at God's Service: Studies in Medieval Cistercian History*, 11 (Kalamazoo, 1987)

—— (ed.) *Bernardus Magister: Papers Celebrating the Nonacentenary of the Birth of Bernard of Clairvaux*, Cistercian Studies Series, 135 (Kalamazoo, 1992)

—— *Bernard of Clairvaux on the Spirituality of Relationship* (Mahwah, 2004)

—— *Aelred of Rievaulx – Pursuing Personal Happiness* (Mahwah, 2005)

STALLEY, R., *The Cistercian Monasteries of Ireland: an Account of the History and Architecture of the White Monks in Ireland from 1142–1540* (London/New Haven, 1987)

STEVENSON, W., 'The Monastic Presence: Berwick in the Twelfth and Thirteenth Centuries', in Lynch *et al.*, *The Scottish Medieval Town*, pp. 99–115

STEVENSON, W. H. and SALTER, H. E. (eds), *The Early History of St John's College Oxford*, Oxford Historical Society, new series, 1 (1939)

STÖBER, K., 'The Role of Late Medieval English Monasteries as Expressions of Patronal Authority: Some Case Studies', in Trio and de Smet, *The Use and Abuse of Sacred Places in Late Medieval Towns*, pp. 189–207

—— 'Social Networks of Late Medieval Welsh Monasteries', in Burton and Stöber, *Monasteries and Society*, pp. 12–24

STOPFORD, J., *Medieval Floor Tiles of Northern England. Pattern and Purpose: Production between the 13th and 16th Centuries* (Oxford, 2005)

SULLIVAN, A., 'An Introduction to the *Vita Beatrici*', in Nichols and Shank, *Hidden Springs*, I, 345–50

SYDAM, M. and ZIEGLER, J. (eds), *Performance and Transformation – New Approaches to Late Medieval Spirituality* (New York, 1999)

SZABÓ, P., *Woodland and Forests in Medieval Hungry*, British Archaeological Reports, International Series, 1348 (Oxford, 2005)

TALBOT, C. H., 'The Account Book of Beaulieu Abbey', *Cîteaux in de Nederlanden* 9 (1958), 189–210

—— 'The English Cistercians and the Universities', *Studia Monastica* 4 (1962), 197–220

THOMAS, D., 'Saint Winifred's Well and Chapel, Holywell', *Journal of the Historical Society of the Church in Wales* 8 (1958), 15–31

THOMPSON, E. M., *The Carthusian Order in England* (London, 1930)

THOMPSON, K., 'The Other Saint Bernard: the "Troubled and Varied Career" of Bernard of Abbeville, Abbot of Tiron', *Journal of Ecclesiastical History* 60 (2009), 657–72

THOMPSON, S., *Women Religious: the Founding of English Nunneries after the Norman Conquest* (Oxford, 1991)

TIMBERLAKE, S., 'Archaeological and Circumstantial Evidence for Early Mining in Wales', *Bulletin of the Peak District Mines Historical Society* 12:3 (1994), 133–43

TRIO, P. and de SMET, M. (eds), *The Use and Abuse of Sacred Places in Late Medieval Towns* (Leuven, 2006)

TRUAX, J. A., '*Miles Christi*: Count Theobald IV of Blois and Saint Bernard of Clairvaux', *Cistercian Studies Quarterly* 44 (2009), 299–320

UNGER, R. (ed.), *Britain and Poland-Lithuania: Contact and Comparison from the Middle Ages to 1795* (Leiden, 2008)

Van DAMME, J.-Baptiste, *The Three Founders of Cîteaux*, trans. N. Groves and C. Carr, Cistercian Studies Series, 176 (Kalamazoo, 1998)

Van ENGEN, J., 'The "Crisis of Cenobitism" Reconsidered: Benedictine Monasticism in the Years 1050–1150', *Speculum* 61 (1986), 269–304

VERNON, R. W., McDONNELL, G. and SCHMIDT, A., 'The Geophysical Evaluation of an Ironworking Complex: Rievaulx and Environs', *North Yorkshire Archaeological Prospection* 5 (1998), 181–201

—— 'An Integrated Geophysical and Analytical Appraisal of Early Iron Working: Three Case Studies', *Journal of the Historical Metallurgy Society* 32: 2 (1998), 67–81

VEYSSIERE, L., 'Les differences de vue et de réalisation chez Étienne Harding et Saint Bernard à propos des premières moniales cisterciennes', in Bouter, *Unanimité et diversité*, pp. 133–47

Victoria History of the Counties of England (London, 1900–)

VINCENT, N., *The Holy Blood: King Henry III and the Westminster Blood Relic* (Cambridge, 2001)

WADDELL, C., 'Abbot Stephan [sic] Reforms the Hymnal', and 'The Molesme – Cistercian Hymnal', in Elder, *The New Monastery*, pp. 78–86

—— 'The Myth of Cistercian Origins: C. H. Berman and the Manuscript Sources', *Cîteaux: Commentarii Cistercienses* 51 (2000), 285–97 and 299–386

WARDROP, J., *Fountains Abbey and its Benefactors 1132–1300*, Cistercian Studies Series, 91 (Kalamazoo, 1987)

WATKINS, W., 'The Life of St Robert of Newminster', *Downside Review* 58 (1939), 137–49

WEILER, B. K. U. and ROWLANDS, I. W. (eds), *England and Europe in the Reign of Henry III* (Aldershot, 2002)

WILDHABER, B., 'Catalogues des établissements cisterciens en Languedoc aux XIIIe et XIVe siècles', in *Les Cisterciens en Languedoc*, pp. 21–44

WILLIAMS, D. H., 'The Welsh Cistercians and Ireland', *Cistercian Studies* 15 (1980), 17–23

—— *The Cistercians in the Early Middle Ages* (Leominster, 1998)

—— (ed.), *Catalogue of Seals in the National Museum of Wales*, vol. 2, *Ecclesiastical, Monastic and Collegiate Seals with a Supplement Concerning Wales* (Cardiff, 1998)

—— *The Welsh Cistercians* (Leominster, 2001)

WILSON, C., *The Gothic Cathedral: the Architecture of the Great Church 1130–1530* (London, 1990; rev. 2000)

—— 'Gothic Architecture Transplanted: the Nave of the Temple Church', in Griffith-Jones and Park, *The Temple Church in London*, pp. 19–44

WINKLESS, D., *Hailes Abbey Gloucestershire: the Story of a Medieval Abbey* (Stocksfield, 1990; repr. London, 2001)

WOLLENBERG, K., 'Die Deutschen Zisterzienserklöster zwischen Rhein und Elbe', in Bouter, *Unanimité et diversité*, pp. 321–44

WOOLGAR, C., SERJEANTSON, D. and WALDRON, T. (eds), *Food in Medieval England: Diet and Nutrition* (Oxford, 2006)

WRATHMELL, S., *The Guest-House at Kirkstall Abbey: a Guide to the Mediaeval Buildings and the Discoveries Made During Recent Excavations* (Yorkshire, 1987)

WRIGHT, R., '"Casting Down the Altars and Levelling Everything before the Ploughshare?" The Expansion and Evolution of the Grange Estates of Kirkstall Abbey', in Prestwich *et al.*, *Thirteenth Century England IX*, pp. 187–200

Theses/Dissertations

BLOUNT, M. N., 'A Critical Edition of the Annals of Hailes (MS Cotton Cleopatra D. iii, ff. 33–59v) with an Examination of their Sources', MA thesis, Manchester, 1974

DENT, E., 'The Impact of Fountains Abbey on Nidderdale', BA dissertation, University College Ripon and York, 1995

McFADDEN, G. J., 'An edition and translation of the Life of Waldef, Abbot of Melrose, by Jocelin of Furness', D. Phil. Dissertation, Columbia University, 1952

Index of Cistercian Houses mentioned in the text

(N) indicates a nunnery

Personnel and granges of Cistercian houses cross referenced here appear in the general index

Abbey Cwmhir (Wales)   46
Abbey Dore (England)   45
Aberconwy (Wales)   46
   abbot of, *see* Dafydd ab Owain
Acre, St Mary Magdalene (N) (Syria)   51
Alcobaça (Portugal)   50, 69, 70, 72, 73,
   79, 191
Altenkamp, *see* Camp
Altzelle (Germany)   75n
Alvastra (Sweden)   48, 49, 94
Amelunxborn (Germany)   36
Aulne (Belgium)   116
   conversus of, *see* Simon
Aunay (France)   133

Balmerino (Scotland) 100, 111n, 112, 131, 133,
   163, 181
Baltinglass (Ireland)
   abbot of 99
Barnoldswick (England), to Kirkstall   60n,
   61
Basingwerk (Wales)   45, 131, 135
Beaubec (France)   180
Beaulieu (England)   40 and n, 64, 65n, 74,
   111, 112, 121, 182, 192
Bebenhausen (Germany)   75
Bective (Ireland)   98
Belleperche (France)   180
Bellevaux (France)   24, 26, 37, 94
Bonnefont (France)
   grange of, *see* Apas
Bonnevaux (France)   26
Bordesley (England)   160, 168, 178
Boulbonne (France)
   conversus of, *see* Pons
Bourras (France)   26
Boxley (England)   40
Boyle (Ireland)   63, 67
Brondolo (Italy)
   grange of, *see* Chioggia
Buckfast (England)   74
Buildwas (England)   60, 131
   abbot of 46
Byarum (N) (Sweden) to Sko   59

Byland (England)   61 and n, 62, 63, 64, 160,
   165, 166, 170, 171n, 173, 179, 185, 186n
   abbot of, *see* Philip
   conversus of, *see* Serlo
   grange of, *see* Old Byland
   monk of, *see* Wimund

Cadouin (France)   26, 27, 28, 36
   abbot of, *see* Henry
Calder (England)   63
Camp / Altenkamp (Germany)   36, 37, 97
Casamari (Italy)   39
Casanova (Italy)   36n
Chaâlis (France)
   abbots of, *see* Simon; William of Bourges
   grange of, *see* Commelles
Cheminon (France)   131
Cherlieu (France)
   abbot of 134
Chiaravalle (Italy)   39
Chiaravalle della Columba (Italy)   39
Cirta (Romania)   128
Cîteaux (France)   1, 6, 7, 9, 11, 13, 14,
   15–20, 21, 22, 23, 24, 25, 26, 27, 28, 31,
   32, 35, 36, 39, 40, 43, 48, 52, 56, 57, 58n,
   82, 88, 90, 91, 95, 100, 101, 111, 135, 190
   abbot of 46, 89, 91, 93, 100; *see also*
      Alberic; Arnold Amaury; Conrad;
      Guy; Raynard du Bar; Robert;
      Stephen Harding; Stephen of
      Lexington
Clairvaux (France)   16 and n, 21n, 23, 24,
   25, 26, 27, 28, 33, 37–9, 40, 45, 47, 48,
   51, 52, 53, 56, 57, 60 and n, 63, 66 and
   n, 73 and n, 74, 76, 82, 91n, 93, 98, 110,
   114, 121, 129, 131, 133–4, 136, 186, 193,
   199, plate 3
   abbot of 84, 89, 94; *see also* Bernard;
      Conrad; Henry de Marcy; Philip;
      Stephen of Lexington
   monks of, *see* Achard; Geoffrey of Ainai;
      Herbert; Rainald; Raynard du Bar;
      Robert
   prior of 105

General Index